"Collins has opened doors in the Scriptures rarely explored, and even more rarely, expl these texts are central to Jesus' teachings. Living as we do in a culture dominated by greed, it is countercultural to be consistently generous, and, even more so, to be radically generous, but that is precisely the lifestyle to which the Gospel calls us. Collins presents each of these texts, explains their meaning in the historical context in which they were first produced, and briefly, at the end of each chapter, exposes our deafness. The Gospel has the power to transform us, and Collins' exegetical study can help to facilitate that transformation. Every Roman Catholic, every Christian, should read this book."

> —Alice L. Laffey
> Professor Emerita
> College of the Holy Cross

"Ray Collins has favored us with a careful examination of what the Bible has to share with us from God's heart about money. *Wealth, Wages, and the Wealthy* is a steady, practical, and inspiring reply to any who would barricade money and its uses and misuses from things spiritual, and a hearty support for Pope Francis's dream for Christians worldwide."

> —Dr. James C. Howell
> Senior Pastor, Myers Park United Methodist Church, Charlotte, NC
> Adjunct Professor, Duke Divinity School

"The final chapter alone in Ray Collins's latest book, *Wealth, Wages, and the Wealthy*, is worth the price of the entire book. But, if you read only the final chapter, you will miss the careful and very accessible scholarship that leads him to conclude that Jesus' teaching and early Christian practice challenge, even condemn, the present economic order of the West, and of the United States in particular, because it oppresses the poor and those on the margins of society, leaving them with no access to justice or to hope. Every pastor needs to have this in his or her library. It will also be of great use in the undergraduate classroom in courses that deal with the practice of Christian morality."

> —Mary Kate Birge, SSJ, PhD
> Associate Professor of Theology
> Mount St. Mary's University

"With candor and brilliance, Ray Collins offers a rigorous study of the New Testament to bring to the fore one of the most pressing issues affecting the common good in the ancient world and today: economic justice. Collins challenges contemporary preachers and leaders to address poverty, wage manipulation, and the misuse of the judicial system, and he has provided the needed information and basis for them to do so. Would that our Sunday sermons and legislation now ring loudly with the prophetic spirit!"

—Carol J. Dempsey, OP
Professor of Theology (Biblical Studies)
University of Portland, OR

Wealth, Wages, and the Wealthy

New Testament Insight for Preachers and Teachers

Raymond F. Collins

A Michael Glazier Book

LITURGICAL PRESS
Collegeville, Minnesota

www.litpress.org

A Michael Glazier Book published by Liturgical Press

Cover design by Monica Bokinskie. Image courtesy of Wikimedia Commons.

Library of Congress Cataloging-in-Publication Data

Names: Collins, Raymond F., 1935– author.
Title: Wealth, wages, and the wealthy : new testament insight for preachers and teachers / Raymond F. Collins.
Description: Collegeville, Minnesota : Liturgical Press, [2017] | "A Michael Glazier Book." | Description based on print version record and CIP data provided by publisher; resource not viewed.
Identifiers: LCCN 2016059610 (print) | LCCN 2017019212 (ebook) | ISBN 9780814687857 (ebook) | ISBN 9780814687840
Subjects: LCSH: Wealth—Biblical teaching. | Bible. New Testament—Criticism, interpretation, etc. | Wealth—Religious aspects—Catholic Church. | Catholic Church—Doctrines.
Classification: LCC BS2545.W37 (ebook) | LCC BS2545.W37 C65 2017 (print) | DDC 241/.68—dc23
LC record available at https://lccn.loc.gov/2016059610

In memory of Henry Shelton,
committed Christian,
tireless advocate for economic justice,
who was born to new life on September 21, 2016

Contents

Abbreviations

AB	Anchor Bible
ABRL	Anchor Bible Reference Library
AER	*American Ecclesiastical Review*
AGJU	Arbeiten zur Geschichte des antiken Judentums und des Urchristentums
AJT	*Asia Journey of Theology*
ANTC	Abingdon New Testament Commentaries
AYBRL	Anchor Yale Bible Reference Library
BDAG	Danker, Frederick W., Walter Bauer, William F. Arndt, and F. Wilbur Gingrich. *Greek-English Lexicon of the New Testament and Other Early Christian Literature.* 3rd ed. Chicago: University of Chicago Press, 2000.
BETL	Bibliotheca Ephemeridum Theologicarum Lovaniensium
Bib	*Biblica*
BibOr	Biblica et Orientalia
BJS	Brown Judaic Studies
BNT	Die Botschaft des Neuen Testaments
BNTC	Black's New Testament Commentaries
BZNW	Beihefte zur Zeitschrift für die neutestamentliche Wissenschaft
CD	Cairo Damascus Document
CSEL	Corpus Scriptorum Ecclesiasticorum Latinorum

CTM	*Concordia Theological Monthly*
Did	*Didaskalia*
EBib	*Etudes bibliques*
ECC	Eerdmans Critical Commentary
ECL	Early Christianity and Its Literature
EDNT	*Exegetical Dictionary of the New Testament*. Edited by Horst Balz and Gerhard Schneider. ET. 3 vols. Grand Rapids: Eerdmans, 1990–1993
EKKNT	Evangelisch-katholischer Kommentar zum Neuen Testament
ETL	*Ephemerides Theologicae Lovanienses*
EvQ	*Evangelical Quarterly*
FR	*The Fourth R*
GNS	*Good News Studies*
HTKNT	Herders Theologischer Kommentar zum Neuen Testament
HTR	*Harvard Theological Review*
IBC	Interpretation: A Bible Commentary for Teaching and Preaching
ICC	International Critical Commentary
Int	*Interpretation*
JBL	*Journal of Biblical Literature*
JDDS	Jian Dao Dissertation Series
JRH	*Journal of Religious History*
JSNT	*Journal for the Study of the New Testament*
JSNTSup	Journal for the Study of the New Testament Supplement Series
KEK	Kritisch-exegetischer Kommentar über das Neue Testament
LNTS	The Library of New Testament Studies
LS	*Louvain Studies*

LSJ	Liddell, Henry George, Robert Scott, Henry Stuart Jones. *A Greek-English Lexicon.* 9th ed. with revised supplement. Oxford: Clarendon, 1996
MdB	*Le Monde de la Bible*
NAB	New American Bible
NAC	New American Commentary
Neot	*Neotestamentica*
NIBCNT	New International Biblical Commentary on the New Testament
NICNT	New International Commentary on the New Testament
NIDB	*New Interpreter's Dictionary of the Bible.* Edited by Katharine Doob Sakenfeld. 5 vols. Nashville: Abingdon, 2006–2009
NIGTC	New International Greek Testament Commentary
NovT	*Novum Testamentum*
NRSV	New Revised Standard Version
NTL	New Testament Library
NTOA	Novum Testamentum et Orbis Antiquus
NTS	*New Testament Studies*
NTTSD	New Testament Tools, Studies, and Documents
PGC	Pelican Gospel Commentary
PW	*Paulys Real-Encyclopädie der classichen Altertumswissenschaft.* New Edition by Georg Wissowa and Wilhelm Kroll. 50 vols. in 84 parts. Stuttgart: Metzler and Druckenmüller, 1894–1980
REB	*Revista eclesiástica brasileira*
RHPR	*Revue d'histoire et de philosophie religieuses*
SBLDS	Society of Biblical Literature Dissertation Series
SBLSP	Society of Biblical Literature Seminar Papers
SBT	Studies in Biblical Theology

Semeia	*Semeia*
SNTW	Studies of the New Testament and Its World
SP	Sacra Pagina
ST	*Studia Theologica*
SubBi	Subsidia Biblica
TJ	*Trinity Journal*
TLNT	*Theological Lexicon of the New Testament.* C. Spicq. Translated and edited by J. D. Ernest. 3 vols. Peabody, MA: Hendrickson, 1994
WBC	Word Biblical Commentary
WUNT	Wissenschaftliche Untersuchungen zum Neuen Testament
ZNW	*Zeitschrift für die neutestamentliche Wissenschaft und die Kunde der älteren Kirche*
ZNT	*Zeitschrift für Neues Testament*

Preface

Hardly had the ink dried on Pope Francis's first encyclical, *Laudato Sì*, "On Care for Our Common Home"[1]—in some cases even before it dried—than the Bishop of Rome was attacked from various quarters. His attackers included some who said that he should stick to spirituality. Catholic pundits on the right said that the pope should concentrate on "morality," by which they seemed to mean abortion and homosexuality, while others strongly argued that economic issues lay beyond the competence of the Magisterium to teach about faith and morals. His opponents claimed that the pope should confine his ministry to the gospel, by which they meant a bowdlerized gospel, sanitized by the removal of its many references to the use and misuse of wealth.

From the very beginning of his pontificate, Pope Francis has repeatedly spoken about the common good and the current state of the economy. In a pathfinding apostolic exhortation that set the tone for his pontificate, *Evangelii Gaudium*, "The Joy of the Gospel,"[2] Francis wrote, "Growth in justice requires more than economic growth, while presupposing such growth: it requires decisions, programs, mechanisms and processes specifically geared to a better distribution of income, the creation of sources of employment and an integral promotion of the poor which goes beyond a simple welfare mentality."[3]

---

[1] The encyclical was dated Pentecost Sunday, May 24, 2015, and was officially published on June 18, 2015. An earlier encyclical, *Lumen Fidei*, dated June 29, 2013, was a joint effort by the recently elected Francis and his predecessor, Pope Emeritus Benedict XVI.

[2] The apostolic exhortation was dated November 24, 2013, the solemnity of our Lord Jesus Christ, King of the Universe.

[3] *Evangelii Gaudium* 204.

Francis returned to this theme in his 2015 encyclical *Laudato Sì*. "We should be particularly indignant at the enormous inequalities in our midst, whereby we continue to tolerate some considering themselves more worthy than others," he wrote. "We fail to see that some are mired in desperate and degrading poverty, with no way out, while others have not the faintest idea of what to do with their possessions."[4]

Before making this plea, Francis echoed the hope of Bartholomew I, the Patriarch of Constantinople, that we be freed from fear, greed, and compulsion and that greed give way to generosity.[5] Among other things, the Bishop of Rome warned that whereas humans have a basic right to water, we are now in a situation where the control of water by large multinational businesses may become a source of conflict,[6] and he lamented that productive land is concentrated in the hands of a few owners.[7] Francis observed that the foreign debt of poor countries has become a way of controlling them.[8] "In the current global system," he wrote, "priority tends to be given to speculation and to financial gain."[9]

Speaking to the Congress of the United States on September 24, 2015, Francis raised a number of related issues. He told the legislators: "Legislative activity is always based on care of the people. . . . Politics . . . cannot be a slave to the economy and finance. Politics is, instead, an expression of our compelling need to live as one in order to build as one the greatest common good." Reiterating what he had said in his apostolic exhortation,[10] Francis stated that business is a noble vocation, directed to producing wealth and improving the world, but he also asked a troubling question. "Why," he asked, "are deadly weapons being sold to those who plan to inflict suffering on individuals and society? Sadly, the answer, as we all know, is simply

---

[4] *Laudato Sì* 90.
[5] *Laudato Sì* 9. Francis referred to Batholomew's *Lecture* at the Monastery of Utstein, Norway, on June 23, 2003.
[6] *Laudato Sì* 31.
[7] *Laudato Sì* 134.
[8] *Laudato Sì* 52.
[9] *Laudato Sì* 56.
[10] *Evangelii Gaudium* 203.

for money, money that is drenched in blood, often innocent blood."[11] In his address to Congress, Francis's words were carefully chosen. He wanted to challenge and not condemn. Nonetheless, his carefully chosen words were to a large extent woven around the themes of the common good and the right use of wealth.

Voicing concern for the common good and a just use of wealth, the pope has generated a fair amount of opposition in certain circles, even—and perhaps especially—within the church of which he is officially the head. He should go back to preaching the gospel, some say. The problem is that the condemnation of greed is an integral part of the gospel. Three passages in the New Testament speak about homosexuality, but nineteen speak about greed, not to mention those that speak about the love of money, the lure of wealth, or the mammon of iniquity. Many of these passages reflect the teaching of Jesus himself.

Greed and the proper use of wealth are, however, not at the top of the list of most preachers' favorite topics. Some would go so far as to say that greed is not seriously sinful. John Howard Yoder once lamented that Christian ethical teaching has largely ignored Jesus.[12] This is glaringly the case where the use of wealth is concerned, a situation that Pope Francis is trying to redress. Francis's voice is not alone, but it may be the loudest on the current world stage. For the greater part of the past century the debate about justice and equity in global economic affairs has been an issue in ecumenical circles.[13] Patriarch Bartholomew has urged people, especially those who espouse orthodoxy, to turn from greed to generosity. The Archbishop of Canterbury is known for his advocacy of greater social justice and the idea that economic growth is not automatically beneficial to all. And he once remarked that if you were to meet Francis, you would be automatically forced to reexamine your attitudes toward poverty.[14]

Francis has made the biblical call for economic justice a touchstone, perhaps the touchstone, of his pontificate. His place on the

[11] Pope Francis, "U.S. Visit: Speech to Congress," *Origins* 48 (2015): 314–18.

[12] Cf. John Howard Yoder, *The Politics of Jesus* (Grand Rapids: Eerdmans, 1972): 15–19.

[13] Cf. Michael Taylor, *Christ and Capital: A Family Debate* (Geneva: World Council of Churches, 2015).

[14] Cf. *The Tablet* (October 31, 2015): 28.

world stage allows his voice to be echoed before all. When he appeared before the General Assembly of the United Nations during its seventieth anniversary celebrations, he spoke with forthrightness as he said to the world's leaders on September 24, 2015: "A selfish and boundless thirst for power and material prosperity leads both to the misuse of available natural resources and to the exclusion of the weak and disadvantaged. . . . Economic and social exclusion is a complete denial of human fraternity and a grave offense against human rights and the environment. . . . This dramatic reality . . . has led me . . . to take stock of my grave responsibility in this regard and to speak out. . . . The baneful consequences of an irresponsible mismanagement of the global economy, guided only by ambition for wealth and power, must serve as a summons to a forthright reflection on man."[15]

The Bishop of Rome believes that his mandate to preach the gospel requires him to speak out about economic justice. Speaking fraternally to the bishops of the United States, as one bishop to others, the Bishop of Rome said, "We all know what it is that the Lord asks of us."[16] What the Lord asks of us is principally spelled out in the memories of the Lord's teaching contained in the twenty-seven books of the New Testament. Each and every one of those books has something to say about wealth. These teachings of the New Testament should inform the Christian conscience with regard to a just use of economic resources. My study intends to enable its readers, especially those readers who are pastors with a mandate to preach the gospel of Jesus Christ, to peruse the pertinent texts of the New Testament with greater insight.

In recent years several short and sometimes challenging books have been written on the New Testament teaching on the use of wealth. Among them I would especially mention Sondra Ely Wheeler's *Wealth as Peril and Obligation*,[17] Luke Timothy Johnson's *Sharing*

---

[15] Pope Francis, "U.S. Visit: Speech at U.N.," *Origins* 48 (2015): 327–31.

[16] Pope Francis, "U.S. Visit: Meeting with U.S. Bishops," *Origins* 48 (2015): 319–22, 320.

[17] Sondra Ely Wheeler, *Wealth as Peril and Obligation: The New Testament on Possessions* (Grand Rapids: Eerdmans, 1995).

Possessions,[18] and Daniel Marguerat's *Dieu et l'argent*.[19] I have learned much from each of these studies and am grateful to their respective authors. For the most part, Johnson, Marguerat, and Wheeler offer a synthetic view of what the New Testament teaches about possessions, with the possibilities and perils that wealth entails. Rarely do they enter upon a detailed study of any of the pertinent texts, which are almost too many to be counted.

Building on and in contrast with what these authors have done, I offer an analytic view of what the New Testament teaches about wealth, wages, and the wealthy within these pages. As a narrative study, this approach leads to the conclusions laid out in the book's final chapter. Concentrating on the understanding of each of the several texts that speak of wealth, wages, and the wealthy, my study is designed to help the pastor who wants to preach on a particular text.

My hope is that the ethical teaching of Jesus with regard to the use of money be not neglected in the preaching of the gospel. As mentioned, Yoder lamented that Christian ethical teaching has largely ignored Jesus. This is so clearly true with regard to the teaching of Jesus on justice and the use of wealth. Preaching on selected passages of the New Testament has enabled Christian pastors, those who might be expected to share Jesus' teaching on economic justice, to hide the ethical teaching of Jesus on the use of financial resources from their congregations. This means that most of Jesus' ethical teaching—arguably, the proper use of money is the dominant ethical theme in the New Testament!—has been hidden in recent decades, perhaps for the past three-quarters of a century.[20] My study is intended to remove the dark shadow and bring the fullness of Jesus' ethical teaching into the light.

I begin with a study of the letters of Paul since these constitute our most ancient Christian witness. The apostle had much to say about wages and greed. Then I treat the Synoptic Gospels according to the

---

[18] Luke Timothy Johnson, *Sharing Possessions: What Faith Demands,* 2nd ed. (Grand Rapids: Eerdmans, 2011).

[19] Daniel Marguerat, *Dieu et l'argent une parole à oser. Parole en liberté* (Bière, Switzerland: Cabédits, 2013).

[20] Cf. Kevin M. Kruse, *One Nation under God: How Corporate America Invented Christian America* (New York: Basic Books, 2015).

generally accepted order of their composition, Mark, Matthew, and Luke. Mark shows how the lure of wealth is a major obstacle to discipleship. Matthew and Luke build on this teaching, adding their own nuances. Luke, in particular, reflects on wealth in its use, especially in his series of stories about "a rich man." Luke's understanding of a use of wealth that is in keeping with discipleship continues in the Acts of the Apostles, where it comes to expression in the evangelist's portrayal of the model Christian community in Jerusalem. Paul's teaching on greed is developed in the writings of his disciples who describe greed as idolatry and speak about the love of money as being the root of all kinds of evil. Among the Catholic Epistles, the Epistle of James stands out because of what it has to say about the rich. Finally, I consider the Johannine literature, with its haunting image of the whore of Babylon. The concluding chapter of my study highlights some of the most important elements on the New Testament teaching on the use of wealth and shows that daily occurrences fly in the face of the Christian Scriptures, almost as if they never existed.

My attempt to weigh the entire New Testament teaching on wealth, wages, and the wealthy has meant—perhaps unfortunately—that my study of the individual texts is not as detailed as it might have been. I am profoundly aware that I have referred to the biblical, that is, "Old Testament," "background" of the New Testament texts only occasionally and as particularly warranted. Attempting to limit the size of this study, I likewise generally avoided the citation of contemporary and early Christian authors whose insights on the use of wealth would have both enriched and nuanced my reflections. In dealing with passages from the so-called triple tradition—that is, passages in Mark that recur in both Matthew and Luke—I limited my study of the updated versions of the Markan text but included them because of my desire to show how the earliest teaching on wealth was preserved and applied to new circumstances during New Testament times. Ultimately, I sacrificed some depth in order to be somewhat concise.

Economic justice is necessarily a joint effort on the part of God's people. My contribution to the discussion of this issue is likewise a joint effort. To the untold number of people throughout the world who have taught me about humanity's misuse of God-given wealth, I owe my profound gratitude. To Timothy, whose encouragement

and prodding saw this project through to completion, even when
the spirit was willing but the flesh was weak, I can only say thanks.
To those who have mentored my studies of the New Testament and
encouraged my scholarship for the past six decades, *eucharistō*, I
thank you. To countless friends who have borne with me as I have
been consumed by this project, I am so grateful. All of you have contributed to its conception.

Others have contributed to its birth in the form of this present study.
Chief among them are Peter Dwyer, Hans Christoffersen, Lauren L.
Murphy, and the entire team at Liturgical Press, without whose support and effort this book would never have seen the light of the
publisher's day—I say thanks. May he who preached the coming of
the kingdom of God bless all of you.

Raymond F. Collins

The Feast of St. Andrew, Apostle

2016

Chapter 1

Paul

The earliest witness to the nascent Christian movement is the apostle Paul, who was called Saul when he was reared in a Hellenistic Jewish community in the city of Tarsus in Asia Minor. He is known to later generations through his letters that have been preserved, especially his masterpiece, the letter to the Romans, along with his letters to the Corinthians, a letter to the Galatians, a letter to the Philippians, a letter to the Thessalonians, and a brief letter to Philemon.[1] In addition, the apostle is known to us through the Acts of the Apostles, whose second and longer "half" is devoted to Paul.

Given his strong desire not to speak about himself,[2] Paul's letters contain few autobiographical details. Words found in the book of Jeremiah the prophet,[3] encapsulated in Paul's pithy, "Let the one who boasts, boast in the Lord,"[4] restrained him from speaking too much about himself. Luke's Acts were written a couple of generations after

[1] Scholars unanimously attribute these seven letters to Paul while they raise questions as to the authenticity of other New Testament letters attributed to Paul: Ephesians, Colossians, 2 Thessalonians, 1 and 2 Timothy, and Titus. Cf. Raymond F. Collins, *Letters That Paul Did Not Write: The Epistle to the Hebrews and the Pauline Pseudepigrapha*, GNS 28 (Wilmington, DE: Glazier, 1988; reprinted Eugene, OR: Wipf & Stock, 2005).

[2] Cf. 1 Cor 1:28, 31; 2 Cor 10:14, 17; 11:16, 21.

[3] Cf. Jer 9:23-24.

[4] Cf. 1 Cor 1:31; 2 Cor 10:17. Cf. Kasper Ho-yee Wong, *Boasting and Foolishness: A Study of 2 Cor 10,12-18 and 1,1a*, JDDS 5; Bible and Literature 3 (Hong Kong: Alliance Bible Seminary, 1998), 172–82.

Paul's death. Luke was a historian who made good use of his sources,[5] but he may not have known the apostle personally.[6] As a consequence of these two factors, the contemporary reader is somewhat limited in trying to write a biography of Paul.

The apostle's letters have nothing to say about his early life, but Luke quotes him as defending himself before a Roman with these words, "I am a Jew, born in Tarsus in Cilicia, but brought up in this city at the feet of Gamaliel, educated strictly according to our ancestral law, being zealous for God, just as all of you are today."[7] This *apologia pro vita sua* suggests that Paul came from a reasonably well-to-do family, at least one sufficiently rich to send the young Saul off to Jerusalem for an education and provide for him during the time of his studies in the Holy City.[8] Moreover, he seems not to have died in poverty. During his two-year house imprisonment in Rome, Paul lived in a rented apartment at his own expense.[9] Writing to the Philippians, Paul acknowledges that he knows what it is to have a lot and be well fed.[10] Paul was, moreover, willing to take on whatever financial obligations toward Philemon that Onesimus, his

---

[5] Cf. Luke 1:1-4; Acts 1:1. Since Luke himself describes Acts as a sequel to his gospel, it is to be presumed that he used the same methodology in composing the second half of his two-part work.

[6] There is a passing reference to "Luke, the beloved physician" in Col 4:14, but that text is probably pseudonymous. The tradition that Luke knew Paul is, for the most part, based on the "we" passages in the Acts of the Apostles. A careful reading of the text shows that these are concentrated in passages that speak about Paul's sea voyages. The first-person plural may have been found in one of the sources used by Luke. If so, they would not indicate that the compiler of Acts was with Paul as he journeyed by water. Cf. Jacques Dupont, *The Sources of Acts* (London: Darton, Longman & Todd, 1964), xxx.

[7] Acts 22:3.

[8] Justin Meggitt has attacked what he calls the myth of Paul's relatively affluent background. He raises some legitimate points, but his statements need to be nuanced and sometimes critiqued. See Justin J. Meggitt, *Paul, Poverty and Survival* (Edinburgh: T & T Clark, 1998), 80–97.

[9] Cf. Acts 28:30; Brian Rapske, *The Book of Acts and Paul in Roman Custody*, The Book of Acts in Its First Century Setting 3 (Grand Rapids: Eerdmans 1994), 236ff.

[10] Phil 4:12, a passage in which the apostle acknowledges that he has also had the opposite experience.

slave, might have accrued.[11] In a magisterial study of the apostle, Udo Schnelle writes that Paul belonged to the urban middle class.[12] This is a fair approximation, but contemporary readers of the New Testament must be wary lest they retroject contemporary categories onto the circumstances of two thousand years ago.

Many years after his studies in Jerusalem, and having accepted Jesus as the Messiah, Paul preached the gospel of salvation in Jesus' name. The circumstantial catalogue of 2 Corinthians 11 suggests that Paul voluntarily embraced a life of poverty for the sake of his mission.[13] Nonetheless, he knew several relatively affluent people on whose support he could count. Among those whom he commended to the Christians of Rome was Phoebe, a deacon of the church of Cenchrae. Paul says that Phoebe was a "benefactor [*prostatis*] of many and of myself as well."[14] In Paul's social world of which the benefaction system was an important element, Phoebe was an important figure in Paul's life. Not only did the fiercely independent Paul accept her material support, he also thought enough of her to describe her as his benefactress. The terminology may have been appropriate to describe the function of Mary Magdalene, Joanna, and Susanna in the life of Jesus,[15] but Phoebe is the only person in the entire New Testament to be identified as a "benefactor." She was not only Paul's personal benefactress, she was also the patron of several people in addition to himself—"many," as Paul says. Phoebe would have been a person of considerable wealth.[16]

Immediately after asking the Romans to help Phoebe in her current endeavor—perhaps helping to prepare for Paul's intended trip to Spain—Paul asks his addressees to greet Prisca and Aquila and the church in their house.[17] Prisca and Aquila were presumably a married

[11] Cf. Phlm 18.
[12] Cf. Udo Schnelle, *Apostle Paul: His Life and Theology* (Grand Rapids: Baker Academic, 2005), 63.
[13] Cf. 2 Cor 11:27; Raymond F. Collins, *Second Corinthians*, Paideia (Grand Rapids: Baker Academic, 2013), 232.
[14] Rom 16:2.
[15] Cf. Luke 8:4.
[16] Cf. Robert Jewett, *Romans*, Hermeneia (Minneapolis: Fortress, 2007), 947–48.
[17] Cf. Rom 16:3, 5a.

couple.[18] That she is listed before him suggests that she was the more affluent of the two. He may well have married "into money," as our contemporaries might say. Although Christians gathered in many different venues,[19] a relatively large house would seem to have been a privileged venue.[20] A large house could accommodate a fairly large number of people; its owner would serve as host and patron of the community that gathered there. Ownership of such a house would require some degree of affluence, especially in a city like Rome where smaller groups of Christians gathered in shops and small tenements.

The farewell greetings of the First Letter of Paul to the Corinthians contain another reference to the church in the house of Prisca and Aquila, although in this instance the names of the married couple are reversed. Paul writes, "Aquila and Prisca, together with the church in their house, greet you warmly in the Lord."[21] This letter was written from Ephesus,[22] the capital of the Roman province of Asia. This indicates that at different times in the mid-first century CE, Prisca and Aquila owned substantial homes in two different cities of the empire, cities that were separated from one another by a distance of more than five thousand miles. This obviously was a considerable distance to travel. That Aquila and Prisca were able to travel such a distance points to their affluence.[23] Impoverished travelers would not have

---

[18] Cf. Mario Barbero, "A First-Century Couple: Priscilla and Aquila: Their House Churches and Missionary Activity" (PhD thesis, The Catholic University of America, 2001); Marie Noël Keller, *Priscilla and Aquila: Paul's Coworkers in Christ Jesus*, Paul's Social Network: Brothers and Sisters in Christ (Collegeville, MN: Liturgical Press, 2010).

[19] Cf. Raymond F. Collins, "The Church in the House," *Corpus Reports* 40, no. 4 (2014): 21–29; Edward Adams, *The Earliest Christian Meeting Places: Almost Exclusively Houses?*, Library of New Testament Studies, JSNTSup 430 (London: Bloomsbury T & T Clark, 2013).

[20] Carolyn Osiek and David L. Balch, *Families in the New Testament World: Households and House Churches*, The Family, Religion, and Culture (Louisville: Westminster John Knox, 1997), 16–17, 21.

[21] 1 Cor 16:19. This is the only passage in the New Testament in which the names Prisca and Aquila appear in this order.

[22] Cf. 1 Cor 16:9.

[23] Gerd Theissen identified four criteria of elevated social status. Prisca and Aquila satisfied two of them: having a house and the ability to travel. The other two criteria are holding office and rendering assistance to the church. Cf. Gerd

been able to traverse such a distance, all the while maintaining what little wealth they might have had.

Another notable traveler who belonged to the early Christian movement was Apollos, the learned and eloquent native of Alexandria. He exercised a ministry in Corinth that Paul presents as being in tandem with his own. Our sources do not indicate when and how they met, if indeed they did. Neither do we know how he came to believe, nor why Apollos's faith was deficient until he met up with Prisca and Aquila in Ephesus.[24]

One thing that we do know about Apollos is that he, like Prisca and Aquila, was a traveler. He was born in Alexandria, at that time the capital of the Roman province of Egypt. From there he made his way to Ephesus, the capital of the province of Asia. Then he moved on to Corinth, the capital of the province of Achaia. Luke tells us that Apollos wanted to go to Achaia, the Western text of Acts 18:27 adding that he was importuned to do so by a group of Corinthians who were staying in Ephesus: to wit, "Now there were some Corinthians sojourning in Ephesus who listened to him and they urged him to go with them to their homeland . . . he agreed with them."[25] All told, Apollos's three-legged journey covered about 850 miles.

In the course of their own much-longer travels, Prisca and Aquila stopped in Corinth, the busy metropolitan center of the province of Achaia. That Paul conveyed their greetings to the church at Corinth shows that they were well known to the Corinthian community. Whether they sojourned in Corinth long enough to have established a house church in that city can only remain a matter of speculation. Perhaps there was no need for them to do so.[26]

Luke's Acts adds a few more details about the couple's stay in Corinth. He tells his readers that the couple arrived in Corinth from Rome, which they had to leave because Claudius had ordered all

---

Theissen, *The Social Setting of Pauline Christianity: Essays on Corinth* (Philadelphia: Fortress, 1982), 73–96.

[24] Cf. Acts 18:25-26.

[25] See the Codex Claromontanus (D) and, apparently, Papyrus 38, dating from around 300 CE.

[26] See below, p. 4.

Jews to leave Rome,[27] and that Paul traveled with them when they journeyed to Ephesus.[28] Such travels were not inexpensive, and Prisca and Aquila had traveled from Rome to Corinth, then to Ephesus, and then back to Rome, where they were living and hosting a house church when Paul wrote to the believers in Rome late in the 50s CE. Their travels had taken them some ten thousand miles, something of a trek even by today's standards. Despite their travels, they had sufficient wealth to accommodate house churches in their homes in Ephesus and in Rome.

We must also rely on Acts for the information that Paul stayed with Prisca and Aquila in Corinth, perhaps for the duration of his eighteen-month stay,[29] and worked with them. By trade they were tent makers, reports Luke.[30] The information is scanty, but Luke seems to suggest that they had their own shop, perhaps one with a dwelling attached. Was it one of the relatively large shops on the agora, the remains of which can be seen in today's "Old Corinth"? That we will probably never know. Nonetheless, their business seems to have flourished enough so that they could add Paul as another hand to their enterprise. It is likely that they worked in leather, though not exclusively tent making.[31] Some scholars have suggested that the identification mark on their shop would have depicted a tent, hence Luke's choice of "tentmakers" to designate the trade of leather workers.

Luke also tells us about another female entrepreneur who was known to Paul and supported his work. When Paul was visiting Philippi, he spoke to a group of women who gathered in a place of prayer outside the city.[32] Among the women who favorably received Paul was Lydia, from Thyatira. Lydia's enterprise was the production

---

[27] Cf. Acts 18:2; Suetonius, *Divus Claudius* 25.4; Orosius, *Historiae adversus paganos* 7.6.15–16.

[28] Cf. Acts 18:18-21.

[29] Cf. Acts 18:11.

[30] Cf. Acts 18:2.

[31] So, various patristic witnesses. Cf. F. F. Bruce, *The Acts of the Apostles*, 3rd ed. (Grand Rapids: Eerdmans, 1990), 392; H. Szsesnat, "What Did the *skēnopoios* Paul Produce?," *Neot* 27 (1993): 391–402.

[32] Cf. Acts 16:11b-15.

and distribution of purple cloth.[33] Her trade would have led people to look upon her as an ordinary craftsperson, but the fact that she was a householder[34] with her own home suggests that she was fairly successful at what she did.[35] She seems to have belonged to a group of people of relatively low social status but of relatively high economic status.[36] Bennema situates her within the "middle class."[37]

Another woman of some means who was known to Paul was Chloe, more than likely a businesswoman from Ephesus. Paul tells us that "her people" (*hypo tōn Chloēs*[38]) brought him the disturbing news that there were serious disagreements among the members of the church of God at Corinth.[39] The odd expression used by Paul suggests that these people were beholden to Chloe, either slaves or freed persons who worked for her,[40] rather than members of her immediate household. That a group of them had been in Ephesus suggests that they had been there to conduct business on behalf of their mistress.

Since Chloe is not mentioned elsewhere in the New Testament, it is impossible to affirm without qualification that she was a believer. In the early days of the Christian mission, it sometimes happened

---

[33] Cf. Mikael C. Parsons, *Acts*, Paideia (Grand Rapids: Baker Academic, 2008), 230.

[34] Acts 16:15 says that Lydia and her household (*ho oikos autēs*) were baptized. For other instances of an entire household being baptized along with the head of the household, see Acts 1:14; 16:31-32; 18:8.

[35] Dunn speaks of her as "a woman with a substantial business in luxury goods"; James D. G. Dunn, *The Acts of the Apostles* (Valley Forge, PA: Trinity Press International, 1996), 219. Florence Gillman writes of her "upward social mobility"; cf. Florence M. Gillman, "Lydia," in *Women Who Knew Paul*, Zacchaeus Studies: New Testament (Collegeville, MN: Liturgical Press, 1992), 30–38, 38.

[36] Cf. Shelley Matthews, "Elite Women, Public Religion, and Christian Propaganda in Acts 16," in *A Feminist Companion to the Acts of the Apostles*, ed. Amy-Jill Levine (London: T & T Clark, 2004), 111–33, 126.

[37] Cf. Cornelis Bennema, *A Theory of Character in New Testament Narrative* (Minneapolis: Augsburg Fortress, 2014), 178.

[38] These three words are all that the New Testament actually tells us about Chloe.

[39] Cf. 1 Cor 1:11.

[40] Cf. Wayne A. Meeks, *The First Urban Christians: The Social World of the Apostle Paul* (New Haven: Yale University Press, 1983), 59, 63.

that some slaves were believers even if the master or mistress was not. On the other hand, were Chloe to have been a believer, it is likely that her slaves would also have belonged to the church. That Paul cites her name is at least a hint that she was a believer.[41] Fitzmyer opines that she was a resident of Corinth—since she was known to the Corinthians—and a believer who had friends in Ephesus,[42] but there is a possibility that she was an Ephesian who did business in the commercial center of Corinth.[43]

Another often-overlooked person in Paul's circle is Philemon. The reason for the relative neglect is obvious. Philemon is known to us only through the relatively short letter that Paul addressed to him. The letter, almost a long note in letter form, contains only twenty-five verses. An excerpt from this letter is read only once every three years in the Lectionary of Sunday readings in the Roman Catholic Church. Paul considers Philemon to be a very dear friend (*agapētō*),[44] a real brother (*adelphe*).[45] Philemon was, moreover, someone with whom Paul had worked closely in the work of evangelization. Paul styles him as a partner (*koinōnon*)[46] and co-worker (*synergō hēmōn*), not only of Paul himself but also of Timothy, who played a role in the composition of this short missive.[47]

This close friend and fellow evangelist was another relatively affluent person in the apostle's entourage.[48] Wayne Meeks says that

---

[41] Cf. Raymond F. Collins, *First Corinthians*, SP 7 (Collegeville, MN: Liturgical Press, 1999).

[42] Joseph A. Fitzmyer, *First Corinthians*, AB 33 (New Haven: Yale University Press, 2008), 141.

[43] So Thiselton suggests, as do Ciampa and Rosner. Ciampa and Rosner also suggest that Chloe may have been a widow. Cf. Anthony C. Thiselton, *The First Epistle to the Corinthians*, NIGTC (Grand Rapids: Eerdmans, 2000), 121; Roy E. Ciampa and Brian S. Rosner, *The First Letter to the Corinthians*, Pillar New Testament Commentary (Grand Rapids: Eerdmans, 2010), 77.

[44] Cf. Phlm 1.

[45] Cf. Phlm 20.

[46] Cf. Phlm 17.

[47] Cf. Phlm 1.

[48] Cf. Peter Arzt-Grabner, "How to Deal with Onesimus? Paul's Solution within the Frame of Ancient Legal and Documentary Sources," in *Philemon in Perspective: Interpreting a Pauline Letter*, ed. D. François Tolmie, BZNW 169 (Berlin: De Gruyter, 2010), 113–42, 119.

Philemon "ranks high at least on the dimension of wealth."[49] As Prisca and Aquila did, he hosted a gathering of believers in his home.[50] His and theirs are the only two "house churches" that Paul mentions using this specifically ecclesial language.[51] Philemon's house was large enough to have a "guest room" (*xenian*),[52] one that Paul wanted Philemon to prepare for him so that he might be able to use it after his desired release from prison. The Greek word *xenia* means "hospitality," but in ancient papyri and in the New Testament[53] the term typically connoted a room or an apartment in which guests, friends, or strangers could be accommodated.[54] James D. G. Dunn opines that Philemon was a successful businessman who probably had several guest rooms.[55]

In addition to these two indications of his relative affluence, there is the fact that Philemon was a slave-owner. We know the name of only one of his slaves, Onesimus, but there is little reason to believe that Onesimus was Philemon's only slave. Evidence from Roman Egypt—unfortunately, similar evidence for Roman Asia has not yet been found—suggests that the majority of slaveholders in urban areas had only one or two slaves. Relatively few had more than six or seven, but Tacitus tells us about the wealthy Pedanius Secundus who owned four hundred slaves.[56]

The entire letter to Philemon is about the relationship between Onesimus and Philemon. Apparently, the slave had availed himself—

[49] Meeks, *Urban Christians*, 60.

[50] Cf. Phlm 1.

[51] Col 3:15 mentions the church in Nympha's house, but that disputed epistle is arguably not something that Paul himself wrote. See Collins, *Letters*, 171–208.

[52] Phlm 22. Fitzmyer notes that *xenia* is "an abstraction used for a concrete term"; Joseph A. Fitzmyer, *Philemon*, AB 34C (New York: Doubleday, 2000), 122.

[53] Cf. Acts 28:33.

[54] Cf. Ceslas Spicq, "*xenia ktl.*," *TLNT* 2:555–60, 559–60; BDAG, 683.

[55] Cf. James D. G. Dunn, *The Epistles to the Colossians and to Philemon*, NIGTC (Grand Rapids: Eerdmans, 1996), 300–301.

[56] Cf. *Ann.* 14.43. Walter Scheidel opines that only a few slave-owners were wealthy enough to own a large number of slaves. Cf. Scheidel, "The Roman Slave Supply," in *The Cambridge World History of Slavery*, vol. 1: *The Ancient Mediterranean World*, ed. Keith Bradley and Paul Cartledge (Cambridge: Cambridge University Press, 2011), 287–310, esp. 291–92.

with Philemon's blessing?—of the *amicus magistri* principle of Roman law, which allowed an aggrieved slave to appeal to one of his master's friends to intervene on his behalf.[57] Onesimus seems not to have been a runaway, as had once been presumed. As for Philemon, in a significant paper delivered to the 2014 Ecumenical Pauline Colloquium, David Horrell argued that we must not overestimate the slave-owner's wealth. Horrell places Philemon in "a 'middling' group whose members live significantly above subsistence level but still with only modest resources."[58]

Prisca and Aquila and Philemon were, of course, not the only relatively wealthy homeowners who furthered the Pauline mission. Writing to the Romans from Corinth, Paul conveys greetings from a man named Gaius, "who is host to me and to the whole church [*ho zenos mou kai hōlēs tēs ekklēsias*]."[59] The name Gaius was not uncommon, even among believers of the New Testament generation,[60] but it is likely that this large homeowner is the Gaius whom Paul recalls having baptized himself.[61] One could plausibly argue that it was in Gaius's large home where the believers at Corinth came together as a church.[62] Although Paul mentions that Prisca and Aquila hosted a church in their homes in Ephesus and Rome, he makes no mention

[57] Cf. Peter Lampe, "Keine 'Sklavenflucht' des Onesimus," *ZNW* 76 (1985): 135–37; Pliny the Younger, *Ep.* 21.

[58] David G. Horrell, "Farewell to Another Wealthy Patron? Reassessing Philemon in the Light of Recent Scholarly Discussion of Socio-Economic Level and Domestic Space," 15. Similarly, "Philemon was among the middling groups in urban society—not destitute but with some surplus resources," 23. The soon-to-be published paper was delivered on September 17, 2014, during the Ecumenical Pauline Colloquium held at Rome's Abbey of St. Paul Outside the Walls, September 15–20, 2014.

[59] Cf. Rom 16:33a. This third-person greeting, followed by a comparable greeting from Erasmus, contains the last words composed by Paul in the dictation of the letter to the Romans. Cf. Raymond F. Collins, "The Case of a Wandering Doxology: Rom 16:25-27," in *New Testament Textual Criticism and Exegesis*, ed. Adelbert Denaux, BETL 161 (Louvain: University Press—Peeters, 2002), 249–59.

[60] Cf. Acts 19:29; 20:4; 3 John 1.

[61] Cf. 1 Cor 1:14.

[62] Cf. 1 Cor 10:17, 18, 20; Anthony J. Blasi, *Early Christianity as a Social Movement*, Toronto Studies in Religion 5 (New York: Lang, 1988), 57.

of a house church under their patronage in Corinth. Perhaps the couple had no need to provide one. Gaius's home would have been a sufficiently large venue in which the city's believers could gather.

In the same breath with which he mentions the baptism of Gaius, Paul also makes note of the fact that he also baptized Crispus,[63] apparently one of the few persons whom Paul baptized personally. Paul mentions Crispus just once in his Corinthian correspondence, but Crispus is undoubtedly the same Crispus described by Luke in Acts 18:8.[64] Luke identifies him as a synagogue official, an *archisynagōgos*.[65] No doubt, Luke mentions Crispus's function to underscore the success of Paul's preaching. The *archisynagōgos* was, in fact, the presiding officer of the synagogue. Not only did he have a role in synagogue services, he also had judicial authority over members of the congregation. He could administer the famous forty lashes minus one[66] and could bar people from the congregation.

Neither Paul nor Luke dwell on the financial status of this synagogue official, but the fact that Paul remembers him in the same breath as Gaius potentially suggests that he belonged to the same class of people. For his part, Luke gives an indication that Crispus too was a householder. The evangelist's narrative says that Crispus was baptized, "together with all his household" (*syn holō tō oikō autou*).[67] Chrys Caragounis notes that he "cannot have lived on existence minimum."[68]

---

[63] Cf. 1 Cor 1:14.

[64] Just before this reference to Crispus, Luke mentions that Paul went to the home of a man named Titius Justus. That he is described as a *sebomenos ton theon*, a "worshiper of God," in reality someone sympathetic to Judaism, and is juxtaposed with Crispus "who became a believer in the Lord," suggests that he was not a believer.

[65] Cf. Mark 5:22, 35, 36, 38; Luke 8:41.

[66] Cf. Deut 25:1-3.

[67] Acts 18:8.

[68] Chrys C. Caragounis, "A House Church in Corinth: An Inquiry into the Structure of Early Corinthian Christianity," in *Saint Paul and Corinth: 1950 Years since the Writing of the Epistles to the Corinthians; International Scholarly Conference Proceedings (Corinth, 23–25 September 2007)*, vol. 1, ed. Constantine J. Belezos (Athens: Psichogios, 2009), 365–418, at 407–8.

Erastus, the city treasurer,[69] was certainly one of the more affluent Corinthians and someone whom Paul knew.[70] The apostle does not mention Erastus in either of his letters to the Corinthians, but the final words of his long letter to the Romans contain greetings on behalf of Erasmus, a person whom the apostle identifies as the city treasurer (*ho oikonomos tos poleōs*).[71]

Erastus seems to be one of the few New Testament characters known to us from extrabiblical sources. The 1929 excavations in Old Corinth yielded an inscription with the name "Erastus" on a paving stone near the entrance to the Roman theater. The two-lined epigraph, dating from around 50 CE, reads, "Erastus, in return for his aedileship, laid this pavement at his own expense [*Erastus pro aedilitate sua pecunia stravit*]."[72] An aedile was generally a very wealthy person who was in overall charge of a city's finances and its public works, including its games, the police, and the city's grain. The aedileship was a higher office than city treasurer, *arcarus*, in Latin; Paul's Erastus seemingly did not hold the office of aedile when Paul wrote to the Romans toward the end of the 50s, but authors such as H. J. Mason and Chrys Caragounis argue that the Greek *oikonomos* was sometimes equivalent to the Latin *aedilis*.[73]

Although we cannot claim with absolute certainty that Paul's Erastus and the inscription's Erastus are one and the same person,[74] it is quite likely that they are. "Erastus" was not a popular name; the name is found, either in Greek or in Latin, only seventy-eight times over the course of perhaps a number of centuries.[75] It would not

---

[69] Acts 19:22; 2 Tim 4:20.

[70] Cf. Fitzmyer, *First Corinthians*, 162, who writes, "Erastus of Rom 16:23 was undoubtedly a man of means."

[71] Cf. Rom 16:33b.

[72] Cf. Henry J. Cadbury, "Erastus of Corinth," *JBL* 50 (1931): 42–58; John McRay, *Archaeology and the New Testament* (Grand Rapids: Baker, 1991), 331–33; Andrew J. Clarke, *Secular and Christian Leadership in Corinth: A Socio-Historical and Exegetical Study of 1 Corinthians 1–6*, AGJU 18 (Leiden: Brill, 1993), 46–56.

[73] Cf. H. J. Mason, *Greek Terms for Roman Institutions: A Lexicon and Analysis* (Toronto: Hajjert, 1974), 71; Caragounis, "House Church," 410n144.

[74] Justin Meggitt argues that they were not the same person, but his arguments have been refuted by Caragounis. Cf. Justin J. Meggitt, "The Social State of Erastus (Rom 16.23)," *NTS* 38 (1996): 218–23; Caragounis, "House Church," 408–10n144.

[75] Caragounis, "House Church," 409n144.

have been likely that two persons with this name held public office at about the same time. Moreover, "rotating chairs" within the empire's officialdom would have made it possible for Erastus to transition from one office to the other. He could have been city treasurer before becoming director of public works or vice versa. In any case, Erastus was a monied man. He paid for the paved esplanade out of his own purse (*sua pecunia*).[76]

This rehearsal of the names of people in Paul's circle who had some wealth suggests that he might have added "rich" to his words on the social stratification of the church of God in Corinth: "Not many of you were wise by human standards, not many were powerful, not many were of noble birth."[77] Not many were wise, powerful, and well born, but some were. Not many would seem to have been rich, but some were.

This situation was not so dissimilar from that of Jesus' own circle a generation earlier. Luke tells us that there were with Jesus and the Twelve "some women who had been cured of evil spirits and infirmities: Mary, called Magdalen . . . and Joanna . . . and Susanna, and others, who provided for them out of their resources."[78] Some of these female patrons even traveled with Jesus to Jerusalem, where he was to be put to death.

It is not appropriate to harmonize the four gospel accounts in an attempt to write a biography of Jesus, but we should note that the Fourth Evangelist tells the story of Mary of Bethany who anointed Jesus' feet with a pound of costly perfume made of pure nard, in anticipation of his burial.[79] The costly perfume had a value of about a year's wages for the ordinary worker.

Matthew adds that on the evening of the day that Jesus was crucified, "there came a rich man from Arimathea, named Joseph, who was also a disciple of Jesus."[80] Having obtained permission from the

---

[76] Ancient inscriptions that honor wealthy benefactors who sponsored public works typically mention that they paid for the works with their own funds. See, for example, Thomas Corsten, *Die Inschriften von Laodikeia am Lykos* (Bonn: Habelt, 1997), inscriptions 9.9; 12.1; 13.7-8; 15.3; 24.3.

[77] 1 Cor 1:26b.

[78] Luke 8:2-3.

[79] Cf. John 12:3-8.

[80] Matt 27:57.

appropriate authority, Joseph took Jesus' body and laid it in a new tomb that belonged to him.

These are only vignettes, but they indicate that the group of Jesus' own disciples included at least a few people of means. Before turning to what the gospels have to say about Jesus' teaching on wealth, wages, and the wealthy, we should examine the letters of Paul since these contain the oldest literary evidence of what the nascent Christian tradition thought about the topic.

So What?[81]

At the conclusion of this rapid overview of the relatively wealthy persons in the early Christian communities, both in Palestine and in the Hellenistic diaspora, it might be useful to reflect on what their example might mean to wealthy believers today. Is affluence an asset or a bane for the contemporary believer?

In a Thursday morning homily in Rome's Casa Santa Marta, where he lives, during Mass on October 19, 2015, Pope Francis reminded the congregation that Jesus was not against wealth.[82] Rather, said the pope, Jesus warned against putting one's security in money and trying to make of religion an "insurance agency."

---

[81] I have decided to add a "So What?" conclusion to each of the chapters in this study. Does the teaching of Jesus have any relevance for today? Does the teaching of the New Testament on wealth, wages, and the wealthy have any bearing on how people act?

Two types of material will be incorporated into these "So What?" sections. One sort of material will illustrate contemporary attitudes toward wealth, wages, and the wealthy by means of newspaper clippings and other news sources. Truth to tell, the collection of this material did not require real "research" on my part. I simply gathered together material that came to my attention in the course of a few months, most often while drinking a second cup of coffee after breakfast. For the most part, this material illustrates an almost total neglect or rejection of New Testament teaching.

The second sort of material assumed into these "So What?" sections will consist of quotations from religious leaders, especially Francis, the Bishop of Rome, as he correctly styles himself. These quotations are intended to show that today's religious leaders continue to proclaim that the teaching of Jesus is indeed relevant and challenging for believers at the dawn of this third millennium.

[82] Cf. Zenit.org, October 19, 2015.

With reference to the Beatitudes, Pope Francis then went on to say that if one has riches, one mustn't be attached to them but must place them at the service of others, "to share, to help many people to make their way."

Although he is not a believer—he is an atheist—Mark Zuckerberg was raised as a Jew and became a bar mitzvah at the age of thirteen. In 2012, he married his college girlfriend, Priscilla Chan, a Vietnamese-Chinese refugee who became a pediatrician. Priscilla suffered three miscarriages, but on December 1, 2015, she gave birth to a healthy daughter, Maxima Chan Zuckerberg. In gratitude, the couple announced that they would launch the Zuckerberg initiative with an initial gift of 99 percent of their Facebook shares, worth about $45 billion, about half of their fortune. Zuckerberg is reputed to be the seventh-wealthiest person in the United States. The new initiative has four foci: personalized learning, curing disease, connecting people, and building strong communities.

Chapter 2

Paul's Letters

It is appropriate that we begin our textual study with an examination of Paul's letters not only because they are the oldest of the New Testament documents but also because they are occasional compositions. They were written to flesh-and-blood communities who were concerned not only with their faith but also with how their faith impacted their lives. Were they to overlook some aspect of their lives that ought to be seen through the lens of their faith, Paul was sure to enlighten them. One aspect of life, then and now, is the use of one's money. Hence, we should expect that the apostle Paul has something to say about wealth, wages, and the wealthy. We are not to be disappointed with this expectation. Paul addresses the topic in one way or another in each of his extant letters.

First Corinthians

"Practically all of the known Corinthians connected with the Church of Corinth," writes Caragounis in one of his cameo reflections on the house church in Corinth, "are shown to be persons of independent means."[1] Such a reflection indicates that it might be well to begin with the Corinthian correspondence in this study of wealth, wages, and the wealthy. Not only is this material some of our oldest

---

[1] Caragounis, "House Church," 409–10; cf. Theissen, *Social Setting*, 95. In his various writings, E. A. Judge has identified at least forty persons at Corinth who belonged to what he describes as the "cultivated social elite." See, among his other publications, "The Early Christians as a Scholastic Community," *JRH* 1 (1960–61): 4–15, 125–37, 128–30.

Christian documentation, but it is also quite extensive. Together, the two letters to the Corinthians comprise twenty-seven chapters, a quantity of material approximately equal to the Gospel of Matthew and exceeded in size only by Luke's two-part work, his gospel and the Acts of the Apostles. Moreover, the Corinthian correspondence is clearly the most hands-on body of material in the New Testament. It deals with real-life issues, including how believers deal with their wealth.

1 Corinthians 1:26

In the first chapter of this correspondence Paul provides his readers with a social analysis of the community. "Consider your own call," he writes, "not many of you were wise by human standards, not many were powerful, not many were of noble birth."[2] Celsus, the second-century critic of Christianity, apparently capitalized on these words, to show his disdain for the upstart group of believers: "By the fact that they themselves admit that these people are worthy of their God, they show that they want and are able to convince only the foolish, dishonorable, and stupid, and only slaves, women, and little children."[3] Celsus certainly exaggerated, but he was only the first in a long line of commentators to assert that early Christianity drew its adherents from the lower classes. Adolf Deissmann was perhaps the most notable commentator to argue along these lines during the historical-critical era of New Testament scholarship.[4]

Paul's thrice-repeated "not many" (*ou polloi*) clearly implies that in his estimation there were at least some members of the church at Corinth who were wise, powerful, and/or of noble birth.[5] The latter

---

[2] 1 Cor 1:26.

[3] From "True Doctrine" (*Alēthēs logos*), as summarized by Origen, *Against Celsus* 3.44, 59, 64. Cf. M. Eugene Boring, Klaus Berge, and Carsten Colpe, eds., *Hellenistic Commentary to the New Testament* (Nashville: Abingdon, 1995), 391–92.

[4] Cf. Adolf Deissmann, *Light from the Ancient East: The New Testament Illustrated by Recently Discovered Texts of the Graeco-Roman World* (New York: George H. Doran, 1927), 8.

[5] See, among classic commentators of the historical-critical era, Johannes Weiss, *Der erste Korintherbrief*, KEK 9 (Göttingen: Vandenhoeck & Ruprecht, 1910), xvi; and Ernest-Bernard Allo, *Saint Paul: Première Épître aux Corinthiens*, 2nd ed., *EBib* (Paris: Gabalda, 1956), 20.

two categories suggest that there were some at Corinth who were relatively affluent, but Paul does not explicitly say anything about the wealthy[6] in his brief reflection on the social status of the members of the community. This would be all the more surprising if, as Gail O'Day has suggested, Jeremiah 9:23 lies behind Paul's social "analysis."[7] The prophet spoke of the wise, the mighty, and the wealthy. So too does the Greek version of 1 Samuel 2:10.

That there are three elements in Paul's description of the social makeup of the community of believers is not surprising in view of his predilection for groups of three. His concern, however, is not in providing his readers with a breakdown of the community of believers. His readers lived in the city and in the community of believers. They would have had experiential knowledge of the social makeup of the city and that part of it that constituted the church of God in Corinth. In the first rhetorical demonstration of the letter—1 Corinthians 1:18–4:21—Paul argues about wisdom. The triad found in 1 Corinthians 1:26 is part of the argument. The emphasis is on wisdom, not power or the circumstances of one's birth.

Despite Paul's omission of the wealthy, there is little reason to doubt, especially in the light of our reflections on Prisca and Aquila, Chloe, Gaius, Crispus, and Erastus, that "the social level of the Corinthian Christians apparently varied from quite poor to rather well-off . . . a fair cross-section of their city."[8] What did Paul have to say to those on the upper half of this spectrum?

1 Corinthians 16:1-4

As Paul, apostle to the Corinthians,[9] is about to complete his letter, he takes up one final topic, the collection for the saints (*peri de tēs*

---

[6] Sanger opines that the powerful (*dynatoi*) are, in fact, the rich whose wealth enabled them to exercise power in the community. Cf. Dieter Sanger, "Die *dynatoi* in 1 Kor 1,26," *ZNW* 76 (1985): 285–91.

[7] Cf. Gail R. O'Day, "Jeremiah 9:22-23 and 1 Corinthians 1:26-31: A Study in Intertextuality," *JBL* 109 (1990): 259–67. Cf. 1 Sam 2:10 [LXX].

[8] Ben Witherington III, *Conflict and Community: A Socio-Rhetorical Commentary on 1 and 2 Corinthians* (Grand Rapids: Eerdmans; Carlisle: Paternoster, 1995), 23.

[9] Cf. 1 Cor 9:2.

logeias tēs eis tous hagious). From time to time throughout the letter Paul uses a classic formula, "now concerning" (*peri de*),[10] to introduce topics on which he had something to say to the Corinthians.[11] For the most part these topics were problematic issues about which Paul had been informed, but this seems not to have been the case in 1 Corinthians 16:1-4. Rather, Paul uses the formula to introduce a topic that was dear to his heart. So he addresses those in the community who have been described as having "disposable income or assets"[12] in these words:

> Now concerning the collection for the saints: you should fol-low the directions that I gave to the churches of Galatia. On the first day of every week, each of you is to put aside and save whatever extra you earn, so that collections need not be taken when I come. And when I arrive, I will send any whom you approve with letters to take your gift to Jerusalem. If it seems advisable that I should go also, they will accompany me.[13]

The Greek phrase that the New Revised Standard Version (NRSV) translates as "whatever extra you earn," *ho ti ean euodōtai*, is difficult to translate with any precision, let alone with a translation that ade-quately takes into account the differences between the economies of the first and twenty-first centuries. The 2011 Common English Bible chose "whatever you can afford from what you earn" to translate the problematic and metaphorical phrase. Earlier, the Revised Stan-dard Version had translated the phrase "as he may prosper."[14] In my commentary on this letter, I rendered the expression as "whatever he or she has gained."[15] BDAG 323 opts for "as much as he gains," while the Revised English Bible interprets the Greek as "whatever he can afford."

---

[10] Cf. Margaret M. Mitchell, "Concerning *peri de* in 1 Corinthians," *NovT* 31 (1989): 221–56.

[11] Cf. 7:1; 8:1, 4; 12:1; 16:12.

[12] Witherington, *Conflict and Community*, 22.

[13] 1 Cor 16:1-4.

[14] Cf. Horst Balz, *"euodoō," EDNT* 2: 81.

[15] Raymond F. Collins, *First Corinthians*, SP 7 (Collegeville, MN: Liturgical Press, 1999), 585, 589.

The verb *euodoomai*, from which *euodōtai* is derived, appears just four times in the New Testament, including one other time in Paul's writings.[16] The verb is related to the noun *hodos*, which means "way" or "road." The prefix *eu* means "good" or "well." So the verb literally means "follow a good path." Used metaphorically, *euodoomai* means "get along well" or "prosper." Applied to finances, the metaphor means "profit." Paul was a master of metaphor and often used metaphors to speak about financial matters.[17]

Paul seems to be implying that the contributions of the members of the community should be in keeping with their relative prosperity.[18] The great patristic commentator on Paul's letters, John Chrysostom, wrote:

> Notice his gentleness even here. He does not say "such and such an amount" but as he may prosper, showing that the resources are from God. Furthermore, by not ordering them to collect it all at one time, he makes the contribution easy. Since it is collected little by little, the offering and the expenditure are imperceptible.[19]

Paul refers to the collection in several of his letters, particularly Romans 15:25-29 and 2 Corinthians 8–9, in addition to 1 Corinthians 16:1-4.[20] In 1 Corinthians 16:1 Paul mentions that he had given appropriate instructions on the collection to the churches of Galatia, but he does not refer to them in his letter to the Galatians,[21] which dealt with a different urgent matter. Given Paul's multiple mentions

---

[16] Rom 1:10; 1 Cor 16:2; 3 John 2 [2x]. All four New Testament uses are metaphorical.

[17] See Raymond F. Collins, *The Power of Images in Paul* (Collegeville, MN: Liturgical Press, 2008), esp. 248–50.

[18] "In keeping with your income" is the fairly accurate NIV interpretation of Paul's metaphor offered by Ciampa and Rosner. Cf. Roy E. Ciampa and Brian S. Rosner, *The First Letter to the Corinthians*, Pillar New Testament Commentary (Grand Rapids: Eerdmans, 2010), 843–44; see also Gordon D. Fee, *The First Epistle to the Corinthians*, NICNT (Grand Rapids: Eerdmans, 1987), 814, who, however, considers "in keeping with your income" too modern.

[19] John Chrysostom, *Homily* 43 (PG 61:368), in *1 Corinthians: Interpreted by Early Christian Commentators*, trans. Judith L. Kovacs, The Church's Bible (Grand Rapids: Eerdmans, 2005), 283.

[20] Cf. 1 Cor 16:15.

[21] Note, however, Gal 2:10.

of the collection both orally and in writing, we can be sure that he considered the collection to be an integral part of his ministry. Keith Nickle's study of the collection[22] highlights its many purposes, including care for the poor, expression of gratitude to the mother church,[23] and unity between Gentile and Jewish believers.[24]

The present study does not warrant a full analysis of the collection, Paul's *logeia*, but a few exegetical observations are in order. First of all, Paul's appeal on behalf of the poor has its roots in his biblical tradition.[25] Many passages could be cited; different interpreters cite different Scriptures. The Greek term *logeia* was commonly used for the collection of taxes, but it could also be used for the collection of voluntary offerings, as it is in 1 Corinthians 16:1-2.[26] Referencing the first day of the week (*kata mian sabbatou*), Paul implicitly invites his addressees to think of the Lord's resurrection, but he does not actually suggest that they are to make a contribution during a liturgical gathering.

Paul's exhortation is addressed to "each of you" (*hekastos hymōn*). This suggests that contributions to the collection should come from each member of the community, not simply from those who had some surplus of wealth. That each one was to set apart some in keeping with his or her income on "the first day of the week" (*kata mian sabbatou*) most likely had an economic as well as a religious purpose. Whether the members of the community were among the more affluent businesspeople or were artisans or slaves, the economy

---

[22] Keith F. Nickle, *The Collection: A Study in Paul's Strategy*, SBT 48 (Naperville, IL: A. R. Allenson, 1966); cf. Dieter Georgi, *Remembering the Poor: The History of Paul's Collection for Jerusalem* (Nashville: Abingdon, 1992).

[23] It is to be noted that Paul does not mention Jerusalem until verse 3. What he puts before the community for their consideration is a collection "for the saints" (*eis tous hagious*). While "the saints" (*hoi hagioi*) eventually came to be used as a designation for all believers (Rom 1:7; 1 Cor 1:2; Phil 1:1; etc.), the terminology seems to have first been used in reference to believers in Jerusalem, "Judeo-Christians" who constituted an eschatological remnant of God's holy people, Israel.

[24] Cf., albeit with an exaggerated political bias, Sze-kar Wan, "Collection for the Saints as an Anti-colonial Act," in *Paul and Politics: Ekklesia, Israel, Imperium, Interpretation; Essays in Honor of Krister Stendahl*, ed. Richard A. Horsley (Harrisburg, PA: Trinity Press International, 2000), 191–215.

[25] Deut 15:7-8 would be one such passage among many.

[26] The twice-used term appears only here in the New Testament.

of the time would have meant that their income fluctuated; it varied from week to week. Setting aside something every week not only makes the collection easier, as Chrysostom suggests, but also ensures that what is set aside is proportionate to one's weekly earnings. Chrysostom rightly observes that there was no specific amount assigned or assessed; the system was not one of taxation.

Finally, Paul has something to say about the delivery of the collection to Jerusalem. He intends that it be carried by a group of people approved by the Corinthians themselves. Paul would write letters of introduction and credence on their behalf, but he did not propose that he should be the one to take the collection to Jerusalem. Nonetheless, he confesses his willingness to go with the group, if the Corinthians should so desire. Having the Corinthians send a delegation to transport the monetary collection had at least two purposes. First of all, it was a kind of insurance intended to ensure the security of the delivery. A single traveler carrying a large sum of money was likely to be a victim of robbery. A group of travelers journeying together lessened that danger considerably. Second, Paul wanted to distance himself from the delivery lest he be accused of dipping into the till for his own purposes. Second Corinthians suggests that such an accusation was later made by somebody or somebodies in the Corinthian community.

1 Corinthians 6:1-9a

Paul's short exhortation with regard to the collection for the saints in 1 Corinthians 16:1-4 tells something about what believers should do with their assets. There are, however, two passages in the epistle that warn against the rich taking advantage of their situation to the disadvantage of the less well-off in the community, namely, 1 Corinthians 6:1-9a and 1 Corinthians 11:17-22. In the first of these, Paul criticizes—and strongly[27]—those who take their fellow believers to a secular court, "before the unrighteous," in Paul's words.[28]

---

[27] Thiselton (*First Epistle*, 423) observes, "The very first word, *tolma*, indemnifies another anomaly which causes Paul to experience a further sense of outrage and disappointment."

[28] Cf. 1 Cor 6:1, *epi tōn adikōn*. Having surveyed various translations of the phrase, Thiselton opts for "where there is questionable justice" and comments,

Archaeological evidence suggests that *duoviri*,[29] chosen from among the city's leading citizens and serving a one-year term, were the highest magistrates in the metropolitan area. Normally, civil cases began in their courts. Aediles heard cases pertaining to business conducted at one or the other marketplace, an agora. The most important cases were heard by the Roman governor himself, as Caesar Augustus had decreed.[30]

The actual administration of justice must, however, be seen within the social situation of the times. The Roman patronage system was an important part of the social fabric. Powerful patrons were able to tip the scales of justice toward themselves, often by means of an appropriate bribe. Civil lawsuits were generally initiated by people of equal and upper social status, generally against those who were less well-off. One exception to the general rule that the plaintiffs were better off than those accused was the plethora of inheritance disputes among siblings that ended up in a court of law. These lawsuits may have provided Paul with the family language that he uses in trying to dissuade his readers from appealing to a court of law to settle their disputes.[31] Typically, the poor had virtually no standing in the eyes of the courts.

Seneca the Elder (54 BCE–39 CE), the scion of a wealthy equestrian, treated the judicial system of the era in one of his two extant writings, the *Controversiae*. A brilliant rhetorician, Seneca enabled his readers to understand the judicial system by offering them a series of short vignettes. In one of them, a rich man is portrayed as taunting a poor man with these words: "Why don't you accuse me, why don't you take me to court?" To which the poor man could only answer, "Am I a poor man, to accuse a rich man?" The purpose of Seneca's

---

"It is safe to conclude that the use of *Roman provincial courts* for *minor* cases and the certainty of a result of *questionable justice* are virtually *synonymous*" (*First Epistle,* 418, 424; his emphasis).

[29] Literally, "two men."

[30] See Collins, *First Corinthians,* 226.

[31] Cf. Michael Peppard, "Brother against Brother: *Controversiae* about Inheritance Disputes and 1 Corinthians 6:1-11," *JBL* 133 (2014): 179–92. Cf. Luke 12:13-15.

story[32] was to show that a powerful and rich man had nothing to fear from the court.

Would, moreover, a poor man even have been able to take a rich man to court? The satirist and courtier Petronius (ca. 27 CE–66 CE) tells a story about Ascyltos who feared going to court because he was without influence. Moreover, he would have had no money with which to bribe the magistrate.[33] Along with patronage, bribery was simply part of the system.[34] Without sufficient wherewithal, the poor were not able to participate.[35]

On the other hand, biblical law demanded the protection of the poor in court.[36] Later Jewish rabbinic tradition was, however, well aware of the bias of the judicial system toward the rich. For example, a rabbinic commentary on the book of Leviticus says, "The usual experience is: two men go before a judge, one of them poor and the other rich; towards whom does the judge turn his face? Is it not toward the rich man?"[37]

Some decades after Paul and writing for a Christian community with a different ethnic constitution from that of the church at Corinth in the mid-50s, the evangelist Matthew urged believers to settle disputes among themselves, one on one. Only as a last resort should the matter be brought to the attention of the entire community.[38] In 1 Corinthians 6:1-9a Paul seems to be of a similar mind. Christians should solve their disputes among themselves. An appeal to a secular court of law is already an acknowledgment of moral failure; it's a defeat for you,[39] says Paul. He speaks to them in this way "to their shame."[40]

---

[32] Cf. *Controversiae* 10.1.2.

[33] Cf. *Satyricon* 14.

[34] Cf. P. Oxyrhynchus 2745, 7–8.

[35] Cf. John K. Chow, *Patronage and Power: A Study of Social Networks in Corinth*, JSNTSup 75 (Sheffield: Sheffield Academic, 1992), 123–41.

[36] Cf. Exod 23:6-8.

[37] *Lev. Rab.* 3:2.

[38] Cf. Matt 18:15-17.

[39] The Greek of 1 Cor 6:7, *ēttēma hymin*, appears elsewhere in the New Testament only in Rom 11:12.

[40] *Pros entropēn*, 1 Cor 6:5. Paul uses the phrase only one other time, namely, in 1 Cor 15:34, when he castigates those who deny the resurrection of the dead.

Paul's language is unusually strong. Believers are a family; they are siblings to one another.[41] Recourse to secular courts shows that something is seriously amiss in the Christian community, even if the disputed matter is rather trivial.[42] Even nonbelievers such as Cicero[43] and Plutarch[44] realized that going to court was not an adequate way of dealing with a troublesome member of the family.

Having argued that believers should resolve their differences among themselves[45] and that it is radically out of order for them to have to resort to secular courts of law, Paul's style leads him to confront those who dared to do such a thing: "Why not rather be wronged? Why not rather be defrauded? But you yourselves wrong and defraud and believers at that. Do you not know that wrongdoers will not inherit the kingdom of God?"[46] The three rhetorical questions are three among the nine that Paul uses in the diatribe of 1 Corinthians 6:1-9a. The first two echo sentiments found among some of the Stoic philosophers,[47] but some authors see in them a reflection of the model of Christ, the innocent one who suffered injustice—at least by human standards, *kata sarka*—on the cross.[48]

Paul reserves his harshest words for those who have used their wealth and power to the detriment of the poorer and less powerful members of the community. He turns the tables on them as he writes, "You yourselves wrong and defraud and believers at that. Do you

---

Paul's use of the phrase in 1 Cor 6:5 points to the seriousness of the matter for one who claims to be a member of the believing church.

[41] Note the use of *adelphos*, "brother," in verses 5 and 6 (and 8). The NRSV's use of "unbeliever" as a translation removes the kinship dimension of Paul's argument.

[42] I have rendered the *critērion elachistōn* as "minor cases" (Collins, *First Corinthians*, 224, 232); the *REB* opts for "trifling cases." Some commentators suggest a comparison with contemporary small-claims courts.

[43] Pertinent quotation cited by Winter.

[44] Cf. Plutarch, "Brotherly Love" (*Moralia* 481E–482C).

[45] Cf. Exod 18:13-27; Deut 1:9-17; 16:18-20.

[46] 1 Cor 6:7b-9a.

[47] Thus, for example, Mussonius Rufus, "He said that he himself would never prosecute anyone for personal injury nor recommend it to anyone else who claimed to be a philosopher" ("Will the Philosopher Prosecute Anyone for Personal Injury?" 10.15, cited in Boring, *Hellenistic Commentary*, 399).

[48] Thus, Thiselton, *First Epistle*, 436–37; Ciampa and Rosner, *First Letter*, 235.

not know that wrongdoers will not inherit the kingdom of God?"[49] Attentive to the concrete social situation in which these kinds of lawsuits took place as well as the various nuances of Paul's choice of verb, Thiselton translates the *adikeite*, the NRSV's "wrong" at the beginning of verse 8, as "deprive of justice."[50] When the wealthy bring those less well-off to court, they effectively deprive them of justice; they defraud the members of their own fictional family.

What is in store for the wealthy folk who do such a thing? Describing them as wrongdoers, Paul uses the final salvo in his arsenal of rhetorical questions to ask, "Do you not know that wrongdoers [*adikioi*[51]] will not inherit the kingdom of God?" To make the point even more forcefully, Paul punctuates this rhetorical question with the third of the three catalogues of vices[52] in 1 Corinthians: "Do not be deceived! Fornicators, idolaters, adulterers, male prostitutes, sodomites, thieves, the greedy, drunkards, revilers, robbers—none of these will inherit the kingdom of God."[53]

The apostle's insertion of "the greedy" into this list of evildoers is telling. In the paired catalogue of vices in the previous chapter, 1 Corinthians 5:9-10, Paul had twice mentioned the greedy.[54] Aelius Aristedes, a popular mid-second-century CE Greek orator, would later say that greed is one of the three most disgraceful things. Greed (*pleonexia*) is not simply a desire to have more than what one already has; it is a desire to have more than what one has a right to have,

---

[49] 1 Cor 6:9a. In similar fashion he will later turn the tables on Jewish Christians who were so ready to accuse Gentiles of all sorts of wrongful conduct. Cf. Rom 2:1.

[50] Cf. Thiselton, *First Epistle*, 437–38. Limbeck observes, "Since to do wrong usually means to damage the one wronged, *adikeō* can take on, specifically in legal and commercial language, the sense of doing damage." Cf. Meinrad Limbeck, "*adikeō, ktl.*," *EDNT* 1:31-33, at 31.

[51] Note the semantic relationship with *adikeō*. "There are good grounds for translating *adikoi* as unjust," writes Thiselton (*First Epistle*, 438; his emphasis).

[52] Cf. 1 Cor 5:10-11; Raymond F. Collins, "Conduct to Be Avoided," chapter 6 in *Sexual Ethics and the New Testament: Behavior and Belief*, Companions to the New Testament (New York: Crossroad, 2000), 73–99.

[53] 1 Cor 6:9b-10.

[54] Cf. Eph 5:5 and Col 3:5 where the authors actually identify greed and idolatry.

particularly what belongs to others.[55] For his part, from among the many vices[56] that he could have chosen for his lists of vices, Paul chose "the greedy"[57] in addition to idolaters (*eidōlolatrai*)[58] as the two kinds of evildoers whose conduct he wanted to underscore with his three lists. Believers, Paul said, echoing his previous and now-lost earlier correspondence, should have nothing to do with them, the greedy and idolaters.

The rhetoric of 1 Corinthians 6:9-10 is masterful. Paul had addressed a sexual matter in the previous chapter, a man's adultery with his own father's wife, and will devote the following chapter to things sexual.[59] It is commonplace for people to disparage the sexual mores of those with whom they disagree. So in 1 Corinthians 6:10 Paul develops a list of those who commit a variety of sexual misdeeds—everyone in the community would have been on board with this!—but the point of his catalogue of vices is the inserted "thieves, the greedy, and robbers," fitting epithets for the wealthy members of the community who have the effrontery to take the less well-off members of the community to a secular court. That may have been their way of life in the past; such conduct has no place in the life of a believer.

1 Corinthians 11:17-22

In 1 Corinthians 11:17-22 Paul addresses another serious matter—one perhaps more serious than the matter of lawsuits before civil courts of law because it strikes at the heart of the celebration of the Eucharist. With regard to the lawsuits, Paul had said that he

[55] Cf. Jennifer Houston McNeel, *Paul as Infant and Nursing Mother: Metaphor, Rhetoric, and Identity in 1 Thessalonians 2:5-8*, ECL 12 (Atlanta: SBL Press, 2014), 49.

[56] All told, 110 different names of vices appear in the catalogues of vices in the New Testament. Philo has one passage in which he lists some 146 vices. Cf. Philo, *Sacrifices* 32.

[57] The nominal form of this vice, *pleonektēs*, appears in all three verses, 1 Cor 5:10, 11; and 6:10.

[58] Cf. 1 Cor 10:14.

[59] Cf. Kenneth E. Bailey, *Paul through Mediterranean Eyes: Cultural Studies in 1 Corinthians* (Downers Grove, IL: IVP Academic, 2011), 178–79.

had spoken to the shame of the Corinthians.[60] Now he describes the situation in words bracketed by the simple and forceful phrase, "I do not commend you" (*ouk epainō*).[61] This rejoinder is all the more significant insofar as Paul uses it after he had written to commend the Corinthians for their fidelity to him and their holding on to the traditions that he had handed down.[62] Moreover, Paul emphasizes the importance of his "I do not commend you" by asking, "Should I commend you?" He wants his addressees to understand that what they are doing is in no way commendable.

What is the matter of such serious concern? Paul gives a description of the situation, as he sees it:

> Now in the following instructions, I do not commend you, because when you come together it is not for the better but for the worse. For, to begin with, when you come together as a church, I hear that there are divisions among you, and to some extent I believe it. Indeed, there have to be factions among you, for only so will it become clear who among you are genuine. When you come together, it is not really to eat the Lord's supper. For when the time comes together to eat, each of you goes ahead with your own supper, and one goes hungry and another becomes drunk. What! Do you not have homes to eat and drink in? Or do you show contempt for the church of God and humiliate those who have nothing? What should I say to you? Should I commend you? In this matter I do not commend you.[63]

Paul's language is strong. The string of rhetorical questions points to his personal investment in the matter. These unanswered questions invite the Corinthians to come to personal decisions about the situation. As Paul tries to correct their practices, which he considers to be out of sync with what the Lord's Supper was meant to recall, he uses

---

[60] Cf. 1 Cor 6:5.

[61] 1 Cor 11:22. The literary inclusion ring construction sets the tone for the whole passage.

[62] Cf. 1 Cor 11:2.

[63] 1 Cor 11:17-22.

the harshest of language. Not only does Paul describe the situation as one that he could not commend, he also says that the Corinthians come together for the worse, not for the better; they are not eating the Lord's Supper; they are showing contempt for the church of God; and they are humiliating those who have nothing. Then, after he has recalled the tradition of the Lord's Supper, the apostle says that they are eating and drinking judgment against themselves.[64] What is the situation that deserves such harsh condemnation?

What is at stake is the Lord's Supper[65] itself. We do not know just who it was that reported the situation to Paul, but we know that someone had told him about it.[66] The members of the Corinthian community were coming together presumably, but not necessarily, in someone's home, perhaps that of Gaius, who was host to the whole church.[67] Paul focuses on their coming together; three times he uses the verb "come together" (*synerchomai*).[68] The Corinthian believers gathered for a meal, as did various associations in the Greco-Roman world.[69] Typically, these religious, trade, and funeral associations gathered for a kind of potluck meal, an *eranos*, to which each participant made a contribution.

Obviously, not everyone who participated in the meal was able to bring the same amount and/or quality of food. Echoing Socrates, the historian Xenophon described what an *eranos* should be like:

[64] Cf. 1 Cor 11:29.

[65] Within the New Testament the expression "the Lord's Supper" (*kyriakon deipnon*) appears only once, namely, in 1 Cor 11:20.

[66] Cf. "I hear" (*akouō*) in verse 18; in 1 Cor 1:11 Paul says that he has received an oral report (*edēlōthē*) about quarrels (*erides*) in the community from Chloe's people. In response, Paul almost commands that there be "no divisions among you" (*mē ē en hymin schismata*). Paul speaks of the divisions (*schismata*) in the community in 1 Cor 11:18. It is, however, impossible to state with any certainty that it was Chloe's people who told Paul about the abuse of the Lord's Supper.

[67] Cf. Rom 16:23.

[68] Verses 17, 18, 20.

[69] Cf. Panayotis Coutsoumpos, *Paul and the Lord's Supper: A Socio-Historical Investigation*, Studies in Biblical Literature 84 (New York: Peter Lang, 2005); Dennis E. Smith, *From Symposium to Eucharist: The Banquet in the Early Christian World* (Minneapolis: Fortress, 2002); Hal Taussig, *In the Beginning Was the Meal: Social Experimentation and Early Christian Identity* (Minneapolis: Fortress, 2009).

> Whenever some of those who came together for dinner brought more meat and fish than others, Socrates would tell the waiter either to put the small contributions into the common stock or to portion them out equally among the diners. So the ones who brought a lot felt obliged not only to take their share of the pool, but to pool their own supplies in return; and so they put their own food also into the common stock. Thus, they got no more than those who brought little with them.[70]

This is what a potluck supper was supposed to be like.

Philosophers from Socrates to Plutarch, Paul's contemporary, urged that the *eranos* truly be a communal meal.[71] Plutarch says that equality among all present (*hē isotēs tois andrasi*) is to be a feature of the common meal.[72] The ideal was not always the reality. Social discrimination did exist. It was not unknown for wealthy patrons to serve simple food and wine for their ordinary clients while they served fine wine and food for their more important clients. The moralists were critical. Pliny, for example, took issue with the practice of a well-to-do person who "lived in splendor combined with economy." He wrote that this wealthy patron "had apportioned in small flagons three different sorts of wine; but you are not to suppose that the guests might take their choice; on the contrary, that they might not choose at all. One was for himself and me; the next for his friends of a lower order (for you must know; he measures out his friendship according to the degrees of quality); and the third for his own freedmen and mine."[73] And Pliny does not even mention slaves, who seem to be completely absent from the meal with three levels of guests.

Drunkenness seems not to have been uncommon during communal meals.[74] Indeed, intoxication was so common that in both Sparta

---

[70] *Memorabilia* 3.14.1.

[71] Much of what the philosophic moralists said about the *eranos* is echoed in the Hellenistic book of Ben Sira, Sir 31:12–32:13.

[72] Cf. "Table Talk," 1.2.5 [*Moralia* 618A]; 1.8.2 [*Moralia* 625E].

[73] *Epistles* 2.6.

[74] See Lucian, *Symposium* 17; Athenaeus, *Deipnosophists* 2.36; Sir 31:29–31.

and Crete the *eranos* was banned for a period of time. And there was always the danger of disorder, about which Plutarch complained.[75]

The meal itself, the *eranos*, was generally followed by a libation to the gods or to a specific deity, the patron of the group.[76] This was the case even in those instances in which the common meal was not celebrated by a religious association or in a hall adjacent to a temple.[77] After the libation, the symposium, the "table talk," could begin. When the rules of proper behavior were not followed, the offending behavior could be construed as an affront to the deity. For example, the statutes of the Guild of Zeus Hypsistos, a first-century CE Egyptian religious association,[78] say that the existence of factions (*schismata synistasthai*) is incompatible with the monthly banquet in honor of Zeus. Roughly a century later, Plutarch complained in this fashion when everyone did not participate in the after-dinner conversation: "Gone is the aim and end of the good fellowship [*koinōnias to telos*] of the party and Dionysius is outraged."[79]

What Paul writes in 1 Corinthians 11:17-30 belongs to this topos. The situation that the apostle describes is one in which house owners, the more affluent members of the community, arrived first, eating the good food and drinking the good wine that they had brought. They ate and drank, even to excess, says Paul. The less well-to-do, probably including slaves—maybe of believing householders—arrived later, perhaps bringing with them some wine of a poorer quality and a paltry amount of food. They went hungry. James Thompson describes the situation in this way: "The wealthy and the poor ate unequal portions while at the same meal; the former ate their own meal composed of what they had brought without sharing with the poor, leaving them to go hungry."[80] For Paul, such a gathering was

---

[75] Cf. "Table Talk," 1.2.1 [*Moralia* 615E]; 1.2.5 [*Moralia* 618C].

[76] Cf. Mark Reasoner, *Roman Imperial Texts: A Source Book* (Minneapolis: Fortress, 2014), 145. Often the patronal deity is portrayed as extending the invitation to the festivities.

[77] These halls were often used as venues for large gatherings of people.

[78] The cult of Zeus Hypsistos may have originated in Macedonia.

[79] "Table Talk," 1.1.5 [*Moralia* 615A].

[80] James W. Thompson, *The Church According to Paul: Rediscovering the Community Conformed to Christ* (Grand Rapids: Baker Academic, 2014), 88; cf. Otfried

not a gathering of the church; those who had come together were not celebrating the Lord's Supper.

Paul says that circumstances like those he describes show contempt for the church of God.[81] The "church of God" was a title of honor that Paul had attributed to the community in 1 Corinthians 1:2. Now he says that the misbehaving, socially divisive community was showing contempt for the church of God. He had intimated as much when he first brought up the topic. He wrote about their coming together,[82] adding a nuance in the following verse when he talked about their coming together as a church.[83] Ironically, they came together as an assembly, an *ekklēsia*, but they were not a genuine assembly. There were divisions (*schismata*)—the very word that appeared in the statutes of the Guild of Zeus—among them.[84] At most, those who came together at Corinth were a crowd, not an assembly, not an *ekklēsia*.

A second, and the most important, criticism that Paul addresses to these people who so blatantly violated the normal rules of social etiquette was that they were not eating the Supper of the Lord. Fitzmyer comments that Paul "will now insist that there can be no real celebration of the Lord's Supper, as long as their liturgical assemblies are marred by unworthy conduct that is divisive and factious and not marked by the same concern 'for others' that Jesus manifested at the Last Supper."[85]

To make his point, Paul offers an etiological narrative of the institution of the Lord's Supper, for which later generations are particularly thankful since 1 Corinthians 11:21-26 is the oldest extant narrative of the institution of the Lord's Supper, the Christian Eucha-

---

Hofius, "The Lord's Supper and the Lord's Supper Tradition: Reflections on 1 Corinthians 11:23b-25," in *One Loaf, One Cup: Ecumenical Studies of 1 Cor 11 and Other Eucharistic Texts; The Cambridge Conference on the Eucharist, August 1988*, New Gospel Studies 6, ed. Ben F. Meyer (Macon, GA: Mercer University Press, 1993), 75–115, 91–93.

[81] *Tēs ekklēsias tou theou kataphroneite*, 1 Cor 11:22.

[82] 1 Cor 1:17.

[83] *Synerchomenōn hymōn en ekklēsia*, 1 Cor 11:18. Cf. 1 Cor 11:20, *synerchomenōn oun hymōn epi to auto.*

[84] Thompson (*Church*, 88) notes, "The divisions are not theological but socioeconomic, and the wealthier members are the offenders."

[85] Fitzmyer, *First Corinthians*, 426.

rist. The narrative is rich and deserves adequate commentary—which, however, exceeds the scope and intent of the present study. I would, however, point to three subtle aspects of Paul's argument.

First of all, Paul clearly contrasts the Corinthians' not eating the Lord's Supper (*kyriakon deipnon*)[86] with their eating their own supper (*idion deipnon*).[87] Each (*hekastos*) ate his own supper rather than the Supper of the Lord. The Corinthians would rather celebrate themselves individually than celebrate the Lord. Second, Paul calls the meal that they do not eat the Lord's Supper (*kyriakon deipnon*), using the adjective derived from *Kyrios*, "Lord." In his rejoinder to the Corinthians, Paul mentions the Lord five times.[88] A "lord" is someone to be obeyed and followed. Clearly, the Corinthians have not done that. The punishment could be severe.[89] Third, at the Last Supper, the Lord had issued a command, "Do this in remembrance of me."[90] The ungracious Corinthians had chosen not to remember the Lord, especially his death, of which the Lord's Supper was a memorial meal. The philosophers taught that pagans offended Zeus or Dionysius when they ate a communal meal and offended the demands of *koinōnia* in doing so; Paul teaches that the Corinthians offended the Lord with their divisive behavior during what should have been a communal meal.

When Paul arrives at his third argument, he has already affirmed that the Corinthians were not a real church when they gathered together. They were not eating the Lord's Supper. What were they doing to one another? Paul says that the uncaring banqueters were humiliating those who had nothing.[91] The "haves" in the community were debasing the "have-nots," the poorer members of the community. To echo what he had said earlier, they were destroying believers for whom Christ died.[92] And this would be for their condemnation.[93] The matter of

---

[86] 1 Cor 11:20.

[87] 1 Cor 11:21.

[88] *Kyrios* in vv. 23 [2x], 26, 27, 32.

[89] See v. 30, "For this reason many of you are weak and ill, and some have died." Cf. Ps 38:3.

[90] *Touto poieite eis tēn emēn anamnēsin*, 1 Cor 11:24.

[91] 1 Cor 11:22c.

[92] Cf. 1 Cor 8:11.

[93] *Eis krima*, 1 Cor 11:34.

social divisiveness in evidence during the celebration of the communal meal was symptomatic of a deeper problem, namely, the way the haves treated the have-nots, the way that the rich treated the poor.[94]

1 Corinthians 9:3-14

Chapter 9 of the letter is sandwiched between two chapters that deal with food offered to idols. Arguing that relatively sophisticated Christians should willingly forgo their right to eat this food, Paul uses a chiastic structure (A-B-A') to establish his point. The central point of the chiasm, B, establishes the ground for his further argumentation. B articulates something of a principle that grounds the applied argumentation (A') in the A-B-A' structure. First Corinthians 9, Paul's *apologia pro vita mea*, serves as the center of the chiasm constituted by 1 Corinthians 8–10.

In this chapter Paul discusses his rights[95] and his willingness to forgo the use of them. The rights in question are his right to food and drink and his right to be accompanied by a believing wife. With regard to the former, Paul argues that the laborer is worth his hire. A series of analogies points to the fact that a worker deserves at least a subsistence level of recompense for his work according to his respective walk in life. With this as a principle, Paul is able to similarly argue that he and Barnabas have a right to be supported by the Corinthians because they have preached the gospel to them.[96] That Paul was willing to forgo that right would prove to be problematic. Some people within the community seem to have considered that any self-respecting person should be paid for their efforts. Paul's willingness to forgo support from the community—something to which he was committed—was "in their face." That aside, the point that Paul makes in 1 Corinthians 9—and on which he bases his right

---

[94] Cf. Stephen Chester, *Conversion at Corinth: Perspectives on Conversion in Paul's Theology and the Corinthian Church*, SNTW (London: T & T Clark, 2003), 249–50.

[95] Note that Paul speaks about "my defense" (*hē emē apologia*) in verse 3 but then immediately switches to the first-person plural so as to include at least Barnabas as a person who also enjoys these rights.

[96] Cf. 1 Thess 2:7, with regard to the support (*en barei*) that Paul, Silvanus, and Timothy might have received from the church of the Thessalonians.

to be supported for his preaching—is that every worker is entitled to a just recompense, in keeping with his walk of life. Paul considers that a given.

Earlier in this letter, he had offered two wonderful examples of the church drawn from everyday life, the field and a building. The pairing was classic in Hellenistic and Jewish literature.[97] Paul uses everyday examples to speak of the unity of the church, in which everyone has a role to play. In each example, albeit only in passing, he affirms that those who labor deserve their pay. Apropos the workers in the field, he writes, "each will receive wages [*misthos*[98]] according to the labor of each."[99] Then in regard to the building, a house that morphs into a temple, Paul says, "the builder will receive a reward [*misthos*]."[100]

In 1 Corinthians 9, while arguing about his own right to receive payment for preaching the gospel, Paul again offers a number of simple examples. Paul's train of thought is worth following. Given his predilection for groups of three, Paul gives three examples.[101] The first is that of the soldier who is not expected to pay his own wages (*opsōniois*[102]) during the time of his military service. The second is that of the vintner.[103] The third is the shepherd. These everyday examples are typical in Hellenistic rhetoric. The short series is enough to make

---

[97] For example, Plato, *Laws* 1.643B; Dio Chrysostom, *Discourses* 71.5; Philo, *Allegorical Interpretation* 3.48; *Cherubim* 100–102; Luke 17:28; Deut 20:5-6; Jer 1:10; 18:7-10; 24:6; 31:28; 42:10; Sir 49:7; 1QS 8:5; 11:5.

[98] For a study of this term, whose ordinary meaning is "pay," "wages," see Spicq, "*misthos, ktl.*," *TLNT* 2:502–15.

[99] 1 Cor 3:8b.

[100] 1 Cor 3:14b.

[101] In v. 10, Paul writes about those who plow and those who thresh.

[102] The Greek *opsōnion* commonly connoted wages or pay, and it is generally used with that connotation so that it is virtually a synonym with *misthos*, "pay." The *ops-* root pertains to preserved fish, prepared for cooking. With regard to a soldier, the term might well mean "rations." Spicq comments, "In a military context [it] is the wage paid in cash to which is added compensation in kind, a certain quantity of grains, i.e., provisions." Cf. Spicq, "*Opsōnion*," *EDNT* 2:600–603, esp. 600–601. The term clearly has this monetary meaning in Luke 3:14. The other two New Testament usages of the term are found in Rom 6:23, a metaphor, and 2 Cor 11:8.

[103] Cf. Deut 20:6; Prov 27:18.

his point. Paul has no need to further multiply examples. Soldiers, vinedressers, and shepherds deserve to be paid. So does Paul.

The three examples given by Paul in 1 Corinthians 9:7 are cited in the form of positively phrased rhetorical questions, suggesting a negative response. The Corinthians themselves are asked to make the commonsense decision that people with different occupations, from soldiers to shepherds, deserve payment for the work that they do. Paul ratifies their implied decision with a scriptural argument, drawn from biblical agricultural law. "You shall not muzzle an ox while it is treading out the grain," he writes in verse 9, and then he immediately comments to the effect that this dictum is not about beasts of burden but about human beings. If mere oxen deserve to be taken care of, so much more should working human beings be properly taken care of.[104] Paul's citation of the Scriptures in this fashion is good rhetoric. Great rhetoricians such as Quintilian were wont to punctuate an argument from reason with one from authority.[105] Paul's Hellenistic Jewish contemporary Philo of Alexandria used a similar rhetorical technique in his letters.[106] For Paul and Philo, the Torah was their authority. It contained the word of God.

Paul's "work" among the Corinthians was the work of evangelization, so he closes out his argument with a double example from the cultic sphere. "Do you not know that those who are employed in the temple service get their food from the temple, and those who serve at the altar share in that which is sacrificed on the altar?"[107] As he did in verse 9, Paul adds an argument from authority to the rhetorical question: "In the same way, the Lord commanded that those who proclaim the gospel should get their living by the gospel."[108] Paul's rhetorical questions speak to Jewish and Gentile believers alike. The Torah contains prescriptions on the portion of sacrifices to

---

[104] The argument *a minore ad majus*, the *qal wa-homer* principle, is classic in rabbinic interpretation of this Scripture.

[105] Cf. Quintilian, *Training of an Orator* 4.5.3.

[106] Cf. Philo, *Epistles* 2.20.9.

[107] 1 Cor 9:13. Interpreters differ among themselves whether this verse is an example of parallelism for the sake of emphasis or whether Paul is referring to two different groups of cultic officers.

[108] 1 Cor 9:14.

which priests are entitled[109] as well as on the tithes given to Levites.[110] Those who served in Greek and Roman temples were also entitled to a share of the temple offerings. Paul's argument would have been understood by all within the community despite the diversity of their ethno-religious backgrounds.

In sum, Paul offers six or seven examples of people in various professions receiving adequate payment for their services. He does not argue that they should be paid an adequate wage. For the apostle, that is a given. They deserve enough recompense for their services to provide for themselves—and, ultimately, for their families. Paul's rhetorical questions invite the Corinthians to reflect on this basic principle of economic justice and affirm it. Only then can he argue that he too has a right to financial support, although he is willing to forgo the use of this right. Without the Corinthians' acceptance of this principle of economic justice, the argument of 1 Corinthians 8–10 falls flat. This principle of economic justice for workers is the lynchpin of these three chapters.

Second Corinthians

Second Corinthians is clearly a different sort of letter from the earlier extant letter of Paul to that community. It goes without saying, therefore, that this letter[111] addresses matters of wealth, wages, and the wealthy in a fashion different from that of its extant predecessor. Perhaps the place with which to begin our examination of this letter is the retort that Paul addresses to the Corinthians in the introduction to the famous Fool's Speech of 2 Corinthians.[112]

[109] Cf. Num 18:8-20; Deut 18:1-5.

[110] Cf. Num 18:21-24.

[111] Many scholars hold that extant 2 Corinthians is a composite text, rather than a single letter written by Paul. See the all-too-brief summary of the discussion in Collins, *Second Corinthians*, 10–12.

[112] Cf. 2 Cor 11:16–12:13.

2 Corinthians 11:7-8

Paul writes:

> Did I commit a sin[113] by humbling myself so that you might
> be exalted, because I proclaimed God's good news to you
> free of charge? I robbed other churches by accepting support
> [*opsōnion*][114] from them in order to serve you.[115]

Almost from the very beginning of 2 Corinthians, Paul is on the
defensive. Sometimes he responds very angrily, sometimes less so.
One of the accusations against his *modus proclamandi* is apparently
echoed in the rhetorical question of verse 7, one of several passages
in the letter in which Paul talks about money matters. Paul uses a
rhetorical question to invite the Corinthians to bring their own judgment to bear on the matter under discussion. The form of his question
suggests that he is inviting them to formulate a strong mental "No."

The question, nonetheless, suggests that there was a problem
with at least some of the Corinthians. These members might have
expected the apostle to receive donations for his speechifying, as
many philosophers did. In the Greco-Roman context, Paul's refusal
of support would have been construed as an insult. Roetzel says that
it would have been as insulting as a refused handshake.[116]

Not only was Paul's refusal to accept financial support from the
Corinthians a violation of the canons of politesse; the Corinthians
may have seen Paul's refusal of support as a refusal to allow them to
participate in his mission, effectively to be partners in the gospel[117]
by providing financial support for it. It may have been that they were
aware that Paul had accepted support from others, such as his patron

---

[113] Apart from the quotation of Ps 32:2 (LXX) in Rom 4:8, this is the only time
that Paul uses the term "sin" (*hamartia*) with the connotation of an individual
offense.

[114] Cf. 1 Cor 9:7 and the remarks above, p. 35.

[115] 2 Cor 11:7-8.

[116] Cf. Calvin J. Roetzel, *2 Corinthians*, ANTC (Nashville: Abingdon, 2007), 105.

[117] Cf. Verlyn D. Verbrugge, *Paul's Style of Church Leadership Illustrated by His
Instructions to the Corinthians on the Collection: To Command or Not to Command* (San Francisco: Mellen Research University Press, 1992), 119. See also
the comment on Phil 2:5.

Phoebe from nearby Cenchrae or some of the Macedonian churches that he had evangelized.[118] Paul downplays and virtually implies a negative moral judgment on the support that he received from other congregations when he compares it to robbery.

Victor Furnish says that the Corinthian community would see Paul's financial independence as a rejection "of their status as a patron congregation."[119] In which case, they would have felt demeaned. But Paul would not allow himself to be beholden to the Corinthians. He did not want to be someone's "house apostle."[120] He was fiercely independent with regard to the preaching of the gospel.[121] Paul preached the gospel free of charge so that he would have to answer to no one save the Lord himself. At issue was the nature of the gospel itself. Was it the free gift of God or something that could be purchased?

The opening thanksgiving of 1 Corinthians is a sure sign that Paul wanted to cultivate their good will, but he did not want to be under obligation to them. In a certain sense, that would have made him socially inferior to them.[122] Paul did not want the dissemination of the Good News to be subject to any human control. The philosopher Seneca writes, "The giving of a benefit is a social act, it wins the good will of someone; it lays someone under obligation."[123] Would

---

[118] Cf. Phil 4:14-18.

[119] Victor P. Furnish, *II Corinthians*, AB 32A (Garden City, NY: Doubleday, 1984), 508. With regard to the system of patronage in Roman Corinth, see John K. Chow, "Patronage in Roman Corinth," in *Paul and Empire: Religion and Power in Roman Imperial Society*, ed. Richard A. Horsley (Harrisburg, PA: Trinity Press International, 1997), 104–25.

[120] The epithet comes from Richard Horsley. Cf. Richard A. Horsley, "1 Corinthians: A Case Study of Paul's Assembly as an Alternative Society," in Horsley, *Paul and Empire*, 242–52, at 250.

[121] Cf. 1 Thess 2:9; 1 Cor 9:12, 18.

[122] To put this into perspective, note the comment of Witherington: "Some opposition [to Paul] was likely coming from wealthier Corinthian Christians who were used to being benefactors and would likely look down on manual workers and servants," he writes (*Conflict and Community*).

[123] Seneca, *Epistles* 81.23. Apropos the situation in Corinth, Mitzi Minor writes, "The Roman practice of patronage was evidently widespread in Corinth. . . . Wealthier Corinthians were accustomed to offering 'favors,' thus buying influence and a loyal group of clients who benefited from the favors"; *2 Corinthians*, Smyth & Helwys Bible Commentary (Macon, GA: Smyth & Helwys, 2009), 211–12.

that have happened were Paul to have accepted a client status under obligation to a wealthy patron? We shall never know. What we do know is that Paul avoided the possibility by refusing to accept the patronage of anyone in the Corinthian community. That irked some members of the community.

It was sufficiently irksome for Paul to see fit to address the matter in two additional passages of his correspondence with the Corinthians, namely, 2 Corinthians 2:17 and 12:13.[124] The latter, "How have you been worse off than the other churches except that I myself did not burden you? Forgive me this wrong," resonates with what Paul says in 11:7, except that Paul uses the language of "wrong," of "injustice" (*adikia*), to speak of his alleged affront to the Corinthians. In the former passage, 2 Corinthians 2:17, Paul states clearly why it is that he does not "peddle" God's word, implicitly contrasting himself with those who are paid for the learned words that they impart. He writes, "For we are not peddlers [*kapēluontes*[125]] of God's word like so many, but in Christ we speak as persons of sincerity, as persons sent from God and standing in his presence." He and his companions are God's emissaries, not the beholden clients of one or another member of the Corinthian community. They are delegates of God (*ek theou*) in whose presence they stand.

As for Greed

Only one catalogue of vices appears in Paul's Second Letter to the Corinthians. That list[126] concentrates on a variety of socially disruptive forms of behavior that Paul has experienced in Corinth and draws attention to the forms of sexual morality that he hopes to be nonexistent when he finally goes to Corinth for a third and presumably last visit. The list does not specifically mention "greed" (*pleonexia*), but the fourth vice on Paul's list is *eritheiai*, the NRSV's "selfishness," whose connotation is "acts with monetary self-interest." The omission of greed from the catalogue of vices in 2 Corinthians 12 does not mean

---

[124] Cf. 1 Cor 9:3-4, 15-18.
[125] Cf. Spicq, "*kapēleuō*," *TLNT* 2:254–57.
[126] Cf. 2 Cor 12:20-21.

that the apostle was unconcerned about greed[127] when he wrote his "second" letter to the Corinthians. On the contrary! In this letter, in which he was so much on the defensive, he repeatedly asserts that neither he nor his co-workers were motivated by greed.

He first does so in 2 Corinthians 7:2 in the course of a poignant plea for the positive affections of the Corinthians, in which he writes, "We have wronged no one, we have corrupted no one, we have taken advantage [*ekpleonektēsamen*] of no one." Paul's verb, *pleonekteō*, has the connotation of "take advantage of,"[128] but the root *pleonek-* shows that etymologically and at bottom the verb signifies depriving another of resources because of one's own greed. Toward the end of the letter, Paul reaffirms his point: "Did I take advantage [*ekpleonektēsa*] of you through any of those whom I sent to you? I urged Timothy to go and sent the brother with him.[129] Titus did not take advantage [*ekpleonektēsen*] of you, did he? Did we not conduct ourselves with the same spirit?"[130] Paul's preaching was never for the sake of greed.[131] He never preached in order to gain some financial advantage or to accrue wealth for himself.

The Ministry to the Saints

Greed was, moreover, not to be a factor in the collection on behalf of Jerusalem's poor,[132] about which Paul had written his earlier letter to the believing community in Corinth.[133] The apostle urged the Corinthians to follow the same set of guidelines that he had proposed to the churches of Galatia, but something happened after that. A crisis arose in Corinth that prompted Paul to change his travel plans.[134] He made a hasty visit to Corinth that did not end well.[135] The interruption of the collection was part of the fallout. A year had passed.[136] Paul

---

[127] Cf. 1 Cor 5:10, 11; see above, pp. 27–29.
[128] Cf. 2 Cor 2:11.
[129] Cf. 2 Cor 9:16-19.
[130] 2 Cor 12:17-18c.
[131] Cf. 1 Cor 2:5.
[132] Cf. 2 Cor 9:5.
[133] Cf. 1 Cor 16:1-4.
[134] Cf. 2 Cor 1:15-17.
[135] Cf. 2 Cor 2:1-2.
[136] Cf. 2 Cor 8:10.

was anxious to get the collection under way again. So he composed chapters 8 and 9 of his Second Letter to the Corinthians.[137]

In 1 Corinthians, Paul had subtly reminded the Corinthians that they were not alone in being asked to support God's poor in Jerusalem. He told them that he was proposing the same guidelines that he had proposed in Galatia. In 2 Corinthians, Paul is not as subtle. He appeals to the Corinthians' pride as he writes about the grace of God at work in the churches of Macedonia. The Macedonian believers were dirt poor. Their poverty overflowed into a wealth of generosity.[138] Voluntarily they gave according to their means—indeed, beyond their means![139] They gave even beyond Paul's fondest expectations.[140]

In addition to citing the tremendous generosity of the Macedonians, Paul pulled out a variety of rhetorical stops in making his appeal to the Corinthians. Chief among them was an appeal to the example of Jesus Christ. We can forgo further analysis of the apostle's rhetorical arguments in order to focus on the practical details of the collection.

First of all, Paul encourages the collection as a voluntary effort.[141] Paul reiterates the notion that contributions to the collection be a freewill offering: "that it might be ready as a voluntary gift [*hōs eulogian*]

---

[137] The relationship between these two chapters and the relationship between them and the rest of 2 Corinthians is a complex and disputed matter. One side of the discussion is well represented by Hans Dieter Betz, *2 Corinthians 8 and 9: A Commentary on Two Administrative Letters of the Apostle Paul*, Hermeneia (Philadelphia: Fortress, 1985). Years previously, Rudolf Bultmann had considered each of these chapters to have been a part of two different letters to the Corinthians; Rudolf Bultmann, *The Second Letter to the Corinthians* (Minneapolis: Augsburg, 1985 [originally in German, 1976]), 18.

[138] 2 Cor 8:2.

[139] Cf. 2 Cor 8:3-4. It is noteworthy that Paul calls attention to the voluntary nature of their contributions in each of these two verses. The *kata dynamin*, "according to their means," of v. 3 suggests the proportionate nature of their response. Each person's contribution was in accordance with their means. In fact, the Macedonians gave beyond their means, as Paul is quick to add.

[140] 2 Cor 8:5.

[141] Cf. 2 Cor 8:10. Bultmann (*Second Corinthians*, 254) remarks, "*thelein* [desire] is the chief thing." The same verb recurs in the following verse where the Greek phrase *hē prothymia tou thelein*, literally, a passion to will, is translated as "eagerness." That the contribution was voluntary was also a characteristic of the collection in Macedonia; cf. 2 Cor 8:3.

and not as an extortion"[142] and again, "Each of you must give as you have made up your mind, not reluctantly or under compulsion, for God loves a cheerful giver."[143]

Second, the apostle says that there is a means-test by which the members of the community should judge the adequacy of their response.[144] Citing a passage from the Exodus tradition as a scriptural proof,[145] Paul explains what he means by this:

> For if the eagerness is there, the gift is acceptable according to what one has—not according to what one does not have. I do not mean that there should be relief for others and pressure on you, but it is a question of a fair balance between our present abundance and their need, so that their abundance may be for your need, in order that there may be a fair balance.[146]

This is a formal explanation on Paul's part; his Greek text begins with a post-positive *gar*, the formal sign of an explicit explanatory statement. Paul did not expect or want Corinthian believers to impoverish themselves so that the Jerusalem saints could become rich. Rather, he was expecting some balance, equity, between the financial situations of the two groups of believers. Kingsley Barrett describes what Paul is proposing as "fair dealing,"[147] dealing fairly with one another in the family of faith. Philo, Paul's Hellenistic Jewish contemporary, says that equity is a "good such that none greater can be found."[148] It is a virtue to be praised.[149]

At bottom is the Jewish ideal, shared by Paul, of equality of conditions among God's people.[150] Sabbatical and jubilee years were

[142] 2 Cor 9:5.
[143] 2 Cor 9:7.
[144] *Ek tou echein*, 2 Cor 8:11; cf. 2 Cor 8:3.
[145] Exod 16:18 in 2 Cor 8:15.
[146] 2 Cor 8:12-14.
[147] Cf. C. K. Barrett, *The Second Epistle to the Corinthians*, BNTC (London: A & C Black, 1973), 227.
[148] *Special Laws* 165.
[149] Cf. Philo, *Joseph* 249; *Rewards* 59; *Decalogue* 162.
[150] Cf. Spicq, "*isos, ktl.*," TLNT 2:223–32, at 230.

institutions that were established in order to promote, if not ensure, the ideal.[151] To support his appeal to the biblical idea of equity, Paul recalls the manna tradition for his Corinthian readers: "The one who had much did not have too much, and the one who had little did not have too little."[152] This citation of Exodus 16:18 functions, in the words of Lawrence Welborn, "to advocate equality between persons of different resources through redistributive action."[153] When Paul cites the Jewish Scriptures in his writing, he does more than offer a proof text taken out of context. Rather, he alludes to the particular Scripture's immediate context. In this case, the evocation of what follows Exodus 16:18—namely, the story of rotting manna in Exodus 16:19-20—is a subtle reminder to the Corinthians that they are not to hoard their resources.[154]

Third, Paul writes about "their need" (*to eikeinōn hysterēma*).[155] Paul returns to this idea in chapter 9, when he writes that "the rendering of this ministry . . . supplies the needs of the saints [*ta hysterēmata tōn hagiōn*]."[156] The collection is a ministry to God's holy people in Jerusalem, but it is not intended to honor them. Nor was it a collection for the sake of a collection. Paul organized the collection in order to help people in poverty. It was a collection on behalf of God's holy people in Jerusalem precisely because they were in need; they lived in poverty, in economically difficult circumstances. Describing this collective effort of believers in Romans 15:26, Paul says that the collection is a matter of sharing resources "with the poor among the saints at Jerusalem."[157] Leander Keck, the former

---

[151] See Lev 25 and *passim* in the Hebrew Bible; Sharon H. Ringe, "Jubilee, Year of," *NIDB* 3:418–19; Mark W. Hamilton, "Sabbatical Year," *NIDB* 5:11–13.

[152] 2 Cor 8:15.

[153] Lawrence L. Welborn, "'That There Be Equality': The Contexts and Consequences of a Pauline Ideal," *NTS* 59 (2013): 73–90, at 88.

[154] Cf. Thomas D. Stegman, "Paul's Use of Scripture in the Collection Discourse (2 Corinthians 8–9)," in *Biblical Essays in Honor of Daniel J. Harrington, SJ, and Richard J. Clifford, SJ: Opportunity for No Little Instruction*, ed. Christopher G. Frechette, Christopher R. Matthews, and Thomas D. Stegman (Mahwah, NJ: Paulist Press, 2014), 153–67, 157.

[155] 2 Cor 8:14.

[156] 2 Cor 9:12.

[157] *Eis tous prochous tōn hagiōn tōn en Ierusalēm.* "The poor" (*hoi ptōchoi*) should not be taken as a nickname for the community; it is a description of their

dean of the Divinity School of Yale University, says that Paul "thinks of them as saints who are now distressingly poor."[158] The collection was intended to alleviate the cause of their distress.

Commenting on the Romans passage, Robert Jewett writes,

> The ethical assumption lying behind this reference is also plain: both in Judaism and early Christianity, it was the obligation of the righteous to share resources with the poor and thereby declare solidarity. Despite subsidiary motives, this obligation remains central in all of Paul's discussions of the Jerusalem offering.[159]

Fourth, Paul expects each member of the community to participate in the collection in accord with his or her ability to do so. The distributive "each" (*hekastos*) of 2 Corinthians 9:7, echoing the "each" of 1 Corinthians 16:2, reminds the members of the community that coming to the aid of their poor siblings in faith in Jerusalem is a duty incumbent upon each and every one in the community.

Conscious that some members of the community had issues with his decision to support himself,[160] Paul made every effort to ensure that there was full transparency[161] in the delivery of the collection. Echoing what he had written in 2 Corinthians 6:3, Paul writes, "We intend that no one should blame us about this generous gift that we are administering for we intend to do what is right not only in the Lord's sight but also in the sight of others."[162] Paul assures the Corinthians that he is not dipping into the till. A three-person team, which does not include Paul, is delegated to take the collection, at

---

economic situation. Most likely the genitive *tōn hagiōn* is a partitive genitive, with reference to the poor among the believers in Jerusalem.

[158] Leander E. Keck, "The Poor among the Saints in Jewish Christianity and Qumran," *ZNW* 57 (1966): 54–78, 122.

[159] Jewett, *Romans*, 930.

[160] Matera opines that the collection itself was "a source of friction." Cf. Frank J. Matera, *II Corinthians*, NTL (Louisville: Westminster John Knox, 2003), 197.

[161] Anni Hentschel, *Diakonia im Neuen Testament: Studien zur Semantik unter besonderer Berücksichtigung der Rolle von Frauen*, WUNT 2/226 (Tübingen: Mohr Siebeck, 2007), 151. Klaiber remarks that the "four eyes principle" was already operative in the New Testament. Cf. Walter Klaiber, *Der zweite Korintherbrief*, BNT (Neukirchen-Vluyn: Neukirchener Theologie, 2012), 189.

[162] 2 Cor 8:20-21.

this point a relatively large sum of money,[163] to Jerusalem. Even before suspicion about his ministry arose in Corinth, Paul was disinclined to be in charge of the delivery of the collection.[164] Recent events made him even more reluctant to be part of the team that would deliver the collected money to Jerusalem.

As the complex letter is drawing to a close, Paul defends himself against charges of financial deceit one last time:

> Let it be assumed that I did not burden you. Nevertheless (you say) since I was crafty, I took you by deceit. Did I take advantage of you through any of those whom I sent to you? I urged Titus to go, and sent the brother with him. Titus did not take advantage of you, did he? Did we not conduct ourselves with the same spirit?[165]

One last time[166] Paul argues against the accusation that he had acted duplicitously. This time the suggestion seems to have been that Paul was clever enough not to dip into the collection directly but to have his agents do so on his behalf. In response, Paul appeals to the experience of the Corinthians themselves. His rhetorical questions beg for them to make their own judgment. The first two require a negative response; the third, a positive response.[167] No more than did Titus did Paul dip into the till. His moral integrity was similar to that of Titus whom the Corinthians knew so well.[168]

En Passant

Given the tense atmosphere that permeates 2 Corinthians, it is not surprising that Paul does not generally make use of parental im-

---

[163] Thus Klaiber, *Zweiter Korintherbrief,* 189.

[164] Cf. 1 Cor 16:3-4.

[165] 2 Cor 12:16-18.

[166] Cf. 2 Cor 1:12; 4:2.

[167] Rhetorically, negatively phrased questions demand a positive response, while affirmatively phrased questions await a negative response.

[168] Titus seems to have visited Corinth on at least three occasions, the first when he initiated the collection "last year" (cf. 2 Cor 8:6, 10), the second when he delivered the tearful letter (2:12-13; 7:5-16), and the third when he completed the collection (8:16–9:5). The matter of which of these visits Paul is alluding to in 12:17-18 is tied up with the thorny issue of the integrity of extant 2 Corinthians.

agery to speak of his relationship with the Corinthians.[169] There is, nonetheless, one passage in which he does so.[170] Preparing for his third visit to Corinth, Paul recalls that he was the apostolic founder of the community, its parent. As a good parent, he does not want or expect financial support from his children. His supporting argument is an ordinary economic principle, "for children ought not to lay up for their parents, but parents for their children."[171] Parents are expected to use their money to provide for their children, not vice versa. It was, as Paul says, an obligation[172] for them to do so.

Romans and Galatians

Paul's letter to the Romans, arguably the chef d'oeuvre among the seven extant letters, is neither as hands-on as 1 Corinthians nor as disjointed and passionate as 2 Corinthians. Consequently, it has not as much to say about the apostle's attitude toward wealth, wages, and the wealthy as did those earlier letters. The use of wealth is, nonetheless, a factor in human life, so it is not surprising that Paul had a few things to say about this in Romans.

Greed

The first chapter of the letter is often quoted—and almost as often taken out of context—by social conservatives who employ Romans 1:24-27 to support their agenda. Omitted from their argument is that Paul continues, "And since they did not see fit to acknowledge God, God gave them up to a debased mind [*eis adokimon noun*] and to things that should not be done. They were filled with every kind of wickedness, evil, covetousness [*pleonexia*]."[173] Thus begins the longest list of vices in the New Testament. Paul would have his readers

---

[169] See, however, 2 Cor 6:13; cf. 1 Cor 3:1-2; 4:14-21.

[170] Cf. 2 Cor 12:14-15.

[171] 2 Cor 12:14c. Note the use of the post-positive *gar* ("for"), as in 2 Cor 8:12.

[172] See the use of *opheilei*, "ought," in v. 14. Cf. Aristotle, *Nicomachean Ethics* 8.14.4; Seneca, *De benefiis* 2.11.5; 3.1.5; 29.1–38.3; 5.5.2; 6.24.1-2.

[173] Rom 1:28-29. While the NRSV translates *pleonexia* as "covetousness," other versions, including the *REB*, employ "greed" as the appropriate translation of the Greek. This is, in fact, the usual translation of *pleonexia* in English-language editions of the New Testament.

know—at this point he is principally appealing to the Jewish-Christian members in the audience—that idolatry leads not only to sexual misconduct but all sorts of immoral and improper conduct.[174] Idolatry, mediated through a debased mind, is the root source of all sorts of greed. With this vision of the origin of greed, it is not surprising that Paul associates greed with idolatry in the catalogues of vices in 1 Corinthians.[175]

Paul then says that, along with others, these greedy idolaters can expect divine wrath rather than eternal life: "For those who are self-seeking [*ex eritheias*] and who obey not the truth but wickedness, there will be wrath and fury."[176] The Greek word *eritheia*, "self-seeking," was a relative newcomer to the Greek lexicon. Virtually unattested before the New Testament,[177] where it occurs seven times including in the vice lists of 2 Corinthians 12:20 and Galatians 5:20,[178] the noun was derived from a Greek verb, *eritheomai*, meaning "work for pay."[179] It came to suggest contriving to gain honor and wealth, the exclusive pursuit of one's own interests,[180] and this is the sense, with a connotation of divisiveness,[181] in which Paul uses the term in Romans 2:8. Those who are devoted first of all to the pursuit of their own monetary advantage can expect to experience God's eschatological wrath and fury—Jew first, but also the Gentile. Unlike the catalogues of vices, in which "greed" is but one among several vices that merit divine punishment, the "self-seeking" are Paul's single focus in Romans 2:8.

---

[174] Cf. Fitzmyer, *Romans*, 288–89. In Rom 2:1 Paul cleverly puts his argument to these Jewish Christians, telling them that they are no less guilty of these things. Cf. 2:21b, "While you preach against stealing, do you steal?"

[175] Cf. 1 Cor 5:10; 5:11; 6:10. The notion is continued in the deutero-Pauline tradition, cf. Eph 5:5.

[176] Rom 2:8.

[177] One notable exception was Aristotle's use of the term in *Politics* 5.2 in reference to the self-serving pursuit of political office by devious means.

[178] Cf. 2 Cor 12:20; Gal 5:20; Phil 1:17; 2:3; Jas 3:14, 16, in addition to Rom 2:8.

[179] The related noun *erithos*, not found in the New Testament, means "day laborer."

[180] Cf. Spicq, "*erethizō, ktl.*," *TLNT* 2:69–72, at 70.

[181] Cf. Jewett, *Romans*, 206.

Wages

In 1 Corinthians, Paul had alluded to the principle of justice that every worker deserves to receive wages (1 Cor 9:14). Every evangelist ought to be paid. He himself deserved payment for his own work of preaching the gospel. In Romans 4:4 he states as a matter of principle, "Wages are not reckoned[182] as a gift but as something due." In a brief commentary on this passage, Fitzmyer writes, "The laborer has a strict right to the profit of his labor; it is a matter of commutative justice."[183] Paul cites the principle, deeply rooted in his Jewish heritage, in order to teach that God imparted righteousness to Abraham as a free gift, not as something to which Abraham had a right because he deserved it as a result of his work.

Throughout the Bible, wages—*śākar* in Hebrew, *misthos* in Greek—are considered a payment justly due. In contrast with service for free, wages are to be paid for labor,[184] goods that have been produced,[185] and services rendered.[186] Depriving a worker of wages was a serious violation of justice. Even deferring wages was deemed to be a serious wrong.[187] The payment of wages was necessary because they allowed the worker to eat and afterward rest.[188] The amount of wages due was a mutually agreed sum.[189]

The writings of Paul's Hellenistic Jewish contemporaries, Philo and Josephus, show that Jewish writers continued to refer to this system of justice during the first century CE. Thus Philo, the Alexandrian philosopher, writes, "Since workmen or laborers are offered wages [*misthoi*] as a reward for their industry and the persons so employed are the needy and not those who have abundance of resources to spare, he [God] orders the employer not to postpone but to

---

[182] Note the use of the bookkeeping term *logizetai*.

[183] Fitzmyer, *Romans*, 374.

[184] Cf. Tob 2:14; 5:3; 12:1; Eccl 4:9; Wis 10:17.

[185] Cf. 2 Chr 15:7; Jer 31:26.

[186] Cf. Exod 2:9, where Pharaoh's daughter says to Moses's mother, "Take this child and nurse it for me, and I will give you your wages." Commenting on the passage, Philo (*Moses* 1.17) writes that Moses's mother agreed to nurse him "ostensibly for wages" (*hōs epi misthō*). Cf. Deut 15:18.

[187] Cf. Lev 19:13; Deut 19:13b; 24:15.

[188] Cf. Sir 11:18-19.

[189] Cf. Tob 5:15-16.

render the stipulated wages [*misthon*] on that very day."[190] Elsewhere, Philo comments on the requirement at some length:

> The following also is one of the commandments promoting humanity. The wages of the poor man are to be paid on the same day, not only because it was felt to be just that one who has rendered the service for which he was engaged should receive in full and without delay the reward for his employment, but also because the manual worker or load carrier, who toils painfully with his whole body like a beast of burden, "lives from day to day," as the phrase goes, and his hopes rest upon his payment.[191]

Josephus, the historian, retelling the story of King Solomon preparing to build the temple, recounts that Solomon wrote to Eiromos (Hiram), king of the Tyranians, "I therefore request you to send some men along with mine to Mount Lebanon to cut timber. . . . And whatever wage [*misthon*] you may fix, I will give it to the woodcutters."[192] Paul shares this vision when he affirms that wages are due[193] but that God's gift of justification to Abraham is freely given. Wages and gifts belong to two different economic registers.

Taxes

About the time that Paul was writing his letter to the Romans, there was considerable unrest in the Roman Empire with regard to taxes.[194] Tacitus, the historian, reports that in the light of complaints coming from many people about the indirect taxes collected by "tax-collectors," Nero thought about abolishing them altogether. His advisors warned him that this would wreak financial havoc on the empire but that some reform was in order.[195] So Nero decreed that tax

---

[190] Philo, *Special Laws* 4.195.

[191] *Virtues* 88.

[192] Josephus, *Antiquities* 8.52; cf. Philo, who writes about "the payment agreed upon" (*diomologēthenta misthon*) in *Flaccus* 140.

[193] *Ho misthos . . . kata opheilēma* in Rom 4:4.

[194] Cf. Philo, *Special Laws* 2.92-95; 3.159-63.

[195] Cf. Tacitus, *Annals* 13.50-51.

regulations should be publicly posted and duly enforced. In addition, he lowered or even abolished some of the more oppressive taxes.[196]

During the era of Neronian rule, Paul wrote the following to believers living in the imperial capital: "Pay to all what is due them—taxes to whom taxes are due, revenue to whom revenue is due, respect to whom respect is due, honor to whom honor is due."[197] The first of Paul's four explanatory exhortations is addressed to those who were not Roman citizens. The Greek term translated as "taxes" by the NRSV is *phoros*,[198] a term that describes "that which is brought in by way of payment, tribute."[199] Those who were not Roman citizens were obliged to pay such tribute, whether they lived in Rome or not. The *phoros* was, as Rebell says, "the direct tribute (property- or head tax) of a subjected people to the foreign ruler."[200] Josephus reports that the inhabitants of Judea were required to pay a tribute consisting of one-quarter of the land's agricultural produce.[201] It has been estimated that approximately thirty thousand Jews were living in Rome at about the time when Paul was writing to the Romans. Some of them were believers in Jesus the Messiah. Some among them may have been Roman citizens, but it is likely that many were not. Someone like Aquila was probably obliged to pay tribute before Claudius forced him out of the city.

The Greek term translated as "revenue" by the NRSV is *telos*,[202] a kind of commercial tax levied on various kinds of transactions, including the payment of rent. More than one hundred different kinds of such taxes were levied, on land, grain, animals, capitation, trade, customs, transport, manumission, and so forth. Payment of this tax was incumbent on all who lived or worked in the empire, citizens and

---

[196] Cf. Suetonius, *Nero* 10.1.

[197] Rom 13:7. Cf. Mark 12:13-17.

[198] The Latin equivalent was *tributum*.

[199] *LSJ*, s.v. *phoros*.

[200] Walter Rebell, "*phoros*," *EDNT* 3:436–37, at 437.

[201] Cf. Josephus, *Antiquites* 14.203; *Against Apion* 1.119.

[202] The word appears dozens of times in the New Testament, but in only one other instance, namely, Matt 17:25, does it have this connotation. The Greek term is cognate with two other words used in the New Testament, "tax collector" (*telōnēs*; cf. Matt 5:46; 9:10, 11; 10:3; 11:19; 18:17; 21:31, 32; Mark 2:15, 16 [2x]; Luke 3:12; 5:27, 29, 30; 7:29, 34; 15:1; 18:10, 11, 13) and "tax booth" (*telōnion*; cf. Matt 9:9; Mark 2:14; Luke 5:27). Its Latin equivalent is *vectigalia*.

noncitizens alike. It fell most heavily, of course, on those who were involved in major commercial transactions, principally, therefore, the well-to-do.

To many readers and some commentators, Romans 13:1-7, the pericope in which Paul's two-pronged exhortation on taxes appears,[203] is a foreign body[204] in a theological letter-essay that is largely concerned with a variety of issues pertaining to the relationship between Gentile and Jewish believers. Paul was, however, a realist. Some Roman believers may have questioned the propriety of paying taxes when the system was corrupt. Paul, however, was fully aware that there is no way of totally escaping contact with evil unless one escapes altogether from this world.[205] Before the Parousia, that is impossible. Believers exist in a compromised world.[206] Hence, apropos our passage, Ernst Käsemann writes, "It is for the sake of this determination of Christian existence in this world that Paul sets himself so passionately against the separation of creation and the new age."[207]

The "Jewish question" may have led Paul to address the practical issue of the payment of taxes. Were not only Jewish-Christian but also Gentile believers to be remiss in the payment of tribute and/or indirect taxes, Jewish believers and other Jews would suffer severely. The edict of Claudius in 50 CE, expelling Jews from Rome, is an indication that Jews were a suspect element within the Roman population. Referencing Marcus Borg, Fitzmyer notes that at the time of Paul's writing of Romans, "Judaism was on the brink of catastrophe as a result of its longstanding resistance to Roman imperialism."[208] Apropos the matter of taxes, Neil Elliott writes, "Popular unrest occasioned by

[203] Jesus' question to Simon in Matt 7:25 would appear to be an allusion to the double system of taxation.

[204] Cf. Leander E. Keck, "What Makes Romans Tick?" in *Pauline Theology*, vol. 3: *Romans*, ed. David M. Hay and E. Elizabeth Johnson (Minneapolis: Fortress, 1995), 14–16.

[205] Cf. 1 Cor 5:10.

[206] Cf. Frank J. Matera, *Romans*, Paideia Commentaries on the New Testament (Grand Rapids: Baker Academic, 2010), 303.

[207] Ernst Käsemann, "Principles of the Interpretation of Romans 13," in *New Testament Questions of Today* (Philadelphia: Fortress, 1969), 196–216, at 211.

[208] Fitzmyer, *Romans*, 664, with reference to Marcus J. Borg, "A New Context for Romans xiii," *NTS* 19 (1972–1973): 205–18.

tax abuses might readily be reflected onto the Jews, who 'by virtue not least of their special privileges regarding the temple tax, would be all the more open to charges of tax evasion.'"[209] Payment of taxes by members of the believing community would help to alleviate dire consequences that might fall on Jews were these taxes not to be paid. Hence, Paul urges the members of the community to "pay up." Taxes must be paid to whom taxes are due.

The Ministry to the Saints

From the beginning of the letter to the Romans, Paul spoke about his desire to visit believers in the imperial capital. He noted his frustration in not having been able to do so.[210] In Romans 15:22-29 Paul again writes about his desire to visit Rome but indicates that something was preventing him from doing so. That was his desire to fulfill his ministry to the saints. "At present, however," he writes, "I am going to Jerusalem in a ministry to the saints; for Macedonia and Achaia have been pleased to share their resources with the poor among the saints at Jerusalem. . . . So, when I have completed this, and have delivered to them what has been collected, I will set out by way of you to Spain."[211] By sharing their resources with the poor among God's holy ones in Jerusalem, believers in Macedonia and Achaia had established a common cause with them, a kind of fellowship.[212]

Paul was eager to go to Rome.[213] He earnestly desired to fulfill the Scriptures by preaching the gospel in Spain, where the Good News had not yet been preached.[214] But all that could be put on hold so

---

[209] Neil Elliott, "Romans 13:1-7 in the Context of Imperial Propaganda," in Horsley, *Paul and Empire*, 184–204, at 191. The quotation is from James D. G. Dunn, "Romans 13:1-7—A Charter for Political Quietism," *Ex Auditu* 2 (1986): 55–68, at 60.

[210] Cf. Rom 1:10-15.

[211] Rom 15:25-26, 28.

[212] See what Paul has to say about equity in 2 Cor 8:13-15. On the meaning of the Greek phrase *koinōnian tina poiēsasthai*, "share their resources" (NRSV), see G. W. Peterman, "Romans 15.24: Make a Contribution or Establish Fellowship," *NTS* 40 (1994): 457–63; and Jewett, *Romans*, 928–29.

[213] Cf. Rom 1:15.

[214] Cf. Rom 15:20-21 with a citation of Isa 52:15.

that he could provide for the needs of the poor in Jerusalem. This was a matter of some urgency. This was his ministry,[215] the service to which God had called him.

Phoebe and Gaius

At this point in our study, nothing more need be said about the collection, but mention must be made of the fact that before Paul conveys second-person greetings[216] to more than two dozen people in Rome, he commends to the Roman believers his sister and patroness, Phoebe.[217] Phoebe was a benefactor to Paul and to many others—or as Paul puts it, to "many as well as myself."[218] She was the "patroness of many" (*prostatis pollōn*). There is no reason to limit those who benefited from her generosity to believers or to assume that Paul was suggesting by this phrase that Phoebe hosted a house church.[219] She may well have done so, but in itself the term "patroness" simply indicates someone who generously shared her financial resources with another. Generous wealthy women were not unknown in the Roman world. They were in the minority to be sure, perhaps numbering about 10 percent of the total number of benefactors, but they played their role personally and out in the open.[220] Phoebe was such a woman, sharing her resources for the sake of God's people, believers and nonbelievers alike.

After his extensive list of second-person greetings, Paul turns his attention to a smaller number of people on whose behalf he wants to send greetings. Among them is the aforementioned Gaius, "who is host to me and to the whole church."[221] In contrast with his

---

[215] Paul uses the term *diakonia*, "ministry" or "service," to describe his task in Rom 15:31.

[216] On the distinction among first-, second-, and third-person greetings, see Jeffrey A. D. Weima, *Neglected Endings: The Significance of the Pauline Letter Closings*, JSNTSup 101 (Sheffield: JSOT Press, 1994), 104–9.

[217] Cf. Rom 16:1-2. On Phoebe, see above, pp. 3–4, 7–8.

[218] Rom 16:2.

[219] So Matera, *Romans*, 339.

[220] Cf. Ramsey MacMullen, "Women in Public in the Roman Empire," *Historia: Zeitschrift für Alte Geschichte* 29 (1980): 208–18.

[221] Rom 16:23.

description of Phoebe, Paul cites himself as being the recipient of Gaius's benefaction before he mentions others. Moreover, he says that Gaius was host to the whole church. Paul says nothing about the generosity that Gaius may have extended to people beyond the pale of the church.

Galatians

Paul's letter to the Galatians treats much of the same material as is covered in the much-longer letter to the Romans, but in contrast with the measured tones of this latter letter, the letter to the Galatians is written by a Paul who describes himself, in what are certainly understatements, as astonished[222] and perplexed.[223] In his anger, Paul omits his customary epistolary thanksgiving; he does not eschew impassioned[224] and harsh language.[225] Given his state of mind, and the subject at hand, it is not surprising that Galatians does not have much to say about money matters. Only two passages need to be entered into the present discussion.

The first is Galatians 2:10, the conclusion of Paul's autobiographical account of his visit to Jerusalem as a believer. On the occasion, an agreement was reached between Paul and the acknowledged leaders[226] of the church in Jerusalem, Peter, James, and John, that they would minister to the circumcised while Paul and Barnabas would go to the Gentiles. Paul ends his narrative of the visit by saying, "They asked only one thing, that we remember the poor, which was actually what I was eager to do."[227] The transition from the first-person plural to the first-person singular is worth noting. Paul mentions his personal eagerness to help the poor. From that eagerness was born the collection on behalf of God's holy ones in Jerusalem, about which he writes in his letter to the Romans and the two extant letters to the Corinthians.

---

[222] Gal 1:6.

[223] Gal 4:20.

[224] Cf. Gal 1:20.

[225] Cf. Gal 5:12. For an expression of his similar sentiments toward those who want Gentile believers to be circumcised, see Phil 3:2.

[226] Cf. Gal 2:2, 6, 9.

[227] Gal 2:10.

The other noteworthy passage is Galatians 5:16, where Paul says, "The only thing that counts is faith working through love." Many are familiar with the classic trilogy, faith, hope, and charity. This trio, which Roman Catholics consider to be the three basic theological virtues, owes its fame to 1 Corinthians 13:13, but in Paul's writing the dyad, faith and love, preceded his use of the triad.[228] In Galatians 5:6, Paul is essentially saying that a dynamic faith (*pistis*) expresses itself in love (*agapē*). Such faith is not merely a sentiment of goodwill toward those inside and those outside the community of believers. For Paul, the love that expresses real faith is love at work.[229]

There is often an element of financial generosity, whose goal is equity between the giver and the recipient, in this kind of love. Contributing to the needs of the poor so that there is some measure of equality between them and those who come to their aid with financial support is proof of one's love.[230] It is a sure sign that love is genuine[231] rather than simply a well-meaning fantasy. Assuring equity in this fashion is not, for Paul, an option. It is, as he says, "the only thing that counts."[232]

Paul reiterates the importance of this kind of love a few verses later when he writes, "Do not use your freedom as an opportunity for self-indulgence,[233] but through love become slaves to one another. For the whole law is summed up in a single commandment, 'You shall love your neighbor as yourself.'"[234] When one realizes that for Paul love is an activity rather than a sentiment, one cannot help but realize that the principle of equity within the community is at issue when Paul cites the biblical precept, the basis for community life within Israel. Paul expects that this same principle should be the

---

[228] Cf. 1 Thess 5:8; 1:3.

[229] See 1 Thess 1:3, where Paul writes about the "labor of love" (*tou kopou tēs agapēs*).

[230] *Tēn . . . endeixin tēs agapēs hymōn*, "proof of your love," Paul writes in 2 Cor 8:24.

[231] *To tēs hymeteras agapēs gnēsion*, "the genuineness of your love," he writes in 2 Cor 8:8.

[232] Gal 5:6.

[233] What Paul calls existence "in the flesh" (*tē sarki*).

[234] Gal 5:14. The quotation is of Lev 19:18.

guiding principle for community life among believers. They must use their assets to take care of and provide for one another.

It is not, therefore, surprising when Paul lists generosity (*agathōsynē*) among the fruits of the Spirit in this letter to the Galatians.[235] He uses this biblical term[236] just twice in the extant correspondence.[237] The term "generosity" designates the virtue, whose power is derived from the Spirit, that "will always take care to obtain for others that which is useful or beneficial."[238] According to J. Louis Martyn, the exhortation to share goods that appears in Galatians 6:6 resonates with the virtue of generosity.[239] Generosity is a virtue that builds and supports community and foreshadows the final words that Paul dictated to the scribe:[240] "Let us work for the good of all, especially for those of the family of faith."[241]

The "all" (*pros pantas*) of this exhortation[242] is extremely important since

> The universal character of God's redemption corresponds to the universality of Christian ethical and social responsibility. If God's redemption in Christ is universal, the Christian community is obliged to disregard all ethnic national, cultural, social, sexual and even religious distinctions within the human community. Since before God there is no partiality, there cannot be partiality in the Christian's attitude towards his fellow man [*sic*].[243]

---

[235] Cf. Gal 5:22.

[236] Spicq observes that the term is unknown in secular Greek and in the papyri. Cf. "*agathopoieō, agathosynē*," *TLNT* 1:1–4, at 3.

[237] Cf. Rom 15:14. In the deutero-Paulines, the term appears in Eph 5:9 and 2 Thess 1:11.

[238] Spicq, "*agathopoieō, agathosynē*," *TLNT* 1:1–4, at 4.

[239] Cf. J. Louis Martyn, *Galatians*, AB 33A (New York: Doubleday, 1997), 543.

[240] The exhortation is immediately followed by the long postscript, written in large letters by Paul's own hand, that appears in Gal 6:11-18.

[241] Gal 6:10.

[242] Cf. Gal 2:16; 3:8, 22, 26-28.

[243] Hans Dieter Betz, *Galatians: A Commentary on Paul's Letter to the Churches in Galatia*, Hermeneia (Philadelphia: Fortress, 1979), 311.

The words of Galatians 6:10 are clearly Paul's conclusion to his earlier discussion.[244] En passant, Paul had urged the Galatians to "bear one another's burdens."[245] These burdens (*ta barē*) may well have included financial burdens,[246] but it is impossible to glean from Paul's words such specificity.[247] Similarly, it is difficult, if not impossible, to find in Galatians 6:6-10 an exhortation to participate in the Jerusalem collection, despite the similarity of vocabulary between that used by Paul in his appeal and the words that he uses as he brings the letter to the Galatians to a close.[248] At the most, one can and probably should affirm that the apostle continues to be on the same wavelength as he is when he appealed for financial help for impoverished believers in the holy city of Jerusalem.

Letters from Prison

Among Paul's shorter letters are two that he wrote while he was imprisoned, his letter to the Philippians and his very short letter to his beloved friend, Philemon.[249]

Philippians

In the Acts of the Apostles, Luke gives a dramatic account of how Paul, in response to divine revelation, left Asia and went to what is now considered the continent of Europe. The apostle's first stop was Philippi, a Roman colony largely inhabited by old soldiers.[250] Ensuing events led to his forcible departure from Philippi and his arrival in

---

[244] Especially in Gal 6:1-10.

[245] Gal 6:2.

[246] Paul employs similar vocabulary with financial connotations in 1 Thess 2:7, 11.

[247] John G. Strelan attempts to do so in "Burden-Bearing and the Law of Christ: A Re-examination of Galatians 6:2," *JBL* 94 (1975). Strelan's argument was rebutted by E. M. Young, "'Fulfil the Law of Christ': An Examination of Galatians 6.2," *Studia biblica et theologica* 7 (1977): 31–42.

[248] See the brief discussion in F. F. Bruce, *Commentary on Galatians*, NIGTC (Grand Rapids: Eerdmans, 1982), 266.

[249] Cf. Phil 1:7, 13, 17; Phlm 9, 10, 13-14, 23; 2 Cor 11:23.

[250] Cf. Phil 2:13; 4:22.

Thessalonica, the capital of the province of Macedonia.[251] Thus, Paul evangelized Philippi before he preached the gospel at Thessalonica.

For the sake of the freedom of the gospel, Paul eschewed receiving financial support from those to whom he was preaching the gospel or those whom he had previously evangelized.[252] For some reason, however, Paul made an exception for the Philippians. He comments on this support in Philippians 4:14-18, writing:

> [I]t was kind of you to share my distress. You Philippians indeed know that in the early days of the gospel when I left Macedonia, no church shared with me in the matter of giving and receiving, except you alone. For even when I was in Thessalonica, you sent me help for my needs more than once. Not that I seek the gift but I seek the profit that accumulates to your account. I have been paid in full and have more than enough; I am fully satisfied, now that I have received from Epaphroditus the gifts you sent a fragrant offering, a sacrifice acceptable and pleasing to God.[253]

The financial support that he received from the Philippians was given to Paul at an early stage in this ministry. It was exceptional and memorable, to the point that Paul was still saying thanks years later.[254]

In the opening thanksgiving of this letter, Paul expresses his gratitude for the Philippians' sharing in the gospel:

[251] Cf. Acts 16:6-17; 1 Thess 2:2.

[252] David E. Briones offers a survey of various scholarly approaches to the background of Paul's attitude in this regard in *Paul's Financial Policy: A Socio-Theological Approach*, LNTS 494 (London: Bloomsbury T & T Clark, 2013), 2-19.

[253] This passage alone qualifies Paul's letter to the Philippians to be an authentic letter from the apostle. In all of these, Paul has something to say about finances. See Mark C. Kiley, *Colossians as Pseudepigraphy*, Biblical Seminar 4 (Sheffield: JSOT, 1986), 46-51, 98-118.

[254] It is difficult to say how many years later. Commenting on the date of composition of the letter, Bonnie Thurston writes, "If the letter is from Rome, it is to be dated in the early 60's; if from Ephesus in the early to mid-50's; if from Caesarea, the late 50's, and if from Corinth, very early, about 50 C.E." See Bonnie B. Thurston, "Philippians," in Bonnie B. Thurston and Judith M. Ryan, *Philippians and Philemon*, SP 10 (Collegeville, MN: Liturgical Press, 2005), 3-163, at 30.

> I thank my God every time I remember you, constantly praying with joy in every one of my prayers for all of you, because of your sharing in the gospel [*epi tē koinōnia hymōn eis to euangelion*] from the first day until now.[255]

Epigraphic evidence and the appearance of words cognate with *koinōnia*[256] indicate that this group of words was often used with financial connotations in the ancient world. The word *koinōnia* itself frequently designated a business partnership.

Julien Ogereau, therefore, argues that Paul was in a kind of business relationship with the Philippians, a *societas* with but one purpose, namely, the preaching of the gospel.[257] If this is indeed the case, it would go a long way to explaining why Paul was willing to accept support from the Philippians while he evangelized the Thessalonians. Paul did not have a client-patron relationship with the Philippians, a relationship that he carefully avoided when dealing with other communities; rather, he had a business deal with them.

Ogereau's suggestion would also explain why Epaphroditus, as a representative of the Philippians, went to care for the imprisoned Paul.[258] It would also help to explain the relative abundance of technical language from the world of finance in Philippians 4:14-18, namely, the apostle's use of "in the matter of giving and receiving" (*eis logon doseōs kai lēmpseōs*) and the bookkeeping expressions "paid in full" (*apechō de panta*) and "fully satisfied" (*peplērōmai*). Moreover, several

---

[255] Phil 1:3-5.

[256] Notably, the verb *koinōneō* and the noun *koinōnos.* Dunn, for example, sees in Paul's use of *koinōnos* in Phlm 17 an echo of legal contracts. Cf. James D. G. Dunn, *The Epistles to the Colossians and to Philemon*, NIGTC (Grand Rapids: Eerdmans, 1996), 337.

[257] Cf. Julien M. Ogereau, "Paul's *Koinōnia* with the Philippians: *Societas* as a Missionary Funding Strategy," *NTS* 60 (2014): 360–78. The article is based on research presented in the form of a doctoral dissertation to Macquarie University in 2014, "Paul's *Koinōnia* with the Philippians: A Socio-Historical Investigation of a Pauline Economic Partnership." See also Bengt Holmberg, *Paul and Power: The Structure of Authority in the Primitive Church as Reflected in the Pauline Epistles* (Lund: Studentlitteratur AB, 1978), 91; J. Paul Sampley, *Pauline Partnership in Christ: Christian Community and Commitment in Light of Roman Law* (Philadelphia: Fortress, 1980), 11–20; Briones, *Paul's Financial Policy*, 71–73.

[258] Cf. Phil 2:25-28.

of the metaphors that Paul, the master of metaphor, employs in the letter to the Philippians are taken from the world of finance.[259] Indeed, he uses the word "profit" (*ton karpon*)[260] as a metaphor in his epistolary thanksgiving.

For the purposes of our study, Paul's financial relationship with the Philippians is an extraordinary subject. We must not, however, overlook the short exhortation that appears in Philippians 2:5, "Let each of you look not to your own interests [*ta heautōn*], but to the interests of others [*ta heterōn*]." The exhortation gathers importance when Paul acknowledges that he knows of people who are on the lookout for their own interests. He writes about some unidentified people, "All of them are seeking their own interests, not those of Jesus Christ."[261] In both of these verses, "interests" is the translation of *ta*, which generally means "things" or "possessions." The reader should not too readily attribute merely a selfish attitudinal outlook to Paul's use of the term in these verses. The exhortation of Philippians 2:5 includes, and perhaps principally so, the thought that the Philippians should share what they own with others.

Philemon

Paul also makes use of technical financial language in his short letter to Philemon, his fellow evangelist. Concluding his plea that Philemon receive Onesimus, no longer as a slave but as a beloved brother,[262] Paul writes, "If he [Onesimus] has wronged you in any way, or owes you anything, charge that to my account. I, Paul, am writing this with my own hand, I will repay it."[263] The short passage includes three financial terms: "owes," "account," and "repay."[264] The first term, "owes" (*ophelei*), was commonly used in reference to debts and financial obligations. The second, "charge to [my] account" (*elloga*),

[259] Cf. Phil 1:11, 21; 3:7-8; 4:19. See Collins, *The Power of Images*, 238–50.
[260] Cf. Phil 1:11.
[261] Phil 2:21.
[262] Cf. Phlm 16.
[263] In the immediately preceding v. 17, Paul's *koinōnos* may be a deliberate and ironic use of a financial term. Cf. Dunn, *Colossians and Philemon*, 337.
[264] Cf. Joseph A. Fitzmyer, *The Letter to Philemon*, AB 34C (New York: Doubleday, 2000), 117–18.

was a technical term used in commerce and was often found in contracts. The third, "repay" (*apotisō*), was used principally in the judicial
sphere in reference to the payment of a fine or the cost of damages.

In effect, Paul's letter to Philemon is a promissory note in which
the apostle commits himself to pay off whatever financial obligations
Onesimus had accrued vis-à-vis his master. Paul's conditional "if"
suggests that he was not sure that there were financial obligations,
but the tenor of his phrase suggests that he believed that there were
some.[265] We do not know whether those debts were large[266] or small.
Nor do we know the source of Onesimus's indebtedness. On both
of these matters, scholars proffer a variety of opinions. Could it be
that Onesimus had robbed Philemon or that Onesimus was being
blamed for something that was not his fault? Was there a debt to be
paid because Philemon was deprived of Onesimus's services for a
period of time? Or had Philemon advanced Onesimus some money
to cover the expenses of his trip to see Paul? We know the answer
to none of these questions; we can only speculate as to what those
answers might be. What we do know is that Paul offered to take care
of whatever Onesimus might have owed. At bottom is the financial
principle that debts must be paid.

Paul's First Letter

The first of the letters written by Paul, the oldest of the written
documents later incorporated into the Christian New Testament,[267]
was written to the church of the Thessalonians midway through the
first century, probably in 50 CE. At the time both Paul and the community to which he was writing were expecting an early Parousia, the
ultimate appearance of Jesus as Lord. As a matter of fact, the First

[265] Fitzmyer writes, "He [Paul] realizes it to be true absolutely" (*Philemon*, 117).
[266] Caird, for example, suggested that Onesimus owed Philemon a considerable
sum of money since he "must have helped himself to at least enough to pay his
way to Rome." Cf. G. B. Caird, *Paul's Letters from Prison (Ephesians, Philippians,
Colossians, Philemon) in the Revised Standard Version* (London: Oxford University
Press, 1976), 222–23. Caird was one of those commentators of an earlier generation who considered Onesimus to have been a runaway slave.
[267] Cf. Raymond F. Collins, *The Birth of the New Testament: The Origin and
Development of the First Christian Generation* (New York: Crossroad, 1993).

Letter to the Thessalonians[268] was written because some believers in the Macedonian capital had died before Christ made his appearance as Lord. Given the fact that neither he nor they expected that the world as they had experienced it was to last much longer, it is not surprising that 1 Thessalonians does not speak about such mundane issues as wealth, wages, and the wealthy. At best, it contains just a few snippets that even allude to financial issues.

The first is Paul's commendation of the Thessalonians' labor of love.[269] The apostle praised the church for its active and demanding love, a love that may have included financial support for the indigent members of the community in Thessalonica and beyond.[270] The second is Paul's reminder that his preaching to the Thessalonians was in no way a pretext for greed.[271] Contrasting himself with charlatans, Paul makes a point of his not being greedy. Later he would regularly list greed among the vices that believers are to avoid.[272] For the moment, in the expected interval of just a short period of human history, Paul affirms that greed (*pleonexia*) is not a motivating factor in the way that he himself lives and acts.

Most striking is that from the very first of his extant letters, Paul affirms that he did not intend to be a financial burden to the Thessalonians,[273] even if as an apostle of Christ he might have a claim to receive financial support from them.[274] Rather than receive their financial support, Paul followed the example of other "rabbis"[275] in working at a trade to support himself. Indeed, his leather-worker's craft gave him an opportunity to proclaim the gospel to visitors even

---

[268] The so-called Second Letter to the Thessalonians is a pseudepigraphic text that will be treated in a later chapter of the present study.

[269] Cf. 1 Thess 1:3.

[270] Cf. 1 Thess 4:9-10.

[271] *En prophasei pleonexias*, 1 Thess 2:5. Paul's assertion in this regard echoes a rhetorical topos. Cf. Abraham J. Malherbe, "Gentle as a Nurse: The Cynic Background to 1 Thessalonians 2," in *Paul and the Popular Philosophers* (Minneapolis: Fortress, 1989), 35–48; *Paul and the Thessalonians* (Philadelphia: Fortress, 1987), 1–4.

[272] See Rom 1:29; 2 Cor 9:2; cf. Eph 4:19; 5:3; Col 3:5.

[273] Cf. 1 Thess 2:7, 9. See Collins, "A Working Visit," in *Birth*, 9–15.

[274] Cf. 1 Cor 9:3-15.

[275] Applied to the first century CE, the term "rabbi" is rather anachronistic.

as he worked in a shop on the marketplace. He would also urge his addressees to work with their own hands and in this way be self-supporting.[276]

Finally, and not to be overlooked, is this snippet from the first Christian Scripture:

> We urge you, beloved, to do so [love all the brothers and sisters throughout Macedonia] more and more, to aspire to live quietly, to mind your own affairs and to work with your hands as we directed you, so that you may behave properly toward outsiders and be dependent on no one.[277]

As he himself was financially independent of those to whom he preached, so Paul urged his beloved Thessalonians to avoid being beholden to others, especially not being financially dependent on them. One might argue that Paul did not want his addressees to be involved in a situation in which they were clients of idol worshipers, but he does not say so explicitly. His exhortation was terse, for the moment, and not designed for the long haul.

In his later letters, as we have already seen, Paul expands and concretizes some of the basic insights expressed in his very first letter. His insights would continue to develop in the thoughts of those who took up the proverbial pen to write in his name, the authors of Ephesians, Colossians, 2 Thessalonians, 1 and 2 Timothy, and Titus. For the most part these pseudepigraphic texts were written toward the end of the first century CE.

Before turning our attention to what these documents have to say about wealth, wages, and the wealthy, it might be useful to look at the oldest of the canonical gospels, that according to Mark, written around 70 CE. In it we already find an echo of what Jesus himself said

---

[276] Older commentators might have been inclined to add to this exhortation a bit of paraenesis found in 1 Thess 5:14, *noutheteite tous ataktous*, translated by the NRSV as "admonish the idlers." Ceslas Spicq has clearly demonstrated that the terminology does not pertain to the idle but to the unruly and disruptive. Cf. Spicq, "Les Thessaloniciens 'inquiets' étaient-ils des paresseux?" *ST* 10 (1956): 1–13; "*Ataktéō, ktl.*," *TLNT* 1:223–26.

[277] 1 Thess 4:10b-12. Cf. Jeffrey A. D. Weima, *1–2 Thessalonians*, Baker Exegetical Commentary on the New Testament (Grand Rapids: Baker, 2014), 295–300.

about wealth, wages, and the wealthy. Somewhat later in this study we can examine the way in which Paul's insights were developed by his second- and third-generation disciples.

So What?

Wages

After perusing what Paul had to say about financial matters, the reader of these pages might be tempted to ask, "So what?" Does what the apostle had to say two thousand years ago have any relevance for the world in which we live, with its different economic system and a global economy? There are obviously some who think that the entire Bible is an ancient text that is irrelevant for contemporary secularists. To them, what Paul had to say about wealth and wages is meaningless, other than as a historical footnote.

One might, however, think that the situation would be different for the contemporary believer. For him or for her, the Bible in its entirety, both the Old Testament and the New, both its message of salvation and its ethical challenge, is considered to be the word of God, having some importance for how the believer views the world and the ethical challenges that he or she faces on a daily basis. For this person, the believer, do Paul's words have any relevance? I would suggest that they do.

Paul speaks about the wages that are owed to those who work. He returns to the topic, of importance to him because of his biblical (Old Testament) legacy and the situations that he and his communities were facing. The withholding of wages not only was a problem years ago but also is a problem in twenty-first-century America, at least in the part of the United States in which I live and where the daily newspaper is *The Providence Journal.*

On May 27, 2015, a front-page article in the *Journal* announced: "Marrocco to pay out $303,000: Probe into Federal Hill holdings found wages owed to 146 workers." The Marrocco is a local nightclub. No criminal charges were filed against its owner. He was not penalized for his withholding of these workers' wages. And just three days later, with regard to another nightclub, a newspaper article by staff reporter Katie Mulvaney had this lead: "Exotic dancer files class-action suit against Foxy Lady: Alleges wage violations, says club classifies dancers as contractors."[278]

The withholding of wages is not limited to the adult-entertainment industry. A blog appearing on the local channel 12 news site, 12WPRI.com, on October 20, 2015, had this to offer: "Autistic Restaurant Worker goes unpaid for about a year."

The next day, with my morning coffee, I read, "A federal judge in California has granted conditional class certification to minor-league baseball players who are suing Major League Baseball teams for failing to pay them minimum wages," reported the *Journal*.[279]

And from the United Kingdom, "church leaders and MPs had joined a fans' campaign for the big Manchester football clubs to pay the voluntary Living Wage to subcontracted stewards, caterers and other staff. . . . Many subcontracted workers are paid the Minimum Wage, currently £6.70 an hour rather than the Living Wage, which is £7.85 an hour."[280]

Particularly egregious is the situation of shrimp workers. "Cheap shrimp at a great human cost: Migrants sold to Thai factories peel 16 hours a day; the seafood ends up in stores, restaurants worldwide" was the headline of a front-page story in the December 15, 2015, edition of *The Providence Journal*. The story began: "Poor migrant workers and children are being sold to factories in Thailand and forced to peel shrimp that ends up in global supply chains, including those of Wal-Mart and Red Lobster, the world's largest retailer and the world's largest seafood restaurant chain, an Associated Press investigation found." The story continued, "At the Gig Peeling Factory, nearly 100 Burmese laborers were trapped, most working for almost nothing."

Better off is the situation of many workers in my home state, even if they aren't paid enough to rent an apartment. For example, another front-page article, this one appearing in the Friday, October 2, 2015, issue of the *Journal*, read: "The median personal income for millennials in Rhode Island, $14,509 in a recent U.S. Census Bureau

---

[278] *The Providence Journal* (Saturday, May 30, 2015): A3.
[279] *The Providence Journal* (Wednesday, October 21, 2015): C4.
[280] *The Tablet* (October 31, 2015): 33.

estimate, is much too low to rent affordably even the average-priced one-bed-room apartment ($928 a month in 2014) in Rhode Island."

From the corporate perspective, I can reference the brief financial report that appeared in my daily newspaper, *The Providence Journal*, at that time owned by the A. J. Belo Company, which later sold the newspaper to another company, Gatehouse Media, its present owner. The chair of the Dallas-based company reported to the stockholders that the company had increased its profitability by 5 percent during the preceding quarter. He explained that this was largely achieved by reducing wages and benefits. The bottom line was that there was a greater profit for the corporate owners because their workers were paid less and received lesser benefits. What was taken from them enriched the corporate owners.

Unfortunately, I did not have to do any research to gather some evidence on how the world has reacted to Paul's teaching that "wages are not reckoned as a gift but as something due," announced as a principle in Romans 4:4 and discussed at length in 1 Corinthians. Seven instances of outright rejection of Paul's traditional teaching were there on the island in my kitchen, right next to my morning coffee as I was completing this study. Could it be that believers no longer accept what the apostle taught as normative for their lives?

Politicians, of course, have their "two cents" to add on the topic. Thus, Robert Reich, secretary of labor under President Clinton, has observed that wage theft from ordinary workers is symptomatic of the contemporary moral crisis. "The moral crisis of our age," he said, "has nothing to do with gay marriage or abortion. It's insider trading, obscene trading, wage theft from ordinary workers, Wall Street's gambling addiction, corporate payoffs to friendly politicians, and the billionaire takeover of our democracy."[281]

---

[281] *Liberal and Proud of It* blog, September 17, 2015.

Chapter 3

Mark

Among New Testament scholars it is almost a commonplace to observe that the Gospel of Mark is not a rich lode from which one can extract an abundance of nuggets of ethical material.[1] The evangelist wrote a story about Jesus and his disciples, and although he observes that people were astounded at Jesus' teaching because he taught them as one having authority and not as the scribes,[2] he generally fails to say much about that teaching. So obvious is the evangelist's relative silence about Jesus' teaching that Matthew filled in the lacuna by offering the entire Sermon on the Mount as the body of teaching that amazed the crowds.[3]

Nonetheless, it is with Mark among the Synoptic Gospels that we must begin in this study of wealth, wages, and the wealthy since Mark is the oldest of these canonical gospels and a major source of the other two. In a stimulating essay, John Donahue notes that this oldest of the New Testament gospels contains two significant bodies of Jesus' teaching.[4] The first is Jesus' teaching in parables of Mark

---

[1] See, for example, Frank J. Matera, *New Testament Ethics: The Legacies of Jesus and Paul* (Louisville: Westminster John Knox, 1996), 13.

[2] Cf. Mark 1:22, 27.

[3] Matt 5:1–7:28.

[4] Cf. John R. Donahue, "The Lure of Wealth: Does Mark Have a Social Gospel?," in *Unity and Diversity in the Gospels and Paul: Essays in Honor of Frank J. Matera*, ed. Christopher W. Skinner and Kelly R. Iverson, ECL 7 (Atlanta: Society of Biblical Literature, 2012), 70–93, at 72.

4:1-34; the second, the apocalyptic discourse of Mark 13. Chapter 4, which contains the teaching in parables, begins with the parable of the Sower[5] that concludes with Jesus' challenge, "Let anyone who has ears to hear listen!"[6]

The Parable of the Sower (Mark 4:1-9; 13-20)

Early Christian tradition considered this parable to be paradigmatic.[7] The evangelist appends to his retelling of the parable a reflection on the purpose of the parables, complete with a scriptural warrant (Isa 6:9-10 in Mark 4:10-12)[8] and an explanation of the parable in Mark 4:13-20. The two-part addendum, albeit not part of Jesus' original teaching,[9] was so significant for those who listened to the parable in the late first century that both Matthew and Luke reprised the material in their later revisions of the Markan text.[10] The emphasis in the little story told by Jesus lies on the fruitfulness of the seed that is sown.[11]

The early church, however, seems to have been more interested in the reasons why God's word did not reach its intended effect. It sought, then, to explain the parable by going into detail about the seed that did not produce fruit. This explanation eventually made its way into the Markan text in this fashion:

> The sower sows the word. These are the ones on the path where the word is sown; when they hear, Satan immediately comes and takes away the word that is sown in them. And

[5] Cf. Mark 4:1-9; Matt 13:1-9; Luke 8:4-8; *G. Thom.* 9.

[6] Mark 4:9.

[7] Note the plural "parables" (*parabolai*) in vv. 10, 11, 13. "This parable," Moloney writes, "is the key to understanding all the parables (4:13) because it describes the proclamation and reception of the gospel." See Francis J. Moloney, *The Gospel of Mark: A Commentary* (Peabody, MA: Hendrickson, 2002), 91.

[8] Cf. Matt 13:10-17; Luke 8:9-10.

[9] See, for example, Vincent Taylor, *The Gospel According to St. Mark* (London: Macmillan, 1963), 258; M. Eugene Boring, *Mark: A Commentary*, NTL (Westminster John Knox, 2006), 129–30.

[10] Cf. Matt 13:18-23; Luke 8:11-15.

[11] Cf. Camille Focant, *The Gospel According to Mark: A Commentary* (Eugene, OR: Pickwick, 2012), 168.

these are the ones sown on rocky ground: when they hear the word, they immediately receive it with joy. But they have no root, and endure only for a while; then when trouble or persecution arises on account of the word, immediately they fall away. And others are those sown among the thorns: these are the ones who hear the word, but the cares of the world, and the lure of wealth, and the desire for other things come in and choke the word, and it yields nothing.[12]

The ecclesiastical interpretation of the parable affirms that the proclaimed word's failure to reach its intended effect is not a simple matter. The different reasons for this apparent failure fall into different categories. Sometimes the failure occurs because of the opposition of superhuman malevolent powers—"Satan," in traditional language.[13] At other times the failure occurs because of outside social pressure, "anything from being ostracized to being executed."[14] A third source of failure lies within the human person him- or herself. The cares of the world, the lure of wealth, and the desire for worldly things choke the word and prevent its fruitfulness. For the evangelist, this is all or nothing; it is not that such cares impede growth; rather, such cares result in the word yielding nothing.[15]

The cares of the world are specified in the other two destructive attitudes of verse 19, namely, the lure of wealth and the desire for other things. The concentric pattern of the Greek phraseology is such that "'lure' and 'desire' bracket the seductive objects, 'wealth' and 'other things' so that the two attitudes or vices are virtually interchangeable and convey a fundamental distortion of values."[16] Joel Barth says, "These things do not permit people a choice but rather *enter into* them like demons and usurp their ability to make a decision

---

[12] Mark 4:14-19.

[13] Cf. T. J. Wray and Gregory Mobley, *The Birth of Satan: Tracing the Devil's Biblical Roots* (New York: Palgrave Macmillan, 2005), 123–24.

[14] Adela Yarbro Collins, *Mark*, Hermeneia (Minneapolis: Fortress, 2007), 252.

[15] The Greek reads *akarpos ginetai*, "is without fruit." This may be rhetorical hyperbole; the evangelist has made his point forcefully.

[16] Donahue, "Lure of Wealth," 75.

for God."[17] The attraction of wealth prevents a person from making a religious decision, a decision for God.

Interpreting the parable as they did, the first generations of believers echoed Jesus' Jewish tradition. The tradition considered the Ten Commandments[18] to be prescriptions of the covenant between God and God's people, Israel. These prescriptions were considered so important that, unlike other divine instructions in the Torah, they are found in two books of the Bible, Exodus and Deuteronomy.[19] Biblical tradition described these commandments as the Ten Words of the Lord,[20] clearly distinct from the legal tradition that was attributed to Moses.

The tenth commandment, the last of the Ten Words of the Lord, was "You shall not covet" your neighbor's house, wife, family, or possessions.[21] The word in the Greek Bible, the Septuagint, translated into English as "covet" is *epithymēseis*, "desire." The verb is related to the "desire" (*epithymiai*) of Mark 4:19. The verb connotes "an inordinate or ungoverned desire that leads to the taking of what is desired."[22] In his study of the Decalogue, Patrick Miller references Exodus 34:24; Deuteronomy 7:25; Joshua 7:21; and Micah 2:1-2 as evidence of such usage. These references include the story of Achan, who confessed, "When I saw among the spoil a beautiful mantle from Shinar, and two hundred shekels of silver, and a bar of gold weighing fifty shekels, then I coveted them and took them." Achan was stoned to death for his crime.[23] The Hebrew Bible also tells the even more famous story of Ahab's desire to possess Naboth's vineyard and the lengths to which Jezebel went in order to fulfill her husband's desire.[24]

---

[17] Joel Marcus, *Mark 1–8*, AB 27 (New York: Doubleday, 2000), 312, his emphasis.

[18] Cf. Raymond F. Collins, "The Ten Commandments in Current Perspective," *AER* 161 (1969): 169–82; "The Ten Commandments and the Christian Response," *LS* 3 (1970–1971): 308–22; Patrick D. Miller, *The Ten Commandments*, IBC (Louisville: Westminster John Knox, 2000); "Ten Commandments," *NIDB* 5:517–22.

[19] Exod 20:1; Deut 5:22.

[20] Cf. Exod 20:2-17; Deut 5:6-21.

[21] Exod 20:17; cf. Deut 5:21.

[22] Miller, *Ten Commandments*, 390.

[23] Cf. Josh 7:20-26.

[24] Cf. 1 Kgs 11:1-16.

In the biblical tradition, inordinate desire for possessions is no small matter. Greed is anathema both to biblical authors and to Greco-Roman moralists. For early Christians, greed, the inordinate desire for money, was the singular human obstacle to the fruitful reception of the word of God. Early Christians were so convinced of this reality that neither Matthew nor Luke in their revisions of the Markan texts mitigated one whit of Mark's explanation of the parable of the Sower.[25]

Matthew writes, "As for what was sown among thorns, this is the one who hears the word, but the cares of the world and the lure of wealth choke the word and it yields nothing."[26] Redacting the Markan text, Matthew has individualized the application[27] and dropped the reference to "the desire for other things" with its rich biblical overtones. Matthew retains Mark's "cares of the world and the lure of wealth" as well as Mark's uncompromising "fruitless" (*akarpos*). Those who hear the word with a heart that is focused on the cares of the world and are seduced by wealth can be sure that the word will produce no beneficial result.

Luke's revision of Mark 4:18-19 is more radical than is Matthew's. Retaining Mark's plural, Luke writes, "As for what fell among the thorns; these are the ones who hear; but as they go on their way, they are choked by the cares and riches and pleasures of life, and their fruit does not mature."[28] Having identified the seed as "the word of God," a specification that is not found in either Mark or Matthew,[29] Luke stresses the seed's inability to come to fruition; its growth is stunted. The reasons are threefold, namely, the cares, riches, and pleasures of life. Luke has displaced the accent from desire and enticement to the actual possession of cares, riches, and pleasures. The possession of wealth impedes the fruition of God's word in those who receive it, says Luke. Luke's attention to the actual possession of wealth is

[25] The interpretation of the parable has not, however, been incorporated into the *Gospel of Thomas*.

[26] Matt 13:22.

[27] Instead of Mark's plural "the ones" (*outoi*), Matthew speaks only of "the one" (*outos*).

[28] Luke 8:14.

[29] Luke 8:11; cf. Matt 13:19; Mark 4:13.

consistent with what he has to say about riches elsewhere in his gospel, as we shall see in chapter 5 of this study.

Mark's relatively short chapter on parables[30] comes to an end with two additional seed parables, the parable of the Seed Growing by Itself in Mark 4:26-29 and the parable of the Mustard Seed in Mark 4:30-32,[31] and a brief conclusion on Jesus' use of parables in Mark 4:33-34.

Almost hidden among the seed parables is the short parable of the Lamp under the Bushel Basket in Mark 4:21-23 and a series of three sayings in Mark 4:24-25 that probably circulated independently of one another prior to their incorporation into Mark's gospel. This group of sayings is virtually a parable in itself insofar as together they constitute an enigmatic or riddling saying.[32]

The last of these three sayings—"For to those who have, more will be given; and from those who have nothing, even what they have will be taken away"[33]—may have some relevance for the present study. In the Markan gospel, the passive voice of the verbs in the sayings is most likely a theological passive; it is God who gives and God who takes away.[34] Those who have the mystery of God will proclaim it and will receive a greater reward, whereas those who don't have the mystery will lose what little they have. As a previously independent saying,[35] the adage might well have reflected proverbial wisdom.[36] The rich get richer and the poor get poorer—what Gundry describes as an economic truism or, better yet, a sociological truism, full of resignation, "for in ancient oriental society as in parts of modern oriental society the already rich are plied with gifts while the last

[30] That is, when compared to Matthew's great discourse in parables, Matt 13.
[31] Cf. Matt 13:31-32; Luke 13:18-19.
[32] Cf. A. Y. Collins, *Mark*, 253. She notes that this corresponds to the Septuagint's understanding of "parable."
[33] Mark 4:25.
[34] In the case of the taking away, Focant suggests that it may be permissible to speak of a "satanic passive." Cf. Focant, *Mark*, 172.
[35] That the saying also appears in Q is an indication that it was originally an independent saying. This is not the only such doublet in the Synoptic Gospels.
[36] Cf. J. Duncan M. Derrett, *Law in the New Testament* (London: Darton, Longman & Todd, 1970), 29–31.

penny is extracted from the destitute."[37] That the version of the saying that appears in the Synoptic Gospels' Sayings Source is found in a story about money[38] seems to confirm that the saying was originally about money.

The Rich Man (Mark 10:17-22)

The Gospel of Mark is noted for its narrative coherence with internal connections and allusions contributing to the literary unity of the narrative. This story is an example that illustrates Mark's interpretation of the parable of the Sower. It illustrates how the lure of wealth is an impediment to discipleship. The parable of the Sower with its appended explanation effectively anticipates and provides the hermeneutical key for the story of the meeting of Jesus with a rich man found in Mark 10:17-22.[39] The story, set in the course of Jesus' journey to Jerusalem,[40] is as follows:

> As he [Jesus] was setting out on a journey, a man ran up and knelt before him, and asked him, "Good Teacher, what must I do to inherit eternal life?" Jesus said to him, "Why do you call me good? No one is good but God alone. You know the commandments: 'You shall not murder; You shall not commit adultery; You shall not steal; You shall not bear false witness; You shall not defraud; Honor your father and mother.'" He said to him, "Teacher, I have kept all these since my youth." Jesus, looking at him, loved him and said, "You lack one thing; go, sell what you own, and give the money[41] to the poor, and you will have treasure in heaven; then come, follow me." When he heard this, he was shocked and went away grieving, for he had many possessions.[42]

[37] Robert H. Gundry, *Mark: A Commentary on His Apology for the Cross* (Grand Rapids: Eerdmans, 1993), 217.

[38] Cf. Luke 19:26; Matt 25:29.

[39] Cf. Donahue, "Lure of Wealth," 77.

[40] Cf. Mark 10:32.

[41] A note in the NRSV indicates that "the money" is not found in the Greek text; the Greek leaves the verb "give" (*dos*) without a direct object.

[42] Mark 10:17-22; cf. Matt 16:19-22; Luke 18:18-23. The traditional title affixed to the scene, "The Rich Young Man," is something of a conflation of details com-

Strikingly, the evangelist does not offer any indication of the precise location of the encounter, nor does he identify Jesus' interlocutor by name. The interlocutor is simply identified as *eis*—literally, "one," but in English, "someone" or "somebody." It is only at the end of the tale, in the guise of an explanatory comment by the evangelist, that the reader is informed that the anonymous interlocutor "had many possessions." The lack of specificity at the beginning of the story invites the reader to ask whether he or she is the "someone" in Mark's story. The evangelist's literary ploy enables the reader to relate to the story even if he or she cannot properly be described as a person with an abundance of resources.

The nameless someone is full of enthusiasm at the sight of Jesus; he appears to be on the verge of discipleship. He runs to Jesus. He kneels[43] before Jesus. Such a reverential gesture would not be extended to any ordinary teacher. He addresses Jesus as "Good Teacher," a double accolade. For the anonymous man, Jesus is not only a teacher[44] but also good. On his knees before Jesus, the man has a question, "What must I do to inherit eternal life?" Before answering the question, Jesus affirms the unique and absolute goodness of God. Neither Jew nor Greek would have normally asserted that God alone is good. This prelude to Jesus' reply contributes a theocentric perspective to the Markan narrative. It is only from God that eternal life comes.

Having made his point, Jesus cites the commandments, those that deal with interactions among men and women, in a nontraditional order. Citing the commandments as he does, Jesus shows that he considers the precepts of the law to be the basis of righteous moral conduct.[45] The fifth commandment[46] comes at the end of the

---

ing from the three versions of the encounter. The final verse of Mark's narrative indicates that the man was rich.

[43] Cf. Mark 1:40.

[44] Cf. Mark 4:38; 9:17, 38; 10:17, 20, 35; 12:14, 19, 32; 13:1.

[45] Cf. Matt 5:17.

[46] In the Catholic tradition, the precept to honor one's parents is counted as the fourth commandment; among Protestants, it is enumerated as the fifth commandment. The discrepancy partially owes to the fact that Deut 5:21 creates two commandments of the single commandment in Exod 20:17. The Markan Jesus paraphrases this commandment as "You shall not defraud," a single commandment.

list rehearsed by Jesus.[47] The six commandments cited are precepts that a ritually observant person might well violate,[48] all the while thinking that he or she is righteous and law-observant in the eyes of God because of adhering to the Jewish identity markers, principally circumcision, Sabbath observance, and dietary regulations.

In his response to his anonymous interlocutor, Mark's Jesus paraphrases the tenth commandment as "You shall not defraud" (*mē aposterēsēs*),[49] using a verb that is found in neither of the Greek versions of the biblical Decalogue but is characteristic of the Deuteronomic teaching on justice, for example, the injunction against defrauding a day laborer of his wages.[50] Given the evangelist's final characterization of the interlocutor, the modification would seem to be significant. "You shall not defraud" stands out because it does not belong to the precepts of the Decalogue otherwise cited by Jesus.

Then, again addressing Jesus as "Teacher" but careful to omit the problematic "good," the nameless interlocutor replies that he has kept all these commandments since his youth.[51] This seems to be a factual response on his part rather than a defensive retort. Jesus does not take issue with the interlocutor's answer. Instead, with a gesture that expresses his love for the anonymous questioner, Jesus focuses his gaze on him. This is, as the Australian biblical scholar Frank

---

Hence, it seems preferable to adhere to the Exodus version of the Ten Words of the Lord. Cf. Collins, "Current Perspective," 171–72.

[47] Cf. Collins, "Christian Response," 311.

[48] Cf. Moloney, *Mark*, 199.

[49] Since the paraphrase is not part of the Decalogue, it does not appear in many ancient manuscripts of Mark. A corrector of the Codex Vaticanus deleted the phrase, which was then reinserted by a later copyist. It is probably because the Markan text deviates in this way from the Greek Bible that neither Matthew nor Luke include the paraphrase in their renditions of Jesus' words (Matt 19:18-19; Luke 18:20). Cf. Bruce M. Metzger, *A Textual Commentary on the Greek New Testament*, 2nd ed. (Stuttgart: Deutsche Bibelgesellschaft, 1994), 89.

[50] Cf. Deut 24:14-15.

[51] The reference to his youth undoubtedly prompted Matthew to refer to him as a "young man" (Matt 19:20, 22). Could it have been that this reviser thought that it would be all but impossible to keep all the commandments, especially as interpreted by Jesus (cf. Matt 5:21-27), into one's advanced age? Donahue, however, says that Mark's reference to youth suggests that the man is no longer a youth. Cf. Donahue, "Lure of Wealth," 83. Similarly, Gundry, *Mark*, 553–54.

Moloney observes, the first indication of a movement from Jesus toward the rich man.[52] Hitherto, it is the anonymous interlocutor who has taken the initiative. Now Jesus does so. Loving the unnamed questioner, Jesus invites—actually commands[53]—the interlocutor to become a disciple. "Come, follow me," says Jesus.

There is one thing standing in the way of the hitherto eager interlocutor's becoming a follower of Jesus. So Jesus prefixes the invitation to discipleship with a condition: "Sell what you own, and give the money to the poor."[54] "A private fortune," writes the British scholar Richard T. France, "was apparently incompatible with membership of the disciple group."[55] Jesus' radical command is found only in Mark.[56] Amazingly, it is addressed to the only person whom Jesus is said to have loved. At this point in the story, the unsuspecting reader does not realize that the interlocutor is rich. He or she knows only that giving the profit of the sale of one's possessions to the poor is a condition of discipleship and that doing so will be of profit in the kingdom of God.[57]

Jesus' command was too much for the once-eager questioner. He was shocked at what Jesus had just said[58] and left Jesus with sadness in his heart. Mark offers an explanation[59] for this unexpected turn

---

[52] Cf. Moloney, *Mark*, 199–200.

[53] The verb is in the imperative; cf. Mark 2:14; 8:34.

[54] Some ancient philosophic texts speak about the importance of divesting oneself from possessions in order to pursue wisdom, but these Hellenistic texts do not suggest that the money should be given to the poor. Aiding the poor in their need is an element of the Jewish ethos.

[55] "God and Mammon," *EvQ* 51 (1979): 3–21, at 13.

[56] Mark is followed closely by Luke 18:22 and conditionally by Mathew (cf. Matt 19:20-21). Since Clement of Alexandria at the beginning of the third century, commentators have taken the sting out of the command by allegorizing it. Cf. Vittorio Fusco, *Povertà e Sequela. Le Pericope sinottica della Chiamata del Ricco (Mc. 10-17-31 Parr.)* (Brescia: Paideia, 1991), 18–37.

[57] Jesus' reference to heaven obliquely responds to the interlocutor's question about inheriting eternal life.

[58] *Ho de stygnasas epi tō logō*, Mark 10:22. Joel Marcus translates the verb as "be indignant" or "resentfully depressed." Cf. Joel Marcus, *Mark 8–16*, AB 27A (New Haven: Yale University Press, 2009), 720, 23, 29.

[59] Note the explanatory *gar* in the evangelist's comment, *ēn gar exhōn ktēmata polla* (Mark 10:22c).

of events. The anonymous interlocutor had many possessions,[60] so he rejected the invitation to discipleship. With this comment, the evangelist concludes his story about the encounter between the interlocutor and the teacher, deemed to be good. The interlocutor's unwillingness to part with his possessions in order to provide for the poor stood in the way of his becoming a disciple. The lure of wealth turned him away from Jesus.

In what is almost an epilogue to the story, the evangelist, as he so often does, then turns his attention to Jesus and the group of disciples,[61] whose number had not been augmented by the once-enthusiastic questioner. Commenting on the scene that they had witnessed, Jesus says, "How hard it will be for those who love wealth to enter the kingdom of heaven."[62] This difficult saying perplexed the disciples. So, addressing the disciples as "children" (*tekna*)—the only such usage in the Synoptic Gospels—Jesus reiterates what he has just said: "How hard it is to enter the kingdom of God."[63] The repetition would have hardly dispelled the disciples' perplexity.

[60] The Greek word *ktēmata*, used by Mark in 10:22, suggests that the interlocutor's wealth may have resulted from oppression of the poor by a wealthy landowner. The Markan Jesus' paraphrase of the tenth commandment intimates that this may well have been the case. The interlocutor was unwilling to forgo his wealth in order to participate in Jesus' new socioeconomic project. See Joseph H. Hellerman, "Wealth and Sacrifice in Early Christianity: Revisiting Mark's Presentation of Jesus' Encounter with the Rich Young Ruler," *TJ* 21 (2000): 143–64; Michael Peppard, "Torah for the Man Who Has Everything: 'Do Not Defraud' in Mark 10:19," *JBL* 134 (2015): 595–604. Peppard (603–4) observes that there were three ways that a person could become wealthy in Roman Galilee: by defrauding the poor, then manipulating them when they could not repay, and perhaps taking control of their land. See also Bruce Malina, "Wealth and Poverty in the New Testament and Its World," *Int* 41 (1987): 354–67, at 355; Dennis E. Nineham, *Saint Mark*, PGC (Baltimore: Penguin, 1963), 274.

[61] Cf. Mark 10:23–27. A feature of the Markan gospel is the clarification of a controversial teaching of Jesus by portraying Jesus as giving further instruction to the disciples, often in response to their questions. See, for example, Mark 10:10-12.

[62] Mark 10:23.

[63] Mark 10:24. That this second logion is less restrictive has led some copyists to add a qualifying "for those who love wealth" to the saying; others, puzzled by the discrepancy, prefer to reorder the sequence of the verses. See, among others, Taylor, *Mark*, 431–32; Metzger, *Textual Commentary*, 89–90; Marcus, *Mark 8–16*, 730; Moloney, *Mark*, 201n159.

To make his point even more forcefully than his reiteration had, Jesus contrasts what is difficult with what is easy in a graphic and hyperbolic example that has elicited a number of fanciful interpretations throughout the ages, saying, "It is easier for a camel to go through the eye of a needle than for someone who is rich to enter the kingdom of God."[64] Jesus' comment astounded the perplexed disciples, prompting them to ask, "Then who can be saved?"[65]

The history of the interpretation of the episode downplays the severity of Jesus' words by suggesting that "the eye of a needle" was one of the gates of the city of Jerusalem. This disingenuous interpretation appears for the first time in the ninth century CE.[66] There was no such gate in Jerusalem at the time of Jesus. Mark 10:25 is simply a logion that features hyperbolic imagery. There is no way for a camel to pass through the eye of a needle; it is simply impossible for a beast of burden of that size to do so. Jesus' point is that neither the accumulation of riches nor anything else that a human does ensures entrance into the kingdom of God. There is nothing that humans can do to achieve salvation or eternal life. Eternal life is beyond the possibilities that humans can achieve. Entrance into the kingdom is a gift that only God can give.

At bottom, Jesus' response to the astonishment of the disciples is a profound lesson about the grace of God, almost a page taken out of one of Paul's letters. Salvation is pure gift, not a reward for what one has done. Despite this assurance, however, the reader of Mark's story of the meeting between Jesus and the anonymous interlocutor and Jesus' teaching on wealth comes away with a reading of the Markan narrative that riches are an impediment to discipleship and make it difficult for a person to inherit eternal life from God who alone is good.

Corban (Mark 7:1-13)

Almost from the very beginning of his tale about Jesus, the evangelist portrays a scenario of opposition to Jesus' proclamation of

---

[64] Mark 10:25.
[65] Mark 10:26.
[66] Cf. Focant, *Mark*, 419.

the coming of the kingdom. The opposition culminates in the death of Jesus and begins with the brief and programmatic scene of Jesus' temptation by Satan.[67] Between this harbinger and the end of Mark's tale come a number of scenes that illustrate the growing opposition to Jesus. Some of these scenes take the form of a verbal debate between Jesus and his opponents. Scholars attentive to the literary structure of Mark's gospel and the kinds of material embodied in this structure describe these verbal debates as controversy stories.[68] Some of these verbal clashes take place early on in the Markan narrative, while Jesus is described as preaching and healing in Galilee; others take place in Jerusalem,[69] as the opposition to Jesus reaches its climax.

Two of the debates, one of which is situated in Galilee while the other is located in Jerusalem, concern the use of one's wealth. The Galilean controversy begins with Pharisees and scribes coming from Jerusalem and picking on Jesus' disciples for not properly washing their hands before eating. The meal setting of the ensuing controversy enables Mark to locate the scene in the bread section of his narrative,[70] virtually bookended by the two feeding narratives.[71] The Pharisees had last been seen in Mark 3:6 when they were presented as plotting with some Herodians as to how they might destroy Jesus. Critical of the disciples' behavior, the Pharisees turn their attention to Jesus, the real focus of their animosity. "Why do your disciples not live according to the tradition of the elders, but eat with defiled hands?"[72] they ask confrontationally. Jesus is up to the challenge. He responds by citing a Scripture from the book of the prophet Isaiah and then forcefully states, "You abandon the commandment of God and hold to human tradition."[73]

With that, the battle is joined, God's commandment versus human traditions, Jesus as God's spokesperson versus the Pharisees speak-

---

[67] Cf. Mark 1:12-13.

[68] See, among others, Joanna Dewey, "The Literary Structure of the Controversy Stories in Mark 2:1–3:6," *JBL* 92 (1973): 394–401; *Markan Public Debate: Literary Technique, Concentric Structure and Theology in Mark 2:1–3:6*, SBLDS 48 (Chico, CA: Scholars, 1980).

[69] Cf. Mark 11:27–12:44.

[70] Cf. Mark 6:30–8:21.

[71] Mark 6:30-44; 8:1-10.

[72] Mark 7:5.

[73] Mark 7:8.

ing in favor of human traditions. Ancient rhetoricians valued the use of examples in making a point. So Jesus offers this example:

> "You have a fine way of rejecting the commandment of God in order to keep your tradition! For Moses said, 'Honor your father and your mother'; and, 'Whoever speaks evil of father or mother must surely die.' But you say that if anyone tells father or mother, 'Whatever support you might have had from me is Corban' (that is, an offering to God)—then you no longer permit doing anything for a father or a mother, thus making void the word of God through your tradition that you have handed on. And you do many things like this."[74]

As an example of the commandment of God, Jesus cites one of Judaism's traditional Ten Words of the Lord, "Honor your father and mother."[75] This time-honored commandment was directed to the people of Israel, to those adults who had taken upon themselves the burden of the Torah. It required that they provide for their parents in their old age.[76] In both biblical versions of the commandment, the precept continues with "so that your days may be long in the land that the Lord your God is giving you."[77] Hence, early Christian tradition considered that the fourth commandment was the first commandment with a promise.[78] The coda to the commandment adds an urgency to the keeping of the commandment. The law of talion comes into play. If adult Israelites expect to have long life, they must provide the material wherewithal for their parents to be able to live a long life. The biblical scholar William Propp comments, "Filial piety is essentially an intergenerational bargain."[79]

---

[74] Mark 7:9-13.

[75] The commandment is included in both biblical versions of the Decalogue, Exod 20:12a and Deut 5:16a, and in Jesus' rehearsal of the commandments in Mark 10:19; cf. Matt 19:19. The Bible describes it as a "word of the Lord" (Exod 20:1; Deut 5:22). In the Catholic tradition, the precept is counted as the fourth commandment; among Protestants, it is enumerated as the fifth commandment.

[76] Cf. 1 Tim 5:4.

[77] Exod 20:12b; cf. Deut 5:16b; Eph 6:3.

[78] Cf. Eph 6:3.

[79] William C. Propp, *Exodus 19–40*, AB 2A (New York: Doubleday, 2006), 178.

God's commandment is clear and unequivocal. Adults must provide financial and material support for their parents. To support further the binding force of the commandment, Jesus adds another Scripture, "Whoever speaks evil of father or mother must surely die."[80] Citing the biblical text, Jesus employs a technique[81] that would become standard rabbinic practice, namely, explaining one passage of Scripture by means of another that contains similar wording. In this instance, the catchphrase is "father and mother." The bottom line is that providing material support for one's parents is, according to the commandment of God, a life-and-death matter. There can be no escape from its obligatory force.

"But," says Jesus, "you say that if anyone tells father or mother, 'Whatever support you might have had from me is Corban.'"[82] Jesus' "you" (*hymeis*) is emphatic. In Greek, use of the pronoun is grammatically unnecessary; it is employed for the sake of emphasis. Jesus creates a contrast between what Moses (*Mōusēs*) said and what these Pharisees and scribes (*hymeis*) are saying.[83] The Pharisees and scribes[84] stand in opposition to the great prophet and lawgiver because of what they say about Corban. The transliterated term "Corban" appears just this once in the New Testament,[85] so it is no wonder that Mark comments on its meaning for the benefit of his Roman and largely Gentile readership. He adds, "that is, an offering to God."[86]

---

[80] Exod 21:17; Lev 20:9.

[81] Jesus employs the *gezerah shavah* principle of interpretation, interpretation by the use of catchwords. The Markan Jesus is also described as using a similar technique in his response to the question about the first commandment. Cf. Mark 12:29-31 (Matt 22:37-39; cf. Luke 10:27).

[82] Mark 7:11.

[83] In his revision of the story, Matthew retains Mark's emphatic *hymeis* but substitutes "God" (*theos*), thereby putting the Pharisees and scribes in direct opposition to God. Cf. Matt 15:4-5.

[84] The presence of the scribes (*hoi grammateis*) adds an important dimension to the scene. Scribes were professionals dedicated to the interpretation of the Scriptures. Jesus turns the tables on them by showing how they nullify God's word.

[85] Cf. Matt 27:6, "But the chief priests, taking the pieces of silver, said, 'It is not lawful to put them into the treasury [*korbanan*].'" Matthew's *korbanan* is derived from the Greek word *korbanas*.

[86] Matt 15:5 paraphrases Jesus' words as this evangelist portrays Jesus as saying, "Whatever support you might have had from me is given to God [*Dōron ho ean ex emou ōphelēthēs*]."

The enigmatic term is found in the Hebrew Bible, but only in the books of Leviticus, Numbers, and Ezekiel. These passages suggest that the term referred to an offering to God that was accompanied by an oath. An Aramaic inscription found on a Jewish ossuary coming from New Testament times confirms that the term—that is, its Aramaic equivalent—continued to be used in first-century Palestine.[87]

What Jesus attacks[88] in the retort of Mark 7:6-16 was a practice whereby people escaped from the financial obligation to support their parents by promising, under oath, to make a religious offering rather than fulfill their obligation of filial piety. Doing so, they rendered the commandment of God null and void.[89] Oaths could not be annulled.[90] Whether or not the dedicated offering was actually made is beyond the pale of the discussion.

Having given this striking example of how human traditions can be used to contravene God's law, Jesus turns his attention from the obstreperous Pharisees and scribes to the crowds, taking up the issue of defilement that the nitpickers had introduced. Mark sums up Jesus' instruction to the crowds in an enigmatic two-part saying, which Mark calls a parable (*parabolē*[91]): "There is nothing outside a person that by going in can defile; but the things that come out are what defile."[92]

Later, when they were back in the house,[93] Jesus' words continued to puzzle his disciples, so they asked for some clarification. What are the things that defile a person, making that person ineligible to approach the Lord in worship? Jesus' answer: "Fornication, theft, murder, adultery, avarice, wickedness, deceit, licentiousness, envy,

---

[87] Cf. Joseph A. Fitzmyer, "The Aramaic Qorban Inscription from Jebel Hallet et-Turi and Mark 7:11/Matt 15:5," *JBL* 78 (1959): 60–65. Fitzmyer translates the epigraph as "All that a man may find to his profit in this ossuary [is] an offering to God from him who is in it."

[88] Gundry observes that Mark's style of writing at this point "heightens the accusatory tone of Jesus' charge." Cf. Robert H. Gundry, *Mark: A Commentary on His Apology for the Cross* (Grand Rapids: Eerdmans, 1993), 353.

[89] Cf. Mark 7:13.

[90] Cf. Num 30:2.

[91] Mark 7:17.

[92] Mark 7:15.

[93] In Mark's gospel, the "house" (*oikos, oikia*) is a privileged place for Jesus' instruction and action.

slander, pride, folly. All these things come from within, and they defile a person."[94]

The list of vices, the only such list in Mark, is classic. It is comparable to the lists of vices found in Paul's letters and in other Christian, Jewish,[95] and contemporary secular literature. Among the vices are two that relate to money: theft and avarice. The corresponding Greek nouns are in the plural. Coming from the heart, as they do, acts of avarice (*pleonexai*), acts of greed, are among those evil realities that separate a person from God.

"Greed" is a staple of early Christian vice lists.[96] It was almost impossible for the first generations of believers to think about moral evil without thinking about greed as one of the most serious of vices.

Paying Taxes (Mark 12:13-17)

In the Galilean controversy over ritual purity leading to Jesus' discussion of the fifth commandment, Jesus' antagonists were a group of Pharisees and scribes who had come from Jerusalem. But the controversy over taxes is set in Jerusalem. The setting makes the scenario all the more dramatic. During Jesus' lifetime, as of 6 CE, Judea was already under direct Roman rule, whereas Galilee was not.[97] As a result, the tax burden seems to have been much greater in Judea than it was in Galilee.[98]

In the controversy over taxes, Jesus' antagonists were a group of Pharisees and Herodians. Theirs was an unlikely alliance and purely political. Typically they were at the opposite ends of the spectrum in

---

[94] Mark 7:21b-23.

[95] Moloney cites Rom 1:29-31; Gal 5:19-21; and 1 Pet 4:3; while Focant references Wis 14-26; 1QS 4:19-11; *T. Rub.* 3:1-7; *T. Gad* 5:1; and Philo, *Sacrifices* 23. Cf. Moloney, *Mark*, 143; Focant, *Mark*, 284 (291-92). See also Rudolf Pesch, *Das Markus-evangelium*, HTKNT II, 1 (Freiburg: Herder, 1976), 381-83.

[96] See, for example, 1 Cor 5:10; 1 Cor 5:11; and 1 Cor 6:10.

[97] Galilee came under direct Roman rule in 44 CE, more than a decade after Jesus' death.

[98] Cf. David A. Fiensy, "Assessing the Economy of Galilee in the Late Second Temple Period: Five Considerations," in *The Galilean Economy in the Time of Jesus*, ed. David A. Fiensy and Ralph K. Hawkins, ECL 11 (Atlanta: SBL, 2013), 165-86, esp. 169.

early first-century Palestine.[99] Throughout Mark's gospel, the Pharisees were bent on discrediting Jesus, but if they were to do away with him, they needed the help of political authority. The Herodians became their allies.

Herod the Great and his descendants were petty kings who owed their political power to Rome, whose favor they sought by means of various gifts and honors. In this classic client-patron relationship, the Palestinian potentates were the clients. They in turn were patrons of those who were loyal to them and sought their favor, the so-called Herodians. The Herodians were a motley group of people that included government officials, royal servants, and supporters of the regime.[100]

The Pharisees could raise questions pertaining to Jewish law, but only political officials could do away with Jesus.[101] Hence, Mark portrays the Herodians, political loyalists, as being in collusion with the Pharisees, who raised the issue of paying taxes to Rome:

> Then they sent to him [Jesus] some Pharisees and some Herodians to trap him in what he said. And they came and said to him, "Teacher, we know that you are sincere, and show deference to no one; for you do not regard people with partiality, but teach the way of God in accordance with truth. Is it lawful to pay taxes to the emperor or not? Should we pay them, or should we not?" But knowing their hypocrisy he said to them, "Why are you putting me to the test? Bring me a denarius and let me see it." And they brought one. Then he said to them, "Whose head is this, and whose title?" They answered, "The emperor's." Jesus said to them, "Give to the emperor the things that are the emperor's, and to God the things that are God's." And they were utterly amazed at him.[102]

[99] Cf. Moloney, *Mark*, 235.

[100] Cf. John P. Meier, "The Historical Jesus and the Historical Herodians," *JBL* 119 (2000): 740–46; *A Marginal Jew: Rethinking the Historical Jesus*, vol. 3: *Companions and Competitors*, AYBRL (New Haven: Yale University Press, 2001), 560–65; Helen K. Bond, "Herodians," *NIDB* 2:813.

[101] Cf. Mark 3:6.

[102] Mark 12:13-17. Cf. Matt 22:15-22; Luke 20:20-26; *G. Thom.* 100.

The instigators of the conflict are the chief priests, scribes, and elders of Mark 11:27; the group of Pharisees and Herodians, their hench-men. The instigators were looking for a way to kill Jesus,[103] but the authority to do so was not theirs. Their relationship with Palestinian imperial authorities was one path that they could follow to achieve that end; using the Herodians was another.

The delegation's obsequious attempt at a *captatio benevolentiae* was an ill-disguised expression of hypocrisy, which Jesus easily saw through. Their question to Jesus was a tricky one, "Is it lawful to pay taxes[104] to the emperor or not?" They wanted a yes or no answer; "Should we pay them, or should we not?" Ostensibly, it was a question about the appli-cation of the Mosaic law, "Is it lawful [*exestin*[105]]?" they asked. Should Jesus have answered with the yes or no that the crafty interrogators demanded, he would inevitably have generated some opposition.

A yes answer would have lost him support among the people who were chafing under the burden of Roman taxation,[106] especially with the way that taxes were then administered in Palestine, where tax collectors made their income by imposing a surcharge on the taxes collected. This practice explains the hostility of the people toward tax collectors in evidence throughout the Synoptic Gospels.[107] Everyone from the age of fourteen until the age of sixty-five was obliged to pay the tax. A yes answer from Jesus would surely have turned the crowds against him, the very crowds whose presence impeded the chief priests and their allies from having Jesus put to death.[108]

---

[103] Cf. Mark 11:18.

[104] The *kensos*.

[105] Cf. Mark 10:2.

[106] Cf. 4Q542, 4-6, "Be careful with the inheritance which has been transmitted to you and which your fathers have given you and do not give your inheritance to foreigners or your heritage to half-breeds." Cf. *Pss. Sol.* 17:21-24.

[107] Mark 2:15, 16 [2x]; Matt 5:46; 9:10, 11; 11:19; 18:17; 21:31-32; Luke 3:12; 5:27, 29, 30; 7:29, 34; 15:1; 18:10, 11, 13. Cf. Emerson B. Powery, "Tax Collector," *NIDB* 5:477–78; Warren Carter, "Taxes, Taxation," *NIDB* 5:478–80; Fabian E. Udoh, *To Caesar What Is Caesar's: Tribute, Taxes, and Imperial Administration in Early Roman Palestine (63 B.C.E–70 C.E.)*, BJS 343 (Providence: Brown Judaic Studies, 2005). According to Josephus, some Pharisees were involved in what might be described as a Palestinian taxpayers revolt. Cf. Josephus, *War* 2.8.1; 5.405-6; cf. Acts 5:37; Josephus, *Antiquities* 18.1-10.

[108] Cf. Mark 12:12.

On the other hand, a no from Jesus' lips would have brought the ire of imperial authorities upon him. It would have put Jesus in conflict with the very authorities who had the power to put him to death. The Herodians probably supported the payment of taxes.[109] Ultimately, they were lackeys of Rome. Herod Agrippa II urged his followers to pay their taxes rather than be in a situation of revolt against Rome, Herod's patron.

Knowing that the interlocutors' real interest was not to obtain his opinion about the relevance of Mosaic law to the payment of taxes to an occupying regime but to trap him, Jesus deflected their question by asking for a coin. Mark specifies that the coin that Jesus asked for was a denarius, a Roman coin.[110] Taxes had to be paid in the coin of the realm,[111] so Jesus asked for a denarius.[112] Jesus wanted to look at it, virtually inviting his questioners to look at it as well, even if only in their imaginations.

On the obverse of the small silver coin, there was an image of a laurel-crowned Emperor (Caesar) Tiberius with the inscription *T Caesar Divi Aug F Augustus*. With the inscription's abbreviations filled out, the inscription reads in English translation, "Tiberius Caesar, Son of the divine Augustus, [also] Augustus." The Latin *augustus*, properly an adjective rather than a proper name, was used in reference to one esteemed worthy of religious awe and service. Such a token of the imperial cult was hardly a welcome sign to pious Jews who held that

---

[109] It can be noted that in Galilee, tax collectors worked on behalf of Herod Antipas, not directly for Rome. Although Mark situates the conflict in Jerusalem, as part of his narrative of increased hostility toward Jesus, the presence of the Herodians in the delegation may reflect their involvement in tax collection.

[110] Cf. Mark 12:15c. Matthew reworks the scene to read, "'Show me the coin used for the tax.' And they brought him a denarius" (Matt 22:19).

[111] Since much of the economy was of the trade and barter variety, money changers were able to exchange goods for Roman currency much in the same fashion as the money changers in the temple were able to provide Jewish (Tyranian) shekels in exchange for goods or Roman coinage.

[112] The value of the denarius was equal to a day's wages for a day laborer. It may be that some of the poorer people had to exchange their copper coins of lesser value for the silver coinage required for the payment of taxes. Two coins worth a denarius were denarii minted during the reign of the emperor Tiberius, but only one of them was in common circulation. Most likely, it was this coin that was shown to Jesus.

the one God was the only one to be worshiped. On the reverse side of the coin was a picture of a seated female, probably representing Pax, in honor of the *pax romana*,[113] with the inscription *Pontif Maxim*, that is, "high priest."

Jesus, who had taken the initiative away from the interlocutors by asking to see the coin, continues to take the initiative by asking his questioners a counterquestion. He asked whose image and whose inscription (*epigraphē*) were on the coin. Those who had confronted Jesus could only answer, "The emperor's [*Kaisaros*]." That the coin bore the image of a human being—and a deified one at that—made it abhorrent to Jews whose tradition banned the production of images of human beings[114] and in turn made the payment of taxes all the more odious.

The response of his questioners led Jesus to utter a memorable comment, "Give to the emperor [*Kaisari*] the things that are the emperor's [*ta Kaisaros*], and to God [*tō theō*] the things that are God's [*ta tou theou*]."[115] Lest the reader think that Jesus was suggesting some sort of divided loyalty, as if some things belonged to the emperor and some things to God,[116] he or she must note that Jesus' aphorism has but a single verb, "give," *apodote*, literally, "give back to."[117] The sense of his words is that what comes from the emperor, *in casu*, the coinage of the realm, must be given back to him, and what comes from God must be given back to God. Taxes are to be paid to the imperial authorities, but both the imposition and the payment of taxes take place under the one God, to whom total allegiance is due.

---

[113] The figure representing the *pax romana* might be that of Livia, the emperor's mother.

[114] Cf. Josephus, *Antiquities* 17.151-52.

[115] Mark 12:17. Commentators often note that there is some ambiguity in Jesus' response. Focant, for instance (*Mark*, 486), writes, "There is an intentional ambiguity in Jesus' answer. It must not be understood as a practical directive authorizing or recommending the payment of the tax but as a theological principle that returns to the interlocutors to construct their own answer by confronting Caesar's purposes and those of God for the Jewish people."

[116] By placing God and Caesar together, Jesus' pronouncement implies that the two realities cannot be considered in isolation from one another. Boring, *Mark*, 336, with reference to Robert C. Tannehill, *The Sword of His Mouth* (Philadelphia: Fortress, 1975), 174.

[117] The idea of "returning" or "giving back" is found in the prefix *apo*.

Clever from a merely human point of view, Jesus' response totally amazes those who sought to trap him. While recognizing peoples' responsibilities to civil authorities, even foreign civil authorities, in the matter of taxation, Jesus proclaimed the absolute sovereignty of God. Marcus comments, "The demands of God transcend those of Caesar. But the demands of these two 'rulers' do not always clash, and when they do not, it is possible to remain loyal to both."[118]

The Parable of the Wicked Tenants (Mark 12:1-12)

We can conclude this study of wealth, wages, and riches in the Gospel of Mark with a brief look at the single parable that Mark's gospel presents as being told in Jerusalem. A study of this parable is not exactly *ad rem*, but it is apropos. We should look at it, if only briefly.

The climax of Mark's story is undoubtedly the account of Jesus' passion and death in Jerusalem. In Mark 11:1-11, the evangelist portrays Jesus entering Jerusalem on the back of a donkey to the hosannas of the crowds. Thereafter, Jesus performed two powerful symbolic gestures. In the presence of his disciples he cursed a fig tree; before those gathered in the temple he chased away the money changers and those selling the turtledoves that the poor were sometimes required to offer. His authority to do such a thing was challenged by the chief priests, the scribes, and the elders. There ensued a controversy between them and Jesus about Jesus' authority.

"Then he began to speak to them in parables."[119] Perhaps Mark was influenced by his own words at Mark 4:2 when he wrote this introduction to the parable of the Wicked Tenants,[120] found in all three Synoptic Gospels.[121] The introduction in Mark 12:1 prefixes only this one parable.[122] Rather than being followed by another parable, the introduction is followed by the controversy over paying taxes to Caesar.[123]

---

[118] Marcus, *Mark 8–16*, 826.

[119] Mark 12:1.

[120] Mark 12:1-12.

[121] Cf. Matt 21:33-46; Luke 20:9-19; *G. Thom.* 65.

[122] Matthew and Luke apparently realize the error in Mark's introductory words and so introduce their version of the parable by speaking only of a parable, *parabolēn*, in the singular. Cf. Matt 22:33; Luke 20:9.

[123] Cf. Mark 12:13-17, and above, pp. 84–89.

In its present allegorized form, the parable hearkens back to the Song of the Vineyard in Isaiah 5. In Mark, it is an *ad hominem* rejoinder directed against the priests, scribes, and elders.[124] It is the story of an absentee landlord who owned a vineyard, traditionally a symbol of Israel. In due time, the owner of the vineyard sent a series of agents to collect his share of the produce. Initially, he sent a slave who was beat up on arrival. Then he sent another slave, who was clobbered on the head and insulted. Then a third slave, who was killed. But that was not the end of the owner's efforts. He sent other slaves, who were either beaten up or killed, perhaps both. But the owner had an ace in the hole, his own beloved son[125] whom he also sent to the vineyard. The son's fate was to be killed and thrown out of the vineyard.

This allegorized parable is a figurative overview of the history of salvation. Israel had repeatedly rejected and maltreated the prophets who had been sent to them. Some were even killed. Finally, God, to whom the vineyard (Israel) belonged, sent his only beloved Son, Jesus, who was also killed. There is no need to go into the details of this allegorized story. It serves as a fitting introduction to the passion narrative. Last in the long line of God's messengers to Israel was the beloved Son, Jesus, identified as the beloved Son of God by God himself according to Mark 9:7. Jesus was killed on Golgotha, a hill outside the city.

Just prior to the quotation of Psalm 118:22-23 in Mark 12:10-11 are veiled references to the destruction of Jerusalem and God's giving Israel's ancestral patrimony to others. The scriptural passage suggests that Jesus is the cornerstone of God's reconstruction of the vineyard. Matthew 21:43 develops this idea. Matthew and Luke, in their respective reworkings of their Markan source, project dire consequences for those for whom the cornerstone becomes a stumbling block.[126]

---

[124] Cf. Mark 12:12.

[125] Cf. Mark 12:6; Mark 9:7.

[126] Cf. Matt 21:43 and Luke 20:18. The Matthean verse is, however, absent from important textual witnesses, particularly some belonging to the Western manuscript tradition.

In its present form, the parable of the Wicked Tenants, a figurative rehearsal of the history of Israel, is not directly pertinent to our study of wealth, wages, and the wealthy. It is, nonetheless, apropos to the study for, at bottom, it is a story of greed that results in violence and murder. The tenants want to retain the entire produce and will go to any lengths, even multiple murders, in order to obtain what they want.[127] Read in this fashion, the parable of the Wicked Tenants is clearly the most graphic description of the consequences of greed in the New Testament.[128]

So What?

"Give to the emperor the things that are the emperor's, and to God the things that are God's."

Jesus' interlocutors were none too keen on paying taxes. Feigning piety, they thought that they had an escape. Their religious beliefs would prevent them from using the coin of the realm to pay the taxes that they loathed. But Jesus recognized the hypocrisy and told them to give to Caesar what belongs to Caesar. The payment of taxes is necessary for the common good in God's plan for human interaction in society. The payment of taxes is required by Jesus' command to give to God what belongs to God.

There are, of course, those who flaunt the law by not paying their taxes. A blog site, *TopStars*, reported that Lindsay Lohan didn't pay taxes in 2012. It further reported that Martin Scorsese owes the government $2.85 million for 2007 and that Nicholas Cage owes $6.2 million for 2007. More subtle than these examples of outright refusal to pay taxes are the ruses used, especially by the wealthy, to avoid paying taxes. Jesus' opponents used a religious ruse to avoid their obligation to pay taxes. Twenty-first-century Americans have been clever in finding other ruses to avoid their divine-mandated social obligations. Taxes? Not for me, they say, finding ways to avoid even the long arm of the law as they neglect God and the society in which God's people live.

[127] Cf. Jas 5:5-6.
[128] Cf. 1 Kgs 21:1-29.

One such ruse is the so-called Captive Insurance Shelter. "The IRS has placed this increasingly popular strategy on its 'Dirty Dozen list' of tax scams" was the headline that introduced an article by Paul Sullivan that appeared in the *Englewood Herald Tribune* on Sunday, April 18, 2015. Reprinted from the *New York Times*, the first paragraph of the article reported: "Many people have been writing checks to the Internal Revenue Service. But not a lawyer in Los Angeles, who last year put all of his earnings, $840,000, into a tax shelter and plans to put $1 million in this year. He doesn't have to pay any income tax."

On August 24, 2014, Ethan Brown reported that according to CBS News, managers of hedge funds typically avoid paying an income tax, currently set at 39.6 percent for top-level earners, and pay a more modest 20 percent via the capital gains tax.

Finally, in an article titled, "Lords, Ladies Rule America," the *Philadelphia Inquirer*'s Harold Johnson writes, "America's political peerage includes both blue bloods who inherited fortunes and commoners who earned them. Most contributed to Republican candidates, which makes sense since that party has all but adopted the 'no new taxes' slogan that has become the mantra for many in the highest tax brackets. That includes the energy tycoon Koch brothers."[129]

The popular idea that the wealthy should pay little or no taxes extends, of course, to the corporations that they own. One tax-avoiding scheme is "the inversion," a procedure that allows a US enterprise to "locate" in a foreign company in order to avoid taxes. One example, cited in the *Journal*,[130] echoed the words of *The Day:*

> Last week came the announcement of Pfizer's $160 billion merger with the Irish-based Allergan. This is another corporate big fish Pfizer, swallowing a smaller one.
>
> Technically, the much smaller Allergan is buying Pfizer. The headquarters of the new merged company will be in Dublin, Ireland. Corporate lawyers, to slash Pfizer's corporate tax rate to the 17 percent charge in Ireland, carefully orchestrated the details of the merger. The U.S. corporate tax rate is 35 percent,

[129] *The Providence Journal* (Saturday, October 31, 2015): A13.
[130] *The Providence Journal* (Wednesday, December 2, 2015): A14. *The Day* is published in New London, CT.

but by using various tax breaks, Pfizer has paid an effective tax rate of 25 percent.

Called inversions, about 80 corporations have renounced their corporate U.S. citizenship to escape their country's taxes, costing the nation 433.6 billion over a decade, according to Congress' Joint Committee on Taxation.

Corporations say that the corporate tax rate of 35 percent in the United States is excessive. In truth, few corporations pay that rate. We also note that the U.S. corporate tax rate helps pay for necessary infrastructure, for a system to regulate and protect fair commerce, and for the largest military that the world has ever known allowing for unfettered global trade.

The move would enable Pfizer to slash its tax rate from around 25 percent this year to about 18 percent. Ireland's lower corporate tax rate would have saved Pfizer nearly $1 billion of the $3.1 billion in U.S. taxes it paid in 2014.

Internet pioneer Yahoo is another major American company. "Under pressure from unhappy shareholders and desperate to avoid a huge investment-related tax bill, will break itself apart—just not in the way it had previously planned."

"For most of the past year, Yahoo had planned instead to spin off the Alibaba stake[131] into a separate holding company. That corporate maneuver was designed to sidestep more than $10 billion in taxes Yahoo might otherwise owe. But the IRS jeopardized that plan by refusing to guarantee a tax exemption."[132]

Jesus' words on the payment of taxes mean nothing to that Los Angeles lawyer. Nor do they mean anything to the executives and board members of those eighty companies that have "located" outside the United States in order to avoid the payment of taxes. Is this an indication that we really do live in a post-Christian society where the teaching of Jesus has no influence on the way that we live? Does it mean that the gospel is without meaning for the world in which we live? If so, how can a believer abide the situation?

[131] Yahoo has a $32 billion stake in the Chinese e-commerce giant.
[132] *The Providence Journal* (Tuesday, December 10, 2015): A12.

The Rich Man

"One cannot live the faith and be attached to wealth," said Pope Francis in his Angelus sermon on October 11, 2015. Earlier in the day, the gospel lesson for the Twenty-Eighth Sunday in Ordinary Time was the story of the Rich Man found in Mark 10:17-27. Francis's sermon was a sharp reminder that the Christian life is incompatible with an attachment to wealth. There is a radical conflict between the two value systems.

Chapter 4

Matthew

The Gospel of Matthew is a revised edition of the Gospel of Mark intended for a Greek-reading Jewish-Christian readership. It retells Mark's story of Jesus in a way that also reflects the experiences of the Matthean church.[1] Although it is impossible to delineate the provenance of the text with any real certainty, it is likely that the text was written in Syria, perhaps in Antioch, in the ninth decade of the Common Era. It was written some fourteen or fifteen years after Mark wrote his pioneering story of Jesus, a little more than a half century after Jesus' death and resurrection.

In addition to his Markan source, Matthew had available to him another text written in Greek, a collection of loosely organized sayings of Jesus, the so-called Sayings Source, also used by the evangelist Luke. In exegetical literature this Sayings Source is generally designated as "Q," from the German word *Quelle*, which means "source." In addition to these literary texts, Matthew also had at his disposition his own special material, for which the letter "M" serves as the common designation. For the most part, this material came to the evangelist via oral tradition.[2] In addition, the discerning reader can also see the work of the evangelist's redactional hand in the text.

---

[1] It is often observed that among the evangelists, Matthew is the only author who actually uses the word "church," *ekklēsia*, in his Greek text. Cf. Matt 16:18; 18:19 [2x].

[2] Ulrich Luz, for example, attributes only the primary antitheses of the Sermon on the Mount and the sayings on almsgiving, prayer, and fasting (Matt 5:21-24,

Gold

Since the development of the social-scientific approach to New Testament texts a few decades ago, commentators have observed that Matthew's church was not completely impoverished.[3] As an indication of this, some have noted that Matthew is the only one of the four gospels to use the word "gold" (*chrysos*). The word "gold" appears five times in his gospel and not at all in the other gospels.

The evangelist's first reference to "gold" is found at the beginning of his story about Jesus, in the tale of the wise men who "offered him [Jesus] gifts of gold, frankincense, and myrrh."[4] Toward the end of the gospel, portraying how Jesus denounced the scribes and the Pharisees in a series of seven woes when he was in Jerusalem, Matthew cites a saying that mentions the gold in the temple three times: "Woe to you, blind guides, who say, 'Whoever swears by the sanctuary is bound by nothing, but whoever swears by the gold of the sanctuary is bound by the oath.' You blind fools! For which is greater, the gold or the sanctuary that has made the gold sacred?"[5] The woe is directed against casuistry in the matter of oaths,[6] but it is clearly a statement about misplaced priorities and a critique of those who attribute more value to gold than to the dwelling place of God. Both of these passages, Matthew 2:11 and 23:16-17, come from Matthew's special material and are not found in the other Synoptic Gospels.

The sixth mention of "gold" is found in a passage that comes from Matthew's Markan source with a parallel in the Gospel of Luke, but Matthew has added "gold" to the words that he found in his source. The passage is important since it is an indication of Matthew's interest in gold and provides his readers with an insight into how he views the economic status of Jesus' disciples. In the mission discourse,[7] the

---

27-28, 33-37; 6:2-6, 16-18) to a written text within Matthew's special material. Cf. Ulrich Luz, *Matthew 1–7*, Hermeneia (Minneapolis: Fortress, 2007), 21.

[3] Among the Synoptics, Matthew alone describes Joseph of Arimathea as both rich and a disciple. Cf. Matt 27:57. The evangelist's Markan source, followed by Luke, describes Joseph as a member of the Sanhedrin. Cf. Mark 15:43; Luke 23:50.

[4] Matt 2:11.

[5] Matt 23:16-17.

[6] Cf. Matt 5:33-37.

[7] For a recent overview of the state of research on the mission discourse, see Christophe Paya, "Le discours d'envoie en mission de Matthieu 10. État de la recherche et perspectives," *RHPR* 90 (2010): 479–99.

Matthean Jesus tells the Twelve, "Take no gold, or silver, or copper in your belts."[8] Matthew's Markan source says simply that Jesus ordered them to take "no money in their belts."[9] Using direct address, as does Matthew, Luke writes, "Take nothing for your journey, no staff, nor bag, nor bread, nor money."[10] The appearance of "gold" in Matthew's version of the missionary charge is a sign that the evangelist considers some of Jesus' disciples to have been sufficiently rich to have gold available for them to use.

Another indication of Matthew's view of the financial situation of Jesus' disciples is his addendum to the parable of the Rich Young Man. The Matthean Jesus says, "And anyone who has left houses [*oikias*], or brothers or sisters . . . for my name's sake, will receive a hundredfold, and will inherit eternal life."[11] The words seem to suggest that some disciples were landlords. The Markan source presents Jesus as saying, "There is no one who has left house [*oikian*, in the singular] or brothers or sisters."[12] The singular also appears in Luke's version of the logion.[13]

Matthew's story about Jesus, nevertheless, contains a strong criticism of wealth. There are at least a half-dozen passages in this gospel that contain a strong caution about possessions. The criticism suggests, as Ulrich Luz notes, "that there may also have been rich persons among the members of the Matthean church."[14] Interestingly, however, in retelling the story of the feeding of the five thousand, Matthew has chosen not to include the disciples' response to Jesus, who told them to give the crowd something to eat. Their retort, "Are we to go and buy two hundred denarii of bread, and give

---

[8] Matt 10:29.

[9] Cf. Mark 6:8.

[10] Luke 9:3. The comparable command in the Lucan missionary charge to the seventy does not specifically mention money. It enjoins those who were sent out from taking a purse or bag but makes no mention of their contents. Cf. Luke 10:4.

[11] Matt 19:29.

[12] Mark 10:29.

[13] Cf. Luke 18:29.

[14] Luz, *Matthew 1–7*, 16. The referenced passages are Matt 6:19-34; 10:9; 13:22; 16:24-26; 19:16-30; and 20:16. Cf. Stefan Alkier, "'Frucht bringen' oder 'Gewinnmaximierung'? Überlegungen zur Gestaltung des Lebens und des Wirtschaftens im Anschluss an des Mattäusevangelium," *ZNT* 16 (2013): 11–20.

them something to eat,"[15] would seem to suggest, if it is not taken as an ironical rejoinder, that among themselves the traveling band had some considerable finances at their disposition.

The Parables of Matthew's Special Material

One of the distinctive features of Matthew's story about Jesus is the way in which he organized many, though not all, of Jesus' teachings into five great discourses or sermons: the Sermon on the Mount in 5:1–7:29, the Mission Discourse in 19:1-42, the Sermon in Parables in 13:1-53, the Ecclesiastical Discourse of 18:1-35, and the Sermon on the Last Things in 24:3–25:46. The evangelist concludes each of the discourses by writing, "When Jesus finished this speech. . . ."[16]

The Sermon in Parables contains seven short stories, coming from various sources including Matthew's special material. Jesus' parables are generally recognized as being one of the most insightful and accurate literary sources of information about day-to-day life in first-century Palestine. History, it is often said, is written by the victor. This old saw is generally true, but the kernel of truth it contains extends beyond the circumstances of war. History generally tends to reflect the positions of those who are dominant; historical literature is generally composed to focus on the interests of the powerful. It tends not to reflect life from below.[17] Those stories told by Jesus known as parables are an exception to the general rule. They reflect the experience of the people to whom they were told and serve as a unique source of history from below for first-century Palestine.

Twin Parables: The Treasure and the Pearl (Matt 13:44-46)

The shortest of the seven parables collated in the Sermon in Parables, the parable of the Hidden Treasure in 13:44 and the parable of the Fine Pearl in 13:45-46, were most probably paired in the oral

---

[15] Mark 6:37. Matthew may have omitted their comeback in the name of brevity. He has a tendency to shorten his use of material found in Mark. The verse is also absent from the Lucan account of the feeding.

[16] Cf. Matt 8:1; 11:1; 13:53; 19:1; 26:1.

[17] Much of the revisionist history of recent decades is an attempt to compensate for that deficiency.

tradition. In Matthew, the two parables are addressed to the disciples[18] rather than to the crowds who had come out to hear Jesus. Each of them speaks about things that human beings consider to be valuable. Belonging to Matthew's special material, they particularly speak to a situation in Matthew's community.

In the first of the twinned parables, the parable of the Hidden Treasure, Jesus tells the story of a man who happens to find a treasure in a field. In a society without the security of modern-day commercial banks with their safe-deposit vaults and with uncertain political conditions, it was common for people to bury their treasure as a way to keep it safe from thieves and marauders.[19] It was not often, but it sometimes happened that someone else found the buried valuables before their owner retrieved them.[20] Stories about lucky finders abounded in antiquity.[21] Aphorisms about hidden treasure are also found in the biblical wisdom tradition.[22]

In Jesus' story an anonymous "someone" (*anthrōpos*) found a treasure buried in a field. He was elated by his find. He did not want to steal this trove, but he did want it for himself. So, rather than publicly announcing his discovery in order to learn the identity of its rightful owner as rabbinic tradition would later require,[23] the lucky finder reburied the treasure. He then sold all his possessions in order to purchase the field. Rabbis would debate whether the owner of a field was entitled to valuables buried in it;[24] Jesus' parable presumes that

---

[18] Cf. Matt 13:10, 51.

[19] Cf. Matt 25:18, 25. The Lucan parallel to the story omits the reference to burying the talent. The practice of burying treasures lest they be stolen or confiscated has continued into modern times. Those who discovered the Dead Sea Scrolls buried many of them, to our loss. Having been preserved from the elements for almost two millennia, the buried fragments were partially destroyed by the soil.

[20] Cf. Josephus, *War* 7.114-15; *Songs Rab.* 4.12.1.

[21] Cf. John D. Crossan, "Hidden Treasure Parables in Later Antiquity," SBLSP (1976): 359–79.

[22] Cf. Prov 2:4; Sir 20:30.

[23] The Mishnah states that the finding of anything valuable, from a small pile of three coins on up, should be publicly announced. Cf. *m. B. Mes.* 2.2.

[24] Cf. *m. B. Bat.* 4.8; *y. B. Mes.* 2, 5, 8c. Cf. Samuel T. Lachs, *A Rabbinic Commentary on the New Testament: The Gospels of Matthew, Mark, and Luke* (Hoboken, NJ: KTAV, 1987), 229.

he was so entitled. As is the case with the other parables of Jesus,[25] the story is concerned not with legal niceties but with the man's action. He did what he had to do in order to achieve his objective.

The second parable, the parable of the Fine Pearl, presumes a slightly different scenario but makes the same point. In this story, a merchant (*anthrōpos, emporos*)[26] is actively looking for valuable pearls. Stories about pearls were a classic topos in Jewish antiquity.[27] Pearls, generally imported from India, were considered to be a luxury item. Pliny the Elder states that pearls were the "top most ranked of all things of price."[28] Because a pearl was so valuable, the pearl often served as a metaphor in Jewish religious literature, where it symbolized Israel or the Torah.[29]

In Jesus' story, the merchant is a buyer and seller of good-quality pearls (*kalous margaritas*), a man of some means.[30] He happens upon one[31] particularly valuable pearl (*hina polutimon margaritēn*) and cashes out all that he owns, not just his stock of pearls[32] but everything that he has, in order to acquire the "pearl of great price." In a sense, it is a possession without further use. The man has no other possessions; only if he sells his precious pearl will he be able to continue with his merchandizing.

Each of the paired stories makes the same point. When a person has an opportunity to acquire a single valuable asset, that person will go to any length in order to acquire it. In a sense, this is commonplace wisdom, reflecting ordinary human experience, but it speaks to

---

[25] Cf. Luke 16:1-8; 18:1-8.

[26] A.-J. Levine makes the point that at the time, merchants were generally considered to be engaged in shady dealings. Cf. Amy-Jill Levine, *Short Stories by Jesus: The Enigmatic Parables of a Controversial Rabbi* (New York: Harper Collins, 2014), 130–34.

[27] *Midr. The.* 28.6; *b. Shabb.* 119a2.

[28] *Nat.* 9, 106.

[29] Cf. Ulrich Luz, *Matthew 8–20*, Hermeneia (Minneapolis: Fortress, 2001), 278.

[30] Cf. Richard T. France, *The Gospel of Matthew*, NIBCNT (Grand Rapids: Eerdmans, 2007), 541.

[31] Luz, *Matthew 8–20*, notes that the parable's "one" (*hina*) is not superfluous. It is necessary because of the referent, the kingdom of heaven.

[32] In the Gnostic parallel to this story found in *G. Thom.* 76, the man is more prudent. He sells only his stock of pearls, not all that he owns.

Matthew's community. Single-minded people will do what they have to do, even selling all that they have in order to acquire something valuable that they really want. The experience is as common today as it was in Matthew's day. In Jesus' story, the valuable reality is the kingdom of heaven, God's reign. The story exploits the reality of human desire to possess valuable things, no matter the cost.

The Parable of the Unforgiving Slave (Matt 18:23-35)

Not all of the parables found in the first gospel have been collected together in the Sermon in Parables. Some of them are found elsewhere in Matthew's gospel. Three of these are of interest to this study and come from the evangelist's special material. One is the parable of the Unforgiving Servant.[33] The parable begins, "The kingdom of heaven may be compared to . . . ," the familiar *incipit* of the parables found in the Sermon in Parables.[34]

Attention is immediately drawn to a king. As the story is told, the king, for reasons unknown—parables are told with relatively few details, just enough to make the point that the storyteller wants to highlight—wanted to be paid up. Most probably Jesus' hearers would have imagined a Gentile king as the story was being told.

A slave who owed the king a huge amount of money, 10,000 talents, was brought to him. The talent (*talantos*) was a unit of weight and measurement of gold or silver and the largest coin of the time. Some scholars estimate the value of a talent to be approximately equal to what a day laborer would earn over the course of twenty years. By today's standards, the indebted slave of the story owed a multimillion-dollar debt.[35] He was no ordinary slave but rather a powerful and rich servant of the king. The slave was not able to pay off his vast debt. The king decided that the slave, his immediate

---

[33] Matt 18:23-25.

[34] Cf. Matt 13:24, 31, 33, 44, 45, 47.

[35] "Today we could express it [the debt] only in the millions, or billions," writes Luz (*Matthew 8–20*, 472–73). A contemporary reading of the parable, applying it to recent economic circumstances, is provided by R. Q. Ford in "Jesus' Parable of the Unforgiving Slave and the Wall Street Crisis of 2008," FR 24 (2011): 15–20, 22.

family,[36] and his possessions were to be sold so that he might recoup some portion of what was owed to him. Falling to his knees, the indebted slave begged for some time, promising that he would pay back all that he owed. How he would do so is another question.

At this point in the story, the tale takes a surprising turn. The wealthy king forgave the indebted man's tremendous debt. Equally surprising is what happens immediately afterward. The slave whose tremendous debt had been forgiven encountered a fellow slave who owed him some money, a hundred denarii, a paltry sum in comparison with the size of the forgiven debt. A denarius was the standard for a day laborer's wage;[37] a hundred denarii was about a third of a year's salary of the ordinary worker. The amount was a large sum, but the debt could reasonably be paid off over time. As had the person to whom he owed this money, this slave begged for time to pay off the debt. But the first slave would have none of this; he was adamant. He had the indebted slave thrown into debtor's prison.[38]

The third scene of the parable says that other slaves saw what had happened and were appalled. They reported the previously indebted slave to the king, who then ordered that slave to be brought back to him. No mention is made of the king's anger, but those who heard the story probably interjected such anger into their hearing of the tale. The king castigated the unforgiving slave for not responding in kind to the tremendous act of generosity that he had received. He handed the slave over to torturers, prepared to torture the unfortunate slave[39] until the last penny of his debt (*pan to opheilomenon*) had been paid. Given the size of his previously forgiven and now

[36] The practice of selling debtors was not unknown in biblical times. Cf. 2 Kgs 4:1; Isa 50:1; Amos 2:6; 8:6; Neh 5:2, 5. Rabbinic lore forbade a man from selling his wife. Cf. *m. Sota* 3.8; *t. Sota* 2.9.

[37] Cf. Tob 5:15.

[38] Matt 18:30 suggests the first slave might even have thrown him into prison himself. When a person was in debtor's prison, the family was forced to pay up. Cf. Josephus, *War* 2.273. Later rabbinic tradition (*Mek. Exod.* 22:2; *b. Qidd.* 18a) would suggest that selling the indebted slave was out of the question since the price of a slave was less than the amount owed.

[39] Torture became common in Palestine during the reign of Herod. Cf. Josephus, *War* 1.548.

restored debt, it was virtually impossible for the slave's punishment ever to come to an end.

The subplot of this story is that of the slave's greed. He had been able to live off the generosity of the king as he amassed debts beyond his ability to pay. The generous king forgave his debt, making him a debt-free independent man, but he did not learn from his experience. In his desire for wealth, he was determined that he was going to get what someone else owed him, no matter the sum.

Within Matthew's gospel, the story of the unforgiving slave is about forgiveness. The story appears in the gospel immediately after Peter's query about how often a member of the community should forgive another member of the community.[40] Matthew's placement of the parable indicates how the evangelist wants his hearers to read the story. In Matthew, and more widely in Jewish literature, the king symbolizes God. Jesus' story is about divine forgiveness and how the experience of being forgiven by God should lead those who have been forgiven to forgive one another. Members of the church are expected to emulate God's forgiveness by forgiving others. As such, the parable virtually serves as a commentary on the fifth petition of the Lord's Prayer, "Forgive us our debts as we also have forgiven our debtors."[41]

The language of debt and forgiveness is common to both the parable and the fifth petition of the prayer. The word "debt," the root *opheil-*, appears in Matthew 6:12 and 18:24, 28 [2x], 30, 34;[42] the word "forgive," the verb *aphiēmi*, in Matthew 6:12 and 18:27, 32, 35. The petition, derived from Matthew's Sayings Source (Q), is also found in the much shorter Lucan version of the Lord's Prayer. Luke 11:4a reads, "And forgive us our sins, for we ourselves forgive everyone indebted to us." The reading "sins" in Luke 11:4a indicates that the first part of the petition was on its way to being understood theologically, in which "debt" is a metaphor for "offense" or "sin," but is such a theological reading of the petition the original one?

---

[40] Matt 18:21-23.

[41] Matt 6:12. Luz notes that the subordinate clause, whose verb is in the aorist, is probably a true condition and cites Matt 5:23-24; 16:14-15; and 7:1 as similar conditions. Cf. Luz, *Matthew 1–7*, 322.

[42] The noun *opheleitēs* appears in Matt 6:12; 18:24; the verb *opheilō* in Matt 18:28 [2x], 30, 34.

Douglas Oakman suggests that the Q tradent of the petition read, "And forgive us our money debts as we forgive those who owe us money."[43] The situation in which Jesus would have spoken these words was an agrarian context in which indebtedness was a major social problem. Debt was pushing the peasantry either off the land entirely or into an oppressive client-patron relationship with increasing insecurity then to be experienced by the day laborer and the tenant farmer.

The petition, addressed to God, had a vertical dimension as well as a horizontal dimension. The horizontal dimension of the petition is found in the comparative clause "as we forgive those who owe us money." As for the vertical dimension, "there were," Oakman suggests, "perhaps two concrete situations in which God might be petitioned to achieve debt forgiveness for the advantage of the petitioner: the temple debt-system"[44] or a court-system, perhaps one in which the *prozbul* held sway. The *prozbul* was a legal fiction, going back to Hillel, in which a person's debts were transferred to the public domain. Private debts were cancelled at the end of the sabbatical year, but public debts were not.[45]

It may be that the *prozbul* was at issue in the conditional clause, the horizontal dimension of the petition. Those who made use of the *prozbul* practice to avoid the remission of debt would not have been able to pray the Lord's Prayer in good conscience.[46] The practice might well have served as a subterfuge to avoid the due obligations of justice, as was the practice of Corban.[47]

---

[43] See Douglas E. Oakman, *Jesus, Debt, and the Lord's Prayer: First-Century Debt and Jesus' Intentions* (Eugene, OR: Cascade, 2014), 51. The Greek would have read *kai aphes hēmin ta opheilēmata hēmōn, kai gar autoi aphēkamen toi opheilonti hēmin.* "Money" as a direct object of the verb *opheilō* is not found in the Greek text; it is, however, the usual connotation of the verb.

[44] Cf. Oakman, *Jesus, Debt, and the Lord's Prayer*, 75.

[45] Cf. *m. Šeb.* 10.2; *b. Giṭ.* 37b. The institution of the *prozbul* enabled a lender to recoup his money. It helped the poor insofar as it freed up money for loans. Lenders had been reluctant to lend to the poor because they would lose any claim to their money at the end of the sabbatical year.

[46] Cf. Lyndon Drake, "Did Jesus Oppose the *prosbul* in the Forgiveness Petition of the Lord's Prayer?," *NovT* 56 (2014): 233–44.

[47] Cf. Matt 15:3-9.

At bottom, the fifth petition of the Lord's Prayer is one for the redress of fiscal insecurity on the condition that the one who prays is willing to forgive the debts of those who are indebted to him or her. This is clearly expressed in the NRSV's literal translation of the petition, "And forgive us our debts, as we also have forgiven our debtors."[48] The initial "and" (*kai*) links the fifth petition to the bread petition, which also speaks about ordinary human need, the need to have something to eat every day. Addressing an economic situation, as it once did and still does, the meaning of the fifth petition is unfolded in the parable of the Unforgiving Slave.

Matthew appends a commentary[49] to the Lord's Prayer, a revision of Mark 11:25-26. The commentary, "For if you forgive others their trespasses, your heavenly Father will also forgive you; but if you do not forgive others; neither will your Father forgive your trespasses,"[50] specifically applies to the fifth petition of the prayer and indicates that within the evangelist's community, the fifth petition was understood metaphorically as a prayer for forgiveness from God on the fulfillment of the pledge that we who pray for forgiveness forgive those who have offended us.[51]

The Parable of the Laborers in the Vineyard (Matt 20:1-16)

The parable of the Laborers in the Vineyard is another short story that comes from Matthew's special material and is best understood within the economic context of first-century Palestine. All too often the story is interpreted on the basis of verse 16, "So the last will be first, and the first will be last." Then the search is on to determine who "the

---

[48] The Roman Catholic NAB renders the petition in similar fashion: "And forgive us our debts, as we forgive our debtors."

[49] The brace of verses, Matt 6:14-15, interrupts the flow of the three-part unit found in Matt 6:1-18.

[50] Matt 6:14-15.

[51] In his study on the fifth petition of the Lord's Prayer, "Understanding the Concept of Sin as Debt in the Lord's Prayer," *Stulos Theological Journal* 16 (2008): 85–93, M. Handayani correctly observes that debt is a metaphor for sin but suggests that in order to obtain forgiveness from God, one must forgive one's debtors. M. J. Nel takes a contrary position in "The Forgiveness of Debt in Matthew 6:12, 14-15," *Neot* 47 (2013): 87–106.

last" are. Are they sinful Jews, in contrast to law-abiding Jews who
have shouldered the onus of the law—who have borne the burden of
the day, as it were? Or are "the last" the Gentiles who did not bear the
yoke of the law and received salvation on the cheap, as it were? The
problem with such interpretations is that the parable is not about the
first and the last; the story is about the equal reward of those who have
worked in the vineyard for different lengths of time. Or is it?

Traditionally, this short story has been and continues to be called
"The Parable of the Laborers in the Vineyard," but is this the best
name for it? Robert Fortna once suggested "The Humane Capitalist"
as an appropriate title for the story.[52] This title would intrigue many
modern readers of the story and allow them to see that the story is
applicable to contemporary circumstances. José David Rodriguez calls
the story "The Parable of the Affirmative Action Employer."[53] Once
again, this suggestion transports us into the contemporary scene,
but does it really capture the point of the parable? In her insightful
study of the story,[54] A.-J. Levine offers a number of other alternatives:
"The Conscientious Boss," "The Last Hired Are the First Paid," "How
to Prevent the Peasants from Unionizing," "Debating a Fair Wage,"
or even "Lessons for Both Management and Employees."[55] These
suggestions readily allow for a contemporary application, all the
while keeping the focus on the vineyard's owner whose conduct is
certainly the most intriguing feature of the parable.

Stories similar to the parable that appears in Matthew 20 are attributed to rabbis of later times, but they attest to an economic system
in which workers are paid according to what their labor produces.
For example, the *Yerusalemi*, the Jerusalem Talmud, preserves the
story of Rabbi Zeira's eulogy for Rabbi Bun bar Hiyya in which he
illustrates the deceased's life by means of a familiar tale:

---

[52] Cf. Robert Fortna, "Exegesis and Theology," *Journal of Theology for Southern Africa* 72 (1960): 66–72, at 72.

[53] Cf. José David Rodriguez, "The Parable of the Affirmative Action Employer," *CTM* 15 (1988): 418–24.

[54] Levine, *Short Stories*, 197–219; Cf. Erin K. Vearncombe, "Redistribution and Reciprocity: A Socio-Economic Interpretation of the Parable of the Labourers in the Vineyard (Matthew 20:1-15)," *JournStudHistJesus* 8 (2010): 199–236.

[55] Levine, *Short Stories*, 199.

A king hired many workers. One worker was excellent in his work. What did the king do? He took him and walked him back and forth [through the rows of crops and did not let him finish his day's work]. Toward evening, when all the workers came to be paid, he gave him a full day's wages along with [the rest of] them. The workers complained and said, "We toiled all day, and this one toiled only two hours, and he gave him a full day's wages!" The king said to them, "This one worked [and accomplished] more in two hours than you did in a whole day."[56]

Rabbi Zeira told the story to say that although Rabbi Bun's lifelong study of the Torah covered a shorter period of time than did that of other scholars, he was able to accomplish as much as they in the time that he did study. The economic principle of a day's wages for a full day's work is preserved in this telling of the story.

Things are different in Jesus' telling of what might be presumed to have been a familiar tale for his audience. The details would have startled his hearers. As Jesus tells the story, it is about a householder (*oikodespotēs*[57]) who owned a vineyard. Later in the story, this character is called the "lord of the vineyard."[58] Early in the morning he went out to the marketplace to hire workers, day laborers. The reader is left to assume that the householder hired sufficient workers for the task at hand. Later in the day, not once but four times—at 9 a.m., noon, 3 p.m., and 5 p.m.—he returned to the market where he found other people who had not found employment. They were jobless,[59] not loafers. Their failure to obtain work was what made them "idle," as those hired at 5 p.m. explained. They were without work "because no one has hired us."[60]

---

[56] *Y. Ber.* 2.7. Cf. *Eccl. Rab.* 5.1; *Tah.* 110; Catherine Hezser, *Lohnmetaphorik und Arbeitswelt in Mt 20, 1-16*, NTOA 15 (Göttingen: Vandenhoeck & Ruprecht, 1990), 301–10.

[57] Cf. Matt 20:1, 11.

[58] Cf. Matt 20:8. The NRSV translates the Greek *ho kyrios tou ampelōnos* as "the owner of the vineyard."

[59] The Greek *argos*, with the alpha privative, which appears in verses 3 and 6, literally means "without work."

[60] Matt 20:7.

The householder struck an agreement[61] with the workers who were hired first that they should be paid a denarius, "the usual daily wage" according to the NRSV. The small silver coin, which was, in fact, the usual daily wage, appears in the story about paying taxes to the emperor[62] and the parable of the Unforgiving Slave.[63] It was enough to purchase about three days' worth of bread, ten to twelve small loaves.[64] It was hardly a great wage. It was basically a subsistence wage, but it was par for the day laborer at the time. No mention is made of wage negotiations between the householder and the later hires, but he is said to have promised a sum that was just (*dikaion*)[65] to those who were hired at nine, noon, and three.[66]

At the end of the workday, when evening came, the householder instructed his manager (*epitropos*)[67] to call the workers and give them their pay.[68] He was to begin payment by paying the last to be hired.[69] These last, who had agreed to work without having been told what they would earn—one can only surmise that they were desperate for work, ready to work for whatever they might earn—received the standard day's wage, the silver denarius. In turn, all the other workers

[61] Cf. Matt 20:2, 13.

[62] Cf. Mark 12:15; Luke 20:14.

[63] Cf. Matt 18:28.

[64] Cf. Luz, *Matthew 8–20*, 530.

[65] Cf. Matt 18:4. A similar amount is implied in the evangelist's observation that the householder did "the same" (*hōsautōs*) for the workers hired at noon and at three (Matt 18:5).

[66] The story makes no reference to the amount that was to be paid to the last hires.

[67] In Luke 8:3, this is the term used to describe the function of Chuza, the husband of Joanna. Matt 20:3 and Luke 8:3 are the only two uses of the word in the four gospels (cf. Gal 4:2). Pier Angelo Perotti notes that a feature of the story is that the manager rather than the householder distributes the day's earnings. Cf. Perotti, "La parabola degli operai della vigna (Mt 19,30–20,16)," BibOr 53 (2011): 19–42.

[68] Cf. Lev 19:13b; Deut 24:15.

[69] Cf. Matt 20:8. The sequence of paying the workers is undoubtedly the reason why the evangelist appended verse 16, "So the last will be first and the first last," to the story. The addition is an editorial feature that serves to accentuate the grumbling of the early hires. It is a product of Matthean redaction (cf. Matt 19:30), but it remains foreign to the point of the story, despite the fact that some have made of it the exegetical key to the interpretation of the parable. The point of the story is equal payment, not the order of payment.

received the same pay, the denarius. For the workers hired at 3 p.m., noon, and 9 a.m., the denarius was what the householder considered to be a just wage. For the workers hired early in the morning, it was the agreed-upon wage.

Then the grumbling began.[70] The first hires expected some kind of a bonus, a sum of money beyond what they had contracted for. Parables typically feature one-to-one dialogue rather than speeches to a group, so the householder spoke to one of them, perhaps their spokesperson[71] or ringleader, although such a role is not indicated in the story. The householder addressed him as "friend"—not *phile*, which would suggest that the householder had some positive affection or love for the worker, but *etaire*, which was a common way of addressing people, something like "my good friend," and was often a form of address used in speaking to comrades and/or subordinates. Matthew alone, among New Testament authors, uses the word *etairos*, some four times all told.[72]

Speaking to the worker, the householder defended himself on two grounds. First of all, he said that he had lived up to the agreement that had been made—and that he did. He paid the usual daily wage to the first group of workers, as he had agreed to do. Second, he was generous in paying those who were hired later the denarius, the amount that they might have expected to receive for a full day's work.

This story must first be read in its Palestinian context within which it was first told. There is a measure of realism in all of Jesus' parables as there is in this parable of the Workers in the Vineyard. Josephus says that when work on the temple had been completed and the more than eighteen thousand laborers were in need, each of them received his pay, even if he had worked only a single hour.[73] Later rabbinic sources indicated that it was a work of piety to provide wages even to those who were not expecting them.[74] In Jesus' story, the householder

---

[70] Grumbling seems to have been a feature of the tale as it was usually told in rabbinic circles. Thus, Rabbi Zeira's eulogistic version of the story speaks about workers' complaints.

[71] Luz, *Matthew 8–20*, 532.

[72] Cf. Matt 11:16; 22:12; 26:50.

[73] Cf. *Ant.* 20.220.

[74] Cf. Craig Keener, *A Commentary on the Gospel of Matthew*, rev. ed. (Grand Rapids: Eerdmans, 2009), 483. Keener also has an IVP commentary on Matthew.

actively seeks to provide employment for jobless workers and to furnish them with a subsistence wage. In this way he demonstrates his generosity, his justice, his desire that people have work and that they receive sufficient pay to live on. In the insightful words of Levine apropos this story, "Those who have should seek out those who need. If the householder can afford it, he should continue to put others on the payroll, pay them a living wage (even if they cannot put in a full day's work), and so allow them to feed their families while keeping their dignity intact. The point is practical, it is edgy"[75]—and it is a great challenge to the church!

The kingdom of heaven[76] may be compared to this scenario developed in the story because the kingdom is not only a matter of the hereafter but also a matter of the here and now. When people show concern for their fellow human beings, alleviating a situation of want, they are responding to the will of God. Through them the reign of God is breaking into human history. What the householder is doing is an act of justice, as the evangelist who tells the story sees it.

Not to be overlooked is the householder's response to the complaints of the day laborers.[77] The punchline of his response appears in verse 15b, "Are you envious because I am generous?" These words point to the generosity and good nature of the owner of the vineyard. He is generous toward his employees. It is, however, a cutting remark that points to the small-mindedness of those workers who were fortunate enough to have been hired for the whole day. Instead of being satisfied with having found work and having been paid what was considered to be a living wage, they complained about others who didn't have similar opportunities and yet were able to obtain work that enabled them to similarly enjoy a living wage, one that would enable them to provide the necessities of life for their families.

---

[75] Cf. Levine, *Short Stories*, 218.

[76] "Kingdom of heaven" does not refer merely to an otherwordly reality. The expression is the evangelist's way of speaking about the kingdom of God. Attentive to the sensitivities of his Jewish-Christian readership, he avoids the usage found in Mark and Luke who speak of the "kingdom of God." Both expressions equally speak of the reign of God, God's rule.

[77] Cf. Matt 20:13-15.

Matthew's editing of the story is readily seen. Its vocabulary is characteristically Matthean, beginning with the introductory lemma, "the kingdom of heaven is like," including such typically Matthean, if not always exclusively Matthean, expressions as householder,[78] vineyard,[79] just,[80] owner of the vineyard,[81] and friend,[82] and concluding with "the last will be first and the first will be last."[83] Obviously, the parable can be read through a theological lens. In Jewish literature, the vineyard is a stock image of Israel.[84] The householder is a ready metaphor for God. Read through this theological lens, the parable warns people not to be resentful of God's generosity to others.[85]

Interestingly, Matthew's version of the parable does not explicitly feature God as the protagonist, as do the later rabbinic renderings of the story. Could it be that he wanted his readers to realize that this example of just behavior was one that they should follow? It matters little. Even if read theologically as an example of how God deals with human beings, some having a short period of time in which to act and work while others have a much longer period of time at their disposal, God's generosity is an example that the people of God are called to follow. The point is well made in the parable of the Unforgiving Servant[86] and is encapsulated in the challenging words of the Sermon on the Mount, "Be perfect, therefore, as your heavenly Father is perfect."[87]

In all there are four parables in Matthew's special material that speak about wealth, wages, and the wealthy. All four of these short

---

[78] *Okodespotēs* in Matt 20:1, 11; cf. Matt 10:25; 13:27, 52; 20:1, 11; 21:33; 24:43. The word occurs only once in Mark and four times in Luke.

[79] *Ampelōn* in Matt 20:1, 2, 4, 7, 8; cf. Matt 21:28, 33, 39, 40, 41. The word occurs five times in Mark and seven times in Luke.

[80] *Dikaios* in Matt 20:4; cf. Matt 1:19; 5:45; 9:13; 10:41; 13:17, 43, 49; 23:28, 29, 35; 25:37, 46; 27:4, 19, 24.

[81] *Kyrios tou ampelōnos* in Matt 20:8. Cf. Matt 21:40; Mark 13:9; Luke 13:1; 15:1.

[82] *Etairos* in Matt 20:13; cf. Matt 11:16; 22:12; 26:50.

[83] Matt 19:30; 20:6. Cf. Mark 10:31; Luke 13:30.

[84] See, for example, the Song of the Vineyard in Isa 5:1-10, a parable reflected in the parable of the Wicked Tenants (Matt 21:33-46; Mark 12:1-12; Luke 20:9-19).

[85] Cf. Nathan Eubank, "What Does Matthew Say about Divine Recompense? On the Misuse of the Parable of the Workers in the Vineyard (20.1-16)," *JSNT* 35 (2013): 242–62. See also 1 Cor 12:11.

[86] Cf. Matt 18:23-35, v. 33.

[87] Matt 5:48. Cf. Lev 19:2.

stories provide the Matthean Jesus with an opportunity to teach about the kingdom of heaven.[88] Two of them speak of the efforts that people will make and the lengths to which they will go in order to acquire something of substantial monetary value, wealth. Jesus uses these examples from ordinary human experience to teach his disciples that they should engage in a similar resolute pursuit in order that God's will be done on earth as it is in heaven.[89]

The parables of the Treasure and of the Pearl speak about the acquisition of wealth. The parables of the Unforgiving Slave and of the Workers in the Vineyard speak about the disposition of wealth. In these stories the focus of the evangelist's Jesus is on the responsibilities of the rich.[90] The parable of the Unforgiving Slave speaks about the forgiveness of debt, whether that should be a large amount or a more manageable sum. The parable of the Workers in the Vineyard speaks about an employer's responsibility to provide people with an opportunity to work and with a wage sufficient for them to live on. From these stories about the responsibilities of the well-to-do can be drawn theological lessons about God's forgiveness and the opportunities that he provides to each of us.

The Sermon on the Mount (Matt 5–7)

In addition to his Markan source and his own proper material,[91] the evangelist had a third source available to him: Q, the Sayings Source. More than two hundred verses from this source have been incorporated into the first gospel as well as into the Gospel of Luke.[92] Scholars generally consider that Luke is more faithful to the material

---

[88] Cf. Matt 13:44, 45; 18:23; 20:1.

[89] Cf. Matt 6:10.

[90] Cf. Levine, *Short Stories*, 218.

[91] German scholars call this body of material the Matthean *Sondergut*.

[92] The actual number would be closer to 235 verses, but it is difficult to count them exactly. Scholars differ among themselves as to whether one or another particular verse comes from Q. Most scholars consider that Q was utilized by Matthew and Luke but not by Mark. Other scholars hold that Q was also available to Mark. See, for example, Jan Lambrecht, "Three More Notes in Response to John P. Meier: Mark 1, 7-8; 3, 27 and 10, 1-10," *ETL* 89 (2013): 397–409; *Understanding What One Reads III. Essays on the Gospels and Paul (2011–2014)*, Annua Nuntia Lovaniensia 71 (Leuven: Peeters, 2015).

content of the sayings than is Matthew. In fact, exegetical literature generally identifies logia in the Sayings Source according to their appearance in Luke.[93] For example, Q 6:30 indicates that a saying in the Sayings Source (Q) is to be found in Luke 6:30.

Both Luke and Matthew have used the various sayings in keeping with their respective literary skills and theological intentions. Luke has put his own twist on some of the material, Matthew more so. Since the material coming from Q consists of sayings of Jesus, it is not surprising that much of it has found its way into one or another of Matthew's five great discourses, the first of which is the Sermon on the Mount. The sermon is about the kingdom of heaven,[94] the fulfillment of the law,[95] and righteousness.[96]

The number of these weighty topics is such that the "sermon" could not have been delivered as a single piece of oratory. The sermon is a literary composition, a collection of sayings that the evangelist has culled from Q and arranged in such a way that they teach about the kingdom of heaven, the fulfillment of the law, and righteousness. Since these sayings concern the types of behavior that are in keeping with the coming of the kingdom, fulfilling the law, and righteousness or justice,[97] it is to be expected that some of them deal with riches and human responsibility.

"Give to everyone who begs from you" (Matt 5:42)

A major section of the Sermon on the Mount is devoted to a series of six antitheses[98] that illustrate how Jesus' teaching fulfills the ancient law. Each of them begins in substantially the same fashion,

[93] See James Robinson and Paul Hoffman, *The Critical Edition of Q: A Synopsis of the Gospels Including Matthew and Luke, Mark and Thomas*, Hermeneia (Minneapolis: Fortress, 2000).

[94] Cf. Matt 5:1.

[95] Cf. Matt 5:18.

[96] Cf. Matt 5:20; see Matt 5:6, 10.

[97] The Greek *dikaiosynē* is a major theme in Matthew's gospel. See the classic study of Albert-Marie Descamps, *Les Justes et la Justice dans les Évangiles et le Christianisme Primitif, Hormis la Doctrine Proprement Paulinienne* (Louvain-Gembloux: Duculot, 1950).

[98] Cf. Matt 5:21-48.

"You have heard that it was said . . . but I say to you."[99] The fifth antithesis contrasts the law of talion, "an eye for an eye,"[100] with Jesus' teaching on nonretaliation. Jesus' teaching is unfolded in four examples, but the fourth illustration appears to be a non sequitur, "Give to everyone who begs from you, and do not refuse anyone who wants to borrow from you."[101]

The evangelist considered the saying to be so important that he incorporated it into the Sermon on the Mount even if it did not quite fit. Ulrich Luz comments, "It [Jesus' command] is part of the tradition of Jewish exhortations to practice charity. It is loosely connected with the situation of the debtor's trial in v. 40, but now it is speaking to the one who has possessions."[102] The saying ratifies the biblical tradition that those who are well-off have financial responsibilities toward those who are not well-off. Deuteronomy 15:10-11, for example, commands, "Give liberally and be ungrudging when you do so. . . . Open your hand to the poor and needy neighbor in your land."[103] Similar exhortations and commands are, in fact, scattered throughout the Bible and other early Jewish literature.[104] The seemingly out-of-place logion in Matthew 5:42 assumes that tradition into the teaching of Jesus and the proclamation of the gospel.

The logion circulated as an independent saying in the earliest generations of the Christian movement before it was assumed into the Sayings Source at Q40, reflected in Luke 6:30, "Give to everyone who begs from you; and if anyone takes away your goods, do not ask for them again." There is an independent version of the saying in the *Gospel of Thomas*: "To the one who asks of you, give; and from the

---

[99] Matt 5:21, 27, 31, 33, 38, 43.

[100] Cf. Exod 21:24; Lev 24:20; Deut 19:21.

[101] Matt 5:42. Talbert opines that a passage in *b. Yoma* 23a, commenting on Lev 19:18a to the effect that the biblical text on revenge and grudges refers to monetary matters, may provide the link between the Q saying and vengeance if indeed the rabbinic tradition were already in circulation in Matthew's time. Cf. Charles H. Talbert, *Matthew*, Paideia Commentaries on the New Testament (Grand Rapids: Baker Academic, 2010), 86.

[102] Luz, *Matthew 1–7*, 275.

[103] Cf. Deut 15:7-8; Sir 29:8-9.

[104] Cf. Exod 22:25; Lev 25:36-37; Prov 28:27; Sir 4:1-10; 29:1-2; Tob 4:7; *T. Job* 9:1–12:4; *T. Zeb.* 7:2.

one who borrows, do not ask back what is yours."[105] The logion does not enjoin the person who responds to the biblical injunction to give everything that is asked for. Nor does the logion imply self-impoverishment. The command suggests only that the just person respond generously and ungrudgingly to those in need.

Matthew's version of the traditional logion is an ethicized[106] and somewhat mitigated version of the saying. Matthew's "give" is the Greek *dos*, an aorist, whereas Luke's—and presumably Q's[107]—"give" is the Greek *didou*, a present tense that has the connotation of a repeated action, "keep on giving." In addition, Matthew has "To the one who asks" (*tō aitounti se*), whereas Luke has an inclusive "Give to everyone who begs." This Matthean modification does not seem to be due to the evangelist's intention to lessen the force of the injunction. Rather, it would appear to be a modification due to the evangelist's editorial desire to make verse 42 parallel with verse 40, "if anyone wants to sue you" (NRSV).[108] A more literal rendering of the Greek *tō theolonti soi krinēthai* would be "to the one who wants to sue."

A caveat to Jesus' demand that those who have possessions respond to the needs of those who ask is to be found in what Matthew writes about almsgiving,[109] the first of the traditional Jewish works of piety: "Beware of practicing your piety before others in order to be seen by them, for then you have no reward from your Father in heaven."[110] Jesus' teaching about the avoidance of self-serving ostentation in giving alms resonates with the teaching of Seneca, the Stoic philosopher, who deemed that gifts could be compromised if a gift-giver shamed the recipient of a gift by drawing attention to the benefaction that he had given.[111] It is important to give alms, but a

---

[105] *G. Thom.* 95. See also *Did.* 5:1a.

[106] Cf. Georg Strecker, *The Sermon on the Mount: An Exegetical Commentary* (Nashville: Abingdon, 1988), 84.

[107] See Robinson and Hoffman, *Critical Edition of Q*, 64.

[108] W. D. Davies and Dale C. Allison Jr., *The Gospel According to Saint Matthew*, vol. 1: *Introduction and Commentary on Matthew I–VII*, ICC (Edinburgh: T & T Clark, 1988), 547.

[109] Cf. Matt 6:1-4.

[110] Matt 6:1.

[111] Cf. *Ben.* 2.5.1; 11.1-2, 16; 13.1; Briones, *Paul's Financial Policy*, 43–45.

person should not be looking over his or her shoulder to see who is watching as he or she gives alms.

"Do Not Store Up for Yourselves Treasures on Earth" (Matt 6:19-21)

The Sayings Source also provided Matthew with a statement about the accumulation of wealth. "Do not," the Matthean Jesus teaches, "store up for yourselves treasures on earth, where moth and rust consume and where thieves break in and steal; but store up for yourselves treasures in heaven, where neither moth nor rust consumes and where thieves do not break in and steal. For where your treasure is, there your heart will be also."[112]

Matthew, who has a predilection for collecting material into literarily organized units, inserts this saying, with its antithetical parallelism and an underlying foundation, into the Sermon on the Mount as the first in a series of three logia that concern priorities. All three involve a contrast between a good choice and a bad choice. They involve an either-or with no room in the middle between the two opposites.

The Matthean saying has a parallel in Luke 12:33-34[113] and an apparently independent parallel in the *Gospel of Thomas* 76.3. The variants among the three versions of the logion are significant. One of the most notable is that the Lucan version of the saying does not contain the negative exhortation, "Do not store up for yourselves treasures on earth, where moth and rust consume and where thieves break in and steal." Luke has only the antithetical positive saying. In this instance, however, it would seem that the Matthean version more closely resembles the Q saying than does Luke.[114]

The saying in Matthew 6:19-21 clearly pertains to the accumulation of wealth; it is not about acquiring one particularly valuable item[115] or retaining a single treasure, as are the parables of the Hidden Treasure and the Fine Pearl. The object of the verb in Matthew 6:19

---

[112] Matt 6:19-21.

[113] The source of the saying is identified as Q 12:33-34.

[114] Cf. Robinson and Hoffman, *Critical Edition of Q*, 328; Davies and Allison, *Matthew*, 1:629.

[115] Cf. Matt 13:44.

is in the plural, "treasures" (*thēsaurous*). The verb is in the present imperative (*thēsaurizete*) with the connotation of "make a habit of storing up treasure."[116] Treasure is inherently perishable; it is subject to the vicissitudes of nature and the desires of other human beings. It can be destroyed by insects or corrosion[117] or taken away by thieves. Do not make a practice of accumulating wealth, Jesus says to his disciples in this part of the Sermon on the Mount. Rather than amassing temporal wealth, says Jesus, his disciple is to store up treasure in heaven. The saying is echoed in the writings of Justin Martyr, one of the early apologetic fathers of the church.[118]

The idea of treasure in heaven was familiar in Jewish thought. The imagery symbolized eschatological reward. Tobit 4:8-9, for example, reads: "If you have many possessions, make your gift from them in proportion; if few, do not be afraid to give according to the little you have. So you will be laying up a good treasure for yourself against the day of necessity."[119] Rabbinic literature continued to use the imagery of treasure in heaven, much in the same way that Matthew did, contrasting temporal wealth with treasure in heaven. The Babylonian Talmud, for example, reports that King Monobaz[120] had said, "My fathers stored in a place that can be tampered with, but I have stored in a place which cannot be tampered with. . . . My fathers gathered for this world, but I have gathered for the world to come."[121]

"For where your treasure is, there your heart will be also," loosely connected to what has just been recorded, intensifies the thought

---

[116] Talbert, *Matthew*, 90.

[117] The Greek word *brōsis*, translated as "rust," denotes "eating." Hence, the connotation of "corrosion" or "rust." However, the Greek manuscript tradition of Mal 3:1 shows evidence of the word as designating a grasshopper. If that is the sense of the term in Matt 6:19, then the treasure envisioned by the logion would consist only of costly fabric. Should the term connote rust, the treasure that is pointed to would be both fabric and metal. The wearing of fancy clothes is a symbol of wealth in virtually all societies, ancient and modern. In either case, the point of the saying's use of imagery remains the same. Treasure is subject to the sometimes destructive forces of nature.

[118] Cf. *First Apology* 15.

[119] Cf. *4 Ezra* 7:77; 8:33, 36; *2 Bar.* 14:12; 24:1.

[120] Monobaz II, a convert to Judaism, renowned for his gifts to the temple in Jerusalem, reigned in the second half of the first century CE.

[121] *b. B. Bat.* 11a; cf. *t. Pe'ah* 4.18.

of the antithetical parallel sayings on treasure. The language of the aphorism[122] is clearly Jewish, but the adage has no parallel in Jewish literature. In Jewish thought, the heart—*kardia* in Greek, *leb* in Hebrew—represents the core of a human being, the very essence of a human person. This additional saying underscores the vital options that a person has to make. Is a person one whose goal, in the very depths of his or her being, is the amassing of wealth and its symbols? Or is a person one who, in the depths of her or his personal reality, makes God and the things of God the focus of his or her being? This is the question that Matthew 6:19-21 raises for the disciples of Jesus.[123]

"You Cannot Serve God and Wealth" (Matt 6:24)

The third of the series of sayings about getting one's priorities straight is found in Matthew 6:24. It concerns money, as did the first saying in the series. The well-known adage calls for a decision on the part of those who hear it.[124] The Matthean version of the saying reads, "No one can serve two masters; for a slave will either hate the one and love the other, or be devoted to the one and despise the other. You cannot serve God and wealth." As was the case with the other sayings on wealth found in the Sermon on the Mount, this saying has a parallel in both Luke[125]—thus leading scholars to the conclusion that it comes from the Sayings Source[126]—and the Gnostic *Gospel of Thomas*.[127]

The almost unforgettable logion, "You cannot serve God and wealth," is the last of a series of three parallel phrases. The sayings

---

[122] A clear indication the aphorism initially circulated independently from the preceding contrast on amassing wealth is that the aphorism is in the second-person singular whereas both members of the contrast are in the second-person plural.

[123] "This [v. 21] is the main point of these verses," Donald Hagner comments in *Matthew 1–13*, WBC 33 (Dallas: Word, 1993), 158.

[124] Cf. Strecker, *Sermon*, 134.

[125] Cf. Luke 16:13.

[126] The logion is identified as Q 16:13.

[127] Cf. *G. Thom.* 47.2. In *G. Thom.* 47, the saying about the impossibility of serving two masters is preceded by "It is impossible for a man to mount two horses or to stretch two bows." These images are not *ad rem* and most likely do not belong to the early tradition of the logion.

are cited by way of explanation[128] of what appears to be a common-sense proverb, "No one can serve two masters." Commentators generally note that the situation of a slave's being owned by two masters was rare but not impossible.[129] Later rabbinic sources postulate the situation of a slave having two owners, perhaps a pair of brothers, and the conflicted situations that arise from this kind of joint ownership.[130] If one of the brothers freed the slave and the other did not, was he half-slave and half-freedman? Joint ownership obviously means that the slave has divided loyalties. Joint ownership means that the slave is not totally devoted to one or the other. The demands of joint owners can create a conflicted situation for a slave. What is a slave to do if his two owners order him to do different things within the same time frame?

The evangelist's commentary on the adage "No one can serve two masters" presents a pair of contrasts: "A slave[131] will either hate [*misēsei*] the one and love the other, or [*ē*] be devoted to the one and despise the other."[132] The evangelist's language may not be as harsh as the English translation seems to imply. Verse 24b reflects a Semitic idiom in which "hate" sometimes means "love less." For example, a Q saying faithfully reproduced in Luke 14:26 reads, "Whoever comes to me and does not hate [*misei*] father and mother, wife and children, brothers and sisters, yes, and even life itself, cannot be my disciple." Interpreting the idiom, Matthew paraphrases the logion as "Whoever loves father and mother more than me is not worthy of me; and whoever loves son or daughter more than me is not worthy of me."[133]

Similarly, the verbs in verse 24c might have softer connotations than the English translation suggests. The contrast may simply be

[128] Note the post-positive *gar*, "for," in v. 24b.

[129] Cf. Acts 16:16, 19, where Luke mentions the "owners" (*kyrioi*) of a possessed female slave in Philippi.

[130] Cf. *m. Gitt.* 4:5; *m. 'Eduy.* 1:13; *b. Qidd.* 90a.

[131] The word "slave," the Greek *doulos*, does not appear in the evangelist's text; it is inferred from the reference to "masters" (*kyriois*) in v. 24a. Luke 16:13a does, however, have an expressed subject of the verb. It is *oiketes*, "slave," or more precisely, "domestic slave," a term not otherwise used in the New Testament gospels.

[132] Matt 6:24b-c.

[133] Matt 10:37. Cf. Robinson and Hoffman, *Critical Edition of Q*, 450–51.

between paying attention to and disregarding. These linguistic niceties are not, however, integral to the understanding of the pair of
parallel sayings. It is the contrast that is important. The Matthean
Jesus is speaking of an either-or situation in which the acceptance
of one, total dedication to the one, implies the rejection of the other.
Only then does he come to the point, the climax of the parallel sayings, "You cannot serve God and wealth [*mammōna*]."

The etymology of the word "mammon" (*mamōnas*), a loan-word
from Aramaic of Canaanite origin, is disputed.[134] What is beyond dispute is that the word rarely appears in ancient literature. In the New
Testament, apart from its Q-sourced appearances in Matthew 6:24
and Luke 16:13, it is found only in Luke 16:9 and 16:11. It does not
appear at all in the Jewish Scriptures except for a single appearance
in the Hebrew text of Sirach 31:8. It appears in three Qumran texts,
making a single appearance in each of them.[135] More than a century
later it appears twice in the Mishnah.[136] It is also found in the Targums
on Deuteronomy 6:5 and Proverbs 3:9.

The loan-word basically means "wealth, property, or possessions."
The term does not have an inherently evil connotation. That this is so
is readily apparent in the Palestinian Targum's version of Deuteronomy
6:5, "You shall love Yahweh your God with all your heart, and with all
your soul, and with all your mammon."[137] "Mammon" is an inherently
neutral designation of wealth that acquires a negative connotation
by means of a qualifying expression—for example, the "dishonest"
(*adikō*) of Luke 16:11[138]—or the context in which it appears.[139]

---

[134] Cf. Harrington, *Matthew*, 101.

[135] Cf. 1QS 6:2; 1Q 272:1; CD 14:20.

[136] Cf. *m. 'Abot.* 2:12; *m. San.* 1:1.

[137] France, "God and Mammon," 10, observes that this is the rendering in both
the Targum of Jonathan and Targum Neofiti 1. The Targum of Prov 3:9 similarly
reads, "Honor God with your Mammon." Targums are Aramaic paraphrases of
biblical texts. They owe their origin to Aramaic oral tradition and seem to have
been written in the Mishnaic period, ca. 200 CE. Cf. Stephen A. Kaufman, "Targums," *NIDB* 5:471–73.

[138] The NRSV's "dishonest wealth" in Luke 16:9 renders the Greek *tou mammōna tēs adikias*, literally, "the wealth of dishonesty," that is, wealth that results
from injustice.

[139] I do not agree with Harrington (*Matthew*, 101) and Luz (*Matthew 1–7*, 334)
that the term has a negative connotation in Matt 6:24.

Saying, "You cannot serve God and wealth," the Matthean Jesus is not making a contrast between allegiance to good and allegiance to evil, between a good relationship and a bad relationship. In Judaism and among the crowds who heard Jesus' teaching,[140] wealth was generally considered to be something good, a gift from God. There was, of course, an exception for ill-gotten wealth, but there is no suggestion of dishonesty in the climactic saying of Matthew 6:24. Rather, Jesus personifies wealth[141] and sets it over and against God as if it were an idol or a god in competition with God himself. Virtually deified with the name of Mammon,[142] wealth is radically incompatible with God.[143] Jesus proclaims that sometimes God's gifts are in competition with God himself for the allegiance of human beings. God demands total allegiance, undivided loyalty. Making wealth the *summum bonum*, the greatest good, makes it impossible for men and women to be totally devoted to God. The issue is not looking on wealth as evil; it is single-minded discipleship and undivided loyalty to God.[144] More often than not, wealth gets in the way.

Another Saying from the Sayings Source: "Laborers Deserve Their Food" (Matt 10:10)

The second of Matthew's five great discourses is the Missionary Discourse of chapter 10. The evangelist has compiled the discourse from material that he has found in Mark and Q. His editorial work in this regard is different from that of Luke. Luke has two missionary discourses, one for the sending out of the Twelve,[145] the other for the sending of seventy other disciples.[146] Luke takes the bulk of the

---

[140] Cf. Matt 7:28; see also Matt 5:1.

[141] The personification of wealth is almost demanded by the reference to "two masters" in v. 24a. God is obviously *kyrios*, lord or master. The other master, competing with God for the allegiance of the human being, is personified wealth.

[142] Cf. Daniel Marguerat, *Dieu et l'argent. Une parole à oser*, Parole en liberté (Bière, Switzerland: Cabédita, 2013), 29–30.

[143] Cf. Batara Sihombing, "A Narrative Approach to God and Mammon (6:19-34) and Its Relevance to the Churches in Indonesia," *AJT* 26 (2012): 25–43; Marguerat, *Dieu et l'argent*, 9.

[144] Cf. Matt 5:8.

[145] Cf. Luke 9:1-6.

[146] Cf. Luke 10:1-20.

material for the first discourse from Mark, while the Sayings Source provides him with material for the second discourse. Matthew's missionary discourse is a literary tapestry woven of material from the two sources.

In the parable of the Workers in the Vineyard, Matthew writes about a householder who agrees to pay his day laborers the usual daily wage, the denarius.[147] Doing so, the owner is acting on a principle of justice. The principle is stated in Q 10:7:[148] "The worker deserves his wages" [my translation] and has earned his pay. The principle, an axiom of social justice at the time, appears three times in the New Testament, always in reference to those who preach the gospel, namely, in Matthew 10:10; Luke 10:7; and 1 Timothy 5:18.

The adage seems to be a popular saying in circulation prior to its incorporation into the Q source. That it is found verbatim in 1 Timothy, which appears to have no knowledge of Q,[149] attests not only to its independence but also to its importance for early Christian communities. The absence of a verb in its six Greek words attests to its proverbial character,[150] as does the post-positive *gar*, "for," in Luke 10:7c. In Luke, the proverb is the punchline of Jesus' exhortation to the seventy disciples, "Remain in the same house, eating and drinking whatever they provide, for [*gar*] the laborer deserves to be paid." Luke's use of the proverb suggests that workers deserve to be paid enough to have a roof over their head and the wherewithal to be able to eat and drink. It was a matter of common wisdom and an article of traditional Jewish righteousness that laborers deserve to be paid. For the evangelists and for the anonymous disciple of Paul who wrote 1 Timothy, this truism was part of the gospel message.

Matthew has a slightly different version of the saying in the Missionary Discourse of chapter 10. The adage is introduced as a foreign body in copy that Matthew has taken over from Mark. After exhorting his disciples to take no money, no bag, and no second tunic, san-

---

[147] Cf. Matt 20:2.

[148] Cf. Robinson and Hoffman, *Critical Edition of Q*, 170–71.

[149] *Pace* Luz (Luz, *Matthew 8–20*, 76n45) who writes, "It is quite possible that Paul [*sic*] knew the saying in its Q form."

[150] Ps.-Phoc. 16; *Did.* 13.1-2, in dependence on Matt 10:10. Cf. 1 Cor 9:14.

dals, or staff,[151] the Matthean Jesus says, "for laborers deserve their food."[152] The Greek word translated as "food" is *trophē*. The word, used four times by Matthew,[153] belongs to a word group derived from the root *troph-* or *treph-* whose words generally connote feeding, although they sometimes acquire the extended connotation of payment. In his commentary on the gospel, Donald Hagner argues that Matthew's choice of words is more original than Luke's and that the Matthean term has the somewhat broader sense of subsistence.[154]

Davies and Allison, however, suggest that Matthew has substituted "food" for "wages" in keeping with the exhortation of Matthew 10:8, "You received without payment; give without payment."[155] This seems to be the more correct interpretation. Matthew's Jesus is urging his disciples to engage in the work of evangelization without expecting any monetary reward. It suffices if they have food to eat.[156] For the evangelist, earning money for preaching the gospel was not the way an apostle was to live.

Parables from the Sayings Source

In the Sermon on Parables, chapter 13 of his story about Jesus, Matthew has collated seven parables. Two of these, the parable of the Treasure and the parable of the Pearl, speak of wealth. Coming from Matthew's own special material, these two short parables have already been covered.[157] Following the time frame of his Markan source, Matthew reserves some parables until the time of Jesus' ministry in Jerusalem prior to his death. One of these is the parable of the Wicked Tenants, which Matthew has taken over from Mark and places within the context of Jesus' Jerusalem ministry, as did Mark.

---

[151] Cf. Matt 10:9-10a. Luz writes about the "plerophorous enumeration" of money.

[152] Matt 10:10.

[153] Cf. 3:4; 6:25; 10:10; 24:45. The word does not appear in Mark and is used only once by Luke (12:23).

[154] Cf. Hagner, *Matthew 1–13*, 272.

[155] Cf. Davies and Allison, *Matthew*, vol. 2: *Commentary on Matthew VIII–XVIII*, ICC (London: T & T Clark, 1991), 174.

[156] Cf. Matt 6:25-34.

[157] See above, pp. 98–101.

Two other parables that also concern wealth came to Matthew via the Sayings Source, Q, and have been located within the Jerusalem ministry. The first, the parable of the Wedding Banquet,[158] follows immediately after Matthew's version of the parable of the Wicked Tenants,[159] while the other, the parable of the Talents,[160] appears a few chapters later in Matthew's story about Jesus.

The Parable of the Wedding Banquet (Matt 22:1-10)

In Matthew, the parable of the Wedding Banquet is bookended by two pieces of Markan material, the parable of the Wicked Talents and the dispute about paying taxes to Caesar.[161] In their *Critical Edition of Q*, James Robinson and Paul Hoffman have chosen "the Parable of the Invited Dinner Guests" as a title for the story.[162] With this nomenclature, the editors draw attention to what is surely one of the most important features of the story, namely, the reaction of the invitees. Similarly, Harrington has observed that "the distinctive motif of Matt 22:1-14 is invitation."[163] Matthew draws singular attention to the invitees by appending to his rendering of the tale the incident of the man who showed up for the gala but was not wearing proper dinner dress.[164]

The editors of the *Critical Edition of Q* note that there is some dispute as to whether or not the story[165] actually comes from the Sayings Source,[166] so great are the differences between the story found in Matthew and the parallel story in Luke. For example, the protagonist in Matthew is a king who throws a wedding banquet,[167] while in Luke

---

[158] Matt 22:1-10. Cf. Luke 14:16-24.

[159] Matt 21:33-46. Cf. Mark 12:1-12; Luke 20:9-19.

[160] Matt 25:14-30. Cf. Luke 19:12-27.

[161] Cf. Matt 22:15-22; Mark 12:13-17; Luke 20:20-26.

[162] Robinson and Hoffman, *Critical Edition of Q*, 432–49.

[163] Harrington, *Matthew*, 307.

[164] Cf. Matt 22:11-14.

[165] Identified in their edition as Q 14:16-18, 19-20, 23.

[166] Cf. Robinson and Hoffman, *Critical Edition of Q*, 432. See also Davies and Allison (*Matthew*, vol. 3: *Commentary on Matthew XIX–XXVIII*, ICC [London: T & T Clark, 1997], 194) who write, "We tentatively assign 22.1-10 to M. Most have instead ascribed the parable to Q."

[167] Cf. Matt 22:2.

the host is "someone," a nondescript *anthrōpos tis*, who gives a big dinner.[168] The *Gospel of Thomas* 64 has preserved yet another version of the story, with again some significant differences from the versions that appear in the canonical gospels. Despite the various differences among the three stories, the provenance of Matthew's parable of the Wedding Banquet appears to be the Sayings Source. Such, at least, is today's scholarly consensus.

Matthew's version of the story is heavily redacted. We recognize his literary hand in the shortened version of the story and his theological interests in a story of a royal wedding banquet.[169] A Jewish-Christian author as he was, he has told a story that belongs to a rich tradition in which the kingdom of God is frequently compared to a banquet. In Matthew's version, the story has become almost an allegorical reflection on salvation history with its mention of the son and the burning of the city.[170]

Key to understanding the story is the king's invitation and the people's response to the invitation. Initially, in verse 3, Matthew writes about a royal invitation and the invitees' declining the invitation. Reprising the motif in verses 4-6, the evangelist embellishes the invitation and differentiates among the responses. Some are indifferent; others are hostile and violent. Those who are indifferent to the invitation have economic concerns on their mind. They went away, one to his farm (*eis ton idion agron*), another to his business (*epi tēn emporian autou*). Offering these two examples of those who made light of the king's invitation, the evangelist highlights that it was their personal economic interests that led the two men to say no to the invitation; he writes about the first one's "own" (*ton idion*) field and the second's own (*autou*, "his") business. The lesson to be drawn from the story is that a person's economic concerns can stand in the way of a serious response to an invitation to be part of the kingdom of heaven, symbolized by the royal wedding banquet.

[168] Cf. Luke 14:16.

[169] See also Matthew's characteristic "kingdom of heaven" in Matt 22:2. The plural number of servants dispatched to invite the guests also comes from Matthean redaction. It reflects not only the royal scenario but also the numerous prophets sent to Israel.

[170] Cf. vv. 2, 7.

The Parable of the Talents (Matt 25:14-30)

Unlike the parable of the Wedding Feast, the parable of the Talents does not have a parallel in the *Gospel of Thomas*. It does, however, have a parallel in Luke 19:11-27, the so-called parable of the Pounds, and is, therefore, safely ascribed to the Sayings Sources as Q 19:11-27. The German Jesuit scholar Gerhard Lohfink styles this story as that of a "Millionaire on a Business Trip."[171]

Matthew's parable of the Talents is the last in a series of three short stories that have to do with the coming of the Son of Man.[172] Like the preceding stories, the parable of the Two Slaves and the parable of the Ten Bridesmaids,[173] the parable of the Talents concerns conduct that is appropriate for the penultimate times, the time before the return of the Master/Son of Man.

In Sunday sermons and homilies, the parable is generally exploited in order to encourage people to use the gifts, material or spiritual, that God has given them. Those who do so can then be contrasted with those who do not use their gifts. Such moralizing is not, however, the gist of the parable that Jesus told. He told a story about taking a risk—something that is praiseworthy and will be rewarded—in contrast with an attitude that plays it safe. The risk that Jesus was talking about was the risk of discipleship, the risk of following him in the time before the coming of the Son of Man, Jesus' Parousia as Lord. Some, however, chose to play it safe, hanging on to what they had rather than taking the risk of discipleship. In the first-century context of Jesus' preaching, the person who did not take the risk was most likely the pious Jew who wanted simply to hang on to his Jewish heritage and failed to take the risk of discipleship.

Like most of the material in the gospels that we read today, the parable told by Jesus was developed during the course of its being handed down orally and then being edited by the evangelist. At the time, the household steward was a domestic slave who enjoyed power and responsibility. It would not have been unlikely for a wealthy per-

---

[171] See Gerhard Lohfink, *Jesus of Nazareth: What He Wanted, Who He Was* (Collegeville, MN: Liturgical Press, 2012), 118.

[172] Cf. Matt 24:45–25:30.

[173] Matt 24:45–25:13.

son who was about to go on a long trip to entrust such a slave with the responsibility of caring for his money.[174]

Matthew has a tendency to exaggerate his financial metaphors in order to describe what humans have received from God and what they owe to God. That tendency seems to have been at work in his redaction of this story. The sum of money first mentioned in the parable is five talents. The wealthy master was something of a braggart; he describes the five talents as "a few things," a trifling sum.[175] A contemporary financier might call it "peanuts." But five talents was a considerable sum of money. Granted, five talents are far less than the ten thousand talents owed by the unforgiving servant of Matthew 18:23-25,[176] but it is still a large amount of money. A talent was worth six thousand denarii; five talents was roughly equal to the pay for a hundred years of work by a day laborer. Two talents was the worth of about forty years of work. Such hefty sums represent the enormity of God's gifts to human beings.

Read on the monetary level,[177] the slaves to whom five and two talents, respectively, were entrusted for the long period while the master was away[178] were able to double the amounts that had been entrusted to them and were rewarded for their efforts. They doubled the master's capital. There was no way that they could do that in ordinary commerce; they must have used unscrupulous means similar to those of their master, who was not only exceedingly rich but also known to have exploited others.[179] In this respect, he was the stereotypical rich person of the times.[180]

---

[174] Cf. Mary Ann Beavis, "Ancient Slavery as an Interpretive Context for the New Testament Servant Parables with Special Reference to the Unjust Steward," *JBL* 111 (1992): 37–54, esp. 40.

[175] *Oliga* in Matt 25:21; cf. v. 23.

[176] See above, p. 101.

[177] In a reading of the parable within its socio-historical context, Justin Ukpong views it as a critique of the rich man and his collaborators in "The Parable of the Talents (Matt 25:14-30): Commendation or Critique of Exploitation? A Social-Historical and Theological Reading," *Neot* 46 (2012): 190–207.

[178] Cf. Matt 25:19.

[179] Cf. Matt 24:24b, 26b.

[180] The rhetoric of Jesus' parables culminates in the point that is made, not on the moral character of the characters in the story. The unsavory character of both the wealthy man and the two servants who made money for him through

The listener is now prepared to hear that the third servant would likewise double the amount that had been entrusted to him and was about to hand over two talents to the returning master. But that was not the case. In a surprising climax in the presentation of the cast of characters, the third slave reports that out of fear of the master, he had buried the talent for safekeeping and had no gain to report. This incurred the wrath of the master, who told the slave that he should have entrusted the talent to the bankers so that the master would have had at least a minimal gain on his money during his absence. This third slave, wicked, lazy, and worthless, was to be thrown into the outer darkness, where there would be weeping and gnashing of teeth, whereas the other two servants were invited to share in their master's joy.[181]

The contrasting fates of the slaves is an example of apocalyptic imagery and serves as a reminder that in its Matthean form and context the story is about preparation for the eschaton. The phrase "after a long time"[182] in verse 19 is a reference to the delay of the Parousia. On his return, the man (*anthrōpos*, v. 14) whose departure was mentioned at the outset of the story (vv. 14-16) had morphed into the master, the Lord (*kyrios*, nine times in vv. 19-26).

The Lord (*kyrios*) reappears in the dialogue of the following parable, The Judgment of the Nations,[183] coming from Matthew's unique material. As in the previous parable, there is a change of designation; the character addressed as Lord (*kyrie*, vv. 34, 37) had been identified as a king (*baslileus*, v. 34). In both parables, the Lord functions as a judge, rewarding those who made good use of their assets and meting out punishment for those who did not.

In the judgment parable, which emphasizes the role of the Lord as judge, both the righteous and the accursed ask the Lord, "When was it that we saw you hungry and gave you food, and gave you something to drink? And when was it that we saw you a stranger and welcomed

---

unscrupulous business practices does not take away from the point of the parable, taking a risk for the sake of the kingdom.

[181] Cf. Matt 25:21, 23; Luke 13:28.

[182] In Greek, the *meta de polyn chronon* of v. 19.

[183] Matt 25:31-46.

you, or naked and gave you clothing?"[184] Principal among the works on which people are to be judged at the Parousia are how they used their material wealth to provide food, drink, and clothing to the poor and how they treated strangers[185] in their midst.

Money and the Temple

The judgment parable, coming from Matthew's special source, is the last of the parables in Matthew's gospel. That does not mean that the evangelist had finished writing about money matters. Money paid to the temple is at issue in two relatively short scenes, one taken from Matthew's special material, the other from the "triple tradition."[186]

The Temple Tax (Matt 17:24-27)

Immediately after Jesus' second prediction of his passion and death,[187] Matthew recounts an incident that is found in none of the other gospels. It is the fanciful tale of the temple tax.[188] The per capita temple tax, whose origins are to be found in a pair of biblical passages, Nehemiah 30:32 and Exodus 30:11-16, was levied on Jews for the support of the temple of Jerusalem and its cult. Babylonian Jews had organized a system for the payment of the tax,[189] but the tax may have been a voluntary tax, as Palestinian Sadducees argued. The Qumranites held that the biblical injunction was satisfied if a person paid the tax once in his lifetime.[190]

After the destruction of the temple in 70 CE the Roman emperor Vespasian diverted the money raised by the tax to the support of the Roman temple of Jupiter Capitolinus[191] and decreed that it be paid by

[184] Matt 25:37-38; cf. v. 44.
[185] *Zenon*, literally, "alien," in vv. 38, 44.
[186] The "triple tradition" is the name given by scholars to material that is found in Mark and that has been taken over by both Matthew and Luke.
[187] Cf. Matt 17:22-23. In Matthew the three passion predictions are found in Matt 17:22-23; 16:21-23; and 20:17-19.
[188] Cf. Matt 17:24-27.
[189] Cf. Josephus, *Antiquities* 18.312.
[190] Cf. 4Q 69:6-7.
[191] Cf. Josephus, *War* 7.218.

all Jews living throughout the empire. This was the so-called *fiscus iudaicus*, the "Jewish tax," whose payment could be enforced by Roman authorities.

Since Matthew wrote his gospel in the final decades of the first century CE, some years after the destruction of the temple, the story in Matthew 17:24-27 must have been preserved by him out of respect for his sources.[192] Might he have included it because it was another story about Peter, who features in the Matthean gospel in singular fashion? In any case, the story was not immediately pertinent to Matthew's audience who did not pay the traditional Jewish "temple tax." Although short, the story raises a number of exegetical issues, especially about Jesus and the members of the church. The episode culminates in a fish story. Fish stories were as common in antiquity[193] as they are now.

What is particular about this story is that at Jesus' direction, Peter caught a fish whose mouth contained a coin whose value was worth twice the amount of the traditional temple tax. The coin, the stater (*statēra*, v. 27), was worth two didrachmas, the equivalent to the Jewish shekel. It was, as Jesus said, enough "for you and me." The temple tax was only a half-shekel. The details of this story and the accompanying exegetical issues are far too many for this study to enter into. We can, however, take away from this story the fact that Jesus and his chief disciple paid a religious tax, although the historical Jesus affirmed that, in principle, he and his disciples were not obliged to pay the tax. They paid taxes even when not obliged to do so.

Matthew's redaction might have served to indicate that at the time of the composition of his gospel, the *fiscus iudaicus* was to be paid in order to keep the peace.[194] Alongside the dispute about paying tribute to Caesar,[195] it is one of two stories about taxes in Matthew's gospel.

---

[192] Gertraud Harb, "Matthew 17.24-27 and Its Value for Historical Jesus Research," *JournStudHistJesus* 8 (2010): 254–74.

[193] See, for example, Herodotus, *Hist.* 3.39-42; *b. Sabb.* 119a.

[194] Cf. Matt 17:27.

[195] Cf. Matt 22:15-22, a story that belongs to the triple tradition.

Money Changers (Matt 21:12-13)

The evangelist's mention of the temple tax with Exodus 30:11-16 lying in the background brings to mind a scene that occurs after Jesus' entrance into Jerusalem, the Cleansing of the Temple in Matthew 21:12-13. Matthew's telling of the story depends on Mark.[196] It has a parallel in the fourth gospel where it is found early on in the narrative.[197] Matthew's account is more sober than that of his source. Here, as so often, Matthew abbreviates what he finds in his written source.

The evangelists describe an action that occurred in the temple's Court of the Gentiles. Matthew's scenario depicts Jesus as driving sellers and buyers out of the temple and overturning their tables. Although the Scripture cited by Matthew, a conflation of Isaiah 56:7 and Jeremiah 7:11, refers to a "den of robbers," there is no suggestion that the sellers and buyers were doing anything immoral.[198] The sellers were simply engaged in facilitating temple offerings; the buyers were obtaining what they needed in order to make an appropriate offering. The scriptural quotation functions in much the same way as do the "fulfillment citations"[199] of Matthew's gospel. They serve to underscore that what has been described is in keeping with the history of salvation.

Two groups of sellers conducted business in the Court of the Gentiles. The first group consisted of money changers, people selling shekels. These traders exchanged the coinage of the realm for Tyranian-minted shekels so that pilgrims could make their temple offerings in the required Jewish coinage.[200] A second group of people conducting business in the temple precincts sold turtledoves in order that the poor and some others would have an acceptable sacrifice.[201] We can hardly imagine how difficult it would have been for Joseph and Mary to carry a pair of turtledoves with them when they traveled from Galilee to the temple in Jerusalem![202]

---

[196] Cf. Mark 11:15-17. See also Luke 19:45-46.

[197] John 2:13-17.

[198] Later rabbinic texts recount stories of protest actions against the greed of some of the temple entrepreneurs. Cf. *m. Ker.* 1.7; *t. Menah.* 13.18-22.

[199] Cf. Matt 1:23; 12:5; etc.

[200] Cf. Exod 30:11-16.

[201] Cf. Lev 5:7; 12:6-8; 14:22; 15:14, 29.

[202] Cf. Luke 2:22-24.

Jesus' action in expelling those engaged in commercial activity within the temple precincts was a prophetic gesture. It was intended to symbolize and anticipate the temple-less and sacrifice-less worship of God that would accompany the coming of the kingdom of God. Nonetheless, it was hardly likely to win the favor of these vendors and their supporters. The cleansing of the temple exacerbated opposition to Jesus[203] and led, soon afterward, to his death.

Jesus' Passion, Death, and Resurrection

Each of the four evangelists describes Jesus' death and burial, but each of them does so in his own particular fashion. Matthew's telling of the story at the heart of the gospel message brings wealth and money into the narrative in a unique manner. Let us first look at how he describes the man who provided for Jesus' burial.

Joseph of Arimathea (Matt 27:57-60)

Matthew, Mark, Luke, and John agree that Joseph of Arimathea provided the dead Jesus with a tomb for his proper burial;[204] of these, only Matthew characterizes Joseph as a rich man (*plousios*).[205] Matthew alone says that Joseph laid Jesus' body in his own (*autou*) tomb. Matthew portrays Joseph as a pious and rich Jew who was attentive to the law of piety that the deceased be provided with a proper burial. He was a good man, despite his wealth. Indeed, his wealth enabled him to own a burial place in the environs of rocky Jerusalem. In providing for Jesus' burial, he put his assets to good use.

There may have been a subplot in Matthew's description of Jesus' burial. The evangelist often uses biblical texts to provide "color" for his narrative. Among the biblical texts employed by Matthew were the Servant Songs of Deutero-Isaiah.[206] Thus he cites Isaiah 53:4, from the Fourth Servant Song, in Matthew 8:17 as a scriptural warrant for Jesus' curing human ailments. When Matthew describes Joseph of

---

[203] Cf. Matt 21:23.
[204] Cf. Matt 27:57-60; Mark 15:42-46; Luke 23:50-53; John 19:38-42.
[205] Matt 27:57.
[206] Cf. Raymond F. Collins, "Servant of the Lord, The," *NIDB* 5:192–95.

Arimathea as a rich man, he may have been influenced by something that the Fourth Servant Song says in regard to the Servant of Yahweh, namely, "They made his grave with the wicked and his tomb with the rich."[207] Matthew may have continued his characterization of Jesus as God's servant by highlighting that Jesus was buried in the tomb of a rich man.

Bribery (Matt 26:14-16; 27:3-10)

Money has a role to play in two other stories related to the death and burial of Jesus in the first gospel. Bribery is the focus of each of the stories. The evangelist does not explicitly bring judgment to bear on those involved in the bribery, but his narrative shows that bribery has no good end.

The first story is the story of the betrayal of Jesus by Judas Iscariot. Matthew shares the first part of the story with his Markan source and with Luke.[208] Three features of Matthew's account are particularly noteworthy. First, Matthew, who highlights the role of the Twelve throughout his gospel, omits the characterization of Judas as one of the Twelve.[209] Second, whereas in Mark and Luke the chief priests made a deal with Judas to give him money for betraying Jesus, in Matthew the betrayer was paid before the betrayal took place. Third, the sum of money paid to Judas was thirty pieces of silver. Neither Mark nor Luke specify the amount of money that was to change hands as a result of the deal to arrest and kill Jesus.

None of the evangelists tell us the source of the money that the chief priests gave to Judas. Was it out of pocket, or was it taken from the temple treasury? Matthew has no interest in answering this question even though Matthew 27:6 seems to suggest that the money had been taken from the temple treasury. For this evangelist, the important thing is the amount of money that Judas received. The evangelist draws attention to this by describing Judas as actually

---

[207] Isa 53:9. Cf. W. Boyd Barrack, "The Rich Man from Arimathea (Matt 27:57-60) and Isaᵃ," *JBL* 96 (1977): 235–39.

[208] Cf. Matt 26:14-16; Mark 14:10-11; Luke 22:3-6. See also John 13:2, 27.

[209] Cf. Matt 26:14; Mark 14:10; Luke 22:3; John 6:70-71.

asking the chief priests, "What will you give me if I betray him to you?"[210] In response, they gave him thirty pieces of silver.

The silver coins reappear in Matthew's account of Judas' suicide.[211] Without parallel in the other gospels, the narrative[212] is derived from Matthew's special material. As the evangelist tells the story, a repentant Judas returns to the chief priests after the death of Jesus and attempts to return the amount of the bribery. The chief priests, in collusion with the elders of the people, will have none of this. In desperation, Judas throws the money on the ground and goes out and hangs himself. The evangelist comments that what had been spoken through the prophet Jeremiah was thus fulfilled.[213] The cited scriptural passage is actually a loosely worded version of Zechariah 11:13,[214] which speaks about thirty silver shekels being thrown into the treasury.[215] As he often does, Matthew has composed his narrative in such a way that the Scripture he cites is "literally" fulfilled.[216] Hence, his account's thirty silver pieces and his mention of Judas' throwing the silver coins to the ground.

The inability to overturn the results of his bribery—Jesus' death—and his own failure to return the bribe that he had received led to Judas' despondency and death. The bribery of Judas had achieved no good purpose; ultimately, it did not even enrich the one who initiated the plot to arrest and kill Jesus.

---

[210] Matt 26:16. The question is Matthew's redactional addition to his Markan source. Neither Mark's nor Luke's account of the bribery notes this detail of the deal.

[211] Cf. Matt 27:3-10.

[212] The account in Acts 1:18-20a is somewhat different. The Field of Blood is a feature of both this and the Matthean narrative.

[213] Cf. Matt 27:9a.

[214] Thus it is not surprising that the manuscript tradition sometimes "corrects" the evangelist by substituting "Zechariah" for "Jeremiah" or by dropping the prophet's name altogether. Some few manuscripts mistakenly correct the text by substituting "Isaiah" for "Jeremiah." Cf. Metzger, *Textual Commentary*, 55.

[215] In Zech 11:12-13, the thirty pieces of silver are a prophet's wages. They were "thrown into" the temple treasury at the Lord's command. In context, the verb means "placed in" the temple treasury rather than being angrily or despondently thrown at the box used for the collection of alms. Cf. Carol L. Meyers and Eric M. Meyers, *Zechariah 9–14*, AB 25C (New York: Doubleday, 1993), 273–77.

[216] See, for example, Matt 1:21-23; 21:4-7.

Matthew 27:62-66; 28:4, 11-15

Another multiphased story of bribery also comes from Matthew's special material, the Matthean account of the guards at the tomb of Jesus. As told by the evangelist, the story has three parts. Part 1 recounts how the chief priests and their allies, some Pharisees, set up a military guard at the tomb.[217] Part 2 describes the soldiers' fear at the appearance of the Lord.[218] Part 3 tells how the chief priests, with the elders, bribed the guards with a concocted story about Jesus' disciples having removed the body from the tomb.[219]

Matthew tells the story for an apologetic purpose. He wanted to discredit the rumor that Jesus had not been raised from the dead, that Jesus' tomb was empty because his disciples were a bunch of grave-robbers who had stolen the body. Fifty years after Jesus' burial and resurrection, this story was still in circulation.[220] Matthew wanted to discredit it once and for all. He does so by writing that the rumor was a concocted story that began to circulate among Jews because of a bribery paid to the soldiers who were on guard at the tomb. Once again, the evangelist does not explicitly bring judgment to bear on the bribery itself, even though lots of money was involved.[221] His readers know that the bribery was done to perpetrate a lie and undermine the resurrection of Jesus, the decisive event in the history of salvation. The misuse of money is accompanied by falsehood, but this compounded evil does not deter God from fulfilling all righteousness.[222]

A Brief Recap

From the gold offered to the infant Jesus by the magi to the bribery offered to Judas and the guards at the time of his death, a focus on money and wealth can be discerned throughout Matthew's gospel. He portrays Jesus' apostles as having little material possessions with no

---

[217] Cf. Matt 27:62-66.
[218] Cf. Matt 28:4.
[219] Cf. Matt 28:11-15.
[220] Cf. Matt 28:15b.
[221] Matt 28:12 mentions a "large sum of money," *agyria ikana*, a "large number of silver pieces."
[222] Cf. Matt 3:15.

coins in their purses or money with which to feed the crowd or pay the temple tax. Indeed, from preaching the gospel they could expect not a monetary payment but only food to eat.

On the other hand, the parables told by Jesus had some significant things to say about money. One of the most significant is that workers deserve a living wage, even if circumstances prevent them from working a normal workday. And workers' debts are to be pardoned.

Matthew tells the story of a rich man who does a work of piety in burying Jesus, but he also tells the story of another rich man whose unscrupulous ways seem to have influenced the conduct of his senior slaves. This man could be said to have fallen victim to the lure of money, to mammon, at whose altar he worshiped while rejecting the vertical dimension of righteousness. He desired to accumulate wealth, thus acting contrary to one of Jesus' memorable injunctions.

This overview of wealth, wages, and the wealthy in the first gospel is all too short. As the reader peruses Matthew's gospel, he or she must rehearse in his or her mind what Mark had said in those passages repeated by Matthew, the later editor. The reader must also prepare him- or herself to hear more about the early Christian view of wealth, wages, and the wealthy as this is reflected in the Sayings Source used by Matthew and by Luke, to whose gospel we can now turn.

So What?

"And anyone who has left houses, or brothers or sisters"

"A German Catholic diocese wants to take episcopal responsibility to a new level," began a July 24, 2004, news release by the Religion News Services,[223] "by making its disgraced former 'bishop of bling' responsible for the 3.9 million euros ($4.9 million) in losses incurred during the luxury makeover of his residence and office."

"Bishop Franz-Peter Tebartz-van Elst earned the "bling" label in 2013 when aides revealed he had spent 31 million euros ($34 million)—over six times the original estimate—on the stately complex opposite the Romanesque cathedral in Limburg, north of Frankfurt."

---

[223] The release was datelined "Paris" and incorporated into a piece by Tom Heneghan.

The Workers in the Vineyard

In the parable of the Workers in the Vineyard of Matthew 20:1-15, Jesus offers to his audience the example of a wealthy landowner who is proactive in providing dignity and ensuring wages to jobless workers. Perhaps the city of Albuquerque's "There's a Better Way" initiative has caught the message.[224] One day in 2015, the mayor of Albuquerque, Richard Berry, was driving through the city when he saw a man holding a sign that said, "Will Work." That gave the mayor the idea of an initiative called "There's a Better Way." Rather than ticketing the jobless for vagrancy or panhandling, the city's program enables Will Cole, an employee of a local homeless shelter, to drive a van twice a week through the city, asking homeless people if they want to work for a day. If they say yes—and 70–85 percent say yes—they are invited to get into the van, where they receive lunch.

Then it's off to work in the city's beautification project. They work five-and-a-half-hour shifts in the city's beautification project at $9 an hour. That adds up to $49.50, hardly a king's ransom, but with a free lunch to spare, the program provides wages almost equal to the federal minimum of $58 for an eight-hour day. At the end of the day they are dropped off at St. Martin's Hospitality Center, where they have access to food, shelter, and other services.

The mayor says, "We want to give the dignity of work for a day. The dignity of a day's work for a day's pay is a very good thing. It helps people stabilize, it helps them with their self-confidence, and it helps them get back on their feet."

On this topic, Pope Francis writes, "Helping the poor financially must always be a provisional solution in the face of pressing needs. The broader objective should always be to allow them a dignified life through work. Yet the orientation of the economy has favored a kind of technological progress in which the costs of production are reduced by laying off workers and replacing them with machines."[225]

The pope's words echo what he had earlier written in *The Joy of the Gospel:* "Welfare projects, which meet certain urgent needs,

---

[224] The blog by Eric March appeared in *Upworthy,* under the date of October 16, 2015.

[225] *Laudato Sì* 128.

should be considered merely temporary responses. As long as the problems of the poor are not radically resolved by rejecting the absolute autonomy of markets and financial speculation and by attacking the structural causes of inequality, no solution will be found for the world's problems or, for that matter, to any problems."

You Cannot Serve God and Wealth

In his morning homily during Mass at the Casa Santa Marta on October 19, 2015, Pope Francis reminded the congregation that we cannot serve two masters. A person serves either God or money, said the pontiff.[226] Drawing from the gospel lection, Pope Francis lamented that attachment to wealth is divisive.

He continued, "Let us consider how many families we know, whose members have fought, who are fighting, who don't [even] say 'Hello!' to each other, who hate each other—all for an inheritance." In these cases, he said, "The love of family, love of children, siblings, parents—none of these is the most important thing—no, it's money—and this destroys. . . . Even wars, wars that we see today: yes, sure there is an ideal [over which people fight], but behind that, there is money; money for arms dealers, the money of those who profit from the war."

---

[226] Cf. Zenit.org, October 19, 2015.

Chapter 5

Luke

The Gospel of Luke, the "third gospel," is more than likely the most recent of the three Synoptic Gospels to have been written. Like Matthew, it may be considered a revised version of Mark, but it was written for a different audience. The prologue to this gospel indicates that Luke was writing for a fairly sophisticated Hellenistic audience.[1] He wrote as a historian *de métier*, carefully consulting eyewitnesses and using various sources that were available to him. Among these sources was the Gospel of Mark and the Sayings Source, which he seems to have quoted even more faithfully than did Matthew.

The evangelist has much to say about riches and the rich and seems to be more trenchant in his judgment of the wealthy than were the other two Synoptic evangelists. For Luke, the attitude of people toward their possessions is a test of their commitment to discipleship.[2] Undoubtedly, many factors contributed to the way that Luke wrote about wealth and the wealthy in his story about Jesus. One of these factors was sociological. Luke, his community, and his potential readership belonged to one of the higher classes. "They are

---

[1] Cf. Luke 1:1-4. The Prologue to the Acts of the Apostles (Acts 1:1-6) indicates that the evangelist construed his gospel to be the first part of a two-part work. Lest the present chapter be unduly long, I shall defer consideration of the traditions contained in Acts until a later chapter.

[2] Cf. François Bovon, *Luke 1: A Commentary on the Gospel of Luke 1:1–9:50*, Hermeneia (Minneapolis: Fortress, 2002), 224.

not exactly poor, and for this reason," notes François Bovon, "they struggle fiercely with the problem of possessions."[3]

Another factor was the evangelist's keen interest in biblical prophecy and the biblical prophets. Many of them—the prophet Amos comes readily to mind—were strong proponents of what might today be called social justice. The evangelist's interest in the Hebrew Bible's prophetic figures was reinforced by his use of the Sayings Source. "Prophetic sayings" were a feature of that ancient text, preserved in the use that Matthew and Luke made of it. Luke preserves many of the Q sayings, as has been noted in the previous chapter. The evangelist's interest in the prophetic tradition is manifest throughout his story, beginning with the literary characters that appear in the so-called infancy narrative, Luke 1–2.

Yet another reason for the Lucan interest in wealth and the wealthy comes from his concern for the marginalized in society. Commentators on the third gospel inevitably note the evangelist's concern with the poor and the extent to which women appear in his narrative. By and large, women lived on the margins of public society in Luke's day. Stories such as the parable of the Widow and the Unjust Judge[4] and that of the Widow's Offering[5] reflect Luke's concern for poor and marginalized women. He has borrowed the story of the widow's offering from Mark but has drawn attention to her poverty by using an adjective meaning "poor"[6] that doesn't appear elsewhere in the New Testament.

This does not mean that the evangelist looked on all women as impoverished and living on the margins of society. Unique to Luke is a brief snippet of information about how Jesus was supported during his public ministry. During the time of his preaching in Galilee and while he was on his way to Jerusalem, Jesus seems not to have functioned as a day laborer using his acquired skills as a builder.[7] The gospels give

---

[3] Ibid., 224. Cf. Robert Karris, "Poor and Rich: The Lukan *Sitz im Leben*," in *Perspectives on Luke–Acts*, ed. Charles H. Talbert (Danville, VA: Association of Baptist Professors of Religion, 1978), 112–25.

[4] Cf. Luke 18:1-8.

[5] Cf. Luke 21:1-4.

[6] *Penikran* in Luke 21:2.

[7] Cf. Mark 6:3.

no indication that he survived by begging for his bread. Occasionally, he was invited to dinner, sometimes even a sumptuous dinner.[8] For the rest, Jesus was accompanied not only by the Twelve but also by some women: "Mary, called Magdalene, from whom seven demons had gone out, and Joanna, the wife of Herod's steward Chuza, and Susanna and many others, who provided for them out of their resources."[9]

These several women had sufficient resources to be able to function as patrons of Jesus and the Twelve as they went from Galilee to Jerusalem to proclaim the kingdom of God. At least one of them was well placed: Joanna—otherwise unnamed in the gospel tradition—who was the wife of Chuza, an administrator or governor (*epitropos*[10]) in the service of Herod Agrippa, grandson of Herod the Great.

Ultimately, Luke's narrative contains just about everything on riches and the rich that is found in Mark's gospel. Luke also contains most of what can be found in Matthew, that is, the material that belongs to the triple tradition and the Q material on wealth and the wealthy. The way in which Luke uses and often expands the traditions that were mediated to him via Mark and the Sayings Source gives the reader a good idea of Luke's theological outlook on wealth, wages, and the wealthy. His own special material gives further insight into his theology in this regard. That special material includes the four canticles that are a feature of the infancy narratives.[11] One of them, the first of the four, is pertinent to the subject of this study.

The *Magnificat* (Luke 1:46-55)

Prior to the birth of Jesus, Luke tells the story of the pregnant Mary's visit to her kinswoman, Elizabeth, an older woman pregnant

---

[8] Cf. Raymond F. Collins, "The Man Who Came to Dinner," in *Luke and His Readers*, ed. R. Bieringer, G. Van Belle, and J. Verheyden, BETL 182 (Leuven: University Press-Peeters, 2004), 151–72.

[9] Luke 8:2b-3; cf. Luke 23:49, 55–24:1.

[10] Cf. Matt 20:3; Gal 4:2.

[11] The four canticles are the *Magnificat* (Luke 1:46-55), the *Benedictus* (1:68-79), the *Gloria* (2:14), and the *Nunc dimittis* (2:29-32), all known by their Latin designations. The nomenclature derives from the first word in the Latin version of the hymns, for example, *Magnificat anima mea Dominum*, "My soul magnifies the Lord" (Luke 1:46).

at the time with John the Baptist. The latter's pregnancy had been announced to Mary[12] by the angel Gabriel as a sign that her own pregnancy was the result of the Holy Spirit's coming upon her. Shortly thereafter, Mary departed Galilee for Judea in order to visit Elizabeth. The evangelist gives no reason for this visit, but one might suggest not only that Mary wanted to confirm the angel's message but also that she wanted to be of help to the older woman in the last weeks of her pregnancy.

On entering the home of Elizabeth and Zachary, Mary was greeted by Elizabeth who, filled with the Holy Spirit, proclaimed Mary to be blessed as the mother of the Messiah and a woman of faith. In response, Mary[13] uttered a joyful hymn of praise. Somewhat reminiscent of the hymns found among the Dead Sea Scrolls, Mary's canticle has traditionally been called the *Magnificat*. In the first part of the hymn (vv. 47-50), largely a celebration of God's attributes, Mary acknowledges the unique blessing that has been given to her. The second part of the paean (vv. 51-55) puts this blessing within the broader perspective of what God has done and will do for his people in fulfillment of the covenantal promises made to Abraham and his descendants. What links the two parts of the hymn of praise together is the idea that what God has done for one lowly woman, a member of the *anawim*,[14] God will likewise do for the entire nation.

The evangelist has purposely placed this hymn of praise on the lips of Mary, the first Christian disciple,[15] at the beginning of the

---

[12] Cf. Luke 1:36-37.

[13] For an evaluation of the textual issues surrounding Luke's attribution of the canticle to Mary, see Metzger, *Textual Commentary*, 109, and Raymond E. Brown, *The Birth of the Messiah: A Commentary on the Infancy Narratives in the Gospels of Matthew and Luke*, rev. ed., ABRL (New York: Doubleday, 1993), 334–36. A strong argument that the canticle is to be placed on the lips of Elizabeth has been advanced by Jeffrey Kloha in "Elizabeth's Magnificat (Luke 1:46)," in *Texts and Traditions: Essays in Honour of J. Keith Elliott*, ed. Peter Doble and Jeffrey Kloha, NTTSD 47 (Leiden: Brill, 2014), 200–219.

[14] The *anawim*—literally, "the poor"—are those with little money, few possessions, and little political influence, who have only God on whom they can rely. The psalms often portray the poor as crying out to God for some redress. See further below, pp. 245–46.

[15] Cf. Brown, *Birth*, 316–19.

narrative. Arguably, Luke added the canticle to his narrative when his story of Jesus was virtually complete.[16] In some ways the hymn encapsulates the entire gospel. The *Magnificat* is programmatic for Luke's story of salvation. What God has done for one person in the coming of the Messiah, he will do for all his people.

Fortunately, the evangelist had a biblical model on which to draw in composing the canticle. That model was the Song of Hannah in 1 Samuel 2:1-10. Barren for most of her life, Hannah conceived Samuel at a relatively advanced age. Having given birth, Hannah presented the infant at the sacred shrine of Shiloh, just as Mary would later present her infant child in the temple at Jerusalem. Hannah's song begins on a note of personal thanksgiving for God's benefaction to her in the birth of her son but segues into a form that celebrates the relationship between God's justice and the human condition. Within this context, Hannah proclaims, "The Lord makes poor and makes rich; he brings low, he also exalts."[17]

Luke's reworking of this text results in "He [the Mighty One] has brought down the powerful from their thrones and lifted up the lowly; he has filled the hungry with good things, and sent the rich away empty."[18] This reversal of fortunes echoes biblical motifs,[19] but it is not without parallels in Hellenistic literature, where similar activity is attributed to Zeus or to the *Moirai*, the Fates. In a strong and forceful yet insightfully accurate theological observation, Bovon comments, "God desires and carries out the overthrow because injustice prevails among peoples. When God inaugurates his reign, he necessarily shakes the mighty from their thrones and demands the money of the rich. If he did not do so, he would be neither just nor good, and thus not God."[20]

[16] Cf. Brown, *Birth*, 339, 454, *passim*.

[17] 1 Sam 2:7.

[18] Luke 1:52-53.

[19] Cf. Édouard Hamel, "Le Magnificat et le renversement des situations: Réflections théologico-bibiques (Lc 1,51-53)," *Greg* 60 (1979): 55–84. Among the pertinent texts are Isa 2:11-17; Jer 17:11; Ezek 21:26, 31; Ps 147:6; Job 12:14-25; 15:29; and Sir 10:14.

[20] Bovon, *Luke 1*, 63.

"The pattern of reversal," writes Luke Timothy Johnson, "that is here begun corresponds to 'the fall and rise of many in Israel' (2:34) fundamental to Luke's narrative."[21] With almost pious emphasis on Mary who proclaimed the announcement of reversal found in the *Magnificat*, Raymond Brown comments, "If for Luke Mary is the first Christian disciple, it is fitting that he place on her lips sentiments that Jesus will make the hallmark of the disciple in the main Gospel story."[22] An examination of the various passages in the third gospel that speak about riches and the wealthy will illustrate the accuracy of this pair of assessments of Luke 1:52-53, the articulation of the evangelist's thesis on the topic. In turn, we shall look at Luke's use of material found in his Markan source, his use of various Q sayings, and passages that are proper to his own narrative.

The Markan Material

The Interpretation of the Parable of the Sower (Luke 8:14)

Key to understanding Mark's attitude toward riches is his interpretation of the first of Jesus' parables, the parable of the Sower. Apropos the seed that fell among thorns, Mark comments, "These are the ones who hear the word, but the cares of the world, and the lure of wealth, and the desire for other things come in and choke the word, and it yields nothing."[23] Luke's revision of Mark 4:18-19 reads, "As for what fell among the thorns; these are the ones who hear; but as they go on their way,[24] they are choked by the cares and riches and pleasures of life, and their fruit does not mature."[25]

Luke changed this part of the interpretation of the parable ever so slightly but quite significantly. First of all, he makes his readers

---

[21] Luke Timothy Johnson, *The Gospel of Luke*, SP 3 (Collegeville, MN: Liturgical Press, 1991), 42.

[22] Brown, *Birth*, 364.

[23] Mark 4:18-19.

[24] Fitzmyer renders the Greek *poreuomenoi* as "in their pursuit of life" and compares the three obstacles to the three nets of Belial that entrap Israel. See Joseph A. Fitzmyer, *The Gospel According to Luke I–IX*, AB 28 (Garden City, NY: Doubleday, 1981), 714. The reference is to CD 4:15–5:10.

[25] Luke 8:14.

think about a journey and a process. The third group of those who hear the word of God initially receive it, but as they go through their life's journey, their concerns, their wealth, and their pleasures prevent the word of God[26] from coming to fruition. The word of God began to grow, but it does not come to maturity. In this way Luke enables the parable to speak to the disciples of Jesus, not simply to those who were never part of Jesus' company. Some disciples receive the word, but their possessions prevent God's word from coming to fruition. They gradually fall away. They began the journey of discipleship, but God's word does not come to maturity in them. Their faith is incomplete, precisely, Bovon comments, "in the realm of ethics."[27]

Second, Luke has shifted the emphasis from Mark's desire and enticement[28] to the actual possession of the objects of a person's desire. The reasons for the nonfruition of God's word are three, namely, the cares, riches, and pleasures of life.[29] Luke has displaced the accent from longing for the good life to the actual possession of riches and pleasures. This is in keeping with the way that Luke portrays wealth throughout his gospel. In Luke's day, prosperity was a dangerous temptation.[30] In expositing the parable, Luke draws attention to this danger. For the evangelist, riches are a real obstacle to the possibility of God's word bearing fruit. In his view, possessions and the pleasures of life prevent the maturation of true religious faith.[31]

In a forceful commentary on Luke 8:14, John Kilgallen writes:

> "The pleasures of life" are universally recognized to be powerful means to corrupt ideals and religious faith. The satisfaction in them tends to make a person think that his

---

[26] Cf. Luke 8:11.

[27] Bovon, *Luke 1*, 310.

[28] Mark's *hē agapē tou ploutou* and *epithymiai*. Cf. Mark 4:19.

[29] *Kai hypo merimnōn kai ploutou kai hēdonōn tou biou*, Luke 8:14. The word *bios*, "life," is a Lucan term. Half of its New Testament usages are in the third gospel. The term connotes not so much physical life itself as it does the material possessions of life; cf. Hans-Joachim Ritz, "*bios, ktl.*," *EDNT* 1:219.

[30] Cf. Bovon, *Luke 1*, 310. See Herm., *Vis.* 33.11.3; 4.2.4-5; *Sim.* 2.5-7; 8.8.5; 8.9.4.

[31] Suggesting that Luke may have wanted to emphasize it, Marshall notes that "riches in themselves constitute a danger to faith." Cf. I. Howard Marshall, *The Gospel of Luke*, NIGTC (Grand Rapids: Eerdmans, 1978), 326.

happiness lies in them. . . . He needs nothing but pleasure to provide happiness and so avoids suffering. If wealth can serve as a source of life, so pleasure can serve as unending causes of happiness. In neither case does one need God or, specifically, a savior. Money or pleasure gives me all I want; I only need them all the time—and nothing or no one else.[32]

A Very Rich Ruler (Luke 18:18-23)

Luke has borrowed the story of the Rich Man from his Markan source.[33] For the most part, the third evangelist has made only a few stylistic changes to the story found in Mark. Yet there are some editorial modifications, and these are noteworthy.

It may be best to begin with the evangelist's last characterization of the man in the story. Luke tells his readers that the forlorn man was very rich (*plousios sphrodra*[34]). He does not mention that the sorrowful man departed from Jesus because of his many possessions, as do Mark and Matthew.[35] Luke simply observes that the man became sad.[36] His sadness appears to result from his perception that accepting the invitation to discipleship and possessing great wealth were incompatible.

Perhaps the evangelist's initial characterization of the interlocutor was partially due to the evangelist's envisioning him as an extremely rich individual. With his riches came political and social clout. Unlike Mark and Matthew who introduce the interlocutor as "someone,"[37] Luke describes the seeker as a man who was a ruler (*tis archōn*),[38] a person of some influence, a leader of people in one sense or another, perhaps a member of the Sanhedrin or a leader among the Phari-

---

[32] John J. Kilgallen, "The Sower and the Seed—8, 5-8 (8, 4-15)," in *Twenty Parables of Jesus in the Gospel of Luke*, SubBi 32 (Rome: Pontifical Biblical Institute, 2008), 17–27, at 26.

[33] Mark 10:17-22.

[34] Cf. Luke 18:23.

[35] *Echōn ktēmata polla* in Mark 10:22; Matt 19:22.

[36] Luke's *perilypos*, used only here in his two-part narrative, connotes profound sadness.

[37] *Eis* in Mark 10:17; Matt 10:17.

[38] Cf. Luke 14:1; 23:13, 35; 24:20; Acts 4:5, 8, 26; 13:27.

sees.[39] Luke may have had some information about the man's social standing, but it is not unlikely that this is a stylistic modification in the narrative chosen to draw attention to the position in society that his substantial wealth afforded him. Luke wanted his readers to imagine the man as a person who was rich and powerful.

From his wealth, this rich ruler had at least provided for the financial needs of his parents, as he acknowledged when he told Jesus that he had honored his father and mother from way back when. The evangelist does not, however, tell us anything about the source of the interlocutor's great wealth, but it is worthy of note that he has dropped "You shall not defraud" from his rehearsal of the precepts of the Decalogue. Does he want to leave his readers with the impression that some of the ruler's wealth was ill-gotten? That was likely the impression that people would have of the wealth of an influential man. Luke might have shared their prejudicial judgment. In Luke 16:11, the evangelist describes wealth as "dishonest wealth," the proverbial "mammon of iniquity" (*mammona tēs adikias*[40]).

At first, the rich man did not go away; unlike Mark and Matthew, Luke doesn't speak about the man's departure.[41] Since the rich man was still in Jesus' presence, Jesus looked at the powerful man now overcome with sadness and told him[42] that it is difficult, indeed impossible, for a rich man (*plousios*) to enter the kingdom of God:

> How hard it is for those who have wealth to enter the kingdom of God! Indeed, it is easier for a camel to go through the eye of a needle than for someone who is rich to enter the kingdom of God.[43]

On this note, which so radically and imaginatively articulates Luke's thoughts about the complete incompatibility between riches

---

[39] He was in any case someone who was knowledgeable about and faithful to the demands of the law.

[40] Luke 16:9; cf. Luke 16:11.

[41] Cf. Mark 10:22; Matt 19:22.

[42] In the parallel narratives, Jesus' words are addressed to the disciples after the departure of the rich man. Cf. Mark 10:23; Matt 19:23.

[43] Luke 18:24-25. Cf. Mark 10:23-25; Matt 19:23-24.

and discipleship,[44] the evangelist terminates his account of the encounter between Jesus and the very rich ruler. Portraying Jesus as addressing these enigmatic words to the rich man, rather than speaking them to the disciples by way of a commentary on his meeting with the rich man,[45] Luke has increased the poignancy of the scene. It is not so much the disciples in general who need to hear these words as those who are rich and powerful.

In the event, Jesus' final words to his interlocutor were as startling to the bystanders[46] who overhear the conversation as they are to contemporary readers of the story. Astonished, the bystanders[47] questioned Jesus, with words similar to those of the disciples in Mark, "Then who can be saved?"[48] Jesus responded with the contrast that only his disciples could understand, "What is impossible for mortals is possible for God." Ultimately, human beings cannot achieve their own salvation. Among other things, riches get in the way. God alone can give the gift of salvation.

In the final analysis, riches—the mammon of iniquity—prove to be deceptive. Riches provide a false sense of security to those who have them,[49] especially those who possess them in a considerable amount, as did the ruler of Luke's story. They are a fragile idol that cannot provide human beings with the gift of salvation; salvation is an ultimate reality that only God can give.

Paying Taxes (Luke 20:20-26)

For completeness' sake in this study of what the third gospel has to say about wealth, wages, and the wealthy, mention must be made of the controversy about paying taxes to Caesar.[50] The celebrated logion "Give to the emperor the things that are the emperor's and to

[44] Luke 10:24 has the verb "enter" (*eiselthein*) in the present tense, indicating present discipleship rather than some future eternal life.
[45] Cf. Mark 10:23; Matt 19:23.
[46] The disciples? Cf. Luke 17:22.
[47] With this editorial modification, Luke generalizes the theological maxim that Jesus is about to utter. It is not only his disciples who need to know that God can accomplish what humans cannot.
[48] Luke 18:24; cf. Mark 10:23; Matt 19:23.
[49] Cf. Marguerat, *Dieu et l'argent*, 33–34.
[50] Cf. Mark 12:13-17; Matt 22:15-22.

God the things that are God's" (Luke 20:25) has been taken verbatim from Mark in the exact same form as it appears in Matthew.[51] The saying has the same meaning and a similar rhetorical force as it does in these earlier gospels.

What Luke has done with his version of the incident is to modify somewhat the narrative context that surrounds the controversy. The setting is that "they," the scribes and chief priests of verse 19, had been keeping an eye on Jesus so that they could turn him over to Pilate. They expected the governor to do what they were not able to do themselves, get Jesus out of the way. To accomplish their plan they sent "spies" (*enkathetous*[52]) hypocritically pretending to be righteous, whose task was to catch Jesus in saying something that could be used against him.[53]

Luke's narrative conclusion adds that the controversy took place in the presence of the people (*tou laou*). Jesus' interlocutors were amazed by his Solomonic answer to their tricky question. In their amazement, they fell silent[54]—a picturesque note that is found only in Luke's version of this story.

Scattered Logia

Luke has not taken over the dispute about Corban and the accompanying vice list that he found in Mark 7:9-13, 21-22.[55] Perhaps this lettered evangelist thought the story too rooted in Jewish customs for his Hellenistic audience to fully understand. The third evangelist did, however, pick up some of the sayings of Jesus on wealth that he found in his Markan source.

One of those sayings is found in Luke 9:25: "What does it profit them if they gain the whole world, but lose or forfeit themselves?"[56]

---

[51] Cf. Mark 12:17; Matt 22:21.

[52] The word occurs only here in the New Testament. When Luke writes that these spies "pretended" to be sincere, he uses a participle, *hypokrinomenous*, related to the English words "hypocrisy" and "hypocrite."

[53] Cf. Luke 20:20, 26.

[54] Cf. Luke 14:4.

[55] Cf. Matt 15:1-9, 19.

[56] To avoid gender-specific language, the NRSV translation of Luke 9:21-27 has replaced the singular number in the Greek texts with a gender-inclusive plural. The result is that v. 25 has lost its aphoristic quality.

Luke has retained the financial language that he found in Mark.[57] "Profit" (*kerdēsas*) and "forfeit" (*zemiōtheis*) are contrasting terms that are often found in financial contracts. The saying implies that financial profit is ultimately of little value. To be sure, "you can't take it with you."[58] Luke teases out the meaning of the saying located at Luke 9:25 in the illustrative parable of the Rich Fool,[59] a short story found only in his gospel.

Of the three Synoptic evangelists, Luke has the greatest interest in the temple in Jerusalem. The account of Zachary's service in the temple and the story of Joseph and Mary taking Jesus to the temple at the age of twelve in the Lucan infancy narrative are but two examples of Luke's fascination with the temple. Thus, it is not surprising that Luke has included an account of the cleansing of the temple in his narration of the events leading up to Jesus' passion and death.[60] His account includes a scriptural conflation that the evangelist took over from Mark 11:17:[61] "It is written, 'My house shall be a house of prayer; but you have made it a den of robbers.'"[62] The reference to the den of robbers is an allusion to Jeremiah 7:11 where the phrase "den of robbers" is found in a long jeremiad in which the prophet complains about those who put their trust in temple worship but do not convert their hearts to the Lord. With the biblical phrase, Luke's Jesus characterizes his cleansing of the temple as a prophetic gesture. Using the temple itself as a venue for the selling of animals for sacrifice and the purchase of shekels for the payment of the temple tax was a relatively new phenomenon at the time of Jesus.[63] Previously, the activity took place in the environs of the temple. Jesus' words were directed at those who were using the temple, a house of prayer,

---

[57] Cf. Mark 8:36; Matt 16:26; 2 *Clem.* 6:2.

[58] Cf. Luke 12:20c. See Ps 49:17 for an expression of Jewish wisdom in this regard.

[59] Cf. Luke 12:16-21; see below, pp. 174–75.

[60] Cf. Luke 19:45-48.

[61] Cf. Matt 21:13. Both Matthew and Luke have dropped the phrase "for all peoples" that Mark had reprised from Isa 56:7.

[62] Luke 19:45.

[63] Cf. François Bovon, *Luke 3: A Commentary on the Gospel of Luke 19:28–24:53*, Hermeneia (Minneapolis: Fortress, 2012), 19.

for the sake of financial gain. Their profits ensured them of protection against financial losses.[64]

In the following chapter, Luke reproduces, with some minor editorial modifications, Jesus' judgment on the scribes found in Mark 12:36b-40. Esteemed for their knowledge of the Scriptures, the scribes were guilty of three offenses: their ostentatious pride,[65] their avarice evidenced in exploiting people who were not rich, and their religious hypocrisy. The widow, whom not only the ruling gentry but also the populace at large were required to protect, is cited as the victim of the scribes' greed. Luke's Jesus, as Mark's, does not give an example of a scribe taking financial advantage of the typical poor widow, but he has strong words for those guilty of such behavior: "Beware of the scribes. . . . They devour[66] widows' houses. . . . They will receive the greater condemnation."[67] Instead of protecting widows as the law required, these scribes took advantage of the widows' lack of protection in order to satisfy their own greed. Hence, their "greater condemnation."

Jesus pronounced this condemnation while he was teaching and preaching in the temple.[68] Immediately[69] after recounting Jesus' condemnation of the scribes for their exploitation of poor widows, Luke writes:

> He [Jesus] looked up and saw rich people putting their gifts into the treasury;[70] he also saw a poor widow put in two small copper coins. He said, "Truly I tell you, this poor widow has

[64] Cf. *m. Šegal.* 1:7.

[65] Cf. Luke 11:43.

[66] One of the Lucan editorial changes is that he has replaced Mark's participle with a third-person plural indicative.

[67] Luke 20:45-47.

[68] Cf. Luke 20:1.

[69] The New Testament was divided into chapters in the thirteenth century. Because of the chapter break after Luke 20:47, the modern reader can easily separate the incident of the poor widow from the condemnation of the scribes even though the two passages immediately follow one another in Luke's story.

[70] Luke's *gazophylakion*, apropos of which Bovon (*Luke 3*, 91) comments, "We would say 'poor box.'" The term *gazophylakion* is a variant of the word found in Mark 12:43. On the "treasury," see further Marshall, *Luke*, 751, and Bovon, *Luke 3*, 94.

put in more than all of them; for all of them have contributed out of their abundance, but she out of her poverty has put in all she had to live on."[71]

Luke links this scene more closely than does Mark to the condemnation of the exploitive scribes. The reader must imagine Jesus as teaching near a spot where the treasury was located and being able to see[72] what alms various people were giving. The contrast throughout is between the rich and the poor widow. The rich are simply identified as being rich (*plousious*, v. 1), while her poverty is highlighted by means of the three different Greek terms that Luke uses to describe her impoverished condition, "poor" (*penikran*, v. 2[73]), "poor" (*ptōchē*, v. 3), and "poverty" (*hysterēmatos*, literally, "lack," v. 4). She is clearly the heroine of the story. The rich put in their gifts,[74] while the impoverished widow put in her "two cents," her *lepta duo*, the smallest coins then in circulation and all that she had. Without condemning the rich,[75] Jesus commends the poor widow for her total generosity. They gave their loose change; she gave all that she had.

Jerusalem Conflicts

This overview of Luke's use of Markan material pertaining to wealth, wages, and the wealthy would not be complete without mention of two tense scenarios in Jerusalem, accounts of which the third evangelist took over from the oldest of the canonical gospels.

---

[71] Luke 21:1-4.

[72] With his use of *eiden*, "saw," Luke portrays Jesus as an observer of what was going on. Commentators generally note that Jesus' superhuman knowledge enabled him to know what people were putting into the treasury.

[73] This word is used in the New Testament just this once.

[74] Using a more general expression, *ta dōra autōn*, "their gifts," than does Mark, Luke downplays the amount of the rich persons' offerings.

[75] There is no need to take these "rich" to be the scribes of Luke 20:47, nor is there any need to read Jesus' words as if they were intended to criticize a practice of the temple. The catchword mentions of a "widow" and "the temple" lead to the placement of the scene at this juncture in the Markan narrative, followed closely by Luke.

The first is the parable of the Wicked Tenants,[76] a story of greed that leads to violence and murder. Luke has simplified the account of the number of victims who suffered at the hands of the malefactors, but he has retained the thrust of the story as he writes about a series of victims, beginning with a slave who is maltreated and ending with the son who is killed.[77] Luke has, however, added one telling remark. After his Jesus describes the punishment that the owner of the vineyard metes out to the perpetrators of so much evil, Luke writes, "When they heard this, they said, 'heaven forbid.'"[78] "No way," our contemporaries might say. Those who heard Jesus tell this story, including those to whom his telling of the story was ultimately directed,[79] were incredulous. They could or would not believe that God would punish greedy people who resorted to murder and violence. Of the three Synoptics, Luke is the only one to add this comment, but he wants his readers to know that some people find the idea that God will severely punish greed, violence, and murder preposterous.

The second scenario is that of the controversy over paying taxes to the emperor.[80] Luke's telling of the story substantially follows Mark, but he has increased the intrigue and drama of the controversy with an introduction of his own crafting: "So they watched him and sent spies who pretended to be honest, in order to trap him by what he said, so as to hand him over to the jurisdiction and authority of the governor." Absent from the scene are Mark's and Matthew's Pharisees and Herodians; in their place is a bevy of anonymous spies (*paratērēresantes*[81]) sent by the scribes and chief priests.[82] Their mission was political. They were to trap Jesus so that the scribes and

---

[76] Luke 20:9-19; Mark 12:1-12; Matt 21:33-46.

[77] Luke has also omitted manifest allusions to Isaiah 5 found in Mark and Matthew.

[78] Luke 20:16b. "Heaven forbid" is the NRSV's rendering of the Greek *mē genoito*, literally, "may it not be." The expression, used by Paul (Rom 3:4, 6; 6:15; etc.) but nowhere else in the gospels, was a feature of Hellenistic diatribe. Cf. Epictetus, *Diatr.* 1.1.13; 1.8.15.

[79] Cf. Luke 20:19; compare with Luke 20:9.

[80] Cf. Luke 20:26; Mark 12:13-17; Matt 22:15-22.

[81] Four of the six uses of this verb in the New Testament are found in Luke–Acts; cf. Luke 6:7; 14:1; Acts 9:24.

[82] Cf. Luke 20:19.

chief priests would have evidence that would warrant their handing Jesus over to the governor, Pontius Pilate.

Luke's account of the controversy itself is similar to that of Mark, but it is somewhat shortened and admits of some Lucan editorial modifications. Luke's concluding comment builds on Mark's and echoes the political overtones of his introduction: "And they [the spies] were not able in the presence of the people to trap him by what he said; and being amazed by his answer, they became silent."[83] Luke draws attention to the utter failure of the mission of the spies. Bovon opines, "Luke . . . delights in noting the inability . . . of the people he had disqualified from the very beginning."[84] The spies were shocked. Not only were they amazed, but they also fell silent (*esigēsan*). In legal matters—and Luke certainly describes the scene as one dealing with law and its political consequences—silence means consent.[85] In public, the taciturn spies are presented as if they were compelled to agree with Jesus' judicious verdict.[86]

Luke's Use of the Markan Material: A Brief Reflection

Luke's story of Jesus does not include Mark's discussion of the tradition of the elders, with its condemnation of a perverse use of the Corban offering, and the ensuing instruction of the disciples.[87] Why? We do not know, although one can speculate that the evangelist might have found that material too rooted in Jewish practice for his Hellenistic readership to fully appreciate. For the rest, he faithfully reproduced the Markan tradition on wealth and the wealthy, adding a few biting comments here and there. His reading of the Gospel of Mark lets his readers know how he understands Jesus' teaching on the rich and their riches.

Luke's Use of the Sayings Source

Further insight into Luke's understanding of this teaching is to be gleaned from the passages that he took over from the Sayings

---

[83] Luke 20:26; cf. Mark 12:17b, "And they were utterly amazed at him."
[84] Bovon, *Luke 3*, 54.
[85] Thus Cicero, *taciturnitas imitatur confessionem.* Cf. *Invention* 1.32.54.
[86] See, nonetheless, Luke 23:2.
[87] Cf. Mark 7:1-23.

Source, Q. Study of these passages is a bit more difficult than was our examination of the Markan material since we do not possess a manuscript of the Sayings Source. What we have is a scholarly consensus on the sometime existence of Q based on a comparison of the sayings material in Matthew and Luke. These same scholars are of the opinion that Luke has preserved the material in a more pristine form than did Matthew. With this in mind, we can proceed to look at what Luke has to say about wealth, wages, and the wealthy in the material that he has taken from Q. All told, this material consists of five short sayings and two short stories.

Giving to Beggars (Luke 6:30)

Matthew inserted four of the Q sayings on riches into the Sermon on the Mount. Only one of them, the logion on giving to beggars,[88] found its way into the parallel discourse in Luke, the Sermon on the Plain.[89] Luke scatters the other sayings throughout his story, generally finding a strategic location in which to place them. We can begin with the saying found in the Sermon on the Plain: "Give to everyone who begs from you; and if anyone takes away your goods, do not ask for them again."[90]

The second part of the saying has to do with a thief.[91] It is at home in a section that deals with love of enemies,[92] illustrated with examples of how to react to a slap in the face and the robbery of one's possessions. The first part of the saying, "Give to everyone who begs from you," is of a different order. It calls for continuous giving and urges that one's generosity be extended to every beggar. The radical command—more radical in Luke's formulation than in its Matthean parallel—illustrates the absolute character of the prophetic charter that is the Sermon on the Plain.[93]

---

[88] Cf. Luke 6:30; Matt 5:42; see above, pp. 113–16.

[89] Luke 6:17-49.

[90] Luke 6:30.

[91] Cf. *Did.* 5:1. The Gnostic *Gospel of Thomas* modifies the saying so that it pertains to someone who has borrowed something. Cf. *G. Thom.* 95.

[92] Luke 6:27-36.

[93] Cf. Johnson, *Luke*, 109.

"The absolute form of the command," notes Joseph Fitzmyer, "excludes any consideration of the person's background or condition or the purpose of the begging. Need must not encounter selfish reserve among disciples of the kingdom."[94] Bovon comments on the relevance of such sayings to Luke's audience as he writes, "His [Jesus'] sayings regain in Luke's time some of their original relevance, since property owners, and even rich people, now belong to the congregation of Christians."[95]

The Laborer Deserves to Be Paid (Luke 10:7)

There are relatively few passages in the New Testament that speak directly about wages, but the Q saying found in Luke 10:7 is so clear that even rich people should be able to understand it: "The laborer deserves to be paid." This principled bit of proverbial wisdom was so important for the early church that it is quoted three times, namely, in Matthew 10:10;[96] 1 Timothy 5:18; and Luke 10:7. In all three instances, the proverb is quoted in reference to those who preach the gospel. Even evangelists deserve a living wage.

Whereas Matthew incorporated the saying into the Missionary Discourse of Matthew 10,[97] Luke has deferred quoting the adage until Jesus' Exhortation to the Seventy Disciples.[98] Doing so, Luke has expanded its relevance beyond the narrow circle of the chosen Twelve. For him, the adage offers sufficient clarification as to why the missionary disciples should remain in the same house, eating and drinking whatever is given to them. The NRSV translates the Greek *axios ho ergatēs tou misthou autou* of Luke 10:7 and 1 Timothy 5:18 as "the laborer deserves to be paid."[99] The adage seems to be a popular

---

[94] Fitzmyer, *Luke I–IX*, 639.

[95] Cf. Bovon, *Luke 1*, 240.

[96] Cf. Matt 10:10b. See above, pp. 121–23.

[97] Matt 10:1-17; cf. Luke 9:1-6.

[98] Luke 10:1-16.

[99] A more literal translation might be "the worker is worthy [*axios*] of his pay," a worker deserves to be paid. In contemporary American English, "laborer" generally connotes a low-skilled manual laborer, but the Greek *ergatēs* is not so restrictive. In fact, the root *erg-* was used throughout the New Testament in reference to the work of preaching the gospel. In 1 Thess 2:9 Paul uses the related verb to speak of his plying his leather-worker's trade.

saying in circulation prior to its incorporation into the Q source. That it is found verbatim in 1 Timothy, whose author would appear to have had no knowledge of Q,[100] attests not only to its independence but also to its importance for early Christian communities. The absence of a verb in the six Greek words attests to its proverbial character,[101] as does the post-positive *gar*, "for," in Luke 10:7c. It was a matter of common wisdom that laborers deserve to be paid. For the evangelists and for the anonymous disciple of Paul who wrote 1 Timothy, this truism was part of the gospel message.

What they deserve is their *misthos*, their wages. The ancient Greek word is found in writings as old as those of Homer.[102] It connotes fixed wages but was not limited to the wages of day laborers or ordinary workers. It was used for the fixed pay given to soldiers and sailors, to jurors and public advocates for a day's service, and for the fee to be paid to a physician. People in all sorts of work deserve adequate pay for the work that they do, the services that they render.

In Luke, the proverb is the punchline of Jesus' exhortation to the seventy disciples, "Remain in the same house, eating and drinking whatever they provide, for [*gar*] the laborer deserves to be paid." Luke's use of the proverb suggests that a worker deserves to be paid enough to have a roof over his head and the wherewithal to be able to eat and drink.

Forgive Us Our Sins, for We Ourselves Forgive Everyone Indebted to Us (Luke 11:4a)

The version of the Lord's Prayer found in Luke 11:2b-4 is shorter than the version found in Matthew 6:9b-13. It appears in a more natural setting in Luke than it does in Matthew. According to Luke, one of Jesus' disciples asked Jesus to teach them how to pray, just as John the Baptist had taught his disciples how to pray. Jesus' response to the disciple's request was the Lord's Prayer. It is truly the Lord's Prayer, and it is truly the disciples' prayer. It is the Lord's Prayer since

[100] *Pace* Luz (Luz, *Matthew 8–20*, 76n45) who, apropos 1 Tim 5:18, writes, "It is quite possible that Paul [*sic*] knew the saying in its Q form."
[101] Ps.-Phoc. 16; *Did.* 13.1-2, in dependence on Matt 10:10. Cf. 1 Cor 9:14.
[102] Cf. *LSJ*, s.v. *misthos*.

it was taught by Jesus himself. Since it is a prayer given to the disciples by the Lord himself, it is the Christian prayer *par excellence*, as so many fathers of the church were happy to note.[103] Matthew's version of the prayer is longer because it has been expanded by elements that were particularly meaningful for a Jewish Christian group.

The fourth petition of Luke's version of the prayer warrants consideration in this study: "And forgive us our sins, for we ourselves forgive everyone indebted to us."[104] The first part of this petition is a request addressed to the Father for the forgiveness of sins. The verb is in the aorist tense (*aphes*), indicative of a punctiliar action, something that happens once rather than an ongoing reality. Uttering the Lord's Prayer, the disciples of Jesus pray for a one-time forgiveness, rather than ongoing or repeated forgiveness. Thus, it is likely that the fourth petition of the Lord's Prayer is a request for forgiveness at the final judgment. This idea is confirmed in the next petition, which asks for deliverance at the eschaton: "And do not bring us to the time of trial."[105]

The fourth petition asks for the forgiveness of sins (*hamartias*) rather than the forgiveness of "debt" found in Matthew 6:12. Given the condition attached to the petition, it is likely that the Q version of the petition spoke of the forgiveness of debt and that Luke "clarified" the meaning of the petition by speaking about sins rather than debts.[106] Given that Matthew's gospel was in more common use in the church from about 200 CE until very recent times,[107] it is not surprising that in the Western tradition some manuscripts of the Lucan text[108] read "debts" (*opheilēmata*) rather than "sins" (*hamartias*),

---

[103] For example, see, Augustine, *Serm.* 56–59; *Serm. Dom.* 2.4.15–11.39. Tertullian (*Or.* 1) says that it is the summary of the entire gospel.

[104] Cf. Matt 6:12.

[105] Luke 11:4b.

[106] Cf. Marshall, *Luke*, 460–61; François Bovon, *Luke 2: A Commentary on the Gospel of Luke 9:51–19:57*, Hermeneia (Minneapolis: Fortress, 2013), 91.

[107] Thus, until the reform of the Roman liturgy after Vatican Council II, Matthew's gospel was read on more Sundays than the Gospels of Mark, Luke, and John combined.

[108] The Codex Bezae Cantrabridgensis (D) and the minuscule 2542. This reading of the Lucan text is reflected in many Old Latin and Vulgate versions of the text. Conversely, the language of "sin" is absent from the textual tradition of Matt 6:11.

undoubtedly under the influence of the more familiar Matthew 6:12.[109] The reading "sins" in Luke 11:4a indicates that the first part of the petition was on its way to being understood theologically, in which "debt" is a metaphor for "offense" or "sin." This is the way that most believers take the petition when they pray the Lord's Prayer individually or in a setting of community worship, but it may not be the original meaning of the petition.[110]

Sell Your Possessions and Give Alms (Luke 12:33-34)

The fourth logion that Luke has taken over from the Sayings Source appears in Luke 12:33-34. As the saying appears in its Matthean parallel,[111] the saying argues against the accumulation of wealth and concludes with what was, at one time, presumably a discrete logion:[112] "For where your treasure is, there your heart will be." In Luke, the Q saying appears in this fashion: "Sell your possession and give alms. Make purses for yourselves that do not wear out, and unfailing treasure in heaven where no thief comes near and no moth destroys. For where your treasure is, there your heart will be."

The concluding and seemingly out-of-place final adage and the previous references to the moth and the thief are sufficient indication to establish that Luke 12:33-34 and Matthew 6:19-21 derive from the same source, but Luke's editorial hand is clearly visible in the saying that appears in his gospel. In English translation, the supportive adage is the same in both Matthew and Luke, but in Luke the qualifying pronouns are in the plural rather than in the singular.[113] Luke apparently wanted the adage to be in the same number as the material to which it was appended.

---

[109] As with all the sayings in Q, the petition would have been handed down in an Aramaic oral tradition before being translated into Greek and consigned to a written form. In Aramaic, the same word, *hôbâ*, means both "debt" and "sin." Cf. Oakman, *Jesus, Debt, and the Lord's Prayer*, 75.

[110] See above, pp. 103–4.

[111] Cf. Matt 6:19-21; see above, pp. 116–18.

[112] Bovon notes that it "has the ring of a proverb." Cf. Bovon, *Luke 2*, 223.

[113] The twice-repeated *hymōn*, in the plural, rather than the double *sou*, in the singular, of Matt 6:21.

Luke's version of the logia is entirely positive, whereas Matthew's begins with a "you shall not," followed by a contrast. Luke opens the small literary unit with a clear and challenging command, "Sell your possessions and give alms." This kind of injunction is a key feature of Luke's theology;[114] he seems to have a special interest in almsgiving. His interest is consistent with the teaching of Greco-Roman philosophic moralists. Herodes Atticus, for example, the second-century CE sophist, aristocrat, and Roman senator, is said to have taught that the "right use of wealth means giving to the needy so that their needs might be met."[115] Almsgiving is a great antidote for greed, but as Herodes Atticus teaches, the purpose of almsgiving is to meet the needs of the poor.

Jewish tradition attached great importance to three kinds of good works: prayer, fasting, and almsgiving.[116] Judaism traces the practice of almsgiving back to the Torah, God's instruction for his people. Later Judaism considered almsgiving as one of the three pillars of the world, along with the Torah itself and temple service.[117] The Mishnah and later rabbinic literature hold that almsgiving brings a reward from God.[118] Luke has reworked the Q material so that he can imaginatively speak of this reward[119] in terms of purses that don't wear out—a striking metaphor on the part of the evangelist that is found only here in the New Testament.

The concluding adage "sums it all up," writes Fitzmyer.[120] Although there are loose parallels in the writings of the philosophic moralists,[121] none are as terse as Jesus' maxim.

Various forms of self-interest are powerfully seductive, but the Lucan Jesus urges his disciples to keep their hearts focused on heavenly treasure. Of itself, the proverbial maxim does not speak of a

---

[114] Cf. Luke 11:41; 14:33; 18:22.

[115] Cf. Philostratus, *Vit. soph.* 2.1.

[116] Cf. Matt 6:1-14. In this passage, Matthew cites almsgiving as the first of these pious activities.

[117] Cf. *m. 'Abot* 2:1.

[118] *Cf. m. Peah* 1:1; *b. Šabb.* 156b; *b. Roš. Haš.* 16b.

[119] Cf. Luke 6:35.

[120] Joseph A. Fitzmyer, *The Gospel According to Luke X–XXIV*, AB 28A (Garden City, NY: Doubleday, 1985), 982.

[121] Cf. Epictetus, *Diatr.* 2.22.19; Sextus Empiricus, *Pyr.* 1.136.

heavenly reward; it does so only in the Q context reflected by Matthew and Luke.

You Cannot Serve God and Wealth (Luke 16:13)

The last of the Q sayings on wealth to appear in the Lucan narrative is the well-known saying that speaks of God and mammon as if they were two masters in competition with one another for the loyalty of human beings. Personified mammon is an idolatrous power that one can serve instead of God.[122] Luke has strategically placed the saying as the climactic conclusion of a section of his narrative that Luke Timothy Johnson has called "Possessions in Parable and Paraenesis."[123]

The saying is one of the rare instances in which a Jesuanic logion appears in both Luke and Matthew[124] with such an exact similarity of wording. The sole difference is that Luke introduces the logion by writing about a "slave" (*oiketēs*)[125]—more precisely, a household slave—who cannot serve two masters.[126] Similarly a very early Christian text, the so-called second letter of Clement—in fact, an ancient and anonymous homily—comments, "Now the Lord says, 'No servant can serve two masters.' If we wish to serve both God and money, it is harmful to us."[127]

The Parable of the Invited Dinner Guests (Luke 14:16-24)

In addition to the various Q logia on wealth and the wealthy scattered at various points throughout his story about Jesus, Luke has incorporated into the Journey Section of his narrative two short

[122] Cf. Luke Timothy Johnson, *Sharing Possessions: What Faith Demands*, 2nd ed. (Grand Rapids: Eerdmans, 2011), 57.

[123] Johnson, *Luke*, 343.

[124] Cf. Matt 6:24; see above, pp. 118–21.

[125] This Lucan term—two of the four uses of this term in the New Testament are in Luke–Acts (Acts 10:7; Rom 14:4; 2 Pet 2:18)—links the logion to the preceding story of the dishonest manager (*oikonomos* in Luke 16:1, 3, 8).

[126] Cf. Luke 16:13a.

[127] *2 Clem.* 6.1, as translated in Michael W. Holmes, *The Apostolic Fathers in English*, 3rd ed. (Grand Rapids: Baker Academic, 2006), 79.

stories focused on economic concerns that come from the Sayings Source. These are the parable of the Invited Dinner Guests in Luke 14:15-24[128] and the parable of the Ten Pounds in Luke 19:11-27.

Luke heavily redacted the material in the Sayings Source[129] so as to create in the parable of the Invited Dinner Guests a story that is uniquely his own. Absent from Luke's version of the story is the hostility and violence found in Matthew's rendition. For Luke, the story is about money. It features the economic concerns of the original invitees and the attitude of the man[130] who wanted to share a sumptuous meal with his friends.

From the outset, Luke provides more details about the invitation and the varied responses to it than does Matthew. Using direct address, the evangelist describes three people offering excuses for their refusal to accept an invitation[131] to the solemn dinner: "The first said to him [the slave who conveyed the invitation], 'I have bought a piece of land, and I must go out and see it; please accept my regrets.' Another said, 'I have bought five yoke of oxen and I am going to try them out; please accept my regrets.' Another said, 'I have just been married, and therefore I cannot come.'"[132] Within a Jewish context, this third excuse may be understandable. Within the culture, newlyweds were exempt from several important social obligations.[133]

The third invitee doesn't offer any apology; he simply states that he is unable to attend the dinner. The other two offer their regrets. Their commercial interests—a desire to check out recent purchases—provide the grounds for their refusals to accept the invitation. Strangely, each of the two wants to see the purchase after it has been made.

---

[128] Cf. Matt 22:1-10; see above, pp. 124–25.

[129] According to Robinson and Hoffman, only verses 16-18, 19-20, and 23 can be attributed to Q.

[130] *Anthrōpos tis* in the Greek of Luke 14:15. In Matthew's allegorized version of the story, the host is a king who has organized a wedding banquet. Cf. Matt 22:2.

[131] Parsons, referencing Plutarch ("Dinner of the Seven Wise Men" 2 [*Moralia* 147E]), Appuleius (*Metam.* 3.12), and Esther (Esth 5:8), suggests that "Come; for everything is ready now" (v. 17b) is a kind of double invitation common in elite circles at that time. Cf. Mikeal C. Parsons, *Luke*, Paideia Commentaries on the New Testament (Grand Rapids: Baker Academic, 2015), 227.

[132] Luke 14:18b-20.

[133] Cf. Deut 24:5.

Perhaps the sale had been negotiated by a third party, an agent, or perhaps the completion of the sale had been made contingent on a later inspection and approval.[134] Whatever the circumstances, their commercial interests led the pair to turn down the invitation.

The threefold rejection of the invitation was a major affront to the host. He was dishonored[135] and angered. He had really wanted to have a full house.[136] In anger, he solemnly declared, "For I tell you,[137] none of those who were invited will taste my dinner."

Two relatively minor points in Luke's narrative deserve further comment. The man who had purchased the field (*agron*) said that he was under some pressure (*anankēn*)[138] to see the field. Compelling financial concerns led to his declining the offered invitation. The second man had purchased five yoke of oxen. This was a man of some means, someone who was in agribusiness. One or two yoke of oxen were enough for the typical small farmer of that time to work his land.[139]

Luke's version of the parable is more detailed than is Matthew's in describing how commercial interests interfere with accepting an invitation—God's invitation in a theological reading of the parable—to join a willing and eager host at dinner. In the words of T. W. Manson, "The claims of mammon take precedence."[140]

The Gnostic *Gospel of Thomas* continues and develops the trajectory of commercial excuses found in Luke:

> He came to the first and said to him, "My master invites you."
> He said to him, "I have bills for some merchants. They are coming to me this evening. I will go and give instructions to

---

[134] Marshall, *Luke*, 589.

[135] The affront was all the more egregious in a society in which honor and shame constituted the poles of social interaction.

[136] Cf. Luke 14:21b, 53c.

[137] This introductory phrase, similar to "Amen, I say to you," indicates that the following dictum represents Jesus' judgment on the reprehensible behavior.

[138] The NRSV translates the Greek, *echō anankēn*, literally, "I have pressure," "I am under constraint," as "I must." Cf. Luke 23:17; 1 Cor 7:37; Heb 7:27.

[139] Cf. Joachim Jeremias, *The Parables of Jesus*, 2nd ed. (New York: Scribner, 1963), 177.

[140] T. W. Manson, *The Sayings of Jesus* (London: SCM, 2012), 130.

them. Excuse me for the dinner." He came to another and
said to him, "My master has invited you." He said to him, "I
have bought a house, and I have been called away for a day. I
will not have time." He went to another and said to him, "My
master invited you." He said to him, "My friend is going to
marry, and I am the one who is going to prepare the meal. I
will not be able to come. Excuse me for the dinner." He came
to another and said to him, "My master invites you." He said
to him, "I have bought a village. Since I am going to collect
the rent, I will not be able to come. Excuse me."[141]

This Gnostic version of the story increases the number and nature of
the excuses. There are now four excuses. All of them suggest an urban
rather than a rural setting, and all of them have to do with monetary
interests. They feature a bill collector, a house buyer, a caterer,[142] and
someone rich enough to own a whole village who wanted to collect
his rent from the inhabitants.

A disdain for material wealth characteristic of the Gnostic tradition is reflected in the *Gospel of Thomas*'s expanded version of the
responses to the invitation, but this later text is at one with the canonical texts in portraying financial interests as preventing people
from accepting a generously offered invitation to dinner.

Luke's version of the parable of the Invited Dinner Guests adds an
important coda. The dishonored man sends his servant throughout
the town to invite the poor, the crippled, the blind, and the lame to
the great dinner that had been prepared. These were marginalized
folks who had no way to reciprocate their host's generous invitation.
But there were still empty places at table. So the master sent the
servant out of town to invite the social outcasts to be found outside
of town. The group might have included prostitutes and beggars[143]
who gathered at the entrance to town. These had to be convinced to

[141] G. *Thom.* 64:2-9. Fitzmyer is of the opinion that this version of the story
comes closer to what might have come from the lips of Jesus himself. Cf. Fitzmyer, *Luke X–XXIV*, 1051.

[142] The shift from someone who was recently married to someone who was
taking care of the wedding dinner is striking, though the reader does not necessarily have to envision the respondent as a commercial caterer.

[143] Cf. Parsons, *Luke*, 228.

come. Their natural reticence to accept an invitation to such a great social event had to be overcome.[144]

This coda, found in Luke alone, offers an example for the disciples of Jesus to follow. In Luke's narrative, the parable of the Invited Dinner Guests follows immediately after Jesus' striking exhortation to a man who had invited him to dinner: "When you give a banquet, invite the poor, the crippled, the lame, and the blind. And you will be blessed because they cannot repay you for you will be repaid at the resurrection of the righteous."[145] Those who have the wherewithal to plan a great dinner are to make sure that the poor, the crippled, the lame, and the blind—those who are socially marginalized—are properly fed. Rather than succumb to what Parsons calls "the vicious circle of reciprocity,"[146] Jesus urges that those who are needy in various ways are to be invited to the banquet. The notion is integral to Luke's recounting of the parable of the Invited Wedding Guests.

The Parable of the Ten Pounds (Luke 19:11-27)

John Kilgallen describes this story as "The Parable about Three Servants and the Final Judgment,"[147] while Mikeal Parsons calls it "The Parable of the Evil Tyrant."[148] The different titles call attention to the different motifs that are intertwined in the story.

The origin of the tale is to be found in the Sayings Source, which includes a story about a rich man who entrusts some of his assets to his servants to take care of while he is away on a journey. In Luke, the rich man tells his servants that they are to make money on his behalf while he is away.[149] While there are only three servants in the

---

[144] The verb "compel" (*anankason*) in v. 23 means to "persuade by compelling argument," as it does in Matt 14:22 and Mark 6:45. Cf. Fitzmyer, *Luke X–XXIV*, 1057.

[145] Luke 14:13-14.

[146] Parsons, *Luke*, 227. The poor, crippled, lame, and blind are contrasted with the friends, siblings, relatives, and rich neighbors of v. 12. There are four groups of people in each of the two listings. The contrast between the rich neighbors (*geitonas plousious*) and the poor (*ptōchous*) is the lynchpin of the chiasm.

[147] Kilgallen, *Twenty Parables*, 157.

[148] Parsons, *Luke*, 280.

[149] Cf. Luke 19:13c. The Matthean parallel does not contain any directive to the servants. They are presumed to know what their master expects of them.

Matthean story,[150] Luke's version speaks of ten servants. All told, the rich man entrusts ten "pounds" to the servants, one pound to each servant. Relatively speaking, the amount is a pittance. A "pound" (*mna*)[151] was the equivalent of one hundred drachmas, about one-sixtieth of a talent, the amount of money featured in Matthew's story. That only three of the servants are called to give an account of their financial endeavors confirms the Q provenance of the story. That the first servant is able to gain a tenfold profit is even more incredible than is the doubling of the entrusted sums found in Matthew. Strikingly, the third servant is not subject to a physical punishment as is the third servant in Matthew's version of the story.[152] His punishment is that the pound with which he had been entrusted is taken away from him and given to the servant with ten pounds. A telling commentary, echoing the wisdom of the ages, follows thereafter: "To all those who have, more will be given; but from those who have nothing, even what they have will be taken away."[153]

As told by Luke, the tale of the ten pounds has been allegorized with a not-so-subtle reference to the story of Archelaus traveling to Rome after the death of his father, Herod the Great, in order to ensure his succession to the throne. The native population of Palestine was opposed to Archelaus's rule. A fifty-member delegation traveled to Rome in an effort to prevent Archelaus from acquiring the crown.[154] Augustus's compromise was to name Archelaus "ethnarch" but not "king." Most probably, the increased number of servants in the story corresponds to the social status of Archelaus, evoked in verses 12, 15, and 27.

---

[150] Cf. Matt 25:14-30; see above, pp. 126–29.

[151] Fitzmyer says that the *mna* would have been worth about $25.00 and that Mark Antony was considered as stingy because he gave a gift of less than two *mna*s. See Fitzmyer, *Luke X–XXIV*, 1235, with reference to Appian, *Bell. civ.* 3.42. The word, which appears nine times in this parable, does not appear elsewhere in the New Testament.

[152] Cf. Matt 25:30.

[153] Luke 19:26; cf. Matt 25:29. The proclamation appears here in a more natural setting than it did in the isolated logion of Luke 8:18 (cf. Mark 4:25; Matt 13:12), where it is seemingly out of place. Luke found the saying in two of his sources, Mark and Q.

[154] Cf. Josephus, *Antiquities* 17.9.1-3; 11.1-2; *War* 2.2.2; 6.1-2.

If the first two levels of the story are about the use of money and the profit to be gained from it and the opposition of a restless people to a new king, the third level is about judgment. Those who rejected the kingly rule of the previously absent nobleman are to be severely punished; they are sentenced to death. "It seems clear," writes Kilgallen, "to identify Jesus as the master who went away to a far-off place to receive a crown only to come back [at the Parousia] for judgment."[155]

Given the complex nature of the Lucan story, it is difficult to draw from it any precise teaching on wealth, wages, and the wealthy with perhaps one exception, which is that even modest amounts of money are to be gainfully used in the time that exists between now and the Parousia.

Luke's Special Material

Luke's special material gives further insight into his theology in regard to wealth, wages, and the wealthy. One of the antithetical statements in the Sermon on the Plain in Luke 6:20-38 is particularly striking.

Woe to You Who Are Rich (Luke 6:24)

One of the peculiarities of the third gospel is a series of four woes[156] that antithetically parallel Luke's short collection of beatitudes.[157] Woes are found in the Hebrew Bible, particularly in the prophetic literature, where they express calamity or displeasure. Luke has adapted the literary form to his own use,[158] clarifying and strengthening his four beatitudes by means of these antithetical statements. The woes are threatening in nature. They are directed to the privileged members

---

[155] Kilgallen, *Twenty Parables*, 164.
[156] Cf. Luke 6:24-26.
[157] Cf. Luke 6:20-23.
[158] Scholarly debate as to whether these woes are traditional or the products of Luke's redactional work continues to this day. Dupont's magisterial three-volume study of the Beatitudes considers that the woes are a product of Luke's literary invention. Cf. Jacques Dupont, *Les Béatitudes*, vol. 1, *Ebib* (Paris: Gabalda, 1969), 299–342.

of Jesus' audience, the rich, well fed, carefree, and those well spoken of, and emphasize the ephemeral nature of such privilege.[159]

The first antithetical pairing is "Blessed are you who are poor,[160] for yours is the kingdom of God. . . . But woe to you who are rich, for you have received your consolation" in Luke 6:20, 24. Daniel Marguerat notes that the woe of Luke 6:24 is a kind of funeral lamentation.[161] Pronouncing a woe upon the rich, Luke's Jesus laments that the rich are on their way to death.[162] They are to be excluded from the kingdom of God, as the antithesis with the preceding beatitude suggests.

The antithesis clearly illustrates Luke's attitude toward the rich and the poor. The poor are those of whom God takes care, as seen in Jesus' many ministrations to the poor and marginalized. On the other hand, the rich enjoy wealth and power and, as Johnson suggests, "a sense of arrogance that does not require the visitation of God."[163] Mistakenly, the wealthy and relatively affluent think that they can make it on their own. The Lucan contrast of beatitude and woe proclaims that this is not the case.

The importance of the antithesis between rich and poor in Luke's narrative should not be overlooked. On the one hand, it harkens back to and repeats the message of Luke 1:52-53 in a different literary form. On the other hand, it anticipates the moving story of the Rich Man and Lazarus.[164]

Lending without Reciprocity (Luke 6:34)

Some few verses later on in the Sermon on the Plain, Luke reports that Jesus said, "If you lend to those from whom you hope to receive,

---

[159] Cf. Fitzmyer, *Luke I–IX*, 636. Luke betrays his conviction about the ephemeral nature of possessions in his revision of Mark 4:25b. Luke writes, "And from those who do not have, even *what they seem to have* [*ho dokei echein*] will be taken away" (Luke 8:14c). Cf. Luke 1:53.

[160] Luke's *hoi ptōchoi*, "poor," clearly designates people who belong to a lower socioeconomic class. Matthew's better-known and secondary *hoi ptōchoi tō pneumati*, "poor in spirit" (Matt 5:3), describes people with a religious attitude, similar to that of the biblical *anawim*.

[161] Cf. Marguerat, *Dieu et l'argent*, 28.

[162] Cf. Jas 5:1.

[163] Johnson, *Luke*, 108.

[164] Luke 16:19-31; see below, pp. 181–83.

what credit [*charis*] is that to you? Even sinners lend to sinners, to receive as much again."[165] Calculating generosity in giving to others has no place in the lives of the disciples of Jesus; giving with no expectation of a monetary return is a trait that distinguishes Jesus' disciples from those whom he characterizes as "sinners" (*hamartōloi*).

Take Care of Him (Luke 10:35)

The parable of the Good Samaritan in Luke 10:25-37, a moving and hauntingly contemporary parable, is found only in Luke. It's a story about being a neighbor, told by Jesus in response to the question, "Who is my neighbor?"[166]

Amy-Jill Levine asks: What does Luke 10:35—"The next day he [the Samaritan] took out two denarii, gave them to the innkeeper, and said, 'Take care of him; and when I come back, I will repay you whatever more you spend'"—contribute to the parable?[167] She responds to her question by saying that the Samaritan has money and that a benevolent reading of the Samaritan's final actions understands him as providing not one-time aid, but long-term care.

Luke does not tell us that the traveling Samaritan was particularly rich. At most, the reader knows that the Samaritan was affluent enough to have a beast of burden with which to travel and sufficient funds to pay for the care of an injured person, who was alien to the Samaritan. The Samaritan appears to have been envisioned as a businessman because he was going to make a return trip. His down payment on the injured man's care was equivalent to two days' wages, real money but not an extravagant amount. If additional sums were required for the injured man's care, he would repay on his way back to Samaria.

Using his riches, however limited they may have been, allows Jesus' interlocutor and today's reader of the Lucan story to conclude that the Samaritan had shown himself to be a neighbor, someone who had fulfilled Leviticus 19:18, one of the two pillars on which the

[165] Luke 6:34.
[166] Luke 10:29.
[167] See Luke 10:2; Levine, *Short Stories*, 103.

entire law and the prophets depend.[168] Doing so, he was, on Jesus' own assurance, expected to live,[169] unlike the rich fool and the rich man of Luke 16:19-31whose fate was death.[170]

The Pharisee and the Tax Collector (Luke 18:9-14)

Another long story that Luke has used from his proper source and that is of some pertinence to this study on wealth is the parable of the Pharisee and the Tax Collector. Jesus told this story to a group of people who considered themselves righteous and held others in contempt.[171] The parable contrasts two caricatures, further distinguished by the places that they take in the temple, their attitudes, and their prayers. The evangelist does not explicitly describe the Pharisee as a rich man. Nonetheless, the reader might consider the story to be one of Luke's tales about rich people if he or she breaks through the gospel caricature of the Pharisee and embraces the social caricature of the tax collector.

Most contemporary readers of the New Testament have an image of the Pharisees that is largely based on Matthew's negative description of them.[172] Luke's description of the Pharisees is still negative but less intensely so.[173] One trait in the Lucan literary portrait of the Pharisees is that they were "lovers of money" (*philargyroi*[174]). This is hardly an accurate reflection of the Pharisees of Jesus' day;[175] rather, it represents the anti-Pharisaic polemic of the early Palestinian gospel tradition. In fact, the Pharisees were adherents of a popular religious movement known for its fidelity to the law. Josephus identified the

---

[168] Cf. Luke 10:27; Matt 22:39-40.

[169] Cf. Luke 10:28.

[170] Cf. Luke 12:20; 16:22-23. See also Luke 6:24a, where an implied death threat is addressed to those who are rich.

[171] Cf. Luke 18:9. Luke Timothy Johnson (*Luke*, 273) says that the parable is addressed "to those unmistakably identifiable as Pharisees," but this interpretation only adds to the negative caricature of the Pharisees.

[172] See, among many places, Matthew 23.

[173] Cf. Luke 5:29-32; 11:16-54; 16:14-15.

[174] The term is hapax in the canonical gospels but is found in 2 Tim 3:2; cf. 1 Tim 6:10.

[175] Cf. Bovon, *Luke 2*, 463.

group as one of the three "philosophies" of the Jews, one in which he himself seems to have had a real interest at one time. Charging intellectual opponents with being lovers of money was a common feature of Hellenistic rhetoric.[176]

What characterizes the Pharisee of Jesus' parable, in addition to the literary contrast with the tax collector, is his supererogatory religiosity and his disdain for others. In his prayer, apparently heard by no human other than himself, he averred that he fasted twice a week and that he paid a tithe on all his income. Both works of piety were above and beyond. Although fasting was an esteemed work of piety in first-century Judaism, mandatory fasting was limited to a few days, such as the Day of Atonement.[177] Deuteronomy 26:12 prescribed a tithe of produce to be given to the Levites, aliens, orphans, and widows every third year, but a tithe on one's entire income was unheard of.[178] By his own confession, this Pharisee was an honest man, generous beyond a fault.

The Pharisee introduced the rehearsal of his own better-than-usual conduct with a negative portrayal of others: "God, I thank you that I am not like other people, thieves [*harpages*], rogues [*adikoi*], adulterers, or even like this tax collector."[179] He may have been correct in his assumption that he had not violated the law;[180] he had, nonetheless, a manifest disdain for others. Not only did he talk about the anonymous group of others—"them" in contemporary parlance—as dishonest, unjust, and sexually immoral; he also looked down on the tax collector (*telōnēs*) who happened to be with him in the temple at the same time.

[176] See, with examples, Luke Timothy Johnson, *The First and Second Letters to Timothy*, AB 35A (New York: Doubleday, 2001), 296.

[177] Cf. Lev 16:19-21; Num 29:7. See also Zech 8:19.

[178] Cf. Luke 11:42 and Matt 23:23, a Q logion, in which Jesus addresses a woe to the Pharisees, castigating them for tithing mint, rue, and cumin while not paying attention to the weightier demands of the law. This woe echoes Amos 4:4, which speaks of those who tithe every three days. Among early Christian communities, as a monetary economic system was developing, money became subject to tithing. Cf. *Did.* 13:7.

[179] Luke 18:11.

[180] Cf. Luke 18:20-21.

At the time, people looked on a tax collector as someone despicable for two prominent reasons. First and foremost, the tax collector was a traitor to his own nation; he collected taxes on behalf of an occupying foreign power. He worked for a government that exploited the temple system. Second, his corruption was presumed to be a given. He made his money by means of a surcharge added to the taxes that were due. That was the system, but it was prone to corruption and the exploitation of those lacking the power to protest. Because of his profession and the way that the profession was looked on, people, including the Pharisee in the temple, would have considered him to be a sinner,[181] as the tax collector himself confessed in his prayer.[182]

The tax collector's problem is, in the words of A.-J. Levine, "that he is a sinner, probably rich, an agent of Rome, and as a tax collector, has likely shown no mercy to others." Luke apparently assumes that tax collectors were fairly affluent. He describes Levi, the tax collector who abandoned his profession in order to be a disciple of Jesus, as having the wherewithal to be able to throw a huge banquet.[183] He describes Zacchaeus, a chief tax collector in Jericho, as a rich man.[184]

The parable of the Pharisee and the Tax Collector is not primarily about wealth, but it does contrast two individuals with some indication of how they dealt with their money. The Pharisee was perhaps overly generous in his tithing, but his loathing of others won him no favor in the Lord's eyes. The tax collector may have made his money by means of some extortion, but he is justified in the Lord's eyes because of his humility in the presence of God.

Stories about Rich Men

One of the features of Luke's gospel is the number of stories that he tells about men who are rich. The evangelist has incorporated

---

[181] Cf. Luke 19:7.

[182] Cf. Luke 18:13.

[183] Cf. Luke 5:29; see also Luke 7:36-50 where there is no mention of the size of the dinner. There are, however, other guests present. The anonymous woman's appearance at Jesus' feet suggests a fairly large house with an atrium.

[184] Cf. Luke 19:2.

these stories into his account of Jesus' Journey to Jerusalem,[185] a unique feature of the third gospel. Most of the Lucan stories about rich men are not to be found in the other Synoptic Gospels.[186] They come from "L," Luke's special material. Because they are so many and are so powerful, they merit discrete consideration in the present study. Taken together, these tales give the reader of his gospel an important perspective on the evangelist's view of the wealthy and the messes that they get into because of their wealth. As a group, they illustrate what Luke has to say about the rich in the *Magnificat* and the first of the woes.[187]

The Rich Fool (Luke 12:13-21)

The parable of the Rich Fool appears in a longer unit that Thomas Stegman has called an "elaborated" *chreia*.[188] The topic is greed. In ancient Hellenistic rhetoric, a *chreia* was a concise saying deemed valuable for life. It was often the conclusion to a longer narrative— its punchline, as it were—and attributed to one of the characters in the narrative.

Luke's long unit on avarice[189] begins with the story of the rich fool. There are two parts to the story, its setting and the parable itself. Each section concludes with a potent statement. "Take care! Be on your guard against all kinds of greed; for one's life does not consist in the abundance of possessions"[190] is one. "You fool! This very night your life is being demanded of you. And the things you

---

[185] Luke 9:51–19:27.

[186] The one exception is the story of the rich young man, Luke 18:18-25, examined above, pp. 146–48. This story comes from Luke's Markan source rather than from Luke's special material. Unlike the stories found in Luke's special material, the story of the young man does not indicate at the outset of the story that he is rich (cf. Luke 18:25), whereas the stories that come from Luke's special material have that distinctive trait.

[187] Cf. Luke 1:53; 6:24.

[188] See Thomas D. Stegman, "Reading Luke 12:13-34 as an Elaboration of a Chreia: How Hermogenes of Tarsus Sheds Light on Luke's Gospel," *NovT* 49 (2007): 328–52, at 332.

[189] Luke 12:13-34.

[190] Luke 12:15.

have prepared, whose will they be? So it is with those who store up treasures for themselves but are not rich toward God"[191] is the other.

Greed was a common topos in ancient rhetoric. Many philosophic moralists condemned avarice in its various forms.[192] Avarice often[193] appeared in the catalogues of vices that they developed, and, as we have seen, the vice has achieved its merited place in the New Testament's list of vices.[194] Luke's gospel does not include any lists of vices such as the one that accompanies the Corban discussion found in Mark and Matthew. Instead, Luke, competent Hellenistic author that he was, has an extended unit on greed that includes the parable of the Rich Fool.

The extended *chreia* begins with a little scene in which an anonymous "someone" (*tis*) asks Jesus to adjudicate a family dispute about an inheritance.[195] The scene described by Luke was not uncommon in the Greco-Roman world. People disputing with one another about an inheritance frequently appealed to an outside authority to arbitrate the dispute.[196] Calling Jesus "teacher" (*didaskale*), the interlocutor recognizes Jesus' authority. But Jesus rejects the role that he was being asked to fulfill. He would not intervene in a dispute between heirs who were siblings.

Jewish law mandated that a firstborn son receive a double share of the inheritance,[197] but neither Jesus nor Luke were interested in the nature of the disputed inheritance, nor were they interested in echoing the biblical tradition. Luke tells this story in order to provide a setting for Jesus' teaching on greed: "Take care! Be on your guard against all kinds of greed [*pasēs pleonexias*]; for one's life does not consist in the abundance of possessions." Verbs in the plural and Luke's introductory "And he said to them" (*eipen de pros autous*) show

[191] Luke 12:20-21.

[192] For example, Dio Chrysostom, "On Covetousness" (*Discourses* 17), and Plutarch, "On Love of Wealth" (*Moralia* 523C–528). See also Hellenistic Jewish writings such as Sir 11:18-19; *T. Jud.* 18-19. Cf. Spicq, "Pleonexia," *TLNT* 3:117–19.

[193] Mark 7:21; Matt 15:19. See above, p. 84.

[194] Cf. Mark 7:22; Rom 1:29; Eph 4:19; 5:3; Col 3:5.

[195] Luke 12:13-15.

[196] See, for example, Polemo in Philostratus, *Vit. soph.* 532. Cf. Peppard, "'Brother against Brother': Corinthians 6:1-11," *JBL* 133 (2014): 179–92.

[197] Cf. Deut 21:15-17; Num 27:1-11; 36:7-9.

that Jesus' teaching on greed was addressed to a wider audience; it was not intended merely as an answer to his interlocutor.

Jesus' "verdict" on wealth is similar to that of Plutarch, who wrote, "Nor is possessing luxuries the same as feeling no need of them."[198] Comparing insatiability and avarice to an almost incurable sickness, the philosopher continues, "He [the greedy person] will never cease to need superfluities—that is, to want what he does not need."[199]

The second part of the extended *chreia* consists of the parable of the Rich Fool. The owner was blessed with a particularly rich harvest, but instead of attributing his good fortune to God and sharing his unexpected wealth with the poor, the rich man dialogued within himself and decided to build a bigger silo so that he could keep his wealth. On two counts he had neglected God,[200] and so God appears, formally addressing him as a "fool" (*aphrōn*), someone who acted as if God did not exist.[201] "This very night," says God, "your life will be demanded of you."[202] The rich man of the story, who had so egregiously neglected God, is condemned to death.

Jesus comments on the short story that he has just told: "So it is with those who store up treasures for themselves but are not rich toward God."[203] In the eyes of the Lucan Jesus, greed is a capital offense. On the other hand, giving alms is a matter of gathering treasure in heaven.[204] Ultimately, the trouble with wealth is that it dispossesses God. As Sandra Wheeler observes, wealth "as a putative source of security . . . usurps God's role as source and measure and guarantor of life."[205]

---

[198] *Love of Wealth* 1 [*Moralia* 523E].

[199] *Love of Wealth* 3 [*Moralia* 524D].

[200] It is noteworthy that Col 3:5 formally equates greed with idolatry.

[201] Cf. Ps 14:1, "Fools say in their hearts, 'There is no God.'"

[202] Luke 12:20b; cf. Jas 1:10b-11; 4:13-14.

[203] Luke 12:22.

[204] Cf. Luke 12:33.

[205] Sandra Ely Wheeler, *Wealth as Peril and Obligation: The New Testament on Possessions* (Grand Rapids: Eerdmans, 1995), 81. Cf. Johnson, *Sharing Possessions*, 56; Thiselton, *First Epistle*, 429.

The Rich Man and the Dishonest Manager (Luke 16:1-8a)

At the beginning of an extended section on money and its consequences[206] is the story of a rich man and his dishonest manager. The
reader should think of some owner of a large estate somewhere in
Palestine. The estate was sufficiently large for the master to appoint
one of his slaves as manager[207] in charge of the property. Luke illustrates the rich man's wealth by the size of the debts that were owed
to him. The evangelist mentions only the hundred jugs of oil and the
hundred containers of wheat. Other debtors lie in the imaginative
background of the story, as the "one by one" (*hena hekaston*) of
verse 5 implies. It is of the nature of parables that only two or three
examples are given to illustrate the point. Further repetition would
be superfluous.

From patristic times the story has proven to be a poser for interpreters. Much of the discussion has focused on the interpretation
of the first part of verse 8. Who is the master, the *kyrios*, who commended the dishonest manager? Is it the rich man,[208] or is it Jesus
who is commenting on the story that he told? What is being praised?
Is it the fraudulent conduct of the dishonest manager or the fact that
he took action in a crisis situation? Although the answers to these
questions continue to be disputed, it is best to think of the rich man
as commending his servant for responding to the crisis of losing a
job.[209]

Mikeal Parsons opines that the Story of the Dishonest Manager
belongs to a body of stories about slaves as tricksters that were widely
circulated in the Greco-Roman world.[210] One such story is told about
Aesop, who was accused of stealing some figs.[211] Like Luke's story of

---

[206] Johnson (*Luke*, 243) entitles this section "Possessions in Parable and Paraenesis (Luke 16:1-13)."

[207] The Greek *oikonomos*, often translated as "steward," was generally a household slave who had a managerial role and was in charge of the other domestic
slaves.

[208] Cf. v. 5.

[209] Cf. Luke 16:2.

[210] Cf. Parsons, *Luke*, 247.

[211] Cf. *Life of Aesop* 3, cited by Mary Ann Beavis in "Ancient Slavery as an Interpretive Context for the New Testament Servant Parables with Special Reference
to the Unjust Steward (Luke 16:1-8)," *JBL* 111 (1992): 37–54, at 46.

the rich man and the dishonest manager, the ancient tale features a master, a slave, stealing, and accusations. In the older story, the tables are turned. The accused is exonerated; the accusers are found guilty. In Luke's story, the accused is proven to be guilty. He has been accused of squandering his master's property; he compounds his guilt by conspiring with his master's creditors to fraudulently reduce the size of their debts. That earns him the epithet "dishonest manager" (*ton oikonomon tēs adikias*)—literally, "a manager of dishonesty."[212] He is a self-serving scoundrel. He has violated the trust that has been placed in him.[213] No more needs to be said.

Appended to the story of the rich man and his dishonest manager, perhaps in a pre-Lucan stage of the gospel tradition, are three lessons or applications, verses 8b-9, 10-12, and 13.[214] The three sayings are tied together by a single catchword, "mammon." All three of them speak about wealth; the first two explicitly describe mammon as iniquitous. Among the three, the Q saying "You cannot serve God and wealth" appears in the climactic final position. The adage hits the nail on the head as far as Luke's understanding of riches is concerned.

Verses 8b-9. The first application adheres most closely to the story of the rich man and the dishonest manager. The words "shrewd" (*phronimōteroi*, v. 8b) and "dishonest" (*adikias*, v. 9) are verbal links between the application of the story and the parable itself, a story of a dishonest manager (*ton oikonomon tēs adikias*) who acted shrewdly (*phronimōs*). "For the children of this age are more shrewd in dealing with their own generation than are the children of light"[215] is Jesus'

---

[212] In New Testament studies, the qualitative genitive is often called a Hebraic genitive because of the Hebrew construct. A qualitative genitive is also found in the following verse where "dishonest wealth" is literally "the wealth of dishonesty" (*tou mammōna tēs adikias*). Cf. Luke 16:11.

[213] Columella, *Rust.* 11.1.7, stressed the importance of loyalty for a person with the responsibilities depicted by Luke. The second application of the parable, vv. 10-12, expands on the theme of loyalty with its threefold use of the adjective *pistos*, "faithful." See, further, 1 Cor 4:2 and Titus 1:6 relative to the loyalty expected of an *oikonomos*.

[214] Fitzmyer, *Luke X–XXIV*, 1105. Fitzmyer considers the first two applications as well as the story itself as having come to the evangelist via his special source.

[215] Luke 16:8b.

commentary on the story that he has told. The comment acknowledges that the devious behavior of the dishonest manager is different from the kind of behavior that is characteristic of Jesus' disciples, the children.

Then the Lucan Jesus adds a piece of paraenetic advice about the use of money: "And I tell you, make friends for yourselves by means of dishonest wealth [*mammōna tēs adikias*] so that when it is gone, they may welcome you into the eternal homes."[216] The evangelist's singular qualification of wealth as dishonest and unrighteous reflects the popular view that those who have money, particularly large amounts of money, have acquired it unjustly and will use it unjustly. The qualification also reflects the evangelist's view that money is an obstacle to a right relationship with God. It stands in the way of true righteousness, that is, a proper relationship with God and with others. The temporal clause, "when it is gone" (*hotan eklipē*), is another Lucanism. It expresses the evangelist's conviction that money and possessions are fleeting.[217]

With his solemn introduction, "And I tell you" (*kai egō hymin legō*), Luke underscores his intention that he wants his readers to view this announcement as coming from Jesus. The saying underlines the importance of almsgiving. The friends of whom Jesus speaks are those who have benefited from the alms of the wealthy.[218] Almsgiving earns a heavenly reward. The form of the saying is similar to that of Luke 12:33. There, the heavenly reward is symbolized by purses that do not wear out; here, it is symbolized by a heavenly welcome, presumably to the eschatological banquet. The "eternal homes"[219] are either the place where the righteous go at the time of their death or the place where the faithful are welcomed at the Parousia.[220]

Verses 10-12. The second application of the story of the rich man and his dishonest manager includes another mammon saying with-

---

[216] Luke 16:9.
[217] Cf. Luke 6:24; 8:14c. Marshall (*Luke*, 621) adds that the verb itself is probably Lucan.
[218] See Bovon, *Luke 2*, 450.
[219] Luke's "homes" is, literally, "tents" (*skēnas*), perhaps reflecting the biblical imagery of God tenting with his people (cf. John 1:14).
[220] Cf. Bovon, *Luke 2*, 451. For similar images, see John 14:22; 2 Cor 5:1-2.

out parallel in Matthew or Mark: "If then you have not been faithful with the dishonest wealth [*tō adikō mammona*], who will entrust to you the true riches?"[221] The saying is clearly Lucan. Of itself, wealth is a neutral reality; it is often understood to be a positive value. Yes, Luke describes wealth as unrighteous, just as it is in the preceding application. Mammon, wealth, is not only dishonest but also of little importance. The preceding verse implies that the evangelist considers mammon to be "very little."[222]

Furthermore, Luke's Jesus suggests in verse 12 that money really belongs to someone else, presumably God, to whom all created reality truly belongs.[223] Commenting on verse 12, Bovon writes that money is, in the eyes of the author, "a possession that is 'alien' to human beings, that we should learn to become independent of and to deprive ourselves of. The text powerfully states that money has a disastrous effect in that it alienates human beings from their true identity as God's creatures."[224]

The mammon logion in 16:11—"If you have not been faithful with the dishonest wealth, who will entrust to you the true riches?"—employs a conditional clause and a rhetorical question whose positive formulation begs a negative response. It contrasts a temporal reality, dishonest wealth, and a heavenly reality, true riches (*to alēthinon*). The contrast almost suggests that money is, after all, unreal. God is subtly introduced into the equation with the author's "who" (*tis*).[225] Those who do not use their money, God's money, in a way that is in keeping with their servant status cannot expect to receive a heavenly reward.

Verse 13. The third application sums up the lesson that Luke has been trying to develop throughout these thirteen verses: "No slave can serve two masters; for a slave[226] will either hate the one and love

---

[221] Luke 16:11. Cf. *2 Clem.* 8:5.
[222] See the Greek *elachistō* in Luke 16:10.
[223] Cf. Luke 20:24; Mark 12:17; Matt 22:22.
[224] Bovon, *Luke 2*, 461.
[225] Ibid.
[226] "Slave" does not appear in the Greek text at this point. The Greek uses verbs in the third-person singular, *misēsei* and *agapēsei*.

the other; or be devoted to the one and despise the other. You cannot serve God and wealth."[227] Devotion to wealth and the service of God are radically incompatible with each other.

On this note, Luke concludes a section of his story about Jesus that specifically focuses on money and its use. Luke has strong views on the subject. For the most part they are articulated in this section, but he has more to say on the subject as he tells other stories about rich men. Before telling these stories, Luke has gathered together a few scattered logia, including statements on the law and divorce.[228] He introduces the sayings by portraying the Pharisees, last seen in 15:2 and well known for their attention to the meaning of the law, as having heard what Jesus said about possessions. Jesus' teaching did not fall on deaf ears, for "the Pharisees, who were lovers of money, heard all this, and they ridiculed[229] him."[230]

The gospel tradition often shows the Pharisees disagreeing with Jesus, but this is the only place in which they are presented as scoffing at Jesus. The way that Luke describes them in this verse serves as a cipher that shows how difficult it is for those who hear Jesus' message about money and its use to accept it. Even presumably religious people, devoted to the law, find Jesus' teaching hard to take.

The evangelist characterizes the scoffing Pharisees as being "lovers of money" (*philagyroi*). This is the only time that Luke uses this characterization to describe the Pharisees. The characterization serves as a literary link to connect what follows with what came before. The love of money (*philagyria*[231]), being greedy, was one of the classic vices in Hellenistic moral thought. Opponents were readily

---

[227] See above, pp. 120–21 (Matt), 179 (Luke).

[228] My study *Divorce in the New Testament, GNS* 38 (Collegeville, MN: Liturgical Press, 1992) has recently been criticized for not paying attention to the impact of finances, for example, the dowry and the wealth of one's love, on divorce in the first century CE. Recent studies on Luke consider this issue and therefore deem the logion on divorce as appropriately located within the Lucan Narrative. Cf. John Nolland, *Luke 9:21–18:34,* WBC 35b (Waco, TX: Word, 1993), 821–22; Parsons, *Luke,* 249.

[229] The verb *exemyktērizon* evokes the image of Jesus' audience turning up their noses at him.

[230] Luke 16:14.

[231] Cf. 1 Tim 6:10; cf. 2 Tim 3:2.

characterized as being money-grubbers.[232] So it is with Luke's Pharisees. There were, of course, no Pharisees, a Palestinian group, in
Luke's Hellenistic readership. Here, "the Pharisees" stands for the
opponents of the Lucan gospel.

The Rich Man and Lazarus (Luke 16:19-31)

The story of the Rich Man and Lazarus is virtually a narrative
commentary on the antithetical beatitude and woe of Luke 6:20b, 24:
"Blessed are you who are poor, for yours is the kingdom of God. . . .
But woe to you who are rich, for you have received your consolation." One of the distinctive features of the parable is that two of the
characters in the story are named. Typically, Jesus' stories are told
in generic fashion, without any of the characters in the story being
named. That is not the case with this story.

The story begins with a presentation of its two main characters.
The first is the rich man (*anthrōpos . . . tis . . . plousios*[233]). We can
capture the flavor of Luke's story if we imagine it to begin, "Once
upon a time there was a rich guy." Rather than simply stating that
this anonymous someone was rich, Luke shares the tokens of his
richness with his readers. The rich man was clothed elegantly. His
attire was fit for a king.[234] And the rich man dined sumptuously. Luke
says that he "feasted" (*euphrainomenos lamprōs*) and that this was
an everyday occurrence (*kath 'hēmeran*).

There are two things that Luke does not say about the rich man.
First, he does not tell us his name. The Latin translation of "rich"
(*plousios*) is *dives*, which led the Latin church to call the anonymous
man Dives, as if the adjective were a proper name. Second, the evangelist does not say that the rich man's wealth was ill-gained, though
that would have been a popular assumption in Jesus' day. Luke simply
wants his readers to conjure up the image of a man living in the lap
of luxury.

---

[232] Dio Chrysostom, *Or.* 32.9; 35.1; Epictetus, *Diatr.* 1, 9, 19-20; Lucian, *Tim.* 56.
[233] This is the same formula as is found in Luke 16:1. The two characters are
alike in their insouciance. The rich fool is oblivious to God; the rich man in this
story is oblivious to the plight of the poor man outside his gate.
[234] Cf. Luke 7:25.

Contrasted with this rich man is a poor man (*ptōchos tis*), who is named. His name is Lazarus, a theophoric name that means "God helps." The symbolism of the name cannot be overlooked as the story unfolds. Lazarus lay at the gates of the rich man's property. Contrasted with the rich man's fine clothing is the covering of sores on the body of the poor man. The pain resulting from the sores was assuaged by the dogs who licked Lazarus's wounds. Contrasted with the rich man's fine dining is the poor man's hunger. He was so hungry that he longed to be able to eat the crumbs and table scraps that came from the rich man's table. Something that is not said about the poor man is any suggestion that his poverty was in any way the result of sin or misuse of what he might have once had.[235]

Eventually, the two men died. After his death, Lazarus, the poor man, was carried off to the bosom of Abraham.[236] After his death, the rich man received a proper burial but ended up in Hades, where he was tormented. He cried out to Abraham for succor. Abraham replied, "Child, remember that during your lifetime you received your good things, and Lazarus in like manner evil things; but now he is comforted here, and you are in agony."[237] Abraham's words echo the words of the beatitude of Luke 6:20 and its accompanying woe.[238]

In the story, no mention is made of how either man died. The evangelist highlights that the one was extravagantly rich, living in opulence, while the other lived in abject poverty. The woe is, however, a kind of funeral lamentation.[239] Pronouncing a woe upon the rich, Jesus laments that the rich are on their way to death. Such is the case of the rich man in this parable. His fate was death with its accompanying torments.

In what then might be seen as an appendix to the parable itself,[240] the dialogue between the deceased rich man and Abraham continues.

---

[235] In this respect Zacchaeus's hunger is quite unlike that of the Prodigal Son. Cf. Luke 15:13b-16.

[236] Abraham is the second individual who is named in the story.

[237] Luke 16:25.

[238] Cf. Luke 6:24.

[239] Cf. Marguerat, *Dieu et l'argent*, 28.

[240] Cf. Ernest van Eck, "When Patrons Are Not Patrons: A Social-Scientific Reading of the Rich Man and Lazarus (Lk. 16:19-26)," *Hervormd Teologiese Studies/ Theological Studies* 65 (2009): 4–5.

The rich man asked that Lazarus be sent to warn the rich man's living siblings. Abraham's response is classic. He did not refer to Jesus' woe and beatitude; there is no reason why the rich man might have been familiar with this teaching. Rather, Abraham told the still-tormented rich man, "They have Moses and the prophets; they should listen to them."[241]

Heeding the biblical tradition with its reiterated demand that the needs of the poor be taken care of as a first demand of justice is something that the rich man's brothers need to do. It is something that the rich man failed to do. He ignored the plight of the poor. He paid for this failure in the flames and torment that caused him to suffer so much.[242] The rich man may have earned his wealth in some morally acceptable manner; his sin was his failure to take care of the poor man at his doorstep. He had not obeyed the law of the Lord. So, woe to him; he had received his consolation in the fine clothes that he was able to wear and the great meals that he enjoyed during his lifetime.

Zacchaeus, the Rich Tax Collector (Luke 19:1-10)

The last of the Lucan stories about a rich man is the story of Zacchaeus, a wealthy tax collector. The story is memorable on several counts, not the least of which is the novelistic detail that the vertically challenged man climbed a tree in order to see Jesus. For the purposes of this study, the reader should note that the story is located in Jericho, a border town on the Jordan River. Located on the border, the city was one in which tax collectors—customs officers, in effect—were employed.[243]

Jesus takes the initiative in inviting himself into Zacchaeus's home. This stirs the indignation of the crowd, who grumble, "He

---

[241] Luke 16:29; cf. v. 31.

[242] The story's apocalyptic imagery should not distract the reader from the point of the story. The point is not "the pains of hell"; it is that failure to rescue the poor from the blight of their poverty will not go unpunished.

[243] Mark locates the scene of the tax collector's call to discipleship in Capernaum, a northern border town. Cf. Mark 2:1, 13-17. Luke omits this detail in his version of the story (Luke 5:27-28).

has gone to be the guest of one who is a sinner."[244] In the popular estimation, there was hardly any doubt that he was a sinner—for the two reasons that Luke suggests in his initial characterization of Zacchaeus. First, he was a tax collector, but not simply an ordinary tax collector; Zacchaeus was a chief tax collector (*architelōnēs*), a major collaborator with the Romans. Second, he was rich (*plousios*), presumably the possessor of ill-gotten wealth. That the object of their disdain was also short may have even added to their negative judgment.[245] He was just a little guy.

Defending himself to Jesus, Zacchaeus says, "Look, half of my possessions, Lord, I will give to the poor; and if I have defrauded anyone of anything, I will pay back four times as much."[246] Without having been asked to do so, he gives an account of his wealth. Although the NRSV translates the verbs (*didōmi and apodidōmi*) as if they were in the future tense, the verbs are in the present. This seems to indicate that Zacchaeus is talking about his habitual behavior.[247] On the other hand, as the NRSV translation suggests, Zacchaeus's words are often taken as if they articulate the resolution of a recent convert,[248] but is the story of Zacchaeus a conversion story? This discussion[249] is ultimately of little import to the present study.

What is important is that Zacchaeus, whether a righteous man or a new convert, is someone who acknowledges Jesus to be Lord[250] and knows what to do with his wealth. In this respect, he can serve as a

---

[244] Luke 19:7.

[245] Cf. Parsons, *Luke*, 278–79, 285–86.

[246] Luke 19:8.

[247] Alan Mitchell, who describes Zacchaeus as an Abraham-like figure because of his hospitality, identifies the two verbs in the present as iterative presents. Cf. Alan C. Mitchell, "Zacchaeus Revisited: Luke 19:8 as a Defense," *Bib* 71 (1990): 153–76; Fitzmyer, *Luke X–XXIV*, 1220–21.

[248] This requires that the present tense of the verbs be taken as futuristic presents. Cf. Dennis Hamm, "Luke 19:8 Once Again: Does Zacchaeus Defend or Resolve?," *JBL* 107 (1998): 431–37; "Zacchaeus Revisited Once More: A Story of Vindication or Conversion?," *Bib* 72 (1991): 248–52.

[249] A large part of the discussion of the encounter between Jesus and Zacchaeus focuses on the literary form of the story. In this regard, Bovon (*Luke 2*, 595) notes, "It can be viewed as a conversion, pardon, salvation, or controversy story."

[250] See the repeated *kyrios*, "Lord," in v. 8, once in Luke's narrative, once on the lips of Zacchaeus.

paradigm for the disciples of Jesus. Half of his wealth is shared with the poor. If he has defrauded anyone, he repays the amount that he has unjustly gained fourfold. The verb "defrauded" (*esykophantēsa*), used only by Luke in the New Testament,[251] is probably to be taken in its technical legal sense in a situation in which a tax collector, not obtaining what he had asked for, could take someone to court, perhaps even using false evidence, to get what he wanted.[252]

Zacchaeus's righteous use of his wealth earns Jesus' commendation: "Today salvation has come to this house, because he too is a son of Abraham."[253] According to the Lucan Jesus, the righteous use of wealth is key to salvation. This is the evangelist's final observation on wealth and the wealthy in his story of Jesus.

So What?

Those Who Store Up Treasures for Themselves but Are Not Rich toward God (Luke 12:21)

In early June 2015, in an article subtitled "Profits without Prosperity,"[254] Robert Whitcomb wrote, "Increasingly selfish execs and their boards take more and more corporate earnings to buy back company shares to boost their prices to enrich themselves at accelerating rates; much of their compensation is in stock. Many senior execs are less embarrassed than their predecessors were 50 years ago about paying themselves so much at the expense of other employees and the communities where they do business."

Just two months later I read, "Fifty years ago, a chief executive commonly was paid about 20 times what the average worker at the same company made. But by 2013, according to the Economic Policy

---

[251] Cf. Luke 3:14.

[252] Cf. Bovon, *Luke 2*, 599.

[253] Luke 19:9. Although the story was derived from Luke's special material, this verse is probably due to the evangelist's redaction of the story. It contains the telltale "today" (*sēmeron*), Luke's day of salvation. Cf. Luke 2:11; 4:21; 5:26; 19:5; 23:43.

[254] Cf. *The Providence Journal* (Saturday, June 6, 2015): A12.

Institute, CEO compensation had soared to nearly $300 for every dollar paid the median-level worker."[255]

Without mentioning specifics such as these, Pope Francis commented, "While the earnings of a minority are growing exponentially, so too is the gap separating the majority from the prosperity enjoyed by those happy few. This imbalance is the result of ideologies which defend the absolute autonomy of the marketplace and financial speculation."[256]

All of Them Have Contributed out of Their Abundance (Luke 21:4)

Commenting on the poor widow whom he saw putting her "mite" into the poor box, Jesus said, "Truly I tell you, this poor widow has put in more than all of them; for all of them have contributed out of their abundance, but she out of her poverty has put in all she had to live on."[257] Jesus' introductory "Truly I tell you"[258] made of his comment something more than an *obiter dictum*. It was a statement whose importance he wanted to underscore for his disciples.

Almost two millennia later, in an article titled "Personal Finance: Don't let church pressure you into giving more," on the second page of the business section of the May 10, 2015, edition of *The Providence Sunday Journal*, Dave Ramsey writes that tithes and offerings are "completely different concepts." "Tithes are first fruits off the top, while offerings are from surplus—meaning that you and your family are doing well financially." Ramsey has been offering financial advice for twenty years. His website bills him as America's financial advisor. His weekly radio show regularly reminds his listeners that wealth comes from God.

His attitude toward giving of one's surplus contrasts with that of Pope Francis who declares that "the sign that tells us we have not fallen into 'this sin of idolatry' is almsgiving, giving to those in

---

[255] M. J. Anderson, "CEO pay soars over average worker's," *The Providence Journal* (Friday, September 18, 2015): A19.

[256] *Evangelii Gaudium* 56.

[257] Luke 21:1-4.

[258] Luke 21:3.

need—and not giving merely of our abundance, but giving until it costs me 'some privation' perhaps because 'it is necessary for me.'"[259]

The Rich Fool (Luke 12:13-21)[260]

Jesus told the story of the rich fool in response to an interlocutor who tried to get Jesus to resolve an inheritance dispute that he had with his brother.[261] In our contemporary American society, social columnists like Ann Landers and Amy Dickinson regularly respond to letters from "aggrieved" persons who have been omitted from a will or who believe that a sibling received more than they deserved. For example, Carolyn Hax responded to a letter that began, "My 88-year-old father recently informed me that he's decided to change his will. I have four sisters and brothers, and three have taken out loans against their share of inheritance. Dad . . . recently decided these loans are to be forgiven and the estate split five equal ways." On a personal note, I remember the will of a deceased person who left equal amounts of money to each of her nieces and nephews, grand-nieces and grandnephews, and the grief caused by an unmarried niece who did not receive her "fair share." On a larger scale, the daily television news during the week of May 24, 2015, regularly reported on the lawsuits initiated on behalf of the families of B. B. King and James Brown.

Without reference to the inheritance dispute that prompted Jesus' telling of the story of the rich fool, Pope Francis insightfully commented on the story itself in his October 19, 2015, homily. "Jesus," he said, "tells the parable of a rich man, 'a good entrepreneur,' whose 'fields had yielded an abundant harvest,' and who was 'full of riches,' and, instead of thinking: 'But I will share this with my workers, with my employees, that they also might have a little more for their families,' thought to himself, 'What shall I do, seeing that I have nowhere to put my crops? Ah, so I will pull down my barns and build bigger ones.' More and more: the thirst that comes from attachment to

---

[259] Homily in the Casa Santa Marta, October 19, 2015.
[260] Cf. *The Providence Journal* (Friday, November 7, 2014): C8.
[261] Cf. Luke 12:13.

riches never ends. If you have your heart attached to wealth—when you have so much—you want more. This is the god of the person who is attached to riches."[262]

There Was a Rich Man Who Was Dressed in Purple and Fine Linen (Luke 16:19)

Jesus began his story of the rich man and the poor man in Luke 16:19-31 with a colorful description of the affluence of the rich man. He followed this up with a vivid description of the poor man. Pope Francis has often spoken and written about such discrepancy between the affluent and the impoverished. In his programmatic encyclical *Evangelii Gaudium* he shared the "big picture" with the faithful: "Nor does true peace act as a pretext so that the more affluent can placidly support their lifestyle while others have to make do as they can. Demands involving the distribution of wealth, concern for the poor and human rights cannot be suppressed under the guise of creating a consensus on paper or a transient peace for a contented minority."[263]

---

[262] Pope Francis, homily on October 19, 2015.
[263] *Evangelii Gaudium* 218.

Chapter 6

Acts

The Gospel of Luke is actually the first part of a two-part work. Luke was not alone among Hellenistic historians in composing a historical work in two parts.[1] Josephus, the evangelist's contemporary, did something similar. The first part of Luke's work was devoted to the story of Jesus, the second part to the early history of the Jesus movement. We speak of the first part of the historical opus as the Gospel of Luke and the second part as the Acts of the Apostles.

In some respects it is regrettable that the dynamics of the formation of the New Testament canon led to the separation of the second part of Luke's work from the first part. It would be useful to read the second part of his work immediately after reading the first part. Luke himself affirms the link between the two parts of his work in the prologue to Acts.[2] The first scene of the second part of his work, the account of the ascension of Jesus in Acts 1:6-11, reprises in fuller detail the final scene in the gospel in Luke 24:50-53, a foreshadowing of the beginning of the story of the Jesus movement, whose plot is established by Jesus in Acts 1:8.

In the prologue of the first part of his work,[3] the evangelist informs his God-loving readers that he is going to provide them with an orderly account that he will write after consulting his written and

---

[1] David L. Mealand adds that the style of Acts is similar to the style of Hellenistic historians. Cf. David L. Mealand, "Hellenistic Historians and the Style of Acts," *ZNW* 82 (1991): 42–66.

[2] Acts 1:1-5.

[3] Luke 1:1-4.

oral sources. Since the gospels according to Matthew and Mark have been preserved, we are able to identify the sources of part one of Luke's work as Mark, Q, and L.

There is no reason to doubt that Luke also used written and oral sources for the second part of his work. Unfortunately, there are no extant sources with which we can compare the Acts of the Apostles, so we can rely only on the evidence of Acts itself to determine what those sources were.[4] Fortunately, we do not need to delve into the issue in this study, but we can rest assured that Luke used both written and oral sources in composing Acts.

There is also no reason to doubt that the theological assessment of wealth, wages, and the wealthy revealed in Luke's account of the story of Jesus would also surface in his story about the spread of the Jesus movement. A look at the pertinent passages will reveal that this is indeed the case.

A Matter of Life or Death

Our study of the Gospel of Luke revealed the evangelist's conviction that the use of wealth is a matter of life and death. A generous sharing of one's wealth leads to life. Retention of one's wealth results in death.

The Death of Judas (Acts 1:18-20a)

Echoing his Markan source, Luke presents Peter as the spokesperson of the disciples of Jesus. After Jesus' ascension, Peter assumes the role of leader of the disciples in Jerusalem. One of his first tasks is to ensure that the group of eleven apostles be restored to its full complement. To set the stage for the eventual selection of Barnabas, Peter gives a short account of the death of Judas:

> Now this man [Judas] acquired a field with the reward of his wickedness; and falling headlong, he burst open in the middle and all his bowels gushed out. This became known to all the

---

[4] See the now dated but then comprehensive study of the issue by Jacques Dupont in *The Sources of Acts* (London: Darton, Longman & Todd, 1964).

residents of Jerusalem, so that the field was called in their language Hakeldama, that is, Field of Blood. For it is written in the book of Psalms, "Let his homestead become desolate, and let there be no one to live in it."[5]

Matthew 27:1-10 gives a parallel account of the death of Judas, but other than the name of the deceased and the name of the field, there is little similarity between the two stories. In the Matthean story a repentant Judas returns the money, which the priests then use to buy a field. The field was named Hakeldama, an Aramaic name that means "Field of Blood," because the field was used as a burying ground for aliens. Scripture enters into the Matthean narrative, not to determine the fate of Judas, who is said to have hanged himself,[6] but to determine the price of the field.[7]

In Luke's account of Judas's death,[8] the betrayer shows no sign of repentance. Instead, he uses his ill-begotten wealth to buy himself a piece of property, probably a small farm.[9] Money for the purchase was the financial gain that resulted from his betrayal of Jesus, the "reward of his wickedness" (*misthou tēs adikias*), says Luke. The expression calls to mind what Luke had written about the mammon of iniquity (*mammona tēs adikias*) in Luke 16:9, 11. Judas had succumbed to Satan and had worked out a deal with the chief priests in order to get the money.[10] Buying the land as he did, Judas further distanced

---

[5] Acts 1:18-20a. The quotation from the Psalms is a conflation of Pss 69:26 and 109:8. Earlier in his speech, Acts 1:15, Luke's Peter alluded to Ps 109:8 in saying that Judas had to be replaced.

[6] Cf. Matt 27:5.

[7] Cf. Zech 11:12-13 in Matt 27:9-10. Matthew mistakenly identifies his prophetic source as "Jeremiah." See the discussion of the textual issue in Metzger, *Textual Commentary*, 55.

[8] Fitzmyer opines that the account is based on a folkloric tradition about Judas and says, "The association of his death with an area near Jerusalem and its Aramaic name are authentic reflections of such a tradition." Cf. Joseph A. Fitzmyer, *The Acts of the Apostles*, AB 31 (New York: Doubleday, 1998), 220.

[9] Seven of the ten uses of the word *chōrion* are found in Acts. Cf. Acts 1:18, 19 [2x]; 4:34; 5:3, 8; 28:7. The Greek term was frequently used of a landed property, an estate. Matthew describes the piece of land as a field (*agros*). Cf. Matt 27:7, 8 [2x], 10.

[10] Cf. Luke 22:3-5.

himself from the ministerial group who had left all things to follow Jesus, a group with whom Judas had once been associated.[11]

While on his property, Judas suffered a severe fall that resulted in a horrible death. Absent from Luke is any suggestion that this was suicidal;[12] rather, the death of Judas seems to be an instance of divine vengeance at work. The blood money indirectly caused Judas's death; ill-gotten wealth leads to death. Hardly had Judas taken ownership of the property than it was taken from him.[13] That the property itself became desolate[14] is a final sign of the judgment of God. Hans Conzelmann says the account of Judas's death belongs to the genre of the death of an opponent of God.[15]

Joseph, Called Barnabas, Ananias, and Sapphira (Acts 4:36–5:11)

Later in his story of the Jesus movement, after a summary description of how the Christians of Jerusalem pooled their resources in order to take care of the needy among them,[16] Luke incorporates a pair of vignettes that illustrate the response of three individuals to the community's ethos.

First, there is Joseph, a Levite[17] from the island of Cyprus, who was nicknamed Barnabas.[18] He was with the program. Doing as other members of the community had done,[19] Barnabas sold a field (*agrou*) that he owned and placed the proceeds of the transaction at the feet

[11] Cf. Acts 1:17.

[12] Cf. Matt 27:5.

[13] Cf. Luke 12:20.

[14] Cf. Ps 69:26 in Acts 1:20a.

[15] Cf. Hans Conzelmann, *Acts of the Apostles*, Hermeneia (Philadelphia: Fortress, 1987), 11. Conzelmann describes the scene as a "name etiology" insofar as it explains why the property was called "Field of Blood."

[16] Acts 4:32–35.

[17] Some biblical texts suggest that Levites did not own property because "the Lord was their inheritance," but in the first century CE Levites were able to own property. Cf. Deut 12:12; 14:29; Josh 14:3, 4; 18:7; Josephus, *Life* 68–83.

[18] In Acts 4:36 Luke incorrectly notes that the name means "son of encouragement." It actually signifies "son of Nebo." Cf. Conzelmann, *Acts*, 56. Parsons suggests that Luke's etymology owes to the role that Barnabas will subsequently play in Acts. Cf. Mikeal C. Parsons, *Acts*, Paideia (Grand Rapids: Baker Academic, 2008), 74.

[19] Cf. Acts 4:34–35.

of the apostles so that the money could be used for the needy members of the group. He exemplified what Jesus asked of the rich ruler.[20]

Nonetheless, as is his wont, Luke devotes more attention to those who have not used their wealth in accordance with God's righteousness; the story of Ananias and his wife, Sapphira, occupies a larger panel of Luke's diptych than does the story of Joseph. Their story is one of greed and deception. As Satan had entered into the heart of Judas, so Satan entered into the heart of Ananias.[21] When he sold a piece of property (*ktēma*) that he owned, Ananias, in collusion with his wife, Sapphira, kept back a portion of the proceeds. That was his greed at work. The rest of the money he laid at the feet of the apostles for all to see. That was his deception. Peter saw through the sham and laid bare Ananias's action. He described what Ananias had done as lying to God. Ananias's offense was not simply against the community; ultimately, his greed and deception were offenses against God. With this revelation, Ananias fell dead. He suffered the lot of the rich fool and the rich man who lived elegantly, whose exemplary stories Luke had told in his gospel.[22]

As the story is told, Ananias's wife, who had agreed to the sale of the property and withholding part of the proceeds from the community and its needs, was unaware of the fate of her husband. Three hours later, she appeared on scene and was immediately confronted by Peter. She continued with the greed and deception that she and her husband had worked out. Peter characterized her action as putting the Spirit of the Lord to the test. Immediately she fell dead and was carried out for burial by the same bearers who had taken her husband for burial just a few hours earlier.

The story of Ananias and Sapphira probably came from a pre-Lucan tradition.[23] How much of it is factual is a matter of scholarly debate.[24] What is beyond debate is that Luke tells the story to illustrate

---

[20] Cf. Luke 18:18-23. Bennema describes him as having been "somewhat affluent" (Bennema, *A Theory of Character*, 175).

[21] Cf. Luke 22:3; Acts 5:3.

[22] Cf. Luke 12:16-21; 16:19-26; above, pp. 150, 181–83.

[23] Cf. Ernst Haenchen, *The Acts of the Apostles: A Commentary* (Philadelphia: Westminster, 1971), 237.

[24] See the discussion in Fitzmyer, *Acts*, 317–20.

the pitfalls of wealth.[25] One cannot serve God and wealth.[26] A choice must be made between the two. Compromise is out of the question.

The Ideal Community in Jerusalem
(Acts 2:42-47; 4:32-35; 5:12-16)

In the opening chapters of Acts, Luke provides his readers with three idealized summaries of the basic characteristics of that church.[27] Raymond Brown once observed, "There was real poverty among the Jerusalem Christians who became the nucleus of the post-resurrection Church."[28] In two of his summaries, Luke describes how that first postresurrection church coped with the financial plight of its members.[29]

Acts 2:42-47

In Acts 2:44-45, Luke writes: "All who believed were together and had all things in common; they would sell their possessions and goods and distribute the proceeds to all, as any had need." Luke's Hellenistic audience would have recognized that when the evangelist writes that the early Jerusalem community held all things in common (*apanta koina*), he was affirming that the community of believers had realized the Greek ideal of friendship.[30] For Luke, such friendship was expressed in the way that the Jerusalem believers took care of one another. In Luke's vision, the Holy Spirit is the ultimate source of the unity manifest in their sharing of wealth.[31]

---

[25] Cf. John B. Polhill, *Acts*, NAC 26 (Nashville: Broadman, 1992), 162.

[26] Cf. Luke 16:13.

[27] Cf. Robrecht Michiels, "The 'Model of Church' in the First Christian Community of Jerusalem: Ideal and Reality," *LS* 10 (1985): 303–23; Andreas Lindemann, "The Beginnings of Christian Life in Jerusalem According to the Summaries in the Acts of the Apostles (2:42-47; 4:32-37; 5:12-16)," in *Common Life in the Early Church: Essays Honoring Graydon F. Snyder*, ed. Julian V. Hills (Harrisburg, PA: Trinity Press International, 1998), 202–18.

[28] Brown, *Birth*, 363.

[29] See the brief excursus, "The Sharing of Property," in Conzelmann, *Acts*, 24.

[30] See, among others, Plato, *Resp.* 4.424a; 5.449c; Aristotle, *Eth. nic.* 8.9; Philo, *Abr.* 235; and Cicero, *Off.* 1.16.51.

[31] Cf. Johnson, *Sharing Possessions*, 122.

Holding all things in common did not mean that the members of the church pooled all of their resources in order to live in some sort of early commune. Rather, the ideal of having all things in common was realized insofar as those who were better off sold some of their property and possessions in order to provide for those in need. The verbs that Luke uses in verse 45, "sell" (*epipraskon*) and "distribute" (*diemerizon*), are in the imperfect tense, indicating that this was a habitual action on the part of the more affluent members of the community, not a onetime clearance sale of all that they owned. These more affluent members of the community took care of the needy members of the church by selling some of their possessions in order to provide for those in need.

Acts 4:32-35

Luke further elaborates on the sharing of possessions in his second summary of the life of the first Christian community, devoted almost exclusively to the economic aspect of the unity of that early church, to wit:

> Now the whole group of those who believed were of one heart and soul, and no one claimed private ownership of any possessions, but everything they owned was held in common. With great power the apostles gave their testimony to the resurrection of the Lord Jesus, and great grace was upon them all. There was not a needy person among them, for as many as owned land or houses sold them and brought the proceeds of what was sold. They laid it at the apostles' feet, and it was distributed to each as any had need.[32]

The vocabulary of this second summary echoes that of the first. The expressions "everything in common" (*apanta koina*) and "as any had need" (*kathoti an tis chreian eichen*) and the verb "sell" (*pipraskomenon*) formally link the two summaries to each other. The narrative demonstrates the economic consequences of the preaching of the resurrection of Jesus from the dead. "It is striking," notes Lindemann,

[32] Acts 4:32-35.

"that the focus is on those who give, not on those who receive. This shows that Luke is more concerned with those in his own time who have possessions than he is with the needy."[33]

Luke begins his narrative by stating that the entire community of believers was one in heart and soul. Then comes the theme of the narrative: "No one claimed private ownership of any possessions, but everything they owned was held in common."[34] This common ownership of property is an expression of the unity of the church, yet no more does it indicate that the members of the community pooled their possessions than did Luke's first summary. What it means is that any overriding claim to the private possessions of goods was renounced for the sake of the common welfare.

Unlike the first account, this second summary focuses on real estate. Those who owned lands or rental properties sold them in order to take care of the needs of impoverished believers. The proceeds of the sales were laid at the feet of the apostles. This striking gesture indicates that the sellers would no longer use the money to satisfy their own needs; it was given to the apostles for them to distribute. The gesture becomes the focal point of the two illustrative stories— one positive, the other negative—appended to this second summary.[35]

By preaching about the resurrection of Jesus, the apostles exercised their role as leaders of the community of believers. Their leadership was further in evidence in their role of distributing the proceeds of the sales of property. They did not distribute the funds at their disposal arbitrarily. Rather, as Luke states,[36] they distributed the money to the members of the community in accordance with their needs.

The result was that there was not a needy person in the community.[37] That the needs of the poorer members of the community are taken care of corresponds to God's will for his community. Commenting on the demands of the sabbatical year, Deuteronomy 5:14 says, "There will be no one in need among you, because the Lord is sure

---

[33] Lindemann, *Beginnings*, 212.
[34] Acts 4:32a.
[35] Cf. Acts 4:37; 5:2. See above, pp. 193–99.
[36] Cf. Acts 4:35b.
[37] Cf. Acts 4:34a.

to bless you." The Deuteronomic promise was fulfilled in the reality of the community of believers. That the needs of the impoverished among God's holy people in Jerusalem are assuaged by the voluntary offerings of the more well-to-do is a sign of God's blessing on the community. God approved of what the apostles were doing; God's favor rested on the community.[38] "A great grace [*charis megalē*] was upon them all."[39]

Luke's third summary of the life of the church in Jerusalem in Acts 5:12-16 has a different focus. It concentrates on the growth of the community and the healing miracles effected by the apostles. Accordingly, it does not require further consideration in this study. What is important for our study is the way in which Luke emphasizes that the rich members' taking care of the poor is a Spirit-inspired characteristic of an ideal community of believers, as his first and second summaries make so clear.

Heroes and Heroines

In Luke's account of the subsequent spread of the Jesus movement, two figures are very much in evidence: Peter, the leader in Jerusalem and Judea, and Paul, whose missionary journeys and his voyage as a prisoner to Rome brought the message of the gospel to the ends of the earth. Early on in his story, Luke portrays Peter and John as going to the temple in midafternoon to pray.[40] A blind beggar who regularly sat at the Beautiful Gate of the temple asking for alms appealed to Peter and John for financial assistance. Ever the spokesperson, Peter replied, "I have no silver or gold, but what I have I give you; in the name of Jesus Christ of Nazareth, stand up and walk."[41] Luke's account of the encounter has the form of a miracle story, and for this reason the incident is important for his narrative scheme. For our purposes, Peter's lack of silver and gold (*argyrion kai chrysion*) is a sign that the leader of the Jerusalem community of believers had

---

[38] Cf. C. K. Barrett, *The Acts of the Apostles*, vol. 1: *Acts 1–14*, ICC (London: T & T Clark, 1994), 254.

[39] Acts 4:33b.

[40] Cf. Acts 3:1-10.

[41] Acts 3:6.

heeded the Lord's command to take no money (*mēte agyrion*)[42] while on the mission of preaching and healing.

Seven Men of Good Standing (Acts 6:1-6)

In addition to Peter and Paul, other characters appear throughout Luke's history, and some of them are not without interest for our study. Among the Jews living in Jerusalem were many, born outside of Palestine, whose primary language was Greek. Some of them, and apparently not a few, were pious Jews who traveled to Jerusalem from the diaspora in their declining years so that they might be buried in the environs of the Holy City. Luke calls these Greek-speaking Jews "Hellenists."[43]

The church of Jerusalem, whose leaders had taken on the responsibility of attending to the needy in the community, had organized a kind of food pantry on behalf of the poor among them. Widows were traditionally among those to whom the righteous would reach out. Elderly widows who had traveled to Jerusalem with their husbands were particularly vulnerable and in need of assistance, especially food from the food bank. Not only were they bereft of their husbands, but they were also without the support of family in the area.

Some of the Greek-speaking believers in Jerusalem felt that Greek-speaking widows were being neglected in the daily distribution of food.[44] Luke does not so much assign blame for this situation as he shows how the Twelve[45] responded to the situation.[46] The Twelve appointed a group of "seven men of good standing" who were to provide for these women. One of the men was Philip, who in Acts 21:8 is identified as "one of the seven," indicating that the Seven were a well-defined group alongside the Twelve. Luke focuses so much on the way that the Twelve responded to the situation of need that

---

[42] Cf. Luke 9:3.

[43] Cf. Acts 6:1.

[44] The complaint of the Hellenists against "the Hebrews" may be a surface indication of the deeper and more widespread tensions between Jewish believers and Hellenistic believers in the early decades of the Christian movement.

[45] Acts 6:2 contains the only explicit mention of the Twelve in Acts.

[46] Cf. Haenchen, *Acts*, 262.

he fails to say that the impoverished widows actually received a full daily ration of food.[47]

Tabitha and Cornelius (Acts 9:36; 10:2)

In Acts 10:1-33, the story of the conversion of Cornelius follows immediately after the account of Peter's raising Tabitha from the dead in Acts 9:36-43. Both accounts are important for the Lucan narrative of the Petrine ministry, but it is the evangelist's characterization of Tabitha and Cornelius that demands a brief mention in the present study.

Tabitha[48] was a female disciple (*mathētria*[49]) living in Joppa, on the Mediterranean coast. After identifying the woman's name and place of residence, Luke continues with his characterization: "She was devoted to [*plērēs*] good works and acts of charity."[50] Luke's Greek is a bit convoluted; his words might be rendered, "She was full of good works and alms which she gave." The last phrase characterizes her as an almsgiver rather than as a recipient of alms. She was a generous person in deed and donation. Among her good deeds were the tunics and other clothing that she had made and given to widows.[51]

Cornelius was a God-fearing centurion stationed in Caesarea Maritima.[52] Luke says of him, "He gave alms generously [*pollas*] to the people and prayed constantly to God."[53] Luke writes of the centurion, as he did of Tabitha, that he was generous in his almsgiving, using the expression *poien eleemosynas* qualified by a term that underscores the generosity of the respective individuals.

God favored Tabitha with the gift of the restored life given to her by Peter; God favored Cornelius with the gift of faith and acceptance

---

[47] Luke Timothy Johnson comments, "Luke has used the dispute and its resolution in order to symbolize through possessions the transfer of spiritual power to the hellenistic missionaries." See *The Literary Function of Possessions in Luke–Acts*, SBLDS 39 (Missoula, MT: Scholars Press, 1977), 213.

[48] The Greek translation of her Aramaic name is Dorcas. The English translation of both of these words is "gazelle."

[49] The word is hapax in the New Testament.

[50] Acts 9:36b.

[51] Cf. Acts 9:40.

[52] Cf. Acts 10:1-2a, 22.

[53] Acts 10:2b.

into the community of believers, using a miraculous vision to enable Peter to break through the cultural divide that had hindered him from welcoming Cornelius as a believer. There is no indication that either Tabitha or Cornelius were particularly wealthy, but in telling their stories, Luke shows that God is gracious toward those who are generous.

Less Noble Individuals

Tabitha and Cornelius were two individuals who used even their limited wealth on behalf of others, thereby earning God's favor. Other characters in Luke's story of the early Christian movement did not use their wealth so generously.

Simon (Acts 8:9-24)

As Luke tells about the spread of the Christian movement in Samaria, the central region of Palestine,[54] he tells the story of a magician named Simon.[55] Simon practiced magic[56] in the city of Samaria and had a good following, leading him to proclaim his own greatness. At that time, magicians typically earned their living from the practice of their art. Things in Samaria began to change when Philip arrived, proclaiming the kingdom of God and the name of Jesus Christ. Many of Simon's followers believed and were baptized. Even Simon himself became a believer and was baptized.

To ensure apostolic approval for the mission to Samaria, the apostles sent Peter and John there. They laid hands on the neophyte believers who then received the gift of the Holy Spirit,[57] manifest

---

[54] Cf. Acts 1:8.

[55] Hence, Simon was called Simon Magus in Patristic tradition. Cf. Eusebius, *Hist. eccl.* 2.1.10.

[56] Philo (3.100-101) distinguishes between true magic and the perversion of the art. The distinction is important for a proper understanding of Luke's account of Simon, the magician.

[57] This passage is important for Christian sacramentology, especially for the relationship between the sacraments of baptism and confirmation. That important discussion lies beyond the scope of the present study.

perhaps in the gift of speaking in tongues.[58] Simon was impressed and offered Peter and John a sum of money so that he too might be able to confer the gift of the Holy Spirit.[59] Having the ability to confer the Spirit would add to his repertoire. Presumably, Simon expected to be paid for the gift that he hoped to confer.[60] Once again, Peter is the spokesman. His reply gave short shrift to Simon's request, saying, "May your silver [*to agyrion sou*] perish with you!"[61] Peter's retort is strong. Translated into today's vernacular, it would be something like "Go to hell, and take your money with you."[62]

In what may seem to be a somewhat calmer tone, Peter explains, "because you thought you could obtain God's gift [*tēn dōrean*] with money. You have no part or share in this, for your heart is not right before God."[63] Continuing with his harsh language, Peter accuses Simon of wickedness and unrighteousness. He calls Simon to change his heart and beg God for forgiveness. Simon heeds the call and asks for Peter and John's prayers.

Just as Peter's conversion of Cornelius foreshadows Paul's mission of preaching the gospel to Gentiles, so Peter's conversion of Simon the magician foreshadows a more extensive conversion of magicians by Paul. To illustrate how the practice of magic lost ground because of Paul's apostolic activity, Luke writes:

> Many of those who became believers confessed and disclosed their practices. A number of those who practiced magic collected their books and burned them publicly; when the value of these books was calculated, it was found to come to fifty thousand silver coins. So the word of the Lord grew mightily and prevailed.[64]

[58] Haenchen, *Acts*, 304. Barrett (*Acts 1–14*, 413) mentions a "perceptible phenomenon" without further speculation.

[59] Commentators note that Simon did not ask to purchase the gift of the Spirit; what he sought was the ability to confer the gift on people, as if doing so could be construed as an act of magic. See, for example, Haenchen, *Acts*, 304.

[60] Cf. Barrett, *Acts 1*, 413.

[61] Acts 8:20a.

[62] Cf. Haenchen, *Acts*, 304; Fitzmyer, *Acts*, 406; Parsons, *Acts*, 117.

[63] Acts 8:20b-21.

[64] Acts 19:18-20.

The critical reader may, with Haenchen,[65] question the historicity of the account. Surely, Luke's interest was in the spread of the gospel message[66] rather than in the details of the book-burning incident.[67] The account may be a popular tale, but it does point to people's ideas about the wealth of magicians. Fifty thousand pieces of silver is a considerable sum of money.[68]

Simon's story is singularly important for our study of wealth and the wealthy. Simon was not in a proper relationship with God because he thought that he could buy God's gifts.[69] His story teaches that God's gifts are gifts and that no amount of money can buy them. God's gifts are freely offered by a beneficent God. God's gifts are not for sale. Any attempt to purchase them is an act of sheer wickedness.

The Owners of a Slave Girl (Acts 16:16-24)

As he recounts the spread of the gospel, Luke pays particular attention to Paul's visit to Philippi, the first step in the evangelization of what is today known as Europe.[70] Paul was welcomed into the home of Lydia, a rich merchant. What happened when he exorcised a slave girl is intriguing. The female slave had a "spirit of divination," a Pythian spirit (*pneuma pythōna*). This language links her to the oracle at Delphi. Her owners (*kyriois*, in the plural[71]) made a fortune (*ergasian pollēn*) from her fortune-telling (*manteuomenē*[72]). They had a lucrative business.[73]

---

[65] Cf. Haenchen, *Acts*, 567.

[66] See Acts 19:20.

[67] In antiquity, book burning was a way to counter the spread of unacceptable ideas. See Josephus, *Antiquities* 10.6.2; Suetonius, *Aug.* 31; and Livy, *Hist.* 39:16; 40:29, for examples. The books to which Luke refers presumably contained magical spells and formulae. Cf. Karl Preisendanz, *Papyri graecae magicae* (Stuttgart: Teubner, 1973–1974).

[68] Following Polhill (*Acts*, 406), Fitzmyer (*Acts*, 651) estimates the amount to be worth about $35,000.

[69] This story serves as the etymological source of the word "simony," the attempt to buy ecclesiastical office.

[70] Cf. Acts 16:6-39.

[71] See also v. 19, "her owners" (*hoi kyrioi autēs*).

[72] The verb is hapax in the New Testament.

[73] The Greek word *ergasia*, which can mean "business" or "profit," is used almost exclusively by Luke in the New Testament. Cf. Luke 12:58; Acts 16:16, 19; 19:24, 25; Eph 4:19.

At no point in his account does Luke indicate that the possessive spirit was evil or impure. Indeed, in the presence of Paul and his companions, she cried out, "These men are the slaves of the Most High God, who proclaim to you a way of salvation."[74] Her repetition of this mantra annoyed Paul, who proceeded to drive the spirit out of the woman. As she was no longer capable of fortune-telling, her owners were deprived of the source of their considerable income. They complained to the civic officials and apparently worked the crowds up to attack Paul and his group. The local magistrate then attempted to restore peace in the city and satisfy the plaintiff's commercial interests by having the missionary group beaten and imprisoned.

Wealth plays a role in this story, as Johnson observes when he writes, "The profit motive figures in the tale."[75] Luke contrasts the attitude of Lydia with that of the owners of the enslaved diviner. The economic aspects of Luke's description of them occasion our interest in the tale. The evangelist, it should be noted, does not negatively portray the seer other than to state that she was an annoyance to Paul. Slavery was part of the economic system of the time; Luke seems not to object. The slave was exploited for the profit that she brought to her owners. When they perceived that they had lost the source of their revenue, they appealed to the magistrate. At the remove of almost two millennia, the contemporary reader can see in this tale not only the exploitation of a slave but also how avarice leads to violence[76] and the misuse of a system of justice in order to protect economic interests.

Demetrius the Silversmith (Acts 19:23-41)

In Acts 19, Luke shares with his readers another story about a profitable business.[77] This one takes place in Ephesus, the capital of the Roman province of Asia and the site of the famous Temple of Artemis [Diana], the daughter of Zeus and Leto. The temple was a

[74] Acts 16:17.
[75] Luke Timothy Johnson, *The Acts of the Apostles*, SP 5 (Collegeville, MN: Liturgical Press, 1992), 298.
[76] Cf. Luke 20:9-19.
[77] The noun *ergasia*, "business," appears in each of the first two verses in Luke's account of the incident at Ephesus. Cf. Acts 19:24, 25.

magnificent edifice and functioned as the center of a financial enterprise. Paulus Fabius Persicus, a well-known scion of a political family, once described the temple as "the ornament of the whole province because of its size, its antiquity, and the abundance of its revenues." An industry developed in conjunction with the cult of Artemis. Archaeological excavations have unearthed terra-cotta replicas of the temple, coins with the image of the temple, and silver statues of the huntress deity. Work and prosperity were afforded by the cult of Artemis.[78]

To date, no silver shrines (*naous argyrous*) of Artemis, about which Luke writes in Acts 19:24, have been found, but there is no doubt that Luke wanted to portray the owner of one of the industries associated with the cult of Artemis in his account of Demetrius, the silversmith. Demetrius was a wealthy man who had several craftsmen in his employ. These craftsmen had more than enough work to do. Demetrius's enterprise, says Luke, "brought no little business to the artisans."[79]

As Luke tells the story, he portrays Demetrius as an entrepreneur who feared that Paul's preaching was undermining the cult of Artemis and the cottage industries that arose in conjunction with the temple. Calling together the members of the silversmiths' guild,[80] Demetrius told them that Paul was drawing people away from Artemis by saying that handmade gods were not really gods.[81] Demetrius was not far off target. A good Jew, Paul had repeatedly condemned idolatry. He urged the people to turn from the worship of idols to the service of the one, living, and true God.[82] Reporting Paul's prototypical appeal to Gentiles in the Areopagus speech,[83] Luke describes Paul as saying, "We ought not to think that the deity is like gold, or silver, or stone, an image formed by the art and imagination of mortals."[84]

---

[78] Cf. C. K. Barrett, *The Acts of the Apostles*, vol. 2: *Acts 15–28*, ICC (London: T & T Clark, 1998), 924.

[79] Acts 19:24.

[80] Luke writes about Demetrius's artisans and "workers of the same trade" in v. 25. Johnson (*Acts*, 247) suggests that the modern reader should think of a guild. In fact, guilds of tradesmen were among the most common associations in the Greco-Roman world. One extant Egyptian papyrus specifically mentions a silversmiths' guild.

[81] Cf. Acts 19:26.

[82] Cf. 1 Thess 1:9; 1 Cor 10:14; Acts 14:15.

[83] Cf. Acts 17:22-31.

[84] Acts 17:29.

Demetrius's appeal to his colleagues was two-pronged. First, he pressed the economic button: "You know that we get our wealth [*hē euporia*[85]] from this business. . . . There is danger that this trade of ours may come into disrepute."[86] Then he added an element of religious motivation: "There is danger . . . that the temple of the great goddess Artemis will be scorned, and she will be deprived of her majesty that brought all Asia and the world to worship her."[87]

In response, Demetrius's audience shouted loudly, "Great is Artemis of the Ephesians!"[88] and a near-riot broke out.[89] It was a mob scene; some did not even know why they were involved.[90] Eventually, the town clerk quieted the unruly mob, which had been shouting, "Great is Artemis of the Ephesians!" for two hours.[91] The city official told the crowd that mob action was not the way to go in a situation like this. Disputes such as this should be handled by the proper authorities, the sitting courts, the proconsuls, and the lawful assembly.[92]

Luke leaves his readers hanging as to what happened afterward. He tells the story to show how the preaching of the gospel was opposed by idol worshipers and those who made a good living from the cult of idols. Luke's sympathy clearly lies with Paul and his companions. They were opposed by wealthy persons who did not want the worship of the one true God to stand in the way of their accumulation of wealth. Their greed led to a near-riot; calm in the city was eventually restored by a city official. The dramatic story of the events in Ephesus is an illustration of how the love of money leads to opposition to the gospel.[93]

---

[85] This word is hapax in the New Testament. Spicq says that the term has only one meaning, namely, "resources, wealth." A related noun that does not appear in the New Testament, *euporos*, is used of a well-to-do person. Cf. Spicq, "*euporeō, euporia*," *TLNT* 2:134–35.

[86] Acts 19:25, 27a.

[87] Acts 19:27b.

[88] Acts 19:25.

[89] Cf. Acts 19:40; 20:1.

[90] Cf. Acts 19:32.

[91] Cf. Acts 19:34.

[92] Luke identifies these as the *agoraioi*, the *antypatoi*, and the *ennomos ekklēsia* in vv. 38-39.

[93] Johnson (*Acts*, 353) comments, "Of special importance here is the way Luke continues one of his major subthemes: the way in which responses to God's visitation are symbolized by attitudes toward material possessions."

Paul

No account of wealth, wages, and the wealthy in the Acts of the Apostles would be complete were it not to include a few words about Paul, the hero of the second part of the book. Arguably, Luke puts his readers on notice that he is about to bring his short history of the young Jesus movement to its conclusion when he includes Paul's Farewell Discourse to the elders of the church of Ephesus who had gathered at Miletus to hear him.

Paul's Farewell Discourse (Acts 20:18b-35)

The speech of "Paul" in Acts 20:18b-35 belongs to the literary genre of the farewell discourse.[94] As such, it records not the words of Paul but what the writer—in this case, Luke—thought about him. Such speeches typically speak about the departure of the literary hero, make provision for succession in office or ministry, and urge those who are being left behind to work together in unison to achieve the goals to which the about-to-depart hero had devoted his life. Monetary considerations are not particularly typical of the genre, but Luke addresses these issues as he concludes Paul's Farewell Discourse:

> I coveted no one's silver or gold or clothing. You know for yourselves that I worked with my own hands to support myself and my companions. In all this I have given you an example that by such work we must support the weak, remembering the words of the Lord Jesus, for he himself said, "It is more blessed to give than to receive."[95]

With this otherwise unattested saying of Jesus,[96] Paul's speech comes to its end.

---

[94] The Farewell Discourses of the Fourth Gospel (John 13–17) are another New Testament example of the genre. *The Testament of the Twelve Patriarchs*, an important piece of Old Testament apocrypha, is a classic example of the genre.

[95] Acts 20:33-35.

[96] Unattested, that is, within the New Testament. For a study of the sayings of Jesus that are not found in the canonical gospels but have some claim to authenticity, see the classic study of Joachim Jeremias, *Unknown Sayings of Jesus* (London: SPCK, 1958), 77–81. Unfortunately, the German original of this work,

Its snippet on wealth and wages contains three related state-ments. First of all, presented explicitly as an example for church leaders, Luke's Paul is a hero who does not covet other people's wealth. In his letters, Paul often defends his own integrity[97] but does not appeal to his refusal to desire others' possessions.[98] Coupled with silver and gold, "clothing" (*himatismou*) apparently refers to expensive or fancy clothing, the kind of clothing that those who had silver and gold might wear.

Second, the departing Paul declares that he worked with his own hands. This echoes what Paul said in the first of his extant letters. Writing to the Thessalonians, he said, "You remember our labor and toil, brothers and sisters; we worked night and day, so that we might not burden any of you while we proclaimed to you the gospel of God."[99] This is the first of many times that Paul asserted that he had supported himself by the work of his hands so as to achieve the financial independence that he wanted for the proclamation of the gospel.[100] In his own writings, the apostle did not suggest that he did so in order to support his fellow evangelists, but Luke does so in Acts 20:34. Luke has modified the tradition of Paul's manual labor in order to provide an example for the elders.

Like many authors in antiquity, Paul presents himself as an ex-emplar to neophyte believers, but he does not propose that they follow his example of manual labor,[101] let alone that they follow his example to work so that they can provide financial support for oth-ers. Second Corinthians 11:27 suggests that Paul barely eked out a subsistence level of existence from his work, hardly enough for him to support himself, let alone others. Luke, however, wants to show that the earliest believers, including Paul, were concerned for the

---

published in 1948, appeared too soon after the Nag Hammadi findings for this important trove to be included in Jeremias's study.

[97] Cf. 1 Cor 9:4-12, 15; 2 Cor 7:2; 11:8-9; Phil 4:10-11.

[98] Cf. Exod 20:17.

[99] 1 Thess 2:9.

[100] Cf. 1 Cor 4:12.

[101] Cf. 1 Cor 11:1; 1 Thess 1:6. See, however, the pseudepigraphic 2 Thess 3:9. After Paul's death, hagiographic writings developed the notion of imitating the apostle. 1 Tim 1:12-17 is an important example (cf. v. 16). As far as Paul himself is considered, the Farewell Discourse of Acts 20 is clearly posthumous.

material well-being of others in the community. So he adds that Paul also helped the weak. This was done, says Luke, because "we must support the weak" (*dei antilambanesthai tōn asthenountōn*[102]). This is a statement of principle. The initial dei means "it is necessary that."[103] Believers must come to the support of those who are impoverished. Paul fulfilled the precept in exemplary fashion, says Luke. From the tradition of Paul's working with his own hands, Luke has created a paradigm,[104] an example of how believers, including their leaders, are to provide for the impoverished members of the community.

The third statement contains the well-known *agraphon*,[105] "It is more blessed to give than to receive."[106] The saying is integral to Luke's argument; it is not simply a literary flourish. Luke's introductory lemma, "remembering the words of the Lord Jesus, for he himself said," underscores the importance of the saying in a number of ways. Remembering (*mnēmoneuein*) is an important motif in paraenesis, Hellenistic moral exhortation. Luke's use of the title Lord (*kyrios*) indicates that Jesus is someone with authority, an unquestionable authority whose will determines what is to be done. The explanatory gar, "for," is used to give the theological basis for the principle enunciated in verse 35a. The grammatically unnecessary but emphatic "himself" (*autos*) reinforces the source of the motivating logion. It

---

[102] The verb *antilambanomai* occurs only three times in the New Testament: here; Luke 1:54; and 1 Tim 6:2. Words derived from the *asthenē-*, a word group that relates to weakness of any sort, are used in the New Testament to speak of the ill or those whose faith is weak. In the Hellenistic world, the words were also used of those who were financially insecure. Cf. Aristophanes, *Pax* 631; Herodotus, *Histories* (2.88 in published ed; see *LSJ*). In a first-century BCE Tebtunis Papyrus, the word group was used to describe those who were unable to pay their taxes.

[103] Soards notes that the *dei* is an important word, "probably indicating divine necessity." Cf. Marion L. Soards, *The Speeches in Acts: Their Content, Context, and Concerns* (Louisville: Westminster John Knox, 1994), 108.

[104] Cf. Jan Lambrecht, "Paul's Farewell-Address at Miletus (Acts 20:17-38)," in *Les Actes des Apôtres: Tradition, rédaction, théologie*, ed. Jacob Kremer, BETL 48 (Gembloux [Belgium]: Duculot, 1979), 307–37, at 321.

[105] This Greek word, literally "un-written" (*a-graphon*), is a technical term used in references to sayings of Jesus that are not preserved in the canonical gospels but enjoy some claim to being authentic.

[106] Acts 20:35b.

was none other than the Lord himself who said, "It is more blessed to give than to receive."[107]

With this example of Paul's exemplarity with regard to the use of wealth, Luke concludes Paul's Farewell Discourse. This is the memory of the apostle that Luke wants his readers to retain. Paul was a hero and example who provided for others out of his own limited means.

Paul and Felix (Acts 24)

The twenty-fourth chapter of Acts is devoted to Paul's appearance before the Roman governor Felix at Caesara Maritima, the site of the Roman garrison on the Mediterranean coast. It contains the second of Luke's three renditions[108] of Paul's *apologia pro vita sua*.[109] This particular version is tailored to a Hellenistic audience, symbolized by the governor, Felix. The three accounts have been especially remembered for the similar yet different stories that they tell about Paul's so-called conversion.[110]

In this second account of Paul's "conversion" there are two references to money. As part of his defense, Paul is reported to have said, "Now after some years I came to bring alms to my nation and to offer sacrifice."[111] Giving money to the poor was a conventional act of Jewish piety,[112] but Luke's statement is easily seen as a reference to the collection on behalf of the saints in Jerusalem.[113] This ready interpretation may stumble on the fact that Luke does not otherwise mention the collection,[114] so integral to Paul's mission. Could it be that Luke simply wants to present Paul as someone who had access

---

[107] Cf. 1 Clem. 2:1. Fitzmyer (*Acts*, 682) notes that a form of the saying may have been common in antiquity.

[108] Cf. Acts 24:10-21; 22:1-21; 26:2-29.

[109] Cf. Acts 14:10 uses the verb *apologymai* in the introduction to "Paul's speech."

[110] Cf. Raymond F. Collins, "Paul's Damascus Experience: Reflections on the Lukan Account," *LS* 11 (1986): 99–118.

[111] Acts 24:17.

[112] Cf. Philo, *Legat.* 216, 313; Matt 6:1-4.

[113] Cf. Rom 15:25-28, 31; Gal 2:10; 1 Cor 16:1-4; 2 Cor 8-9. See above, pp. 41–46, 53–54.

[114] Cf. Johnson, *Acts*, 413–14.

to money? Luke was a competent writer. Did he simply want to set the scene for the second reference to money in his account of Paul and Felix?

After Paul's *apologia*, the wily governor deferred judgment. In the meantime, Paul was consigned to the custody of a centurion of the guard with some limited liberty that allowed his friends to provide for his needs.[115] A few days later, Felix, accompanied by his Jewish wife, Drusilla, came to visit Paul. Luke seems to imply that the woman might have been interested in what Paul had to say about a religious matter. Luke tells his readers that similar visits on the part of Felix were not unusual. Felix hoped that he would get some money from Paul,[116] either for the latter's freedom or as an expression of gratitude for his less-than-severe circumstances. Roman law forbade the taking of bribes from prisoners,[117] but the practice was not unknown[118] and would seem to have been in keeping with Felix's well-known greed, whose desire for what did not belong to him included the successful coveting of other men's wives,[119] one of whom was Drusilla, previously the wife of Azizus, a Syrian king.

Paul, who coveted neither precious metals nor extravagant clothing,[120] did not succumb to Felix's expectations, despite the latter's repeated conversations with his prisoner. It is unlikely that Paul possessed the wherewithal to provide the governor with the money he wanted, but Luke seems to be more interested in presenting Paul as a man of financial integrity. Unlike some of the other religious figures who appear in Luke's story of the Jesus movement,[121] his Paul is a man whose conduct with regard to money was exemplary. Even his companions, Gaius and Aristarchus,[122] who became involved in a minor riot over the worship of the goddess Diana, whose cult was

---

[115] As another example of this type of custody, see Josephus, *Antiquities* 18.235.
[116] Cf. Acts 24:26.
[117] Cf. *Lex Iulia de pecuniis repetundis* (PW 12.2389-2; cf. Fitzmyer, *Acts*, 740).
[118] Cf. Josephus, *War* 1.14.1.
[119] Cf. Josephus, *Antiquities* 19.9.1; 20.7.1-2; *J.W.* 2.11.6; Suetonius, *Claud.* 28; Tacitus, *Ann.* 12.54; *Hist.* 5.9.
[120] Cf. Acts 20:34.
[121] Cf. Acts 19:24-27.
[122] Cf. Acts 19:29.

profitable for the city of Ephesus, were declared to be exonerated of temple-robbing[123] by none other than the town clerk himself.[124]

House Arrest (Acts 28:30-31)

The final two chapters of Acts feature three social customs of antiquity that provide a social setting for our study, namely, philanthropy, friendship, and hospitality.[125] It concludes on an upbeat note:

> He [Paul] lived there two whole years at his own expense and welcomed all who came to him, proclaiming the kingdom of God and teaching about the Lord Jesus Christ with all boldness and without hindrance.[126]

The modern reader of Luke's account of the early Jesus movement would like to know what happened next, but Luke remains silent on the issue.

Commentators have advanced various theories as to why the second book of Luke's magnificent opus ends on this note. None of the explanations fully satisfy. Perhaps the best explanation is that Luke has completed the exposition of his theme. The risen Jesus had ordained that there be witnesses to him in Jerusalem, all Judea, Samaria, and the ends of the earth.[127] With Paul's arrival and preaching in Rome, the gospel was preached at the end of the earth, the capital of the empire.

The NRSV translation somewhat softens the force of the Greek *enemeinen*, which literally means that "he stayed" there, arguably under a type of custody similar to the circumstances under which Paul had been in custody in Caesarea. These circumstances were not harsh, but they were not of Paul's own volition. In Acts, a period of two years is a significant amount of time.

---

[123] The noun *hierosylos*, literally "temple-robber," but occasionally meaning "perpetrator of sacrilege," is hapax in the New Testament at Acts 19:37.

[124] Cf. Acts 19:35.

[125] Cf. Parsons, *Acts*, 367–70.

[126] Acts 28:30-31.

[127] Cf. Acts 1:8. "To the ends of the earth" (NRSV) renders the Greek *eōs eschatou tēs gēs*, an expression in the singular number, arguably denoting Rome.

While in Rome, Paul stayed "at his own expense." This translation of the Greek phrase *en idiō misthōmati* seems to suggest that Paul was able to exercise his trade and earn a sufficient living to support himself while he proclaimed the kingdom of God. Although he was in custody, Paul carried on his life in almost the same circumstances as he previously had. He worked as a leather-worker and preached the gospel. It could be, however, that the Greek phrase *en idiō misthōmati* is simply a reference to lodging that Paul had personally rented.[128]

Show and Tell

"Show and tell" is part of every child's school experience. It is also part of any author's technique. Sometimes an author will communicate a message by stating it in straightforward fashion. At other times, the same author will proclaim the message in illustrative vignettes. Luke is an ancient author who made use of both techniques.

In the first part of his two-part opus, the Gospel of Luke, the evangelist stated a Christian vision of money, wealth, and possessions straight out. He also incorporated into his story about Jesus a number of stories that articulate various aspects of that vision. In the second part of his work, the Acts of the Apostles, the evangelist employs another technique. His account of the spread of the Christian message is comprised of many different vignettes, many of which bear upon the use of money; Acts contains hardly any explicit teaching on wealth and the wealthy. Rather, Luke's stories show how greed and the pursuit of wealth lead to death. Dramatically, the evangelist shows how the pursuit of wealth leads to opposition to the gospel. The other side of the coin is that some characters in his story, people like Joseph, Tabitha, and Cornelius, use their wealth righteously and merit God's favor. Luke portrays an ecclesial ideal in which poverty is eradicated and the needs of all are attended to. In all of this, the

---

[128] Cf. Spicq, "*Misthōma*," *TLNT* 2:516–17, at 517. The Greek word, hapax in the New Testament, is related to *misthos*, "wage." In the papyri, the term designates an agreed-upon wage or price, sometimes referring to a price agreed upon in a lease. Although opting for a rented dwelling place as the better interpretation of the Greek, Spicq does not reject out of hand the possibility of an "at his own expense" interpretation.

evangelist uses narrative to proclaim a theological vision of how money is to be used and how it is not to be used.

The narrative continues in the story of Paul. The economic vision appears in Luke's account of various incidents. The apostle's conduct with regard to wealth is exemplary. Only once does Luke resort to telling the message in so many words. He does so by way of a conclusion to Paul's Farewell Discourse: "We must support the weak, remembering the words of the Lord Jesus, for he himself said, 'It is more blessed to give than to receive.'"[129] For Luke, this is Paul's legacy to the church.

So What?

All Who Believed Were Together and Had All Things in Common

Luke describes the ideal church in Jerusalem as one in which its members held all things in common.[130] Pope Francis, for his part, describes the common good as "a central and unifying principle of social ethics." He makes his own the definition of the common good found in Vatican Council II's Pastoral Constitution on the Church in the Modern World. "The common good," he writes, "is 'the sum of those conditions of social life which allow social groups and their individual members relatively thorough and ready access to their own fulfilment.'"[131]

Earlier in his short pontificate, Francis wrote about the common good that "the dignity of the human person and the common good rank higher than the comfort of those who refuse to renounce their privileges. When these values are threatened a prophetic voice must be raised."[132]

[129] Acts 20:35b.
[130] Acts 2:44; cf. Acts 4:32.
[131] *Laudato Sì* 156, quoting *Gaudium et Spes* 26.
[132] *Evangelii Gaudium* 218.

Chapter 7

The Deutero-Pauline Texts

The Epistles to the Ephesians and to the Colossians, the Second Epistle to the Thessalonians, the two Epistles to Timothy, and the Epistle to Titus are generally considered to be pseudepigraphic.[1] Although bearing Paul's name—signed by him, if you will—they were probably not written by the apostle. Seeking neutrality on a matter that has now been discussed for more than two centuries, some scholars prefer to call these texts the disputed letters. I, however, have come to the conclusion that none of the six were written by Paul and so do not hesitate to call them pseudepigraphic, or deutero-Pauline, that is, Pauline in a secondary sense. I also call them epistles, to distinguish these six from the undisputed Pauline letters: Romans, 1 and 2 Corinthians, Galatians, Philippians, 1 Thessalonians, and Philemon.[2]

It can generally be said that the common purpose of these epistles is to continue the legacy of Paul in circumstances that arose after the apostle's death. The circumstances of the texts vary from one epistle to another. Consequently, it will be necessary for me to say something about the circumstances of composition of each text before I examine what the epistle has to say about wealth, wages, or

---

[1] Cf. Raymond F. Collins, *Letters That Paul Did Not Write: The Epistle to the Hebrews and the Pauline Pseudepigrapha*, GNS 28 (Wilmington, DE: Glazier, 1988).

[2] What the seven letters tell us about the believing Paul's appreciation of wealth, wages, and the wealthy was the subject of the second chapter of this study.

the wealthy. These circumstances are complex and are the subject of scholarly debate. In the present work, I will provide only a few words to situate the text in a plausible context before moving to an examination of the respective epistle from the angle that is of interest to the present study.

Before proceeding further, it is necessary for me to state that all six epistles belong to the Canon of the New Testament recognized by the Christian churches. What they have to say remains authoritative for the believer, notwithstanding the fact that they do not represent the work of the apostle himself. For the believer, the six epistles are authoritative and inspired.

Second Thessalonians

Although there are serious problems with attributing 2 Thessalonians to Paul, there remains a good number of authors who think the epistle is authentically his.[3] Whether written by Paul or by a second-generation disciple of the apostle, the epistle seems to have been written in order to refocus the eschatology of 1 Thessalonians. This letter seems to imply that the Parousia of the Lord Jesus would occur relatively soon, even during the apostle's life. Second Thessalonians reworks the eschatology. Instead of assuming that the Parousia would take place while the author was still alive, 2 Thessalonians postulates a series of occurrences that must take place before the Parousia occurs. The scenario that is presented employs a rich and sometimes mysterious symbolism that is characteristic of apocalyptic literature.

Following the model of the outline of 1 Thessalonians, 2 Thessalonians concludes with a hortatory section in which we read:

> Now we command you, beloved, in the name of our Lord Jesus Christ, to keep away from believers who are living in idleness and not according to the tradition that they received from us. For you yourselves know how you ought to imitate us; we were not idle when we were with you and we did not eat any one's bread without paying for it; but with toil and labor we worked day and night, so that we might not burden

[3] Among them, Fee, Green, Malherbe, and Weima, in their respective commentaries.

any of you. This was not because we do not have that right, but in order to give you an example to imitate. For even when we were with you, we gave you this command: Anyone unwilling to work should not eat. For we hear that some of you are living in idleness, mere busybodies, not doing any work. Now such persons we command and exhort in the Lord Jesus Christ to do their work quietly and to earn their own living. Brothers and sisters, do not be weary in doing what is right.[4]

Of itself, this passage, the only one in 2 Thessalonians that speaks of financial matters, should not be included in this study of wealth and the wealthy.[5] The passage is, however, widely quoted by those who claim that the indigent should not be provided with (public) funds for their support, not even at a subsistence level. The argument goes something like this: Scripture says that people who do not work should not receive food to eat. The flaw in the argument is that the author speaks of "anyone unwilling to work" (*tis ou thelei ergazesthai*). The author's stress is on the will not to work, on a decision not to work.[6] In contemporary society, many of those who do not work either cannot find a job or are unable to work.

The passage echoes not only the Pauline motif that the apostle worked at his trade in order to be self-supporting while he preached the gospel but also an idea that appeared in Acts, namely, that the apostle's work should be seen as an example to be followed. In the past, the passage was often taken to be a rebuke of those who, in the expectation of an imminent Parousia, decided not to work anymore. Why work when the end is at hand?

Studies by Ceslaus Spicq have shown that words belonging to the *atakt-* word group connote disorderly behavior rather than idleness as such.[7] Citing the authority of the Lord Jesus Christ, the author of

---

[4] 2 Thess 3:6-13.

[5] At most, the passage might be included because it urges its readers to earn their own wages.

[6] Cf. Béda Rigaux, *Saint Paul: Les épîtres aux Thessaloniens*, EBib (Paris: Gabalda, 1956), 709; Abraham J. Malherbe, *The Letters to the Thessalonians*, AB 32B (New York: Doubleday, 2000), 452.

[7] See Spicq, "*atakteō, ataktos, ataktōs*," *TLNT* 1:223–26, for a succinct synopsis of this work.

2 Thessalonians urges the community to avoid disorderly behavior. One particular issue, of which the author claims to have been apprised, is that some within the community are not spending their time in working to support themselves but are engaged in busybodying. Busybodies are a classic topos in the Hellenistic world.[8] The author of 2 Thessalonians uses a pun, difficult to retain in English,[9] to describe the situation. His response is that the members of the community should follow Paul's example and be gainfully employed. An orderly community is one in which its members provide for themselves and their families. They should earn their own wages.

Colossians and Ephesians

Some commentators continue to hold that Colossians was written by the apostle Paul. For some decades now, however, the consensus among scholars is that Colossians is a pseudepigraphic composition. The question then becomes that of the relationship between the Epistle to the Colossians and the Epistle to the Ephesians. The issue is necessarily raised since there is considerable similarity of vocabulary between the two, a rather similar outline, and even some similarity of discrete passages in the two epistles. My view is that Ephesians is a revised and expanded edition of Colossians, expanded in such a way that the later text becomes almost a focused treatise on the church.

Colossians 3:5

Writing about new life in Christ, the consequence of sharing in Christ's resurrection, the author of the Epistle to the Colossians exhorts his readers, "Set your minds on things that are above, not on things that are on earth."[10] Almost immediately thereafter he specifies

[8] See, for example, Plutarch, *On Being a Busybody* (*Moralia* 516A); Lucian, *Icaromenippus.*

[9] The NRSV renders the Greek *mēden ergazomenous alla periergazonemous* of v. 11 as "mere busybodies, not doing any work." Moffatt's translation attempts to retain the pun with "busybodies" instead of "busy."

[10] Col 3:2.

these earthly realities[11] as he writes, "Put to death, therefore, whatever in you is earthly: fornication, impurity, passion, evil desire, and greed (which is idolatry)."[12] Such behavior incurs the wrath of God.[13] These earthly realities are inconsistent with the new life in Christ, with sharing in Christ's resurrection.

The epistle writer employs the classic topos of a catalogue of vices[14] to illustrate the earthly realities that should have no place in the life of the believer. The first four are of a sexual nature. Then comes greed, which can be interpreted as the source of the previously cited sexual evils.[15] Greed (*pleonexia*) is always an inordinate desire for something more,[16] hence it can easily lead to a desire for more in the area of sexual activity.[17] Because of the almost inevitable connection between the two vices, Plutarch linked greed with debauchery.[18]

The philosophic moralists considered greed to be one of the most serious of vices, detrimental to both the individual and the community. Menander, for example, declares, "Greed is a very great evil for humans."[19] In an era roughly contemporary with that of the epistle writer, the philosopher Dio Chrysostom spoke of greed as "the worst of deities."[20] Spicq says that greed is not only insatiable and excessive but also aggressive.[21]

---

[11] The same Greek phrase, *ta epi tēs gēs*, is translated as "things that are on earth" in v. 2 and as "whatever is earthly" in v. 5.

[12] Col 3:5.

[13] Cf. Col 3:6.

[14] See above, pp. 26–27. The author of Colossians complements the list of vices in 3:5 with another five-item list in 3:8.

[15] Charles H. Talbert, *Ephesians and Colossians*, Paideia Commentaries on the New Testament Series (Grand Rapids: Baker Academic, 2007), 227; cf. Jean-Noël Aletti, *Saint Paul: Épître aux Colossiens*, EBib (Paris: Gabalda, 1993), 225.

[16] Etymologically, the Greek term *pleon-exia* means to have or to want more.

[17] Sumney notes that another's wife is included in the biblical prohibition of covetousness. Cf. Exod 20:17; Jerry L. Sumney, *Colossians*, NTL (Louisville: Westminster John Knox, 2008), 190.

[18] Cf. Plutarch, *Agis* 3:1; 10:5.

[19] Cf. Curt Wachsuth and Otto Hense, *Joannis Stobaei Anthologium* (Berlin: Weidman, 1894–1923), 3:408. Wachsuth and Hense's work is the modern edition of the fifth-century collection of sayings that Stobaeus compiled for his son Septimius.

[20] Dio Chrysostom, *Discourses* 17.1.

[21] See Spicq, "*pleonexia*," TLNT 3:117–19, at 117.

Thus far, the use of the vice list in Colossians is in keeping with then-contemporary thought about sexual immorality and greed, but then the author adds the phrase "which is idolatry" (*ētis estin eidōlolatria*) to clarify what greed really means. The notion of idolatry comes from the Jewish world even if the term itself, "idolatry" (*eidōlolatria*), may be a Christian formulation.[22] The apostle Paul himself may well have been the first person to use the term.[23] In any case, "idolatry" is a derogatory term used to speak of polytheistic religious practices and beliefs. When the author of Colossians 3:5 identifies greed as a form of idolatry, he echoes a notion found in various Jewish texts and builds on the close association of greed and idolatry in Paul's own lists of vices.[24] In the postbiblical Jewish world, texts such as *T. Levi.* 17.11; *T. Jud.* 18.2 and 19.2; Philo's *Spec. Laws* 1.23-27; and Qumran's 1QpHab 6.1 and 8.11-12 relate greed and idolatry. Margaret MacDonald suggests that within the epistle writer's community greed could be equated with idolatry because of group identity. In their pursuit of wealth, the affluent members of the community might have become closely associated with nonbelievers and adopted some of their practices.[25]

For a monotheist, idolatry is the most serious of sins.[26] In the Jewish world, it is the most deadly divergence from the way of the one true God.[27] Idolatry constitutes a rejection of the one God, the Lord and creator of all. By identifying greed as a form of idolatry—of the five vices listed in Colossians 3:5, greed is the only one so identified—the epistle writer designates greed as one of the most serious of sins. It places wealth in the stead of God. The pursuit of wealth replaces the worship of God as the priority in one's life. In the words of James Dunn, "'Greed' is a form of idolatry because it projects

---

[22] Cf. James D. G. Dunn, *The Epistles to the Colossians and to Philemon*, NIGTC (Grand Rapids: Eerdmans, 1996), 215.

[23] That is, in 1 Cor 10:14 and Gal 5:20. The other New Testament use of the term is to be found in 1 Pet 4:3.

[24] See especially 1 Cor 5:9, 10; above, p. 26.

[25] Cf. Margaret Y. MacDonald, *Colossians and Ephesians*, SP 17 (Collegeville, MN: Liturgical Press, 2000), 135, 149–50.

[26] Cf. Exod 20:4-5; Deut 5:8-9.

[27] Thus, Ernest Best in *Ephesians*, ICC (London: T & T Clark, 1998), 481.

acquisitiveness and personal satisfaction as objective go(o)ds to be praised and served."[28] The identification of greed with wealth belongs to the same matrix of thought as does the Synoptics' "You cannot serve God and wealth."[29] The service of wealth is incompatible with the worship of the one true God.

Ephesians 5:5

One of the similarities between Colossians and Ephesians is their common identification of greed as idolatry. The author of the Epistle to the Ephesians writes, "Be sure of this, that no fornicator or impure person, or one who is greedy (that is, an idolater [*ho estin eidōlatrēs*]), has any inheritance in the kingdom of Christ and of God."[30] The passage, embedded within a long exhortation urging that evil has no place in the lives of believers, is clearly reliant on Colossians 3:5. In both cases, there is a catalogue of vices, the list consists of sexual vices and greed, and there is the interpretive aside[31] on idolatry. The author of Ephesians has used personal forms in his list rather than the abstract forms found in Colossians, but that does not change the thrust of his words.

What is of more importance is that the epistle writer has modified the paraenetic exhortation of Colossians 3:5 so that it has become a declarative statement, whose importance the writer has empha-sized with the introductory lemma "Be sure of this" (*touto gar iste ginōskontes*). The writer wants his readers to know the importance of what he is about to say. His words are virtually a command. There can be no mistake as to what he has to say.

What he has to say is that those guilty of any one of three serious vices—fornication, impurity, and greed, which is idolatry—have no inheritance in the kingdom of God and his Christ. The kingdom of God is a traditional biblical motif and the object of Jesus' preaching.

---

[28] Dunn, *Colossians and Philemon*, 216.
[29] Cf. Matt 6:24; Luke 16:13. See above, pp. 120–21, 177–79.
[30] Eph 5:5.
[31] Punctuation was not used in ancient manuscripts. The parentheses found in Col 3:5 and Eph 5:5 (NRSV) are the editor's way of identifying the function of the enclosed clauses.

The kingdom of Christ is a relatively new idea, whose source may be the apostle Paul himself,[32] consistent with the epistle writer's notion of the cosmic Christ.[33] In the New Testament, the double expression "the kingdom of Christ and of God" is proper to Ephesians 5:5. Using the notion of inheritance, the author speaks of the exclusion of greedy persons from the kingdom.[34] Because of their avarice, the greedy reject the reign of God and the reign of Christ.

Lest the audience not get the message, the author adds another threat to the warning of deprivation from God's benevolent rule, realized in Christ, articulated in 5:5. Reprising an idea found in Colossians, he writes, "The wrath of God comes on those who are disobedient."[35] This second threat is the other side of the coin of exclusion from the kingdom. It expresses in positive terms what exclusion expresses in negative terms.

No more than did the author of Colossians does the author of Ephesians speak of the plight of those who have been harmed by another's greed. He has not written a moral treatise. His epistle is mainly concerned with the church, which is to be holy and unsullied.[36] In Ephesians 5:5, the epistle writer's concern is for the good of the church. The threats of verses 5 and 6 are directed to those whose idolatrous behavior, expressed in greed, defiles the church. Using threats, the epistle writer urges them to change their ways.

Ephesians 4:28

The author's ecclesial interest results in his not writing much about wealth, wages, and the wealthy. His epistle does, however, include a short passage in which he writes about earning a livelihood and what

---

[32] Cf. 1 Cor 15:24.

[33] Cf. Eph 1:20-23.

[34] Some exegetes and some theologians entertain a discussion as to whether the epistle writer is referring to the future, eschatological reign of God or to God's present kingdom. Peter O'Brien suggests that the double formulation refers to both the future reign (of God) and God's present reign (of Christ). Cf. Peter T. O'Brien, *The Letter to the Ephesians*, Pillar New Testament Commentary (Grand Rapids: Eerdmans, 1999), 364.

[35] Cf. Col 3:6.

[36] Cf. Eph 5:25b-27.

a person should do with the compensation that he earns: "Thieves must give up stealing; rather let them labor and work honestly, so as to have something to share with the needy."³⁷ This Scripture, often overlooked in studies of the epistle, is germane to the present study. The exhortation to avoid stealing echoes the Decalogue;³⁸ the accompanying positive exhortation is what merits particular attention.

The author first addresses thieving members within the community. For the most part, the economy of the time was principally a barter economy, based on an exchange of goods rather than on an exchange of money for goods. Most likely, then, these thieves were involved in the stealing of goods that belonged to others rather than in the stealing of money. The author urges these thieves to give up their stealing and work honestly and gainfully (*to agathon*) at a manual trade.³⁹ His exhortation echoes the paraenesis of the Thessalonian correspondence.⁴⁰ Within Judaism, manual labor was well regarded. Both Jesus and Paul were engaged in manual labor.

The epistle writer then appends a reason why former thieves should be engaged in gainful employment. Unlike 2 Thessalonians, the purpose that he alleges is not the imitation of Paul; rather, he says, sometime thieves should work so as to have something to share with someone who is in need (*tō chreian echonti*).⁴¹ In the epistle writer's eyes, responsibility for taking care of the needy falls on each member of the community, not simply on the rich. If thieves have no money, they should stop stealing and get some work so that they can provide for the needy.

---

³⁷ Eph 4:28.

³⁸ Cf. Exod 20:17; Deut 5:21; Lev 19:11; Isa 1:23; Jer 7:9. Exod 20:15 originally pertained to depriving an Israelite of his freedom, selling a member of the covenanted people into slavery.

³⁹ Textual problems in this verse may have arisen from a presumed incompatibility of "good" (*agathon*) with manual labor (*tais idiais chersin*). One or the other of these Greek expressions is absent from some ancient manuscripts. Cf. Metzger, *Textual Commentary*, 537–38. The language, says O'Brien (*Ephesians*, 343) does not mean that only manual labor is recommended. While undoubtedly true, the remark seems extraneous to the circumstances envisioned by the epistle writer.

⁴⁰ 1 Thess 4:11; 2 Thess 3:12.

⁴¹ The phrase is formulated in the singular, not in the plural as the NRSV's "the needy" might seem to suggest.

Ernest Best draws attention to the communitarian dimension of the exhortation when he writes, "Thieves fail to play their part in the life of the community, not because they steal from fellow members, but because they make no financial contribution to it; the new conduct demanded of them would positively benefit the community."[42] The epistle writer's exhortation is not so much a "thou shalt not" as it is a "thou shalt." His concern is for the well-being of the church. In pursuit of that aim, he instructs his audience as to how they should use their income. "Labor is necessary," writes Markus Barth, "in order that the needy may live!"[43]

The Pastoral Epistles

The two epistles addressed to Timothy and that addressed to Titus are generally grouped together under the name Pastoral Epistles. The nomenclature derives from an old presumption that these texts were pastoral directives written to Paul's closest co-workers, his "assistants," who were to succeed him in the pastoral ministry. Timothy and Titus were then considered to be "pastors," Timothy in Ephesus, Titus on Crete.[44]

Discussions about the authorship of these epistles continue until the present day. I, along with most scholars, hold that all three epistles were written after the death of Paul, perhaps by different authors who belonged to the same school. Similar vocabulary and ideology[45] characterize the three texts in such a way that the reader cannot escape the conclusion that there is some relationship among them.

The three epistles were written late in the first century CE, but they do not belong to the same literary genre. First Timothy and Titus are documents of church order. For the most part they give instructions for how members of the household of God are to conduct themselves

---

[42] Best, *Ephesians*, 453.

[43] Markus Barth, *Ephesians 4–6*, AB 36A (Garden City, NY: Doubleday, 1974), 517.

[44] Cf. 1 Tim 1:3; Titus 1:5.

[45] Notably, the singular emphasis on Paul and his authority (e.g., Titus 1:1-3), the "the saying is sure" refrain (e.g., 1 Tim 1:3), and the "manifestation" (*epiphaneia*) Christology (e.g., 2 Tim 1:10).

in the circumstances of that time.[46] The Parousia of the Lord Jesus Christ had not yet occurred; the church had to settle in for the long haul, to establish itself as a viable and respectable community in the Greco-Roman world. Second Timothy, on the other hand, is a testament. It is a disciple's reflection on the significance of the apostle Paul, written more than a generation after his death. It captures the memory of an important figure and apostolic authority for believers in the late first century.

First Timothy

The six chapters of this epistle make it the longest of the three Pastoral Epistles. Since it is a document that deals with ecclesiastical regulation,[47] it is to be expected that it would have a considerable amount to say about wealth, wages, and the wealthy.

First Timothy 3:3

One of the features of 1 Timothy and Titus is that they set out a profile of qualities expected of those who are to assume positions of leadership in the church, its "overseers" (*episkopoi*) and the "assistants" (*diakonoi*).[48] Of the two positions, that of overseer was the most important. First Timothy 3:1-7 spells out what an overseer must be, with a list of sixteen qualifications that a would-be overseer should have. Such lists were not unknown in Hellenistic literature. For example, the philosopher Onasander spells out the qualifications of a military officer. He must be chosen because "he is temperate, self-restrained, vigilant, frugal, hardened to labor, alert, free from avarice."[49]

---

[46] Cf. 1 Tim 3:15.

[47] Cf. Raymond F. Collins, "The Origins of Church Law," *The Jurist* 61 (2001): 134–56.

[48] The Greek terms *episkopoi* and *diakonoi* generally appear in English translation as "bishops" and "deacons," respectively. Given the role played by bishops and deacons in contemporary churches, these translations of the two words lead to anachronistic interpretations of the ancient text.

[49] Onasander, *The General* 1.1. Cf. Yann Redalié, *Paul après Paul: Le temps, le salut, la morale selon les épîtres à Timothée et à Tite*, MdB 31 (Geneva: Labor et Fides, 1994), 342–43.

Two of the qualifications for leadership on Onasander's list have to do with a proper use of wealth, namely, that the leader be frugal and that he be free from avarice. With regard to being free from greed, the philosopher writes, "This quality of freedom from avarice [*aphilargyron*] will be valued most highly, since it is largely responsible for the incorruptible and large-minded management of affairs."[50] Extolling the qualities of Atoninus, the second-century CE Roman emperor,[51] Marcus Aurelius is reported to have said, "In the first place, he had a love of wisdom; in the second place, he did not love money [*to deuteron aphilargyros*]; and in the third place, he loved virtue."[52]

Among the expected qualifications of the ecclesiastical overseer is that he similarly be not a lover of money (*aphilagyron*).[53] The word itself—which Spicq says echoes Matthew 6:34, "you cannot serve God and wealth"[54]—occurs just twice in the New Testament, here and in Hebrews 13:5. Philo considers the love of money to be a disease and unholy.[55] The appearance of "not a lover of money" among the overseer's qualifications is a sign that the leaders of a community seeking to establish its place in society should be as incorruptible in their leadership as were other leaders in society. For them, as for the overseer in the church, a love of money would easily lead to various forms of corruption.[56] Within the church, it is particularly important that the overseer not exploit the community to his own profit.[57]

First Timothy 3:8

Like the overseer, the assistant would have had some responsibility for offerings made by members of the community. Hence, it is required that he not be a person who is greedy for money (*mē aischrokerdeis*).[58] At the time when the Pastoral Epistles were written,

---

[50] *General* 1.8.
[51] Antoninus Pius reigned from 138 to 161 CE.
[52] *P. Oxy.* 33.II.11.
[53] Cf. 1 Tim 3:3.
[54] Cf. Spicq, "*aphilagyros*," *TLNT* 1:245–46, at 245.
[55] Cf. Philo, *Laws* 1.24, 281.
[56] Cf. Pol. *Phil.* 6:1.
[57] *T. Levi* 17:1 identifies love of money as a vice of priests.
[58] Cf. 1 Tim 3:8.

greed for money was a particularly evil form of love for money. It was the pursuit of sordid gain.[59] Demosthenes, the great Athenian orator, linked it with villainy,[60] while Aristotle portrayed it as a vice against honor and moral beauty.[61]

That assistants in the household of God not have this vice and, on the other hand, that they be models of financial integrity were crucial given their role in the distribution of goods to the needy.[62] Widows, particularly, were in a vulnerable situation; they were easily exploited. First Timothy 5:3-6 describes how women who were true widows—widows without other means of support—are to be supported by the church.[63] It details how these widows are to be cared for. It begins with the formal exhortation, "Honor widows who are really widows."[64] "Honor" (*tima*) does not simply mean "hold in high regard"; rather, it means "provide for, take care of," just as it does in the precept to honor one's father and mother.[65] Elderly parents were not able to support themselves, hence, their families were bound to support them.

The biblical commandment remained in force in the Pastoral Epistles' household of God. The author of 1 Timothy begins his exposition on the support of widows by saying, "If a widow has children or grand-children, they should first learn their religious duty to their own family and make some repayment to their parents"[66] and concludes, "If any believing woman has relatives who are really widows, let her assist them; let the church not be burdened, so that it can assist those who are really widows."[67] Primary responsibility for

---

[59] See Theophrastus, *Char.* 30.1-2.

[60] Cf. Demosthenes, *3 Aphob.* 4.

[61] Cf. Aristotle, *Eth. nic.* 4.33.1121[b7] ff.

[62] Cf. Acts 6:3.

[63] Kidd describes these women as "*destitute* widows" [his emphasis]. Cf. Reggie M. Kidd, *Wealth and Beneficence in the Pastoral Epistles: A "Bourgeois" Form of Early Christianity?*, SBLDS 122 (Atlanta: Scholars Press, 1990), 103.

[64] 1 Tim 5:3.

[65] Cf. Exod 20:12 [LXX]; Deut 5:16 [LXX]; cf. Raymond F. Collins, "Obedience, Children and the Fourth Commandment—A New Testament Note," *LS* 4 (1972–1973): 157–73.

[66] 1 Tim 5:4.

[67] 1 Tim 5:16.

caring for elderly widows falls on their progeny. If they do not have children and grandchildren to take care of them, it falls to the church to take care of these widows. It is not unlikely that "assistants" were involved in the administration of this support.

In sum, it is required that church officials be characterized by financial integrity not only because such integrity was required of other leaders in society[68] but also, and particularly, because of their role in the distribution of money and goods for the support of the needy.[69]

First Timothy 5:17-18

The longest of the Pastoral Epistles is not only concerned with the qualifications and responsibilities of church leaders; it also has something to say about their support. In a short passage known as "The Elders' Bill of Rights,"[70] the author writes:

> Let the elders who rule[71] well be considered worthy of double honor, especially those who labor in preaching and teaching; for the scripture says, "You shall not muzzle an ox while it is treading out the grain," and, "The laborer deserves to be paid."[72]

The financial compensation of church leaders is the point of this brace of verses. Its author pays special attention to those ministries of preaching and teaching. Those who are engaged in this pair of ministries are especially worthy of "double honor" (*diplēs timēs*).

In this passage, 1 Timothy 5:2–6:2b, words formed from the tim-root have an economic connotation,[73] while in the doxologies of

---

[68] 1 Tim 3:7a stipulates that leaders of the church should be held in high regard by outside observers.

[69] Cf. Spicq, "*aischrokerdēs, aphilargyros*," *TLNT* 1:46–48, at 47n10; Jürgen Roloff, *Der erste Brief an Timotheus*, EKKNT 15 (Zurich: Benziger; Neukirchen-Vluyn: Neukirchener Verlag, 1988), 162.

[70] 1 Tim 5:17-22.

[71] "Rule" is an overly strong translation of the Greek *proestōtes*. "Preside" or "lead" would be more appropriate.

[72] 1 Tim 5:17-18.

[73] Cf. 1 Tim 5:3, 17; 6:1; Deborah Krause, *1 Timothy* (London: T & T Clark, 2004), 116.

1 Timothy 1:17 and 6:16, the noun *timē* retains the broader connotation of honor. Because of this ambiguity, it is not entirely clear that the author has "double pay"[74] or "double compensation" in mind. Moreover, the financial strictures of the community[75] might suggest that the community would not be so extravagant in the expenditure of its money as a double stipend would imply. It is preferable, I think, to envision the author as urging the members of the household of God to extend a double form of honor to their leaders, that is, both esteem and adequate financial support.[76]

The author's emphasis is, nonetheless, on the financial compensation of church leaders. In dependence on 1 Corinthians 9, he cites two maxims that support his directive to the community. As did Paul in 1 Corinthians 9:9,[77] the author cites an item of agricultural law, Deuteronomy 25:4, in a *qal va-homer* argument, from the lesser to the greater, to support the directive. That the author of 1 Timothy does not generally cite Scripture in this fashion makes it rather clear that he depends on Paul at this point in his text.[78] The author confirms the scriptural argument with the adage found in Luke 10:7,[79] "The laborer deserves to be paid." This gnomic maxim affirms that all workers deserve to be paid. The author of 1 Timothy appropriates the general affirmation and applies it to the elders in his community, especially those involved in the ministries of preaching and teaching. If all workers have a right to a fair wage, he argues, so too do ministers in the church have a right to adequate compensation.

---

[74] Thus, Jerome D. Quinn and William C. Wacker, *The First and Second Letters to Timothy*, ECC (Grand Rapids: Eerdmans, 2000), 460; Robert W. Wall with Richard B. Steele, *1 and 2 Timothy and Titus*, Two Horizons New Testament Commentary (Grand Rapids: Eerdmans, 2012), 132.

[75] Cf. 1 Tim 5:16.

[76] Also Ambrosiaster, *Commentary on 1 Tim*, CSEL 81.3:284; Raymond F. Collins, *I and II Timothy and Titus: A Commentary*, NTL (Louisville: Westminster John Knox, 2002), 144–45; Benjamin Fiore, *The Pastoral Epistles: First Timothy, Second Timothy, Titus*, SP 12 (Collegeville, MN: Liturgical Press, 2007), n111.

[77] See above, p. 36.

[78] Krause argues at length that the author is more concerned with Paul's text than he is with Paul's example and authority. Cf. Krause, *1 Timothy*, 111, 147–56.

[79] See above, p. 122.

First Timothy 6:6-10

A little later in this epistle, the author of 1 Timothy, whom I have called the pastor because of his desire to address pastoral directives to his flock,[80] concludes a sweeping condemnation of false teachers by saying that they seek to make money from religion; they imagine piety to be a "source of gain."[81] This prompts him to share with his audience some serious reflection on money.[82] He first addresses the avaricious who want to be wealthy,[83] then he addresses those who are wealthy.[84]

In the first of these passages the author of 1 Timothy counters the notion that naked wealth confers the right to lead, says Reggie.[85] His statement needs some nuance. In 1 Timothy 6:6-8, the pastor draws on popular philosophic ideas to affirm that godliness, accompanied by self-sufficiency, is advantageous. The NRSV translates what the author has written in this fashion: "Of course, there is great gain in godliness [*hē eusebeia*] combined with contentment [*autarkeias*]."[86] To an English-language reader, the translation suggests that the author is using a word that belongs to the same word group from which he draws when he writes about being content (*arkesthēsometha*) in verse 8, but this is not the case.

A more serious difficulty with the translation is that it neglects the importance of the virtue of self-sufficiency (*autarkeia*) in Hellenistic moral thought. Plato[87] and Marcus Aurelius[88] extolled the virtue of self-sufficiency. Self-sufficiency is a common topos in Hellenistic moral discourse. Socrates is said to have spurned the king's offer of riches, for he preferred self-sufficiency to riches.[89] The self-sufficient

---

[80] See Collins, *I and II Timothy*, passim.

[81] 1 Tim 6:5. Cf. 1QpHab 8:3-13; CD 4:15-19.

[82] Similarly, W. Hulitt Gloer and Perry L. Stepp, *Reading Paul's Letters to Individuals: A Literary and Theological Commentary on Paul's Letters to Philemon, Titus, and Timothy* (Macon, GA: Smyth & Helwys, 2008), 197.

[83] 1 Tim 6:6-10.

[84] 1 Tim 6:17-19.

[85] Cf. Kidd, *Wealth and Beneficence*, 100.

[86] 1 Tim 6:6.

[87] Plato, *Lysis* 215A.

[88] Marcus Aurelius, *Meditations* 4.25; 10.1.1; 11.15.4-6.

[89] Cf. *Joannis Stobaei Anthologium* 4.33.28.

person is satisfied with him- or herself and with what he or she has. That person is independent, not having a need to rely on others or wanting to accumulate more than what he or she has. At its core, self-sufficiency is a matter of self-satisfaction. That is an ideal for the philosophic moralists and an important virtue for the author of 1 Timothy.

For the pastor, the antithesis of self-sufficiency (*autarkeia*) is the love of money (*philagyria*), about which he writes devastatingly in 1 Timothy 6:9-10:

> But those who want to be rich fall into temptation and are trapped by many senseless and harmful[90] desires that plunge people into ruin and destruction.[91] For the love of money is a root of all kinds of evil, and in their eagerness to be rich some have wandered away from the faith and pierced themselves with many pains.

The words are addressed to those who want to climb out of their socioeconomic condition by amassing wealth. To fully understand what the author wants his readers to understand, it is useful to break down what he writes into three movements of thought.

Apropos those who want to be rich (*hoi de boulomenoi ploutein*), the pastor first of all declares that they fall into temptation (*eis peirasmon*). This phrase, familiar to most readers because of its appearance in the Lord's Prayer,[92] is to be taken with utmost seriousness. Temptation is not a matter of being attracted to one or another wrong action. Rather, it is a matter of ultimate temptation. It is a test of one's loyalties; to fall into temptation is to be in a situation in which one's allegiance to God is at stake. It is temptation with eschatological consequences.

Having echoed the early Christian understanding of temptation as a pitfall of those who want to be rich, the pastor speaks of the desire to be rich from a point of view that echoes the philosophic moralists.

---

[90] The Greek adjective *blaberas* is a strong word that occurs only here in the New Testament.

[91] In Greek, this verse is characterized by paronomasia; the "p" sound occurs nine times.

[92] Matt 6:13.

Those who desire to be rich fall into the trap of desire.[93] The Stoics had a rather negative view of "desire." For these moralists, "desire" (*epithymia*) is not simply wanting to have food or sex; rather, it is any kind of inordinate and uncontrolled desire. Those who want to be rich fall into any number of desires, says the pastor. He characterizes these desires as senseless and harmful. These desires prevent people from reaching the fullness of truth and lead to disastrous deterioration. The result? Those who want to be rich fall into utter and final ruin, eschatological ruin, the work of Satan.[94]

The pastor underscores his reflection on those who want to be rich with a foundational statement of principle:[95] "For the love of money is a root[96] of all kinds of evil [*rixa . . . pantōn tōn kakōn*]." Just as there are core virtues, virtues that come to fruition in other virtues, there are also root vices, vices that give rise to other vices. Philo considered that desire, inequality, pride, and falsehood were such vices.[97] With this second movement of his thought, the pastor enters into the philosophic discussion by affirming that a love of money (*hē philargyria*) is the source of all kinds of evil; it is a root vice. First Timothy 6:10 is the only passage in the New Testament that explicitly speaks of the love of money, using the word *philargyria*.[98] The maxim[99] resonates with that of Bion of Borysthenes, the

---

[93] The author's Greek phrase, *eis peirasmon kai pagida kai epithymias pollas anoētous kai blaberas*, coordinates "temptation" (*peirasmon*), "trap" (*pagida*), and "many senseless and harmful desires" (*epithymias pollas anoētous kai blaberas*), joining each of the three nouns by *kai*, "and." Some important Western manuscripts, perhaps under the influence of 1 Tim 3:7, add "of the devil" (*tou diabolou*) to qualify "trap." The "desire" phrase should be taken epexegetically, as an attempt to clarify the meaning of the author's "trap."

[94] See Collins, *I and II Timothy*, 158–59.

[95] See the explanatory *gar*, "for," in v. 10.

[96] The NRSV translation leaves open the issue of other root vices and respects the anarthous character—there is no qualifying article—of the Greek *rixa*. The popular translation of the pastor's explanation, "the love of money is the root of all evil," seems to suggest that he is affirming that there is only one root vice.

[97] References can be found in Collins, *I and II Timothy*, 159.

[98] The related adjective appears in 2 Tim 3:2 and Luke 16:4, apropos the Pharisees (see above, p. 170). The antonym appears in 1 Tim 3:3, in the list of qualifications of the overseer (see above, p. 225), and in Heb 13:5.

[99] Roloff, *Der erste Brief*, 338; Redalié (*Paul après Paul*, 453) describes the author's saying as a proverb.

third-century BCE philosopher, who said, "The love of money is the mother city of all evils."[100] In turn, the pastor's thought was echoed by Polycarp of Smyrna, who wrote, "The love of money is the beginning of all troubles."[101]

In his third movement of thought, the author of 1 Timothy adds a kind of peroration. With reference to the "sound words of our Lord Jesus Christ and the teaching that is in accordance with godliness," the content of the faith of the church, he says that "in their eagerness to be rich some [*hēs tines oregomenoi*] have wandered away from the faith and pierced themselves with many pains." Not all, but some (*tines*) have abandoned the faith because of their cupidity, their desire for wealth, and have stabbed themselves (*heautous periepeiran*), causing pain. The metaphor[102] dramatically portrays what these people have done to themselves; their love of money is a kind of self-mutilation that causes much pain.

First Timothy 6:17-19

In the accompanying exhortation, the pastor speaks to the wealthy. That his final exhortation is addressed to the affluent is an indication not only that there were a number of well-to-do in his community but also that he considered some of their conduct to be problematic. In 1 Timothy 6:6-10 he issues them a warning; in 1 Timothy 6:17-18 he offers them advice as to how they ought to use their wealth. He uses the rhetorical device of paronomasia, the repetition of a same sound, to make his point. Those who listened to the reading of his epistle[103] would have heard the sound of "riches," the Greek root *plout-*, echo throughout this final exhortation:

> As for those who in the present age are rich [*tois plousiois*], command them not to be haughty, or to set their hopes on the

---

[100] Cf. *Joannis Stobaei Anthologium* 3.10.37. A similar saying has also been attributed to the Cynic, Diogenes of Sinope. Cf. Diogenes Laertius, *Lives* 7.111, 6.50.

[101] *Phil.* 4:1. The Greek reads *archē de pantōn chalepōn philargyria*.

[102] Cf. Philo, *Flacc.* 1.

[103] In the largely nonliterate societies of the first century CE texts such as 1 Timothy were read to the congregation. The reception of these texts was an auditory rather than a visual experience.

uncertainty of riches [*ploutou*], but rather on God who richly [*plousiōs*] provides us with everything for our enjoyment. They are to do good, to be rich [*ploutiein*] in good works, generous and ready to share, thus storing up for themselves the treasure of a good foundation for the future, so that they may take hold of the life that really is life.[104]

As the author is coming to the end of his writing, his style affects the mode of a personal letter. He adopts the persona of Paul writing to his son, Timothy.[105] He does not address the rich directly; rather, he instructs his Timothy to give a command in the name of the apostle Paul.

Two contrasts envelop the author's central exhortation. The first is between the present (*en tō nyn aiōni*) and the future (*eis to mellon*). What takes place in the present has an impact on the future. The second contrast is between riches (*ploutou*) and God (*theō*). The contrast recalls the dichotomy between God and wealth set out in the aphorism of Luke 16:23,[106] "You cannot serve God and wealth." Those who are wealthy should not be conceited. Rather than place their trust in wealth, by nature ephemeral,[107] they are to trust in God who provides us with all that we need. Wealth is given for our enjoyment (*eis apolausin*[108]). The phrase cuts both ways. It counters the idea that only an ill-advised voluntary poverty is pleasing to God, and, on the other hand, wealth is given to us to make the most of it. Philo and Josephus had used the phrase referring to enjoyment with regard to food, sustenance, and the necessities of everyday life.[109] What the author says about wealth in 1 Timothy 6:17-18 comes from the same matrix of thought as what he had to say about marriage and food in 1 Timothy 4:3-4.

God's gifts are given for a reason. The philosophic moralists deemed wealth a means to an end. Amassing wealth for its own

---

[104] 1 Tim 6:17-19.
[105] Cf. 1 Tim 1:2.
[106] Cf. Matt 6:24.
[107] Cf. Luke 12:16-22.
[108] The word appears only twice in the New Testament, here and in Heb 11:25.
[109] Cf. Philo, *Mos* 2.70; *Rewards* 135; Josephus, *Antiquities* 1.1.4; 8.6.1.

sake was considered greedy and evil.[110] How are those who listened to the reading of the author's missive to make the most of the wealth that they have received from the riches of God? They are to do good, abound in good works, be generous, and share their wealth with others. This is the pastor's program of reform,[111] an ethical responsibility for believers.[112]

To "do good" (*agathoergein*) is to perform a good deed for someone else. To be "rich in good works" (*ploutein en ergois kalois*) means that they should be as lavish in sharing their possessions as God is in sharing the goods of his creation. To "be generous" (*eumetadotous einai*) is to give what one has to another. Finally, in a kind of hendiadys,[113] the author wraps up his exhortation with the idea that the rich should be "ready to share" (*koinōnikous*). They should be attentive to the common good. The pastor's final phrase echoes the Lucan idea that members of the believing community should share what they have so that there is no needy person among them.[114] His fourfold iteration is intended to make the point with utter clarity.

Then, in a kind of peroration, the author urges his rich listeners to think about the future. If they heed his advice to use their God-given wealth "for enjoyment," as he has explained the term, they will be storing up treasure for the future. They will be investing in the future, where they will enjoy the "true life" (*tēs ontōs zōēs*), life eternal. The pastor's words about a future treasure reflect a common motif in early Christian thought about wealth, found not only in the Q saying of Luke 12:32-34 (Matt 6:19-21)[115] but also in James 5:2-3.[116]

The pastor's thought is not particularly novel, nor is it particularly Christian. Some four centuries before the pastor had dictated

---

[110] Cf. *Love of Wealth* 4 [*Moralia* 525A]; 5 [*Moralia* 526BC].

[111] The expression comes from Fiore, *The Pastoral Epistles*, 124.

[112] Cf. Roloff, *Der erste Brief*, 368.

[113] Dornier notes that "be generous" and "be ready to share" are almost synonymous. He says that the first, "generous," is applicable to someone who gives without being asked while the second, "share," connotes a constant desire to help everyone. Cf. Pierre Dornier, *Les Épîtres pastorales*, SB (Paris: Gabalda, 1969), 110.

[114] Cf. Acts 2:44-45; 4:32-34. See above, pp. 194–95.

[115] See above, pp. 116–18.

[116] See below, pp. 255–57.

his epistle to an anonymous scribe, the dramatist Menander had incorporated into his prize-winning *Dyscolos* (*The Grouch*), the only one of his plays to have survived almost in its entirety, this dialogue between the sage Sostratos and his grouchy father:

> *Sostratos:* You speak of money an unstable substance. If you know that it will stay with you forever, guard it and don't share it with anyone. But where your title is not absolute all is on lease from Fortune,[117] not your own, why grudge someone a share in it? . . . So long as you control it, use it generously, aid everyone, and by your acts enrich all whom you can. Such conduct never dies.
> *Kallippides:* . . . . No need for sermons. You may dispose, and give, and share.[118]

The pastor has incorporated traditional moral wisdom into his final exhortation, adding to it the theological vision of the one God who is the source of all good[119] and the eschatological conviction that the one God rewards people in accordance with how they have used his gifts, specifically, the gift of wealth that God has given to them.

The Epistle to Titus

The other Pastoral Epistles, 2 Timothy and Titus, are much shorter than 1 Timothy and obviously lack the two-part digression on wealth that characterizes the final chapter of 1 Timothy. Of the two shorter epistles, it is probably best to look at the Epistle to Titus first since it shares with 1 Timothy the literary genre of a document of church order.

Titus contains but two references to the desire for wealth. One of them, as one who has previously read 1 Timothy might expect, is to be found in the author's list of qualifications for church leaders.[120] The leader of whom he writes is an elder (*presbyteros*) who has the function of overseer (*episkopos*), God's steward. All told, the author

[117] The goddess, Tyche.
[118] *Dysk.* 797-817.
[119] Cf. Krause, *1 Timothy*, 130-31.
[120] Cf. Titus 1:5-9.

cites fifteen qualities required of the person who is to fulfill this important function. The author gathers them into three groups. First, there is a short list of three qualities required of one who is deemed to be an elder. Then, there is a list of six negatively phrased qualifications of the overseer. Finally, the author provides a list of six positively phrased qualifications, leading up to the specifically Christian concern that he have a firm grasp of the word.[121]

As for what the leader of the community should not be, "he must be blameless, he must not be arrogant or quick-tempered or addicted to wine or violent or greedy for gain [*mē aischrokerdē*]."[122] This last phrase is found among the qualifications for assistants in 1 Timothy 3:8. No upright person should be tainted by any of these things, let alone someone with responsibility for overseeing God's household. No respectable person should be a money-grubber,[123] a fortiori the overseer and steward.

The author provides perspective on this requirement by what he writes next. The overseer must have a firm grasp of the word not only so that he might preach it but also so that he can refute those who contradict it, for[124] "there are also many rebellious people, idle talkers and deceivers, especially those of the circumcision; they must be silenced, since they are upsetting whole families by teaching for sordid gain what it is not right to teach."[125]

In Greco-Roman society, many teachers earned their livelihood from the fees that their teaching brought. Those whom the overseer is to silence are those who teach things that ought not be taught. They seem to have been making inroads into believing families.[126] These folks are charlatans and must be silenced. Their motive is unworthy of a respected leader of a believing community. They do what they do for the sake of sordid gain (*aischrou kerdous charin*).

---

[121] Cf. Titus 1:9.

[122] Titus 1:7. It is possible to read the list as one general negative, "blameless," followed by five specifics, as I have done in my commentary, *I and II Timothy*, 324.

[123] Titus is presumably on Crete (Titus 1:5). On the proverbial *aischrokerdeia* of the Cretans, see Polybius, *Hist.* 6.46.1-4.

[124] The explanatory *gar*, "for," of Titus 1:10 is not translated in the NRSV.

[125] Titus 1:10-11.

[126] Cf. Josephus, *Antiquities* 13.400-402.

Poets and dramatists used the word "gain" (*kerdos*) to speak of economic advantage.[127] The author's "sordid" (*aischros*) characterizes the wealth gained from teaching what ought not be taught as base and ill-gotten. The leader of the community is to utterly avoid such a way of making money.

Second Timothy

For the most part, the Second Epistle to Timothy is a reflection on Paul's life and ministry, directed to "Timothy" who is depicted as being about to succeed Paul in his ministry of evangelization. Interspersed in the epistle are a number of exhortations directed to Timothy.

Second Timothy 2:1-7 contains the second exhortation.[128] Appropriating the occupational imagery found in 1 Corinthians 9:7-10, 24-27, the author writes, "It is the farmer who does the work who ought to have the first share of the crops."[129] Agricultural images are relatively rare in the Pastoral Epistles; here, as elsewhere, the images are borrowed from Paul. Like his hero, Paul, the author of 1 Timothy 5:18 uses a passage from Jewish agricultural law in support of the idea that one who works deserves his pay. The author of 2 Timothy uses another agrarian image to speak of the compensation due to church leaders. "It is the farmer who does the work who ought to have the first share of the crops," he writes.

"The farmer who does the work" is an understatement. The Greek ton *kopionta geōrgon* really means "the hard-working farmer." The verb *kopiaō* has the connotation of toil or labor. "Ought" is also something of an understatement. The Greek *dei* generally suggests necessity; it refers to something that must be done.[130] What must be done? Hardworking farmers must be paid first and appropriately. They are

---

[127] Cf. Pindar, *Pyth.* 3.54 and Sophocles, *Ant.* 222, for example.

[128] The first exhortation appears in 2 Tim 1:6.

[129] 2 Tim 2:6.

[130] Quinn and Wacker (*First and Second Letters*, 622) observe that in the Pastoral Epistles the verb *dei* always occurs in passages about what *ought* (their emphasis) to be first.

due the first share of the produce (*protōn tōn karpōn*).[131] They are not to receive their wages from what is left over.

Applied to church leaders, as exemplified by the author's Timothy, their hard work is the suffering that they endure.[132] The image suggests that these leaders must be paid promptly and justly.[133]

One more passage in this epistle has some interest for our study. In 2 Timothy 3:2-4, the author uses a long catalogue of vices, the second longest of the lists in the New Testament,[134] to describe the rampant evil of the last days. The list begins with selfishness; people will be lovers of themselves (*philautoi*), says the author. Next, the author says that people will be greedy; they will be lovers of money (*philagyroi*[135]). After these two root vices come an additional sixteen vices.[136] The author of 2 Timothy apparently wants his readers to understand that the first two vices on his list are root vices, the source of many of the evils that he is about to pass in review.[137]

The Epistle to the Hebrews

The magnificent "Epistle to the Hebrews" is not a letter.[138] It is, as its anonymous author states, "a word of exhortation," a hortatory

---

[131] Weiser opines that *first* fruits is to be understood simply as part of the image without further ado. Cf. Alfons Weiser, *Der zweite Brief an Timotheus*, EKKNT 16/1 (Zurich: Benziger; Neukirchen-Vluyn: Neukirchener Verlag, 2003), 163.

[132] Cf. 2 Tim 2:2.

[133] Paul used the images of the soldier and the farmer in 1 Cor 9:7-10 to say that, although workers deserve to be paid for their work, he himself has resolved to forgo being paid for his work of evangelization. The author of 2 Timothy uses these same images to make another point, namely, that the one who proclaims the gospel deserves a proper recompense.

[134] Rom 1:29-31 is the longest of these lists in the New Testament.

[135] Cf. 1 Tim 6:10.

[136] "Holding to the outward form of godliness but denying its power" (2 Tim 3:5) is certainly an evil, but I hesitate to cite it as a nineteenth vice on the list because its formulation differs from that of the other eighteen vices.

[137] See above, p. 231. Weiser (*Der zweite Brief*, 247) notes that money-grubbing is seen as the source of multiple evils even more in Stoicism, Cynicism, and Hellenistic Judaism than it is here.

[138] See chapter 1, "The Epistle to the Hebrews," in Collins, *Letters That Paul Did Not Write*, 19–56.

address.[139] Since it does not have the form of a letter, it does not claim Pauline authorship. For centuries it has been appended to the thirteen Pauline letters in the canon. Some of its hortatory remarks merit its inclusion in this study. Taking a cue from the tradition, I have decided to add it as an appendix to my study of the letters that Paul did not write.

The author's christological reflection capitalizes on various biblical texts and motifs to portray a unique image of Christ as high priest and son of God. En passant, the unknown author writes about the inheritance,[140] a last will and testament,[141] and tithing.[142] These subjects are of only tangential interest for our study.

Interspersed with the author's christological passages are hortatory passages. Two of these are important for our study of wealth, wages, and the wealthy. Both are to be found in chapter 13, the epistle's final chapter.

Hebrews 13:5-6

Hebrews 13:1-7 describes a life pleasing to God. Having exhorted his listeners to hold marriage in high regard, the homilist concludes his reflection with these words: "Keep your lives free from the love of money [*aphilagyros*[143]], and be content with what you have; for he has said, 'I will never leave you or forsake you.' So we can say with confidence, 'The Lord is my helper; I will not be afraid. What can anyone do to me?'"[144]

It is not surprising that the author writes about money. Some members of his community were robbed because of their steadfastness to their faith.[145] His exhortation is almost a maxim. In Greek, the advice contains only six words.[146] Each of the two parts of the adage

---

[139] Cf. Heb 13:22.
[140] Cf. Heb 11:8 and *passim*.
[141] Cf. Heb 9:15-17.
[142] Cf. Heb 7:4-10.
[143] Cf. 1 Tim 3:3, above, p. 225.
[144] Heb 13:5-6.
[145] Cf. Heb 10:34.
[146] *Aphilagyros ho tropos, arkoumenoi tois parousin.*

advice begins with an alpha; neither contains a verb. So terse is the maxim that the NRSV requires sixteen words, "keep your lives free from the love of money, and be content with what you have," to render the author's succinct exhortation. The warning against avarice is, as we have seen, a common theme in early Christian and contemporary literature. For the author of Hebrews, greed is antithetical to caring for one another and taking care of strangers, which the author urges in the first two verses of his exhortation.[147]

That his audience be content with what they have is consistent with what the pastor had written in 1 Timothy 6:6 and echoes the importance of the esteemed virtue of self-sufficiency (*autarkeia*), with one considerable difference. Whereas the Stoics' understanding of self-sufficiency proceeded from a sense of asceticism and self-control,[148] the author of Hebrews, comments Craig Koester, urges people to be content for the sake of serving others.[149]

Throughout his address, the author of Hebrews cites Scripture almost with abandon. As he comes to the end of his discourse, he makes one final appeal to Scripture. His audience should be content with what they possess for the Scriptures affirm that God will take care of them. His conflation of Deuteronomy 31:6 and Psalm 118:6, designed to bolster his audience's confidence, serves to make his point.[150] The audience should not trust in an accumulation of wealth; rather, they are to trust in God who will take care of them.[151] Trust in God is the antidote to greed.

[147] Heb 13:1-2.

[148] Although he is not a Stoic, Philo also counsels self-control to counter the love of money. Cf. Philo, *Names* 226–27.

[149] Cf. Craig R. Koester, *Hebrews*, AB 36 (New York: Doubleday, 2001), 559; cf. Luke Timothy Johnson, *Hebrews*, NTL (Louisville: Westminster John Knox, 2006), 343.

[150] The citation of Ps 118:6 is according to the Septuagint (=Ps 117:6). The citation of Deut 31:6 is not an exact citation. Similar wording appears in Deut 31:8 and 1 Chr 28:20. See the discussion in Johnson, *Hebrews*, 343–45.

[151] Koester (*Hebrews*, 559) writes about a "future reward," but an eschatological note is not at all apparent in the Scriptures that the author cites.

Hebrews 13:16

Worship is an important motif in the Epistle to the Hebrews. The heavenly cult provides a major image for the author's Christology. Before bringing his final exhortation to a close, the homilist reminds his audience of the importance of praising God through Jesus Christ[152] but immediately adds, "Do not neglect to do good and to share what you have, for such sacrifices are pleasing to God."[153] Worship has its practical counterpart in doing good[154] to others and sharing one's possessions.[155] Providing for others in this way is a form of worship, an acceptable sacrifice pleasing to God.[156]

So What?

"Greed (which is idolatry)"

"The current financial crisis can make us overlook the fact that it originated in a profound human crisis; the denial of the primacy of the human person! We have created new idols. The worship of the ancient golden calf (cf. Exod 32:1-35) has returned in a new and ruthless guise in the idolatry of money and the dictatorship of an impersonal economy lacking a truly human purpose."[157] So wrote Pope Francis in his apostolic exhortation *Evangelii Gaudium.*

"The sign that tells us we have not fallen into 'this sin of idolatry,'" said Pope Francis in his early morning homily at Casa Santa Marta on October 19, 2015, "is almsgiving, giving to those in need—and not giving merely of our abundance, but giving until it costs."[158]

---

[152] Cf. Heb 13:15.

[153] Heb 13:16.

[154] The noun *eupoiia*, hapax in the New Testament, can mean any form of doing good, but it often has the specific connotation of performing an act of beneficence, as it does here. Cf. Diogenes Laertius, *Lives* 10.10.

[155] Cf. Alan C. Mitchell, *Hebrews*, SP 13 (Collegeville, MN: Liturgical Press, 2007), 304–5.

[156] Cf. James W. Thompson, *Hebrews*, Paideia Commentaries on the New Testament (Grand Rapids: Baker Academic, 2008), 284. The idea that moral behavior can be seen as a form of worship appears in Rom 12:1-2.

[157] Pope Francis, *Evangelii Gaudium* 55.

[158] Cf. Zenit.org, October 19, 2015.

The Love of Money Is a Root of All Kinds of Evil

Echoing a long philosophic tradition, the pastor had said that the love of money is a root of all kinds of evil.[159] His words presaged the headline that jumped out at me as I entered the checkout line on November 4, 2015. In bold print, black and white, the front page of the tabloid simply said, "Power, Greed, and Lots of Corruption."

In the words of Pope Francis, "Inequality is the root of social ills."[160]

[159] Cf. 1 Tim 6:10.
[160] *Evangelii Gaudium* 202.

Chapter 8

The Catholic Epistles

The Epistle of James, the First and Second Epistles of Peter, the First, Second, and Third Epistles of John, and the Epistle of Jude appear in the canonical New Testament between the Epistle to the Hebrews and the book of Revelation. They are usually grouped together under the title of General, Catholic, or Universal Epistles because, unlike Paul's letters and those written in his name, they are not addressed to any particular local church or specific individual.[1] They appear to be pseudepigraphic even if the authorship of James remains a moot issue among mainstream scholars.

The epistles known as 1, 2, and 3 John belong to the corpus of Johannine Literature. Along with the Gospel of John and the book of Revelation, the three texts will be examined in the next chapter of this study. The present chapter will deal only with the four other Catholic Epistles, James, 1–2 Peter, and Jude. Of these, the Epistle of James is of most importance for our study.

The Epistle of James

The Epistle of James is a book of the church insofar as it describes the practical life of a community. Surprisingly, although it has much

---

[1] This characterization is not entirely accurate. Second John is addressed to a local church, metaphorically described as the elect lady and her children (2 John 1), while 3 John is addressed to Gaius (3 John 1).

to say about God,[2] the epistle contains only two mentions of Jesus Christ.[3] Evincing features of Greco-Roman rhetoric, the epistle has similarities with Jewish wisdom tradition[4] and draws heavily on the New Testament tradition of the sayings of Jesus. As one might expect of a text that deals with the practicalities of life within a community, the rich and the poor are a major focus of the author's concern. Indeed, the discrepancy between the two socioeconomic classes seems to be the principal topic addressed by the epistle.[5] The epistle rejects the biblical Wisdom tradition that prosperity is a blessing from God[6] and espouses the Jesus tradition's view that wealth is problematic for a person's relationship with God.

James 1:9-11

The author of the epistle abruptly introduces the topic of the rich and the poor in a passage replete with floral imagery that speaks of the exaltation of the poor and the humiliation of the rich.[7] In some ways, the reversal of fortunes of which the passage speaks recalls the words of Mary's canticle in Luke 1:52, but there the focus was on God's action. In James, attention is drawn to the object of a believer's boasting.

The pericope begins with an apparent aphorism, "Let the believer who is lowly boast in being raised up and the rich in being brought low."[8] The rest of the passage uses the image of the flower to speak about the fate of the rich. Who are the lowly and the rich? The author clearly describes the lowly person as a believer, using the traditional

---

[2] See the table of Propositions about God in Mark Allan Powell, *Introducing the New Testament: A Historical, Literary, and Theological Survey* (Grand Rapids: Baker Academic, 2009), 454.

[3] Cf. Jas 1:1; 2:1. James 5:7-9 describes the coming of the Lord as judge but does not mention the name of Jesus.

[4] Cf. Patrick J. Hartin, *James*, SP 14 (Collegeville, MN: Liturgical Press, 2003), 77–81.

[5] Cf. Dirk G. Van der Merwe, "Rich Man, Poor Man in Jerusalem According to the Letter of James," *Acta patristica et byzantina* 21 (2010): 18–46.

[6] Cf. Prov 8:18; 10:4, 22; 13:21; 22:4; Sir 44:2-5. See, however, Prov 21:6-7; 28:20-22; 30:7-9.

[7] Jas 1:9-11.

[8] Jas 1:8-10a.

metaphorical designation of "brother and sister" to describe him or her as a member of the believing community. This believer is said to be lowly (*ho tapeinos*).[9] Given the term's antithetical relationship with the rich (*ho plousios*) in verse 10, the "lowly" surely means the poor person. The parallelism between the rich person and the poor person clarifies who is meant by "the rich." Grammatically, the rich man appears to be one of the brothers and sisters, a member of the family of believers.

The poor man does not boast in his poverty; rather, he boasts because of his exaltation (*en tō hypsei autou*). Given the fact that the New Testament motif of role reversal generally has an eschatological focus, the poor man's exaltation might take place in the eschatological future. On the other hand, the author of James speaks of the poor as being rich in faith and heirs of the kingdom of God when he compares the poor and the rich later in his epistle.[10] From this perspective, the exaltation of the lowly might well mean the richness of their faith and their participation in the kingdom. In which case, the aphorism may well not refer to the eschatological future nor suggest a reversal of the poor and the rich's respective financial statuses.[11] The poor do not boast in becoming nouveaux riches, nor do the rich boast in becoming impoverished. The rich boast in "being brought low" (*en tē tapeinōsei*).[12] The rich person boasts in being associated with the poor, the tapeinos of verse 8. Both belong to the community of the baptized, the new anawim.

The *anawim* are well known in the author's biblical tradition. "Seek the Lord, all you humble [*anawim*] of the land who do his commands, seek righteousness, seek humility; perhaps you may be hidden on the day of the Lord's wrath," says Zephaniah 2:3. The *anawim* are the poor and lowly who remain faithful to the Lord in times of personal and national difficulty, awaiting salvation from the Lord, their only Savior. Many of the biblical psalms speak of this group

---

[9] Cf. Luke 1:52.

[10] Cf. Jas 2:1-7.

[11] Cf. James Painter and David A. de Silva, *James and Jude*, Paideia Commentaries on the New Testament (Grand Rapids: Baker Academic, 2012), 69.

[12] In Greek, *tapeinōsei* is the dative of the noun *tapeinōsis*, not a gerund or other verbal form. It might be translated as "lowliness" (cf. Luke 1:48).

of people.[13] Typical is Psalm 18:27, which speaks of the reversal of their fortunes in comparison with that of the rich, "For you deliver a humble people, but the haughty eyes you bring down." Mary of the *Magnificat* is often described as a representative of the *anawim*. Concerned with the rich, the author of James reworks the biblical motif of the *anawim* in James 1:9-10a.

While the poor can boast of the riches of their faith, the rich can boast of their association with the *anawim*. The apostle Paul is well known for his considerations on boasting, particularly for what he writes about boasting in 2 Corinthians.[14] "Let the one who boasts, boast in the Lord" is key to his reflections.[15] Like Paul, the author of James criticizes some boasting, writing in condemnatory fashion, "You boast in your arrogance; all such boasting is evil."[16] Yet, like Paul and the philosophic moralists,[17] the author of James recognizes that some boasting can be legitimate. When a poor man boasts in the riches of his faith and the rich man boasts in his lowliness, they are boasting of what the Lord has made possible.

After the author's reflection on the respective justifiable boasting of the poor and the rich comes his floral imagery:

> because the rich will disappear like a flower in the field. For the sun rises with its scorching heat and withers the field; its flower falls, and its beauty perishes. It is the same way with the rich; in the midst of a busy life, they will wither away.[18]

The initial "because" (*hoti*) suggests that what follows is a description of the fate of the rich.[19] Like a flower, the rich person is destined to

---

[13] See, for example, Pss 34:18; 82:3; 102:17.

[14] Cf. Wong, *Boasting and Foolishness*; Collins, *Second Corinthians, passim.*

[15] Cf. Jer 9:22-23; 1 Cor 1:31; 2 Cor 10:17.

[16] Jas 4:16; cf. Jas 3:14.

[17] Cf. Painter and de Silva, *James and Jude*, 68–69.

[18] Jas 1:10b-11.

[19] In this passage the word "rich" appears only once, namely, in verse 10, *plousiois*, "the rich" in the plural. "The rich" of the NRSV's verse 10b is a specification of the indeterminate subject of the metaphorical expression "like a flower of the field, he will disappear." "Or possibly," writes Johnson, "'it will pass away,' referring to the wealth rather than to the person." Cf. Luke Timothy Johnson, *The Letter of James*, AB 37A (Garden City, NY: Doubleday, 1995), 186.

disappear. To explain the comparison,[20] the author borrows the imagery of Isaiah 40:6-8. With such imagery, the gnomic sayings speak of the ephemeral nature of the flower and its beauty. As the flower is not able to endure, so too the rich cannot survive, despite their active pursuit of wealth. If, however, they withstand the test as the lowly do, they can expect to receive the crown of life that the Lord has promised to those who love him.[21]

Authentic Religion (Jas 1:27)

Much of the first chapter of James criticizes those who cannot control their anger, those who only hear the word and do not act accordingly, and those who cannot control their tongues. The author concludes his criticism on a positive note, a definition of true religion, to wit, "Religion that is pure and undefiled before God, the Father, is this: to care for [*episkeptesthai*] orphans and widows in their distress, and to keep oneself unstained by the world."[22]

This is one of the few references to "religion" (*thrēskeia*)[23] in the New Testament.[24] Related to the verb *thrēskeuo*, "observe religious practices," which does not appear in the New Testament, the word indicates the outward manifestation of an internal relationship with God. Writing as he does, the author of James indicates that he shares with the apostle Paul and the writer of the Epistle to the Hebrews the idea that acting ethically is a form of worship.[25] While the author of Hebrews says that doing good and sharing—without indicating the intended recipients of these acts—are acts of worship, the author of James cites the traditional biblical pair of widows and orphans as

[20] Note the explanatory *gar*, "for," in v. 11.

[21] Cf. Jas 1:12. Virtually all the commentators on Jas 1:9-11 point to the difficulty of understanding who really is meant by the "rich" in the passage, especially in the light of the author's negative judgment on the rich in the rest of the letter. Is the rich person a member of the community or an outsider? I have interpreted the passage as referring to the believing wealthy while seeing in the floral imagery a reflection of the author's condemnatory attitude toward the rich and riches.

[22] Jas 1:27.

[23] Cf. Spicq, "*thrēskeia, thrēskos,*" *TLNT* 2:200–204.

[24] Cf. Acts 26:5; Col 2:18; and Jas 2:17.

[25] Cf. Rom 12:1-2; Heb 13:6.

those for whom the God-observant are to care. His words are not necessarily addressed only to rich believers; his words define religion for all who are in a right relationship with God.

In the biblical tradition, widows and orphans who lacked a protective male figure in their family were singled out as particular recipients of God's care.[26] The psalmist describes God as the "father of orphans and protector of widows."[27] Israelites were expected to manifest their loyalty to God by taking care of orphans and widows. Commenting on useless sacrifices and the futile celebration of festivals, an oracle in the first chapter of the book of Isaiah proclaims, "Seek justice, rescue the oppressed, defend the orphan, plead for the widow."[28] The neglect of virtually helpless orphans and widows or their oppression was roundly condemned in the prophetic tradition.[29]

In the Greek Bible, the verb *episkeptomai*, "visit," was used almost as a technical term to describe God's gracious visitation of his people in need.[30] Luke uses the verb in this traditional sense in the Canticle of Zechariah.[31] The verb means to go to visit a person with helpful intent, in order to be of assistance.[32] Hence, the NRSV's translation of *episkeptesthai* in James 1:27 as "assist." James's definition of religion in this verse echoes the biblical tradition. Someone who is in a right relationship with God emulates God in "visiting" the orphan and the widow. He or she is a "visitor" on God's behalf. The author of the epistle also echoes the biblical tradition of such visiting when he places it within the oversight of God, designated "Father" in James 1:27.

The ultimate source of the assistance provided to orphans and widows is God. Shortly before offering his definition of pure and undefiled religion, the author of this paraenetic text had written, "Every generous act of giving, with every perfect gift, is from heaven above,

---

[26] Cf. Pss 10:14, 18; 22:22-23.
[27] Ps 85:5.
[28] Isa 1:17; cf. Isa 1:12-17.
[29] Cf. Jer 5:28; Ezek 22:7; Zech 7:10.
[30] See the references in Johnson, *James*, 212.
[31] Cf. Luke 1:68, 78.
[32] Cf. BDAG, 378.

coming down from the Father of lights."[33] The correlative terms, "act of giving" (*pasa dosis*) and "every gift" (*pan dōrēma*), are virtually synonymous. If a distinction is to be made between them, the first expression draws attention to the action while the second highlights the gift itself. Assisting orphans and widows is not only a manifestation of one's relationship with God but also a matter of following the divine example made possible by God the Father himself.

Partiality toward the Rich (Jas 2:1-7)

By putting the care of orphans and widows at the core of authentic religion, the author of the epistle prepares for his critique of partiality toward the rich, which follows immediately after his description of pure and undefiled religion. The scene that he sets, as he writes, resembles a religious gathering:

> My brothers and sisters, do you with your acts of favoritism really believe in our glorious Lord Jesus Christ? For if a person with gold rings and in fine clothes comes into your assembly, and if a person in dirty clothes also comes in, and if you take notice of the one wearing the fine clothes and say, "Have a seat here, please," while to the one who is poor you say, "Stand there," or, "Sit at my feet," have you not made distinctions among yourselves, and become judges with evil thoughts?[34]

The rhetorical question of the first verse expresses the thesis, the *prothesis* of Hellenistic rhetoric, of the discussion, the *probatio* that follows. Having defined authentic religion, the author asks a question about Christian faith, faith (*tēn pistin*) in our glorious Lord Jesus Christ. The positive phrasing of the question awaits a negative response. Someone who shows partiality (*en prosopolympsiais*)[35]

---

[33] Jas 1:17.

[34] Jas 2:1-4.

[35] The Greek word occurs only four times in the New Testament, here and Rom 2:11; Eph 6:9; Col 3:25. Vocabulary belonging to the word group is more common in Hellenistic Jewish writings. Actions described by this vocabulary are always regarded negatively. Cf. Klaus Berger, "*prosōpolēmpsia*," *EDNT* 3:179-80.

does not have faith in the Lord Jesus Christ. Evidence of partiality is incompatible with true faith.

The use of examples is an important feature of Hellenistic rhetoric. Accordingly, the author provides an explanatory example in verses 2-4. The setting of the hypothetical example[36] is the assembly, the *synagōgē*.[37] The two characters in the example are distinguished from one another by their apparel:[38] the rich man by his luxurious clothes and gold rings;[39] the other person, specifically identified as a poor man, a *ptōchos*, by the dirty rags that he is wearing. The example appears to portray them as strangers to the assembly since they are told where to position themselves. The assembly instructs the rich man[40] to take a seat, while the poor man is told to either remain standing or sit on the floor. The unequal treatment is a blatant example of discrimination, of favoritism toward the rich.

It is generally assumed that the author of James has in mind a kind of liturgical assembly,[41] a gathering for worship, but citing the judicial use of words belonging to the *prosopolympsi-* word group, the singular usage of the term *synagōgē*, and a number of later rabbinic parallels, Roy Bowen Ward argues that the envisioned assembly convened for a judicial purpose.[42] To his arguments could be added the rhetorical questions of verses 4 and 6, which speak of judges (*kritai*)

---

[36] Cf. Martin Dibelius, *James: A Commentary on the Epistle of James*, Hermeneia (Philadelphia: Fortress, 1976), 135.

[37] This is the only time in the New Testament that the word *synagōgē* is used of a Christian assembly. It may suggest that the community has come together for some sort of a judicial process.

[38] Cf. Luke 16:19-31, another story of a rich man and a poor man.

[39] The compound adjective "wearing gold rings," *chrysodaktylios*, may have been coined by the author of the epistle. Cf. Dale C. Allison Jr., *The Epistle of James*, ICC (New York: Bloomsbury T & T Clark, 2013), 85.

[40] The instruction would normally be given by the president of the assembly, but the author of the example uses a plural verb, "you say," *eipēte*, to indicate that the members of the assembly are responsible for the discriminating directive.

[41] In 1 Cor 11:17-34 Paul severely criticized discrimination against the poor by believers who gathered for fellowship and worship. See above, pp. 27–34.

[42] Cf. Roy Bowen Ward, "Partiality in the Assembly: James 2:2-4," *HTR* 62 (1969): 87–97; Johnson, *James*, 225; Hartin, *James*, 118. Allison (*James*, 386–88) opines that the author of James is suggesting a synagogue building being used for a judicial convocation.

and courts (*kritēria*), respectively. Ultimately, whether the community has gathered for a liturgical purpose, a judicial purpose, or an instructional session matters little. The author's hypothetical example has been formulated simply to offer a blatant example of partiality in an assembly of believers. The brunt of his rhetorical proof lies in the series of rhetorical questions that follow the example.

Employing the rhetorical device of the diatribe, the author shares his views on the rich and the poor, suggesting by the questions that he raises, questions that demand mental responses from his audience, that its members come to a decision with regard to the issues that he raises. The first of the five rhetorical questions—"Have you not made distinctions among yourselves, and become judges with evil thoughts?"[43]—embodies a pun[44] and serves as the apodosis to the conditional clause of verse 3. By acting as the example suggests, hasn't the community established a double standard for itself? Haven't its members become judges with scheming designs?[45] "Yes, they have," is the implication of the negative form of the question. In the client-patron society of the times, these scheming designs may have been focused on some financial return in exchange for the preferential treatment extended to the rich in the assembly.[46]

Then, reprising the familial formula of direct address from verse 1, the author issues a prophetic call to hear as he expands his horizon beyond the example of verses 2-3 to speak more generally about the poor and the rich:

> Listen, my beloved brothers and sisters. Has God not chosen the poor in the world to be rich in faith and to be heirs of the kingdom that he has promised to those who love him? But

[43] Cf. Lev 19:15; 1 Cor 4:3.

[44] "You have made *distinctions* (*diakrinesthai*) and you have become *distinguishers* (*kritai*, 'judges') with evil motives," writes Dibelius in *James*, 136. He (*James*, 135) compares this pun with those used by Paul in Rom 14:23 and 1 Cor 11:31.

[45] The NRSV translates the Greek *dialogismōn* as "thoughts." In the New Testament the word is always used with negative connotations. Cf. Matt 15:19; Mark 7:21; Luke 5:22; 6:8; 9:46-47; 24:38; Rom 1:21; 14:1; 1 Cor 3:20; Phil 2:14; 1 Tim 2:8; Gerd Petzge, "*dialogizomai, dialogismos*," *EDNT* 1:308.

[46] Cf. Johnson, *James*, 224.

you have dishonored the poor. Is it not the rich who oppress you? Is it not they who drag you into court? Is it not they who blaspheme the excellent name that was invoked over you?[47]

The author begins with the poor. His question infers that God has chosen the poor to be rich in faith, a significant paradox, and heirs of the kingdom. This mention of the kingdom is the only time in the entire epistle that the author speaks of it. His words echo the first beatitude[48] and Jesus' words about inheriting the kingdom.[49] Mention of the kingdom probably includes an eschatological nuance, the future kingdom in contrast with this world in which the poor now live. In this world the poor are rich in faith; they are heirs of the kingdom to come.

The writer then accuses the community of dishonoring the poor man, thereby repudiating God's election of the poor. They have done the opposite of what God has done.[50]

Having spoken about the community's treatment of the poor, the author turns his attention to the treatment they have received at the hands of the rich. He uses three negatively formulated rhetorical questions to make his point. All three of them demand a positive response. First, he asks in a general way, "Don't the rich oppress you?" "Don't you suffer at the hands of the rich?" "We surely do," is the expected answer. Then, turning his attention to the almost legendary abuse of the judicial system by the rich, he asks, "Don't the rich take you to court, perhaps for trivial offenses?"[51] "That's the way it is," the audience is expected to answer; "that's the way the system works." The author's final salvo asks, "Don't the rich blaspheme the name invoked over you in baptism, the name of Jesus?" Dibelius warned against seeing in these three questions evidence of a persecution of

---

[47] Jas 2:5-7.

[48] Luke 6:20; Matt 5:3; *G. Thom.* 54.

[49] Cf. Matt 25:34; 5:5; 1 Cor 6:9, 10; 15:50.

[50] Verse 5 speaks of the "poor" (*tous ptōchous*) in the plural; verse 6a speaks of "the poor" (*ton ptōchon*) in the singular, "the poor man," perhaps harkening back to the example given in verses 2-3.

[51] Cf. 1 Cor 6:1-8. Paul writes specifically about rich believers taking poor believers to court. James's third rhetorical question seems to imply that he is thinking about the rich who are not believers.

poor believers by rich nonbelievers.[52] Evincing the author's antipathy to the rich, the questions simply evoke the mistreatment that the less well-off suffer at the hands of the rich and powerful.

The Works of Faith (Jas 2:14-17)

Martin Luther is often quoted for remarking that the Epistle of James is a letter of straw. The observation is based on the epistle's assumed opposition to the apostle Paul's teaching on faith without works. Contemporary scholarship takes a more nuanced view of the issue. When writing about works, Paul specifically had in mind the identity markers of contemporary Judaism, especially Sabbath observance and the observance of dietary restrictions. James, on the other hand, was writing about activity that manifests the reality of an active faith.[53]

The author of the Epistle of James writes about works in James 2:14-17. The writer does not specifically address himself to the rich in the community. His words are applicable to all believers, the less well-off and the rich alike, as he writes:

> If a brother or sister is naked[54] and lacks daily food [*tēs ephēmerou trophēs*], and one of you says to them, "Go in peace; keep warm and eat your fill," and yet you do not supply their bodily needs, what is the good of that?[55]

Once again, the author uses an example and a rhetorical question[56] to make his point.[57] This time, the answer is "It is no good." It is useless to tell a naked[58] and cold person to stay warm. It is useless

---

[52] Cf. Dibelius, *James*, 2, 45–47, 139–40.

[53] Cf. Jas 1:27; above, pp. 247–49.

[54] The Greek *ean adelphos ē adelphē gymnoi hyparchōsin* of Jas 2:15 is in the plural and specifically mentions both the brother (*adelphos*) and the sister (*adelphē*).

[55] Jas 2:15-16.

[56] For an overview of the importance of rhetorical questions in the Epistle of James, see Painter and de Silva, *James and Jude*, 93.

[57] Cf. Jas 2:2-4.

[58] Writing about the "naked," *gymnoi*, in the plural, the author was most likely thinking of persons who were dressed in rags rather than people who were totally nude.

to tell a hungry person to eat up when he or she has no food for that day's meals.

Examples are an important feature of Hellenistic rhetoric.[59] The point of the author's example is that just as words without action are inane, so faith without works is meaningless. The author's example speaks about the basic necessities of life, food and clothing.[60] If a fellow believer, male or female, lacks the basic necessities of life and the members of the community[61] do not respond by providing these necessities of life, their faith is in vain, their faith is useless. Their faith is not the dynamic faith, an essential characteristic of a believing community, about which Paul writes in 1 Thessalonians 1:3. At the very least, a believer must ensure that fellow believers possess the basic necessities of life.[62]

Ephemeral Wealth (Jas 4:13-14)

The Epistle of James, dealing with ethics as it does, is a book of practical wisdom. Its author uses simple hypothetical examples to make his point. Another such example[63] is found in James 4:13-14. The example is that of merchants and traders who think about making their fortune without taking into account just how little control they have over their future:

> Come now, you who say "Today or tomorrow we will go to such and such a town and spend a year there, doing business and making money [*emporeusometha kai kerdēsomen*]." Yet you do not even know what tomorrow will bring. What is your life? For you are a mist that appears for a little while and then vanishes.[64]

[59] Cf. Aristotle, *Rhet.* 2.20; Anaximenes, *Rhet. Alex.* 8.

[60] Cf. Matt 6:25.

[61] On the communal concern of the epistle, see Roy Bowen Ward, "The Communal Concern of the Epistle of James" (PhD diss., Harvard University, 1966); Johnson, *James*, 82–83.

[62] Cf. 1 John 3:17; Matt 25:35-39, 42-44.

[63] Like the examples of Jas 2:2-4 and Jas 2:15-16, this example is also hypothetical. Cf. Johnson, *James*, 295.

[64] Jas 4:13-14.

In their soliloquy, these merchants think about their future business and making money. The Greek verbs connote buying and selling and making a profit while engaged in this activity. The merchants in this example might not be among the truly rich in the author's world, but as the Australian biblical scholar James Painter suggests, perhaps those on the way up, on the way to making a fortune before settling down at ease in luxurious circumstances."[65] They belonged to the mercantile class of traveling traders.[66]

These people are willing to devote an entire year in making their small fortune. The moralist who wrote the epistle does not condemn their plans to make money, nor does he say that their money is ill-begotten or the source of evils. His admonition is simply that these people overlook the fact that they cannot control their own future. They have just about cut God out of the mix.

For the author of this epistle, money is of no value beyond the grave. Wealth is as ephemeral[67] as life itself is fleeting.[68]

Judgment on the Rich (Jas 5:1-6)

The section of the epistle that has been titled "Denunciations of the Prosperous"[69] began with the author's reflection on ephemeral wealth in James 4:13-14. It opens with the imperatival interjection "come now" (*age nyn*), an old Greek expression that marks a shift in emphasis. It spoke about people who want to be rich.

A new unit begins in James 5:1. It likewise begins "come now" (*age nyn*), marking a shift in focus. The focus of this unit, James 5:1-6, is on the landed aristocracy, those who have inherited their wealth.[70] Wealthy property owners were well known throughout the Roman Empire. Often they inherited an estate and then schemed to acquire

---

[65] Painter and de Silva, *James and Jude*, 151.

[66] Cf. Allison, *James*, 653.

[67] Cf. Jas 5:2-3c.

[68] Cf. Jas 1:10-11. The image of the mist recalls such passages as Pss 37:20; 39:11; 90:10.

[69] Cf. Allison, *James*, 640–88.

[70] Cf. ibid., 650, 667.

other property, often at the expense of the poor.[71] They were known to defraud the poor, manipulate them when they were unable to pay, and then seize their property, their only wealth and the source of their sustenance.[72]

Josephus tells the story of Herod's killing of the Hasmonians and seizing of their property, which he was then able to distribute to his favorites.[73] The philosophic moralists of the Hellenistic world saw such despoliation of another's lands as a moral evil. Seneca, for example writes:

> It was avarice that introduced poverty and, by craving much, lost all. And so, although she now tries to make good her loss, although she adds one estate to another, evicting a neighbor either by buying him out or by wronging him, although she extends her country-seats to the size of provinces and defines ownership as meaning extensive travel through one's own property—in spite of all these efforts of hers, no enlargement of our boundaries will bring us back to the condition from which we have departed.[74]

The author of the epistle develops his own thoughts on such landed and often corrupt landowners in two movements of thought. Before developing a list of sins of which the rich (*plousioi*) are presumed to be guilty in verses 4-6, the author prophetically speaks of the eschatological woes that will come upon these rich: "You rich people, weep and wail for the miseries that are coming to you."[75] The initial vocative "you rich people" (*hoi plousioi*) shows that the writer is speaking directly to the rich.

He speaks about their "coming miseries" (*tais palaipōriais hymōn tais erchomenais*) to describe the future, eschatological punishment of these rich people. His threat places the judgment on the rich within the context of the coming of the Lord, the subject of the epistle's

---

[71] The story of Ahab, Jezebel, and Naboth is a well-known biblical example of the phenomenon. Cf. 1 Kgs 21:1-29.

[72] Cf. Peppard, "Torah for the Man Who Has Everything," 603–4.

[73] Cf. Josephus, *War* 1.358-60; *Antiquities* 15.5-6; 17.305-7.

[74] Seneca, *Ep.* 90.38-39.

[75] Jas 5:1.

next pericope,[76] the penultimate subunit of the text. The prophetic threat includes vocabulary rarely found in the New Testament.[77] The severity of the threat corresponds to the severity of divine judgment on "the rich."

The eschatological tenor of the condemnation of the rich continues into verses 2 and 3. What will then happen to their wealth? "Your riches have rotted, and your clothes are moth-eaten. Your gold and silver have rusted, and their rust will be evidence against you and it will eat your flesh like fire."[78] All signs of their luxurious lifestyle will disappear,[79] not only their fine clothing but also their gold and silver.[80] Metallurgists know well that these precious metals do not oxidize, but at the time the epistle was written the rusting of gold and silver was a proverbial image[81] used to speak of the waste of valuable resources. These tokens of wealth, soon to disappear, provide quasi-judicial evidence against the rich.[82]

The overarching accusation is that the rich have amassed wealth rather than using their wealth to help the poor.[83] Their resources should have been used to provide alms for the poor.[84] In the eschaton, this misused wealth will disappear and the fires of gehenna[85] will consume their flesh: "and it will eat your flesh like fire."[86] In the final salvo of his tale of future horrors, the author addresses an ironic

---

[76] Jas 5:7-12.

[77] The word "wail" is used in Isa 6:13 (cf. Isa 14:31; 15:3) in reference to the coming of the Day of the Lord, but it is hapax in the New Testament. "Miseries" is found only here and in Rom 3:16. Allison suggests that the author's eschatological threat is modeled after traditional eschatological expressions. Cf. Allison, *James*, 669.

[78] Jas 5:2-3c.

[79] The three verbs, "have rotted" (*sesēpen*), "are moth-eaten" (*sētobrōta gegonen*), and "have rusted" (*katiōtai*) are in the perfect tense, indicating that the destruction is complete.

[80] Cf. Ep Jer 10-11.

[81] Cf. Sir 29:10-11.

[82] Cf. Ezek 7:19; *1 En.* 94:6.

[83] Cf. Wheeler, *Wealth*, 105.

[84] The imagery and content of these verses, Jas 5:2-3c, resonates with that of Sir 28:8-12.

[85] Cf. Jas 3:6.

[86] Jas 5:3c.

peroration to the rich: "You have laid up treasure for the last days."[87] What treasure! The loss of their finery and their valuable coins and the destruction of their flesh by fire is the treasure that they have stored up for themselves.

Having spoken of the eschatological fate of the rich in verses 1-3, the author develops an almost prosecutorial bill of particulars, detailing their misdeeds, in verses 4-6. The list begins with another summons, "Listen" (*idou*[88]). The first accusation[89] is that they have defrauded laborers of their wages: "The wages of the laborers[90] who mowed your fields, which you kept back by fraud, cry out, and the cries of the harvesters have reached the ears of the Lord of hosts."[91] By defrauding the laborers of their wages, the rich have violated one of the foundational laws of society that Yahweh had given to his people:

> You shall not withhold the wages of poor and needy laborers, whether other Israelites or aliens who reside in your land in one of your towns. You shall pay them their wages daily before sunset, because they are poor and their livelihood depends on them; otherwise they might cry to the Lord against you, and you would incur guilt.[92]

Jesus said, "The laborer deserves to be paid,"[93] but these wealthy landholders violated this basic principle of social justice.

The second accusation is the other side of the coin. While these probably absent agricultural barons defrauded their workers of their

---

[87] Jas 5:3d.

[88] Cf. Jas 3:4; 5:7, 9, 11.

[89] All told, there are four accusations in the indictment. Because of the *idou* in verse 4, marking a transition, I take the four to be one accusation followed by a series of three accusations.

[90] Hartin notes that the word "laborers" (*ergatōn*) appears in later texts of the Greek Bible, reflecting a situation where day laborers worked the fields of mostly absentee landlords. Cf. Hartin, *James*, 229; Johnson, *James*, 301.

[91] Jas 5:4.

[92] Deut 24:14-15. Cf. Lev 19:13; Josephus, *Antiquities* 4.288. Deut 24:5-22 contains a number of laws that are basic to Israel's social existence. Its final words, "I am commanding you to do this," constitute a formal appeal for their observance.

[93] Luke 10:7; cf. 1 Tim 5:18; see above, pp. 122, 237.

wages, they themselves lived in the lap of luxury: "You have lived on the earth in luxury and in pleasure: you have fattened your hearts in a day of slaughter."[94] The accusation has the ring of a prosecutor spelling out charges against an accused criminal, but it echoes even more the words of Israel's prophets of social justice.[95] Ironically, in what may seem a reversal of fortunes, the rich who received favored treatment in the judicial setting of James 2:2-3 now stand accused of serious wrongdoing. They have lived sumptuously,[96] fattening themselves like an animal is fattened before being slaughtered for a festive celebration. But "a day of slaughter"[97] may have another connotation. Allison suggests that it is a reference to the eschatological assize.[98] Those who lived so sumptuously on earth[99] may have unwittingly prepared themselves for their own slaughter. Martin Dibelius offers a somewhat different interpretation of the text. In his reading, the sense of the accusation may be that the rich live riotously while it goes badly for the pious.[100]

The author of the epistle has reserved the most serious accusation against the rich until the end. In good rhetorical fashion, the climax of his series of accusations is: "You have condemned and murdered the righteous one, who does not resist you."[101] A judicial setting continues to be in evidence. The word "condemned" (*katedikasate*)

---

[94] Jas 5:5.

[95] Reicke once observed that the entire passage "conforms to the pattern of the prophetic oracle of doom." Cf. Bo Reicke, *The Epistles of James, Peter, and Jude*, AB 37 (Garden City, NY: Doubleday, 1964), 50.

[96] In Painter and de Silva (*James and Jude*, 155), Painter comments, "This piling up of language is supposed to communicate a level of luxury that is obscene especially when seen in relation to the poverty of those whose exploitation made that luxury possible."

[97] The phrase comes from Jer 12:3.

[98] Cf. Allison, *James*, 683; Painter and de Silva, *James and Jude*, 151.

[99] Might the seemingly superfluous phrase "on the earth" (*epi tēs gēs*) have been attracted by way of contrast with the "Lord of hosts," an image of the Lord with his heavenly armies? Or could it be due to the influence of Q 13:22-34 (Luke 13:33-34; Matt 6:19-21), a saying of Jesus that seems to have influenced much of the imagery of this passage in James?

[100] Cf. Dibelius, *James*, 239. Nonetheless, he avers that "the words are spoken from the viewpoint of an eschatological position at the End of the time."

[101] Jas 5:6.

seems to retain its full legal sense.[102] The rich have used the courts to condemn the innocent (*ton dikaion*). In some cases, the skewed courts may have condemned the innocent to death. The actions of the rich would then have been tantamount to murder.[103] Those who have lost their lives were unable to defend themselves. They were unable to offer resistance to those who oppressed them, a situation that aggravates the crime of the rich.

Raymond Brown opines that the Epistle of James, "with its eloquent denunciations of the rich (5:1-6) may represent Christianity in Diaspora Judaism."[104] In fact, the Sitz im Leben of the epistle is a subject of debate among New Testament scholars. Likewise moot is the question of whether the author of the text has the nonbelieving rich in mind or whether he is thinking of rich believers who oppress the poorer members of the community. What cannot be doubted is that the author has compiled a serious indictment of the rich, though his examples may well be hypothetical. For him, the rich do not use their wealth properly. They amass riches for their own pleasures, paying little heed to the needs of the poor. Indeed they exploit the less well-off to their own advantage and even employ the judicial system to accomplish their self-serving purposes. There is, says the author, another judicial system. With the arrival of the eschatological assize on the Day of the Lord, the tables will be definitively turned, and the rich will be subject to judgment.

First Peter

Whereas virtually all commentators agree that in the Epistle of James, a person's relationship to wealth is a "litmus test" for their relationship to God,[105] the matter of wealth, wages, and the wealthy is not one that occupies the attention of other authors of the Catholic Epistles. For example, the First Epistle of Peter, not much shorter than James, has only a few things to say about the subject. We can begin

---

[102] Allison, *James*, 684. Cf. Johnson, *James*, 304.
[103] The case of Naboth comes to mind; cf. 1 Kgs 21:1-29.
[104] Brown, *Birth*, 363.
[105] Cf. Allison, *James*, 641, with a quotation of Kanell, *Economics*, 157.

with what he has to say about gold and silver, the precious metals that are generally considered to be a sign of wealth.

Gold and Silver

The metals are mentioned in 1 Peter 1:18-19a to underscore the singular value of Christ the Redeemer: "You know that you were ransomed[106] from the futile ways inherited from your ancestors, not with perishable things like silver or gold, but with the precious[107] blood of Christ." Hebrew tradition was familiar with the use of coins to secure redemption.[108] Because of their value, gold and silver were commonly used in redemption transactions in both the Jewish and the Greco-Roman world. In comparison with Christ, these precious metals are only "perishable things" (*phthartois*). Of themselves, they defy corruption, but they provide a negative example of the singular importance of redemption effected through the blood of Christ.

Another reference to gold appears in what seems to be a small unit taken from a household code in 1 Peter 3:1-7. The unit has more to say about wives than it does about husbands. Among other things, wives are urged, "Do not adorn yourselves outwardly by braiding your hair, and by wearing gold ornaments or fine clothing; rather, let your adornment be the innermost self with the lasting beauty of a gentle and quiet spirit, which is very precious in God's sight."[109]

Women's attire may not be the real issue in the subunit; perhaps the author includes it only to substantiate his idea that women should be subordinate to their men.[110] Nevertheless, the way that women

---

[106] The verb "ransom" (*elytrōthēte*) was typically used for the manumission of slaves or the redemption of prisoners.

[107] The adjective "precious" (*timiō*) naturally applied to metals like gold and silver is now applied to the blood of Christ while the "precious" metals are said to be perishable. Cf. 1 Pet 1:7.

[108] Cf. Exod 30:12-16.

[109] 1 Pet 3:3-4.

[110] For Donelson, the real issue is submission. For Achtemeier, the issue is more narrowly the subordination of Christian wives to unbelieving husbands. Cf. Lewis R. Donelson, *I & II Peter and Jude: A Commentary*, NTL (Louisville: Westminster John Knox, 2010), 91; Paul J. Achtemeier, *1 Peter*, Hermeneia (Minneapolis: Fortress, 1996), 208–9.

should appear in public was a classic topos for Hellenistic and Jewish philosophic moralists who urged women to avoid ostentation and dress simply.[111] The author of 1 Peter echoes this topos when he urges the wives of nonbelieving husbands to avoid the kind of ostentation associated with the wearing of gold ornaments.

Shun Ill-Gotten Wealth

In the midst of a long exhortation on suffering as a Christian,[112] 1 Peter has something to say about other kinds of suffering, the kind that should not be found in a believer: "But let none of you suffer as a murderer, a thief, a criminal, or even as a mischief-maker."[113] This rhetorical aside barely deserves mention in our study of wealth, wages, and the wealthy, but it is worthy of note that in a text that really does not treat these matters, the author nonetheless echoes the Decalogue's prohibition of stealing. One can only speculate whether theft might have been a temptation for some members of his community. In any case, the author is at one with other New Testament authors as seeing the acquisition of another's possessions as a moral evil.[114]

Responsibility of the Elder

The final passage of 1 Peter that is even remotely pertinent to the subject of this study is one that echoes the catalogues of virtues that the author(s) of 1 Timothy and Titus used to describe the qualifications of church leaders. In a similar vein, the author of 1 Peter writes, "I exhort the elders [*presbyterous*] among you to tend the flock of God that is in your charge, exercising the oversight [*episkopountes*], not under compulsion but willingly, as God would have you do—

---

[111] The subject is mainly treated in works written by men. Cf. *T. Reub.* 5.1, 5; Philo, *Sacrifices* 21.6-27; *Virt.* 39-40; Plutarch, *Conj. Praec.* 26 [*Moralia* 141 E]; Pliny the Younger, *Pan.* 83.7; Juvenal, *Sat.* 3.180-81; see also 1 Tim 2:9-11. The topic also appears in the more limited number of works by women. Cf. Perictione, *On the Harmony of a Woman* 143.10-14, 26-28; Phintys, *Concerning the Temperance of a Woman* 153.15-28.

[112] Cf. 1 Pet 4:12-19.

[113] 1 Pet 4:15.

[114] Cf. Matt 19:18; Rom 2:21; 1 Cor 6:10; Eph 4.28.

not for sordid gain [*mēde aischrokerdōs*] but eagerly."[115] The adverb *aischrokerdōs*, translated as "for sordid gain," is hapax in the New Testament. It is related to the adjective *aischrokerdēs*, "greedy for gain," which appears just twice in the New Testament, namely, in the list of qualifications of assistants at 1 Timothy 3:8 and of the overseer at Titus 1:7, both times qualified by the simple negative "not" (*mē*).

John Elliott judiciously notes that in the context of 1 Peter, "not for sordid gain" is not so much a qualification as it is an attitude with which elders are to lead and shepherd the flock.[116] It is the central one of three attitudinal descriptions of a proper exercise of oversight that the author spells out in the three antitheses of 1 Peter 5:2b-3. It is encompassed by "not under compulsion but willingly" and "not lord it over them . . . but be examples to the flock." The financial admonition[117] is appropriate. Leaders of a believing community generally received some sort of compensation for their role in leading the community, but the acquisition of money through the perks of office is considered shameful.[118]

Even in the early days of the Christian movement, some church leaders lacked financial integrity. For example, Polycarp, citing the case of Valens, warns the Philippians to "avoid love of money."[119] The *Didache* teaches, "If anyone should say in the spirit 'Give me money' or anything else, do not listen to him."[120] It also warns against the person who trades on Christ, the *christemporos*, one who trafficks on Christ.[121]

---

[115] 1 Pet 5:1c-2.

[116] Cf. John H. Elliott, *1 Peter*, AB 37B (New York: Doubleday, 2000), 815, 827, 829. Elliott (815) also notes, "The elders do not occupy positions in a hierarchalized organizational structure, of which there is no hint in 1 Peter."

[117] Cf. 1 Cor 9:7; Gal 6:6; 1 Tim 6:5; *Did.* 12:5.

[118] Cf. Donelson, *I & II Peter and Jude*, 145.

[119] Cf. Polycarp, *Phil.* 11.1.

[120] *Did.* 11.12a. "But if he tells you to give on behalf of others who are in need, let no one judge him" (*Did.* 11.12b) immediately follows the exhortation, clearly suggesting that the first exhortation was in reference to those who were seeking money for themselves.

[121] Lightfoot in J. B. Lightfoot and J. R. Harmer, eds., *The Apostolic Fathers* (Grand Rapids: Baker, 1984), 234. Kurt Niederwimmer translates the word as "using Christ to make a living" and provides an excursus on the expression.

Jude

With only twenty-five verses, the Epistle of Jude is one of the shortest texts in the New Testament. Its length leads to its appearing in the canonical New Testament after the other Catholic Epistles. It was probably written before 2 Peter, whose second chapter is largely dependent on Jude. Accordingly, we should take a look at it before turning to 2 Peter, arguably the last New Testament text to have been written.

For the most part, the Epistle of Jude is an exhortation against false teachers, who appear to be Christians who wormed their way into the community. The text, designed to build up the community, is largely devoid of references to financial matters, but in a rapid-firing salvo, the author of the epistle accuses the intruders, saying that they "are grumblers and malcontents; they indulge their own lusts; they are bombastic in speech, flattering people to their own advantage [*ōpheileias charin*]."[122] This final accusation may suggest that the false teachers flatter people in order to weasel money out of them. The reader must not, however, too readily conclude that the author was primarily thinking of monetary gain. The word "advantage" (*ōpheileia*), rarely used in the New Testament,[123] indicates any kind of advantage, including honor and position.[124]

The language of "flattering people" (*thaumazontes prosōpa*) seems to echo the Greek of Leviticus 19:15 and Deuteronomy 10:17. God does not show partiality,[125] but the false teachers do. In Hellenistic rhetoric, the charge was a stock accusation against one's opponents. The Hebrew Scriptures held that showing flattery was reprehensible.[126]

Cf. Kurt Niederwimmer, *The Didache*, Hermeneia (Minneapolis: Fortress, 1988), 186–87.

[122] Jude 16.

[123] Only here and Rom 3:1.

[124] Cultural norms generally precluded patrons from paying their clients in cash. Cf. Jerome H. Neyrey, *2 Peter, Jude*, AB 37C (New York: Doubleday, 1993), 82. Neyrey references A. R. Hands's *Charities and Social Aid in Greece and Rome* (London: Thames and Hudson, 1968).

[125] Cf. Deut 10:17; 2 Chr 19:7; Sir 35:12-13.

[126] Deut 16:19; Job 13:10; Ps 82:1-4; Prov 18:5; see also Jas 2:1.

Witherington suggests that the author's concern is partiality shown to potential patrons in order to curry their favor.[127] This proposed scenario makes sense in a client-patron environment in which teachers are often supported by their patrons. As they hear something that appeals to their egos,[128] their beneficence to their teachers is increased.

Second Peter

First Peter's admonition to elders that they exercise their service "not for sordid gain" provides a good segue into something that the anonymous author of 2 Peter says about false prophets.[129] Characterizing them as false teachers (*pseudodidaskaloi*), the nameless author[130] draws attention to the inaccuracy of what they were teaching. By describing his opponents as false prophets (*pseudoprophētai*) in 2 Peter 2:1, the author places these teachers alongside the false prophets who had led Israel astray, citing Balaam as an example.[131] In Jewish tradition Balaam was noted for his avarice and greed.[132]

"In their greed [*en pleonexia*]," the Petrine author writes, "they will exploit you with deceptive words."[133] In contrast with real apostles who carefully eschew cleverly devised myths,[134] false prophets "make up" their teaching. The adjective "deceptive" (*plastois*), hapax in the New Testament, was typically used of something that was shaped, molded in clay or wax.[135] Used metaphorically, as it is here, it means fabricated or sham.[136]

---

[127] Ben Witherington III, *Letters and Homilies for Jewish Christians: A Socio-Rhetorical Commentary on Hebrews, James and Jude* (Downers Grove, IL: IVP Academic, 2007), 625.

[128] Cf. 2 Tim 4:3.

[129] Cf. 2 Pet 2:1.

[130] The "Simon Peter" of 2 Pet 1:1 is a pseudonym.

[131] Cf. 2 Pet 2:15b-16; Num 22.

[132] Cf. Philo, *Mos.* 1.267-68; *Cher.* 33-34.

[133] 2 Pet 2:3.

[134] Cf. 2 Pet 1:16.

[135] See, for example, Philo, *Leg.* 2.54-55.

[136] Cf. *LSJ*, s.v. *plastos*.

According to the author, their imparting of sham teaching was due to their greed. Their hearts, he would write later, were "trained in greed" (*kardian gegymnasmenēn pleonexias*).[137] Whether or not these false prophets were really charlatans is a moot question. A stock accusation in Hellenistic rhetoric was that one's opponents were teaching as they did in order to make money.[138]

Despite this caveat about the foundation of the accusation, 2 Peter's two verses on greed are important for our query. First of all, by twice citing greed as a motivator of the false prophets, the author, under the aegis of Simon Peter, clearly characterizes greed as serious evil. Second, he shares with his readers two important thoughts about his understanding of greed. Greed is, he implies in 2 Peter 2:14c, a deep-seated vice. It affects the human heart, the *kardia*, the very core of the human person. Moreover, greed is a root vice. It leads to other vices.[139] It leads to deceptive teaching, false doctrine.

These words about greed are the last of the New Testament's teaching on the corrosive vice. Thoughts on greed (*pleonexia*) appear in seven other New Testament texts—Mark, Luke, Romans, 2 Corinthians, Ephesians, Colossians, and 1 Thessalonians[140]—but 2 Peter is the last of the New Testament texts to have been written. The characterization of greed that first appeared in the oldest book of the New Testament, 1 Thessalonians, written about 50 CE, carries through until the New Testament is complete, around 135 CE.

So What?

Religion That Is Pure and Undefiled before God, the Father, Is . . .

The author of the Epistle of James spoke about the nature of authentic religion. Pope Francis continued the discussion of the nature

---

[137] Cf. 2 Pet 2:14c.

[138] Cf. Daniel J. Harrington, "Jude and 2 Peter," 262; Donelson, *I & II Peter and Jude*, 239.

[139] Cf. 2 Pet 2:14a-b, 15-16a. This destructively generative power of greed has drawn the attention of Pope Francis who, in an address on June 19, 2015, said, "If you have greed in your heart, all other vices will follow."

[140] The related verb, "be greedy for" (*pleonekteō*), appears in 2 Cor and 1 Thess. The related noun, "greedy person" (*pleonektēs*), appears in 1 Cor and Eph.

of true religion in his inaugural encyclical, *The Joy of the Gospel*, as he wrote: "It is no longer possible to claim that religion should be restricted to the private sphere and that it exists only to prepare souls for heaven. . . . No one can demand that religion should be relegated to the inner sanctum or personal life, without influence on societal and national life, without concern for the soundness of civil institutions."[141]

Acts of Favoritism in the Judicial System

In 2013, sixteen-year-old Ethan Crouch, who had previously been convicted as a juvenile of drunken driving, was convicted of killing four people while driving drunk. He had slammed into a twenty-four-year-old woman who had stopped to change a flat tire, killing her along with three people who had stopped to help her. He was found guilty, but his defense had argued that Couch suffered from "affluenza," a condition they said impaired his judgment because of his wealth and privileged upbringing. In December 2013 Judge Jean Boyd sentenced the youth to ten years' probation and required that he attend rehabilitation, not drive, drink alcohol, or use drugs during the time of his probation.

Two years later, in another jurisdiction, twenty-three-year-old Daniel Gautreau was sentenced to four years in prison, followed by four years of home confinement, followed by seven years of probation, during the first five years of which his license would be suspended.[142] He was fined five thousand dollars and was required to undergo substance-abuse evaluation. His offense was that in June 2014 while driving drunk, he crashed his car, killing a twenty-one-year-old passenger and injuring another person.

Although no death was involved, America News posted a blog by Ray Brown on December 9, 2015, which reported, "After a New Jersey police chief[143] drove drunk, hit a parked car, fled the scene of an accident, and then lied about it, he will be given more than $260,000 in

---

[141] *Evangelii Gaudium* 182, 183.

[142] *The Providence Journal* (Saturday, December 5, 2015): A3.

[143] William C. King was the South Bound Brook, NJ, police chief at the time. The incident appeared on the April 4, 2015, police blotter of the town.

compensation plus one year's pay and be allowed to retire in good standing." And "he won't face any criminal charges."

Large corporations are especially privileged by the courts. They and their executives are virtually immune to the judicial system. For example, the Tenet corporation—which, among other ventures, operated several private hospitals in the state of Florida—participated in the state's Medicare and Medicaid programs. In 2006, the corporation agreed to pay $7 million to settle claims by the Florida attorney general's office that it had inflated prices to obtain more than $1 billion in excess Medicare payments. The penalty was seven dollars per thousand, less than 1 percent.[144] Would a young African American who stole one thousand dollars be subject only to a seven-dollar fine?

Corporations are generally immune to the judicial systems because of their complex and tiered management structure, which immunizes individuals from blame. While billions of dollars in fines were levied against banks and brokerage firms in the wake of the 2008 economic meltdown that left millions without a job and caused many to lose their homes because of reckless lending and shady securities dealings, executives were subject to neither fines nor imprisonment. Responsibility for wrongdoing is virtually impossible to determine, while reward for wrongdoing is readily given to the executives of companies that profit from wrongdoing.

Moreover, many corporations are charged with crimes under a deferred prosecution agreement. This means that if they do not engage in wrongdoing—or are not caught engaging in wrongdoing—the slate is wiped clean. The legal loophole was developed ninety years ago, at the time of the Great Depression, in order to give juveniles a second chance. Because corporations are able to exploit this loophole, a column by investigative reporter and editorial board member M. J. Anderson received the telling title, "At GM, it's just us delinquents."[145]

---

[144] The following year the corporation named the former governor of Florida to its board and paid him $2 million over an eight-year period.

[145] *The Providence Journal* (Friday, October 2, 2015): A5.

Wages which You Kept Back by Fraud

The author of the Epistle of James had harsh words to address to rich and generally absentee landlords who deprived the laborers who worked their fields of the just reward of their labor. The problem that he addressed remains to this day. During the first week of the 2015 Roman Synod on the Family, Cardinal Berhaneyesus Soura-phiel, the archbishop of Addis Ababa, said, "The issues in Africa are poverty, migration, people dispersed, war . . . and degradation of the environment." He then specifically mentioned foreign companies that practice mineral extraction in African countries, leaving local communities without adequate benefit from the work.

Wealthy Landowners

Taking a small landowner's property, the issue addressed in James 5:1-6, was also addressed by Pope Francis in *Laudato Sì*, almost two millennia after the author of the epistle wrote his harsh warning. The pope wrote, "Economies of scale, especially in the agricultural sector, end up forcing smallholders to sell their land or to abandon their traditional crops."[146] And further: "In many places, following the introduction of these crops, productive land is concentrated in the hands of a few owners due to 'the progressive disappearance of small producers, who, as a consequence of the loss of the exploited lands, are obliged to withdraw from direct production.' The most vulnerable of these become temporary laborers, and many rural workers end up moving to poverty-stricken urban areas."

Wages Kept Back by Fraud

Karen Lee Ziner listed "a sampling of recent wage-theft cases in R.I." in an article that appeared on page A15 of the Sunday, November 15, 2015, issue of *The Providence Journal.* She writes,

> Recent wage-theft cases in Rhode Island have involved food works, construction workers and garbage collectors Among

---

[146] Pope Francis, *Laudato Sì* 129.

them: Gourmet Heaven . . . The suit alleges [Chung] Cho violated state wage law—in some cases pay $360 to $400 for as many as 84 hours of work per week—and violated the federal Fair Labor Standards Act by denying overtime wages. . . . Cilantro Mexican Grill . . . The Rhode Island restaurant chain was ordered to pay $100,417 in back wages and damages to 32 restaurant workers in May after federal investigators found that it violated federal wage and hour laws by failing to pay overtime. . . . Cardoso Construction . . . [Joaquim] Cardoso agreed to pay 32 workers a total of $351,812 and an equal penalty to the DLT, plus a fine of $27,000 for drywall work at the University of Rhode Island. Investigators found that Cardoso misclassified the employees as independent contractors. . . . Marrocco Group . . . Entrepreneur Gianfranco Marrocco and his businesses agreed to pay $303,000 in back wages and damages to 146 low-wage workers after a U.S. Department of Labor investigation found "numerous payment schemes" that deprived cooks and dishwashers of overtime pay. . . . And this is just a sampling!

$\mathscr{X}$

Chapter 9

The Johannine Corpus

The last group of New Testament texts to be examined in this study are the Gospel of John, the three epistles of John, and the book of Revelation. For long periods in the history of the church each of these five texts has been attributed to John, one of the Twelve. For the most part, the attribution to that apostle has been abandoned by modern scholarship. There are, however, sufficient similarities of vocabulary and ideology to affirm that the five texts have emanated from authors who had some relationship with one another. Because of these affinities and the traditional attribution of authorship, these texts can be gathered together under the rubric of the Johannine Corpus. They were written in the waning years of the first century CE.

John

The Gospel of John is quite different from the gospels according to Matthew, Mark, and Luke, the similar narratives known collectively as the Synoptic Gospels. One striking difference is that the account of Jesus' "cleansing" of the temple, a prelude to the passion narrative in the Synoptic accounts,[1] appears in John 2:14-22, toward the beginning of the evangelist's story of Jesus. As such, the cleansing of the temple initiates a series of scenes in which traditional Jewish feasts are recast so that they point to Jesus. In the Johannine account,

---

[1] Matt 21:12-13; Mark 11:15-17; Luke 19:45-46. See above, pp. 131–32.

the core narrative of the cleansing of the temple, John 2:14-16, is expanded by discourse material that speaks about the resurrection of Jesus.

A citation of Psalm 69:9, "It is zeal for your house that has consumed me," which the disciples of Jesus are said to have remembered sometime later,[2] enables the evangelist to attribute Jesus' prophetic action to Jesus' zeal for the Father's house. As the evangelist describes Jesus' action, he specifically mentions that Jesus poured out the coins (*execheen to kerma*) of the money changers, a detail that does not appear in the Synoptic accounts. The word "coins" does not appear elsewhere in the New Testament. In the Johannine story, "coins" refers to the shekels and half-shekels used to buy offerings and pay the temple tax and the imperial coinage received in exchange, but the term generally designated the hard cash used for regular purchases.[3]

The evangelist closes his account of what Jesus had done by portraying Jesus as saying that the temple should not be a marketplace, a trading mart.[4] Jesus' words may have prompted the evangelist to shy away from speaking about financial matters in the remainder of his story about Jesus. He has, for example, failed to mention Judas's thirty pieces of silver or the fact that Joseph of Arimathea, who lent a tomb to Jesus, was a rich man. The New Testament's fourth evangelist has, in fact, very little to say about wealth, wages, and the wealthy in his narrative.

Wages

This is not to say that the evangelist is totally oblivious to these matters. Speaking to his disciples about the already present eschaton, Jesus says, "The reaper is already receiving wages [*misthon lambanei*] and is gathering fruit for eternal life."[5] That the reaper is already getting paid means that the harvest has begun. This illustrates the

---

[2] Cf. John 2:17.

[3] Cf. Spicq, "*Kermatistēs, kollybistēs, trapezitēs,*" *TLNT* 2:313–18, esp. 313.

[4] The Greek *oikon emporiou* takes the place of the "den of thieves" (*spēlaion lēstōn*) found in Matt 21:13; Mark 11:17; and Luke 19:46.

[5] John 4:36a.

realized eschatology of the fourth gospel, a fascinating topic the pursuit of which would take us far beyond our present inquiry.[6]

The reader of the NRSV's account of the story of the feeding of the five thousand finds another reference to wages in Philip's response to Jesus before the sign took place. Philip answered Jesus, "Six months' wages would not buy enough bread for each of them to get a little."[7] The NRSV translators have taken a bit of literary license at this point in their work. The evangelist wrote *diakosiōn dēnariōn*, "two hundred denarii," the equivalent of two hundred days' pay, but he didn't really speak about wages (*misthos*) as such.

Germane to our study is the appearance of Mary of Bethany and Judas Iscariot in John 12:3-8. Comparison and contrast is one of the techniques used by the evangelist in his characterization of the literary figures who appear in his narrative.[8] Their respective genders obviously distinguish Mary from Judas, but their attitude toward wealth distinguishes them even more clearly from each other and is important for our study. Although the evangelist does not say so explicitly, Mary was a woman of some means. Taking a container of fragrant and costly perfume, she anointed Jesus' feet. The anointing would have consisted of her pouring the perfume over Jesus' feet. The evangelist specifies that it was "costly" (*polytimou*).[9] Judas proclaimed its value to be three hundred denarii,[10] about a year's wages for the ordinary worker. The perfume was indeed valuable. Even more valuable were the spices that Nicodemus brought to be wrapped, along with the body, in Jesus' burial shroud. The mixture of myrrh and aloes was "worth a fortune."[11]

---

[6] It is an oversimplification to say simply that the fourth gospel is concerned with present salvation whereas the Synoptics are concerned with the future coming of the kingdom, but that is the heart of the issue.

[7] John 6:7.

[8] Cf. Raymond F. Collins, "'Who Are You?' Comparison/Contrast and Fourth Gospel Characterization," in Skinner, *Characters and Characterization*, 77–93.

[9] Cf. Matt 26:7.

[10] Cf. John 12:5.

[11] Bennema, *A Theory of Character*, 148. With reference to 2 Chr 16:14 and Josephus, *Ant.* 15:61 and 17:199, he explains that the extraordinary amount of expensive spices, "about a hundred pounds" (John 19:39, NRSV), was only used for a royal burial (151).

Feigning concern for the poor, Judas said that the perfume with which Mary anointed Jesus' feet should have been sold and the money given to the poor. The evangelist discounts this argument by saying that Judas was a thief (*kleptēs*[12]). He served as the bursar for the group of disciples who traveled with Jesus, but he dipped into the common till. He really didn't have any interest at all in the poor; perhaps he simply wanted to increase the amount of money that he had at his disposal. In contrast, the relatively affluent Mary was concerned with Jesus. She didn't talk about him, as Judas talked about the poor. Rather, she acted on his behalf. Her action, said Jesus, was in anticipation of his burial. It was connected to the salvific reality of Jesus' death, burial,[13] and resurrection. Her extravagant action proclaimed the "value" of Jesus. As for the poor, they would survive Jesus' death and resurrection and would need to be taken care of by Jesus' disciples. There is no disparagement of the poor in Jesus' statement, "You always have the poor with you, but you do not always have me."[14] The anointing of Jesus' body for burial was a matter of some urgency; caring for the poor was a perpetual issue that needed to be attended to after his death and resurrection.

The Johannine Epistles

First, Second, and Third John are three short texts that constitute the minicorpus called the Johannine Epistles. Second and Third John appear to be genuine letters written by a person who styles himself "the elder" (*ho presbyteros*), addressing himself respectively to a church designated as the "elect lady" (*eklektē kyria*) and to a man named Gaius. First John, with its five chapters, is a longer text that does not have an epistolary format. Rather, 1 John appears to be a short treatise that rehearses and expands on themes found in the Gospel of John.

---

[12] Cf. John 10:10.

[13] It is to be noted that whereas Mark 16:1, followed by Luke 24:1, indicates that the women's Easter visit to the tomb had as its purpose the anointing of Jesus' body, there is no such mention in the fourth gospel; cf. John 20:1. There was no need for Jesus' body to be anointed; Mary of Bethany had taken care of that.

[14] John 12:8.

Of these three texts, only 1 John is of particular interest to our study. First John 2:16 says, "For all that is in the world—the desire of the flesh, the desire of the eyes, the pride in riches—comes not from the Father but from the world." This statement clarifies what the Johannine author means when he writes about loving the world and the things of the world, a love that is antithetical to love of the Father.[15] Johannine texts generally evince a negative attitude toward "the world" (*ho kosmos*) but are not specific in spelling out the temptations that come from the world.

He first writes about sexual desire, lust,[16] and then about "pride in riches" (*hē alazoneia tou biou*). Whether there be two or three vices that the author has in mind, together they constitute what Witherington has called "the reigning value system of the larger culture."[17] At the time, the vice of "pride" (*alazoneia*) was widely condemned by moralists, but each author who writes about pride puts his own spin on the precise nuance of the term.

Striking is the colorful description of the "proud man" (*ho alazōn*) provided by Theophrastus, the student of Plato and Aristotle. "The *alazōn*," he writes, "is the kind of person who will stand on the rostrum and tell perfect strangers what a lot of money he has at sea, and discourses about his investments, how large they are, and what gains and losses he has had, and as he spins his tales, he will send his servant to the bank—his balance being a denarius."[18] The description is obviously a caricature, but the reader understands what the ancient philosopher thought about the proud man. The proud man boasts about his wealth.

---

[15] Cf. 1 John 2:15.

[16] Bultmann notes that what distinguishes the "desire of the flesh" from the "desire of the eyes" can scarcely be determined. Cf. Rudolf Bultmann, *The Johannine Epistles*, Hermeneia (Philadelphia: Fortress, 1973), 34.

[17] Ben Witherington III, *Letters and Homilies for Hellenized Christians*, vol. 1: *A Socio-Rhetorical Commentary on Titus, 1–2 Timothy and 1–3 John* (Downers Grove, IL: IVP Academic, 2006), 478. Apropos the triad in 1 John 2:16, Dwight Moody Smith comments, "Translating this as 'sex, money, and power,' may not miss the mark by much." Cf. D. Moody Smith, *First, Second, and Third John*, Interpretation (Louisville: John Knox, 1991), 66.

[18] Theophrastus, *Characters* 23, translated by Witherington in *Titus, 1–2 Timothy and 1–3 John*, 379.

In the book of Wisdom and in the writings of Philo, pride was a vice of the rich and of those in the public eye.[19] Hellenistic Judaism often warned against the lure of sex and money.[20] So too does the author of 1 John 2:16. The author complements his words about the desire of the flesh and the desire of the eyes with the pride of riches. He contrasts the love of God with pride in one's possessions. In effect, the dichotomy between love of the Father and love of the world manifest in the "pride in riches" that the Johannine author sets out in 1 John 2:16 is functionally equivalent to the Sayings Source's "You cannot serve God and wealth"[21] and the deutero-Pauline "greed (which is idolatry)."[22]

In 1 John 2:16, the epistle's author writes somewhat philosophically about money. In the following chapter, he adopts the viewpoint of a moralist: "How does God's love abide in anyone who has the world's goods and sees a brother or sister in need and yet refuses help?"[23] The person who "has the world's goods" (*echē ton bion tou kosmou*) is not necessarily someone who is particularly affluent or has a surplus of wealth. Someone who has the world's goods is anyone who has possessions.[24]

The careful reader immediately recognizes that the rhetorical question of 1 John 3:17 begs for an immediate negative response. There is no way that God's love can abide in a person who has possessions and turns his or her back on a believer in need. "It is absurd," writes Bultmann, "that the 'love of God abides' in one who is not compassionate."[25] A single act of compassion is proof positive of one's love of God or, perhaps better yet, proof positive that God's love is at work in the compassionate person.

---

[19] Thus Spicq, "*alazoneia, alazōn*," *TLNT* 1:63–65, at 63, with references to Wis 5:8 and Philo's *Virtues* 16:2.

[20] Cf. *T. Jud.* 17.1.

[21] Cf. Luke 16:13; Matt 6:24. See above, pp. 118–21, 161. Cf. Raymond E. Brown, *The Epistles of John*, AB 30 (Garden City, NY: Doubleday, 1982), 449.

[22] Cf. Col 3:5. See above, pp. 217–20.

[23] 1 John 3:17.

[24] Brown (*Epistles*, 441, 449) renders the Greek, "when someone has enough of this world's livelihood." Cf. Witherington, *Titus, 1–2 Timothy and 1–3 John*, 512.

[25] Cf. Bultmann, *Johannine Epistles*, 56.

The reader should not overlook the pathos in the writer's admonition. The person seen to be in need is a member of the family (*ton adelophon autou*)—that is, a member of the fictive family of believers—a brother or sister. The person lacking compassion is said to have closed off his or her innards (*kleise ta splanchna autou*), their gut feelings, toward the needy person. "The author," writes Raymond Brown, envisions "a situation where a person not only does not help his brother in need, but actually shuts off a feeling of compassion that the needy would instinctively arouse."[26] That person immunizes himself against compassion. If a person has steeled his feelings against the needy, especially a needy member of the believing community, God's love is inoperative within him or her.

The Book of Revelation

The book of Revelation, most probably written in the waning years of the first century CE as a product of an inspired author's religious imagination, has been called the most enigmatic book of the Bible. It may well be that. It is almost inordinately full of symbolism and symbolic numbers. Gold, one of its most prominent symbols, is used to qualify heavenly realities.[27]

Typically, apocalyptic literature is written by an author whose identity we cannot determine. The hero of the author's narrative is a seer from the past. In the case of the book of Revelation, the seer is a man called John[28] who is said to have experienced a vison while on the island of Patmos.[29] Like all books that belong to the apocalyptic genre,[30] Revelation is a book written to convey hope to a people suffering oppression and trauma. From this perspective, the book's final two chapters, chapters 21–22, might be the core of the author's message. The vision encourages believers persecuted during the reign of Domitian to remain steadfast.

---

[26] Brown, *Epistles*, 450.

[27] Cf. Rev 1:12, 13, 20; 2:1; 4:4; 5:8; 8:3 [2x]; 9:13, 20; 14:14; 15:6, 7; 17:4; 21:15.

[28] Cf. Rev 1:2, 4, 9; 22:8. The author of the book does not identify his John with either the son of Zebedee nor with the author of the fourth gospel.

[29] Cf. Rev 1:9.

[30] See the definition of the apocalyptic genre by John J. Collins in "Toward the Morphology of a Genre," *Semeia* 14 (1979): 1–19, at 9.

The Letters to Smyrna and Laodicea

The first major section of the book of Revelation consists of letters that the seer is to write to the angels of seven churches in Asia Minor. In the letter destined for Smyrna, modern-day Izmir, a heavenly figure, "the first and the last,"[31] says of the congregation, "I know your affliction and your poverty, even though you are rich."[32] Despite suffering persecution and its ensuing poverty, the community was spiritually rich.[33] The port city of Smyrna was rich; its persecuted believers were poor. Perhaps their goods had been taken from them. Their poverty was a sign that they had not succumbed to their persecutors. Despite their material poverty, they were rich in faith and the promise of future blessings.[34]

In the letter to the church of Laodicea, another affluent city, the Christ figure—"the Amen, the faithful and true witness, the origin of God's creation"—confronts the church in this fashion: "'For you say, I am rich,[35] I have prospered, and I need nothing.' You do not realize that you are wretched, pitiable, poor, blind, and naked. Therefore I counsel you to buy from me gold refined by fire so that you may be rich."[36]

The financial metaphors are appropriate. Laodicea was a financial center whose population included a number of quite wealthy inhabitants. These affluent believers of Laodicea were deluding themselves. With their wealth, they thought that they had everything they wanted, but the Christ figure reveals their real indigence. They are really wretched, pitiable, blind, naked, and poor.[37] The community that thinks itself to be rich (*plousios*) is actually poor (*ptōchos*). Unlike the Smyrnians, the Laodiceans are spiritually poor. To be rich, they need to obtain from Christ gold refined by fire. The biblical image of

---

[31] The expression appears three times in Revelation, always in reference to Christ. Cf. Rev 1:17; 22:13.

[32] Rev 2:9a.

[33] Cf. 2 Cor 6:10; Jas 2:5.

[34] Cf. Rev 2:10e.

[35] Cf. Hos 12:9; Zech 11:5; *1 En.* 97:8-9.

[36] Rev 3:17-18a.

[37] Rhetorical assonance, the repetition of the *os* sound at the end of each of the five adjectives, links the five negatives together.

refined gold generally connoted a life purified of sin,[38] but it is likely that here the image suggests persecution.[39] The Laodiceans' monetary wealth conceals their real poverty; only Christ provides true riches.

The Heavenly Liturgy

One of the features of the book of Revelation is its narrative account of the seer's vision of heavenly liturgies. In Revelation 5:9-10, four living creatures and twenty-four elders sing a "new song" that proclaims the worthiness of the Lamb.[40] In the immediately following vision, the seer sees and hears[41] untold numbers of angels sing of what the Lamb is worthy to receive. They sing, "Worthy is the Lamb that was slaughtered to receive power and wealth and wisdom and might and honor and glory and blessing."[42] God is the source of these gifts. The seven rights, which together constitute a complex unity, are royal prerogatives.

Seven is a number of plenitude. Among the Lamb's prerogatives is "wealth" (*plouton*), a gift of God.[43] In God's plan, wealth belongs to the Lamb. This vision explains why the Laodiceans should realize that they must obtain their wealth from Christ.[44]

Exorbitant Prices

The sixth chapter of the book of Revelation contains the seer's vision of the Lamb opening six of a set of seven seals.[45] That the Lamb opens these seals is a sign that the whole scenario is under God's control. Nonetheless, the unsealing of the first four seals unleashes tremendous harm upon humankind. These are penultimate eschatological

---

[38] Cf. Job 23:10; Prov 27:21; Mal 3:2-3; Pss. Sol. 17:42-43, 51.

[39] Cf. Zech 13:9; 1 Pet 1:6-9.

[40] Cf. Rev 4:11.

[41] Cf. Rev 5:11, "I looked and I heard" (*kai eidon kai ēkousa*).

[42] Rev 5:12.

[43] Cf. 1 Chr 29:11-12. This is the only instance in the book of Revelation where "wealth" is specifically attributed to God or to Christ.

[44] Cf. Rev 3:18a.

[45] The seventh seal is opened in Rev 8:1, a prelude to the vision of the seven trumpets (Rev 8:2–11:18).

misfortunes that precede the final establishment of the reign of God. The coming of these misfortunes is symbolized by the arrival of four terrifying horsemen.[46]

The third horseman rides a black horse. Its ominous color symbolizes a famine that comes over the earth.[47] The rider holds a set of scales in his hands. At a time of hunger, food was carefully rationed. Bread was weighed rather than being handed over in approximately equal units. The prices in this vision of end-time misfortune are exorbitant. The denarius was the amount of the ordinary daily wage. Now it costs a day's wage for a quart of wheat; a day's wage for three quarts of barley. The ominous voice, probably God's voice,[48] speaks, "A quart of wheat for a day's pay [*dēnariou*], and three quarts of barley for a day's pay [*dēnariou*] but do not damage the olive oil and the wine."[49]

The "quart of wheat" was a day's ration of wheat for a Roman soldier. At the marketplace, a denarius would usually be enough to buy eight quarts of wheat. During the famine, ordinary wheat is severely overpriced. Barley loaves served as the staple of the poor. The people's poverty did not allow them to buy the better-quality loaves of wheat bread. But now, even the price of barley is outrageous. Normally, a denarius would be enough to buy sixteen quarts of barley. Now, in the midst of this tremendous famine, a denarius could buy only three quarts of barley. Ironically, the olive oil and the wine seem to have been spared. At the time, wealthy landlords devoted their lands to the production of oil and wine, thinking that these would bring bigger profits.

Craig Koester has this to say about this ominous picture: "The exorbitant grain prices in Rev 6:6 point to the failure of an economic system to provide for people. Even though oil and wine remain avail-

---

[46] Cf. Rev 5:1-8; Zech 1:7-11; 6:1-8.

[47] Cf. Rev 6:8.

[48] Cf. Brian K. Blount, *Revelation*, NTL (Louisville: Westminster John Knox, 2009), 127.

[49] Rev 6:6b. Aune comments, "One liter of wheat and three liters of barley are mentioned together here because it is the appropriate ration for a cavalryman and his mount, or for an individual and his domestic animals." Cf. David E. Aune, *Revelation 6–16*, WBC 52B (Nashville: Thomas Nelson, 1998), 397.

able, they are unaffordable for those who must spend their day's wage of a denarius to buy enough grain for themselves. . . . The shortages ushered in by the third horseman point to the limits of an economic system to guarantee prosperity."[50]

Cowering in Fear

The war-induced famine particularly affected those who eked out a subsistent living, while apparently sparing the produce of the economically powerful. When, however, the sixth seal is opened and the eschatological timetable is about to be realized, the rich and powerful read the signs of the times and realize that the end is near. The cosmic upheaval described in Revelation 6:12-14 announces the imminent judgment of God:[51]

> Then the kings of the earth and the magnates and the gen-
> erals and the rich and the powerful, and everyone slave and
> free,[52] hid in the caves and among the rocks of the mountains
> calling to the mountains and rocks, "Fall on us and hide us
> from the face of the one seated on the throne and from the
> wrath of the Lamb; for the great day of their wrath has come,
> and who is able to stand?"[53]

Along with other powerful persons,[54] the rich must face the judgment of God. A hasty departure for the mountains will not provide refuge.[55]

---

[50] Craig R. Koester, *Revelation*, AB 38A (New Haven: Yale University Press, 2014), 408.

[51] Cf. Mark 13:1-27. Aune rehearses a large number of biblical and extrabiblical parallels in *Revelation 6–16*, 413–19.

[52] "Everyone slave and free" (*pas doulos kai eleutheros*) may be a reference to those who serve the powerful. So, apparently, G. K. Beale, *The Book of Revelation*, NIGTC (Grand Rapids: Eerdmans, 1999), 130. On the other hand, the expression may signify that "social distinctions will be forgotten in the frantic attempt to escape." So, Wilfred J. Harrington, *Revelation*, SP 16 (Collegeville, MN: Liturgical Press, 1993), 96. For Aune (*Revelation 6–16*, 410), the phrase is "a complex way of saying 'everyone,'" reflecting the Hebrew idiom of pairing opposites to express universality. Cf. Rev 13:16.

[53] Rev 6:15-17.

[54] Cf. Isa 34:12.

[55] Cf. Matt 24:16-22; Luke 21:20-22.

"These groups of people," writes Beale, "undergo divine judgment because they are an essential part of the corrupt world system, which must be destroyed."[56] Despite their efforts to hide from God's wrath, they cannot escape.[57]

Babylon, the Whore

One of the most dramatic scenes in the book of Revelation speaks directly to the theme of our present inquiry. The two-part vision begins:

> Then one of the seven angels who had the seven bowls came and said to me, "Come, I will show you the judgement of the great whore who is seated on many waters, with whom the kings of the earth have committed fornication, and with the wine of whose fornication the inhabitants of the earth have become drunk." So he carried me away in the spirit into a wilderness, and I saw a woman sitting on a scarlet beast that was full of blasphemous names, and it had seven heads and ten horns. The woman was clothed in purple and scarlet, and adorned with gold and jewels and pearls, holding in her hand a golden cup full of abominations and the impurities of her fornication and on her forehead was written a name, a mystery: "Babylon the great, mother of whores and of earth's abominations." And I saw that the woman was drunk with the blood of the saints and the blood of the witnesses to Jesus. When I saw her, I was greatly amazed.[58]

Most commentators on Revelation hold that the woman is a symbol of Rome. The seer's amazing vision is that of a rich courtesan. Despite the fact that she is a very expensive call girl, the author still outfits her with the trappings of a street hooker, says Brian Blount.[59] Her name is tattooed on her forehead.

---

[56] Beale, *Revelation*, 399.

[57] Koester (*Revelation*, 412) notes: "The vision has a satirical quality as it depicts those who claimed high dignity for themselves indecorously seeking to hide in the caves and rocks of the mountains."

[58] Rev 17:1-6.

[59] Cf. Blount, *Revelation*, 315.

The depicted scene draws on a similar scene in Jeremiah 51:7[60] "where the people of the world have imbibed so heavily of Babylon's economy that their lust of a greater and greater stake in her profits has driven them mad."[61] Part two of the author's diptych develops Jeremiah 51:8: "Suddenly Babylon has fallen and is shattered; wail for her!" The reworking of this Scripture occupies the entire eighteenth chapter of the book of Revelation, 18:1-24, in which a compilation of prophecies of doom create an image of the judgment announced in Revelation 17:1.

An angel different from the angels with the seven bowls comes on scene and announces, "Fallen, fallen is Babylon the great! . . . For all the nations have drunk of the wine of the wrath of her fornication, and the kings of the earth have committed fornication with her, and the merchants of the earth have grown rich from the power of her luxury."[62] Kings and merchants have fallen victim to her allure. These merchants are most likely the "magnates" of Revelation 6:15[63] who attempt to hide from the wrath of God.

After a divine voice, that of either God or Christ, urges people to escape from the woman's clutches and her punishment, comes the weeping and wailing:[64] "And the kings of the earth who committed fornication and lived in luxury with her, will weep and wail over her."[65] They can utter only a mournful lament: "Alas, alas [*ouai, ouai*], the great city, Babylon, the mighty city! For in one hour your judgment has come."[66] "And the merchants of the earth weep and mourn for her."[67]

These merchants traded in extravagant goods, as the list—which includes trafficking in human persons—in Revelation 18:11-13 makes clear. Suddenly, their market was lost, and with it their own wealth disappeared. The divine voice addresses them: "The fruit for which

---

[60] One of the features of the book of Revelation is its reworking of biblical motifs. The two-part vision of Babylon, the whore, in Rev 17–18 is a good example of the author's technique.

[61] Blount, *Revelation*, 313.

[62] Rev 18:2a, 3.

[63] Cf. Rev 18:23. See Koester, *Revelation*, 412.

[64] Cf. Jer 51:8.

[65] Rev 18:9a.

[66] Rev 18:10b.

[67] Rev 18:11a.

your soul longed has gone from you, and all your dainties and your splendor are lost to you, never to be found again!"[68] Distancing themselves from the situation, their tale was a tale of woe: "Alas, alas [*ouai, ouai*], the great city, clothed in fine linen, purple and scarlet, adorned with gold, with jewels and with pearls! For in one hour all this wealth [*ho tosoutos ploutos*] has been laid waste."[69]

Babylon, the great whore, had "seduced the kings and merchants of the earth into an idolatrous mercantile tryst."[70] When it came to an end, they could only weep and mourn and wail their tale of woe. There was, in addition, a third group of people caught up in the vicious web woven by the lure of wealth. These were the seafarers, the merchant marine, who also "wept and mourned."[71] The sailors' tale of woe echoed that of the merchants: "Alas, alas [*ouai, ouai*], the great city, where all who had ships at sea grew rich by her wealth! For in one hour she has been laid waste."[72]

Then the unnamed voice of verse 4 utters a final comment,[73] a prelude to the triumphant canticle of Revelation 19:1-8: "Rejoice over her, O heaven, you saints and apostles and prophets! For God has given judgment for you against her."[74] At the end, those who have actively resisted the lure of wealth can rejoice.

The vision of Revelation 18 is colorful, taunting, and dramatic. Ultimately, it speaks of the fall of Rome.[75] Losers along with Rome were the kings, merchants, and seagoing traders who were led astray by the great city's wealth. God's judgment fell not only on Rome but also on these wealthy hangers-on. Unscathed in God's judgment, although scarred by their treatment at the hands of the great whore

---

[68] Rev 18:14.

[69] Rev 18:16-17.

[70] Blount, *Revelation*, 335.

[71] Rev 18:19.

[72] Rev 18:19b.

[73] Cf. Adela Yarbro Collins, "Revelation 18: Taunt-Song or Dirge," in *L'Apocalypse johannique et l'Apocalyptique dans le Nouveau Testament*, ed. Jan Lambrecht, BETL 53 (Louvain: University Press, 1980), 185–204, esp. 193.

[74] Rev 18:20.

[75] Cf. Tina Pippin, "Of Metaphors and Monsters: The Body of the Whore of Babylon in the Apocalypse of John," *Classical Bulletin* 86 (2010): 156–72.

and her clients,[76] are those who resisted the seductive lure of the whore's wealth.

So What?

Exorbitant Prices (Rev 6:6)

In an article titled, "Big Pharma Owes a Debt to Society,"[77] Mariana Mazzucato, professor in economics of innovation at the University of Sussex, writes, "When Martin Shkreli of Turing Pharmaceutical raised the price of Daraprim[78] by 5,455 percent,[79] he put drug pricing on the agenda for the leading 2016 presidential candidates. . . . Studies looking at cancer treatments have shown no correlation between the price of cancer drugs and the benefits they provide. Peter Bach, a renowned oncologist, has found that, for most drugs, a value-based cost is actually lower than the current market-based price.

"This state of affairs is not simply a huge failure of the so-called free-market; it is a long con. The supposed partnership between public and private sectors is increasingly parasitic, hurting innovation and fueling inequality through reduced investment, exorbitant prices for consumers and more money siphoned off for stockholders."

An example is Sovaldi, a hepatitis C drug that sells for $84,000 for a twelve-week course of treatment. The drug could have sold between $50,000 and $115,000. The price decided on by the executives of Gilead Sciences was not based on the cost of research and development; rather, company executives believed that setting the cost at the lower end of the scale would have resulted in "significant foregone revenue." "By raising the price of the new standard of care set by Sovaldi, Gilead intended to raise the price floor for all future hepatitis C treatments,[80] including its follow-on drugs and those of

---

[76] Cf. Rev 18:4; 19:2.

[77] Cf. *The Providence Journal* (Tuesday, November 3, 2015): A15.

[78] The sixty-two-year-old drug is the only approved treatment for toxoplasmosis, a parasitic disease that mainly strikes pregnant women, cancer patients, and AIDS patients.

[79] The price of the drug went from $13.50 per tablet to $750.

[80] The company's next hepatitis C drug, Harvonim, was priced at $94,500.

its competitors," said a US Senate Science Committee report. "Documents show it was always Gilead's plan to max out revenue, and that accessibility and affordability were pretty much an afterthought," said Senator Ron Wyden who led the Senate investigation. Indeed, noted an article in the *Washington Post*,[81] patients were warehoused in order to limit access to Sovaldi.

---

[81] The article by Carolyn V. Johnson and Brady Dennis was reprinted in the Sunday, December 6, 2015, issue of *The Providence Journal*, F1, 3, with the title "How an $84,000 drug got its price."

Concluding Thoughts

This study of the passages in the New Testament that treat of wealth, wages, and the wealthy leads to one singularly important conclusion, namely, that there is a remarkable consistency among the various authors and their different writings with regard to wealth, wages, and the wealthy. Before summarizing these thoughts as a conclusion to this study, some caveats relative to the use of New Testament texts in developing a contemporary Christian economic ethic are in order.

The Prosperity Gospel

First of all, something should be said about "The Prosperity Gospel," a enticing body of thought that misconstrues the gospel teaching as if material prosperity is the true measure of God's favor and economic indigence is a sign of divine condemnation.

The ideology, sometimes known as "Prosperity Theology," derives from the faith-healing revivals of the mid-twentieth century. It was popularized by the televangelism of the 1970s and 1980s. Among the founders of the movement are Kenneth Hagin, Kenneth Copeland, and Frederick K. C. Price. Its best-known proponents are the televangelists Oral Roberts, Jim Bakker, and Joel Osteen. The first-named combined his televangelism with faith-healing.

The core message of this "gospel" is that wealth is a blessing from God. Those who possess material wealth are those who have been blessed by God. The ideology is rooted in an individualistic concept of salvation, a sign of the ideology's origins in the individual experience of television watching. Nonetheless, the ideology has given rise to many mega-churches that promote professing one's faith with the expectation that God will respond to whatever they desire. Generous donations are encouraged since God will reward those who give generously.

Proponents of the prosperity gospel have a limited list of selected scriptural passages to which they appeal. "Bring the full tithe into the storehouse so that there may be food in my house, and thus put me to the test, says the Lord of hosts; see if I will not open the window of heaven for you and pour down for you an overflowing blessing"[1] is one of the most frequently cited passages. A popular New Testament text is a Johannine mission statement, "I came that they may have life, and have it abundantly," notwithstanding the fact that the life of which the evangelist speaks is eternal life, which, in the Johannine gospel, has little if anything to do with material wealth.

With the text of Malachi as a virtual slogan, some versions of the prosperity gospel see the relationship between God and the believer as a contract bearing on wealth. In fact, there is little doubt that the Bible does look upon wealth as a gift of God. The story of the righteous Job dramatically portrays this belief and concludes with the Lord's giving to Job twice as much as he had before his ordeal: fourteen thousand sheep, six thousand camels, one thousand yoke of oxen, and one thousand donkeys, not to mention his seven sons and three daughters.[2] The aphorisms of Proverbs 10:4, "Prosperity rewards the righteous," and 10:22, "The blessing of the Lord makes rich," articulate this belief in memorable sayings. First-century rabbinic teachers continued to hold that prosperity and material blessings were signs of God's favor.

Without denying that wealth was a gift from God, Jesus' reform movement had, however, another view of wealth. Wealth was potentially the source of considerable danger for one's relationship with God. To counter the popular view of wealth, Jesus said, "It is easier

---

[1] Mal 3:10.
[2] Job 42:10-13.

for a camel to go through the eye of a needle than for someone who is rich to enter the kingdom of God."[3]

Later, the Epistle of James confronted head-on views later expounded in the prosperity gospel. It is little wonder that preachers of this gospel are no more fond of the book of James than they are of the Gospel of Luke. Indeed, one commentator on the Acts of the Apostles, sympathetic to the prosperity gospel, carefully omitted those passages that described the ideal community of believers as sharing all things in common.[4]

Proof-texting

The development of a biblical and specifically a New Testament understanding of wealth requires more than an assemblage of a few selected passages extrapolated from their biblical contexts, as proponents of the prosperity gospel have done. The practice of proof-texting is dangerous, out of order, and often misleading.

In recent years, a few New Testament texts have been repeatedly cited in order to establish what writers want to establish as a Christian position on gay marriage. In addition to two biblical (Old Testament) texts, three New Testament texts are generally cited. Rarely, if ever, are these texts cited in their New Testament context. Words are omitted from scriptural passages in order to make them work on behalf of the ideology that is being supported. Such a use of Scripture is an affront to what the believer considers to be the word of God. The believing interpreter must not dictate in a priori fashion the meaning of the text.

What needs to be taken into consideration is the entirety of the scriptural witness. It is for this reason that the present study has attempted to examine the entirety of what the New Testament has to say about wealth, wages, and the wealthy. Hopefully, no pertinent text has been omitted from our study. Moreover, a study of economic justice in the New Testament requires that the texts be seen in their scriptural contexts, both in the individual book in which they appear

[3] Mark 10:25; Matt 19:24; Luke 18:25. See above, p. 79.
[4] Cf. Acts 2:42-47; 4:32-35.

and in the New Testament as a whole. When this is done, a remarkable New Testament consensus emerges with regard to wealth, wages, and the wealthy.

Translation

Among the many pitfalls of proof-texting is the assumption that words, particularly words that appear in a translation, have the same meaning as the translated words had in the linguistic and social context of two millennia ago. Words reflect a culture. The culture of the New Testament texts that we have rehearsed is the Greco-Roman society of the first century CE. That culture is quite different from those of the many cultures of the early third millennium. Even words that appear to be adequate translations are, at best, approximately equivalent. The ancient word and its contemporary counterpart have different connotations.

Economies

An important feature of any culture is its economic system. A world of difference exists between the trade and barter system of the agricultural and urban societies of the New Testament era and contemporary capitalism. Fortunately, a number of recent studies have exploited not only textual evidence but also archeological evidence, including numismatic finds as well as the location and sizes and shapes of buildings, to better understand the economic realities of yesteryear.

One feature of the worldview of New Testament times was that this world's goods existed in a finite, fixed amount. The corollary of one person owning a large amount of goods was that others had fewer possessions. This led to the widespread antagonism of the poor toward the rich. The poor considered that they were deprived because the rich had amassed more than their share of things. From this followed the idea that the very rich were thieves. In many respects this notion was an a priori assumption. In fact, however, many did become rich by fraud and exploitation.

We now live in a global economy. Contemporary capitalism enjoys a naïve belief that the amount of this world's goods is infinite. This belief, says Pope Francis, is based on a lie.[5] I am neither a physicist nor an economist and so have no competence to enter into a fully informed discussion of the world's finitude. Neither can I discuss with any particular competence the details of the capitalistic economic system, which, in any case, results from choices made by men and women throughout the world. The free market does not exist independently of human beings. The free market may well be today's version of mammon, an idol created and maintained by human beings.

Anecdotal evidence shows a correlation between the wealth of some and the poverty of others, of individuals and of nations, and a correlation between the amassing and use of goods by some and the inability of others to avail themselves of these goods. Even in a global economy, "we fail to see," writes Francis, "that some are mired in desperate and degrading poverty, with no way out, while others have not the faintest idea of what to do with their possessions, vainly showing off their supposed superiority and leaving behind them so much waste which, if it were the case everywhere, would destroy the planet."[6]

Although there are obvious differences between the economies of the New Testament era and the global economy of today, there are also significant analogies between the two. These analogies must be pursued if the teaching of the New Testament is to be considered relevant to the twenty-first century. Aware of these differences and sensitive to these analogies, we can bring this study of wealth, wages, and the wealthy to a close with a summary of the consensus teaching of the New Testament, a partial unfolding of the implications of the kingdom of God proclaimed by Jesus.

Wealth

To begin, wealth is alluring; it is seductive. Mark preserves the tradition of the early Jesus movement when he writes about the lure

---

[5] He writes, "The idea of infinite or unlimited growth, which proves so attractive to economists, financiers and experts in technology . . . is based on the lie that there is an infinite supply of the earth's goods, and this leads to the planet being squeezed dry beyond every limit" (*Laudato Sì* 106).

[6] *Laudato Sì* 90.

of wealth in his appendix to the parable of the Sower. The seductive quality of wealth is graphically portrayed by the author of Revelation, who presents Babylon as a rich and seductive courtesan to whom kings, merchants, and seafarers fall victim.

The reality is that wealth becomes for many people the overarching focus of their lives, the god to whose service they devote themselves. The New Testament authors speak of wealth as the virtually divinized "Mammon," in competition with the God of Israel for the allegiance of human beings. This view of wealth is encapsulated in the terse and memorable adage "You cannot serve God and Wealth [Mammon]." While the saying is found only in Matthew and Luke, other texts concur in teaching about the incompatibility of the service of God and the service of wealth. Colossians and Ephesians agree in identifying greed, the inordinate pursuit of wealth, with idolatry.

This identification of greed with idolatry puts an exclamation point on the condemnation of greed that appears throughout the New Testament, from Paul to 2 Peter, with reiteration by Mark and Luke. Apart from the amorphous "sexual immorality,"[7] greed (*pleonexia*) is the vice that is most often condemned in the New Testament. In the clearest of terms, Paul says that the greedy cannot inherit the kingdom of God.[8] The story of the Rich Young Man is a dramatic illustration of the obstacle that substantial possessions place in the way of discipleship. The man's walking away from Jesus is a gesture that dramatizes that truth. The parable of the Invited Guests, particularly in its Lucan version,[9] is another story that illustrates how financial interests prevent a person from responding to the call to discipleship. For his part, the author of 2 Peter argues that greed motivates false prophets, teachers who veer from the truth and lead others away from it.

Greed

From a theological perspective, greed, the seductive pursuit of wealth, can lead to the creation and worship of the idol of mammon. It is a form of idolatry, a rejection of God and his Christ. From an

---

[7] *Porneia* in Greek.
[8] 1 Cor 6:9-10.
[9] Luke 14:15-24.

ethical perspective, greed is a root vice; it breeds other vices. Hence, the pastor declares, "For the love of money is a root of all kinds of evil."[10] Greed does not exist in a vacuum; it actively generates other vices. The author of 2 Peter concurs with this assessment of greed.[11] For this author, one of the fruits of greed is the denial of the Master. The Synoptic authors prefer to echo the stories told by Jesus, the upstart rabbi, but Mark recalls that when challenged about the interpretation of the commandments, this upstart taught that greed was one of the things that defiles the human being.[12]

One of Jesus' stories is the parable of the Wicked Tenants, a captivating tale of how greed leads to untold violence and murder. Greed is not constrained in its capacity to produce other vices, including murder, taking another person's life. The lesson of this old story was so important for the early church that it appears in all three Synoptic Gospels, early Christian texts that were written for different readerships.[13]

That the love of money is an impediment to discipleship and the source of untold evils does not mean that money is inherently evil. Whether wealth is evil or not depends on the use that one makes of one's resources. Mammon can become an idol that draws a person's full attention and allegiance, usurping the place of God in one's life, but mammon can be put to use in the service of God. The Palestinian Targum paraphrased the biblical challenge to love God completely[14] with "You shall love Yahweh your God with all your heart, and with all your soul, and with all your mammon."

Wealth in the Service of God and God's People

As the total orientation of one's heart and soul toward God is the way to love God completely, the use of one's wealth in the service of God is a manifestation of one's love of God. Jesus is reported to have said, "And I tell you, make friends for yourselves by means of

---

[10] 1 Tim 6:10.
[11] Cf. 2 Pet 2:1-3, 14.
[12] Cf. Mark 7:21-23.
[13] Cf. Mark 12:1-12; Matt 21:33-46; Luke 20:9-19.
[14] Cf. Deut 6:5.

dishonest wealth [*mammōna tēs adikias*[15]] so that when it is gone, they may welcome you into the eternal homes."[16] The poor have a special claim to God's love and protection. They are, in the words of the beatitudinal affirmation, blessed, for theirs is the kingdom of God. Received into the heavenly dwelling place, they can welcome those who are their friends, those who have shown them understanding and compassion by their almsgiving.

Responsibility for taking care of the poor falls not only on individuals but also on communities, on groups of people. Three series of texts confirm that as the community of believers became organized as a church, organized efforts were made to provide for the needy. The oldest group of texts comes from the apostle Paul who wrote often, at length, and in some detail about the collection for the poor in Jerusalem.[17] The Acts of the Apostles offers glimpses of the early church organizing its efforts in order to provide for the needy among them.[18] Luke tells how failure to participate in this communal effort is a mortal offense, just as he showed in the story of the Rich Man and Lazarus that failure to respond to the needs of the poor was a death-resulting moral failure.[19] Finally, the deutero-Pauline First Epistle to Timothy provides guidance as to how the church should coordinate its efforts to provide support for elderly widows who are without other means of financial support.[20]

Norms for Almsgiving

The New Testament offers two important norms for the giving of alms. These are the alleviation of need and the establishment of equity among God's people. That the alleviation and eradication of need should be the believer's goal in sharing his or her assets is made

---

[15] The dishonesty of which this logion speaks is not only an indication of the use to which much wealth is put but also a reflection of the popular assumption—the truth of which can only be shown anecdotally—that wealth is generally dishonestly gained and often dishonestly used.

[16] Luke 16:9.

[17] Cf. Rom 15:25-32; 1 Cor 16:1-4; 2 Cor 8-9.

[18] Cf. Acts 2:42-47; 4:32-38; 6:1-6.

[19] Cf. Acts 5:1-11; Luke 16:19-31.

[20] Cf. 1 Tim 5:3-16.

clear in Luke's description of the ideal community of believers. The evangelist writes about this community as one that shares all things in common. This is not a socialistic or communist community but one in which members are ready to dispose of their personal assets and distribute the proceeds to everyone in accordance with their needs. The goal of selling one's assets is the alleviation of poverty.[21] There was not, writes Luke, "a needy person among them, for as many as owned land or houses sold them and brought the proceeds of what was sold . . . and it was distributed to each as any had need."[22] The lesson to be drawn from this picture, limned in somewhat simplified fashion, is that the goal of almsgiving is the alleviation of individual and collective poverty.

The alleviation of the poverty of the believing community in Jerusalem was a concern for the apostle Paul, who writes about this issue in his three longest letters. He offers a number of reasons why believers should come to the assistance of the poor in Jerusalem— the most basic of which is the obligation of the righteous to share resources with the poor, as a token of solidarity—but he also offers a norm for such almsgiving. He does not expect that those who give alms should inflict poverty on themselves in order to lift others out of poverty. Rather, says Paul, the aim of almsgiving is equity, a fair balance between our abundance—he was writing to the somewhat affluent community of believers in Corinth[23]—and the needs of others. Citing Scripture as an argument for this redistribution of wealth, Paul roots the moral demand of equity in the biblical tradition. The call for equity is not a new idea on Paul's part; a demand for equity is inherent in the age-old witness of the Jewish Scriptures.

The demand to share resources with the poor in order to eliminate poverty and create equity among God's people is the principal demand that Jesus and the New Testament authors address to believers in regard to their wealth. Each of these criteria focuses on the recipient of the believer's almsgiving. As far as the donor is concerned, Paul commends the Macedonians who gave according

---

[21] Cf. Acts 2:44-45.
[22] Acts 4:34-35.
[23] *Ek tou echein*, 2 Cor 8:11; cf. 2 Cor 8:3.

to their means.[24] His Greek *para dynamin* suggests that he lauds them because they gave in accordance with their ability to do so. He reminds the Corinthians that a gift is acceptable if it is given in accordance with what one has.[25] Echoing the Scriptures, Paul writes that the one who sows sparingly will also reap sparingly.[26] An acceptable gift is not taken from what is extra, what is surplus.[27] Jesus makes a similar point with regard to temple donations.[28] Having seen the rich make their large contributions, Jesus observes that they gave out of their abundance. He reserves his commendation for the widow who contributed more than they did, for she gave from her livelihood.

Filial Responsibility

Need, equity, and capability are three criteria that determine whether one's giving to the poor is acceptable to the Lord. Providing for the poor is not, however, the sole obligation of the believer with regard to his or her wealth. In addition, the New Testament reiterates one particular responsibility in the use of one's wealth that has been taken over from ancient Jewish and biblical tradition. That is the responsibility to "honor your father and mother,"[29] to take care of them and provide for them in their declining and nonproductive years. Jesus did not dispute that the "rich young man" had kept this commandment.[30] He did, however, have harsh words to say about people who employ legalistic casuistry and feign religious devotion in order to escape from providing financial support for their aged parents.[31] Jesus describes their conduct as an attempt to annul the word of God.[32] The obligation that falls on the able-bodied to provide for their elderly parents, and even grandparents, is reaffirmed in 1 Timothy's

[24] 2 Cor 8:3.
[25] 2 Cor 8:12.
[26] 2 Cor 9:6.
[27] See the discussion on the NRSV's misleading translation of 1 Cor 16:2, "put aside and save whatever extra you earn," above, pp. 19–20.
[28] Mark 12:41-44; Luke 21:1-4.
[29] Exod 20:12; Deut 5:16.
[30] Cf. Mark 10:19; Matt 19:19; Luke 19:20.
[31] Cf. Mark 7:6-13; Matt 15:39.
[32] Cf. Mark 7:13.

instruction on the care of widows.[33] Their care is to be provided by their descendants, rather than by the church at large.

The Payment of Taxes

The New Testament strongly affirms that taxes are to be paid, despite the general disregard in which tax collectors in Palestine were held because of the fact that they worked for an occupying power and had a system of support that was prone to corruption. The Jerusalem dispute between Jesus and a coalition of Pharisees and Herodians is found in each of the three Synoptic Gospels.[34] As described by the evangelists, the scene is one in which a tax-revolt was virtually called for. The dispute takes place virtually in the shadow of the temple, the conversation was at least superficially about the interpretation of the Mosaic law, and the coin of the realm in which taxes were to be paid was idolatrous. Jesus takes the initiative in asking for the coin that symbolizes the system of taxation and brings the discussion to an amazing conclusion, "Give to the emperor the things that are the emperor's, and to God the things that are God's." Taxes are to be paid, despite the case to the contrary that might be made.

The Jerusalem dispute makes it clear that taxes are to be paid by those who accept the teaching of Jesus. A correlative argument for the payment of taxes can be found in the fact that despite the umbrage taken at his conduct by learned Pharisees, Jesus did not hesitate to call a tax collector as one of his disciples.[35] Rather than condemn tax collectors, popularly considered to be sinners of the worst sort, Jesus made a tax collector the hero of one of his short stories.[36] He even invited himself into the home of a well-known tax collector, much to the chagrin of those who saw what had happened.[37] Among the evangelists, Luke has the most to say about tax collectors. In his narrative, they are not condemned, but they are urged not to exploit people.[38]

[33] 1 Tim 5:3-16, especially vv. 4, 16.
[34] Cf. Mark 12:13-17; Matt 22:15-22; Luke 21:20-26.
[35] Cf. Mark 4:13-17; Matt 8:9-13; Luke 5:27-32.
[36] Cf. Luke 18:9-14.
[37] Cf. Luke 19:1-10.
[38] Cf. Luke 3:12-13.

For his part, the apostle Paul, addressing himself to the issue of taxes in another politically heated situation where there was considerable dispute about the payment of taxes, urged God's people in Rome, "Pay to all what is due them—taxes to whom taxes are due, revenue to whom revenue is due."[39] Paul had two forms of taxation in mind. The first was the tribute due to the emperor and incumbent on non-Roman citizens not only in Rome but also throughout the empire. This could be a hefty sum, to be paid to Nero, the despicable reigning emperor. The second was the commercial tax levied on a wide variety of commercial transactions. The "tax code" was not simple; more than a hundred different kinds of commercial taxes were levied. This sort of tax liability fell on all who lived within the empire, but it fell most heavily upon the wealthy who were involved in major financial transactions. Some decades later, the author of 1 Peter, who did not specifically raise the issue of taxes, was on the same wavelength as Paul had been[40] when he wrote, "For the Lord's sake accept the institution of every human institution, whether of the emperor as supreme or of governors. . . . Fear God. Honor the emperor."[41]

In sum, taxes are to be paid to civic authorities. Neither Jesus nor the epistolary authors entered into the reasons why these taxes were to be paid, but all five witnesses (Matthew, Mark, Luke, Paul, and the author of 1 Peter) make it clear that believers have a religious obligation to pay taxes. Civic authorities impose taxes; believers pay taxes not only because of the police power of the state but also because they consider that under God they have an obligation to do so.

By and large, New Testament texts fail to say much of anything about the payment of religious taxes. One somewhat fanciful anecdote is an exception to the general rule. In the Matthean story about the payment of the temple tax,[42] Jesus resolves the issue as to whether he himself paid the temple tax by wonderfully producing a coin of sufficient value to pay the tax for himself and for Simon Peter, one of

---

[39] Rom 13:7.
[40] Cf. Rom 13:1-7.
[41] 1 Pet 2:13-14, 17.
[42] Cf. Matt 17:24-27.

the disciples—a disciple who at this point in the Matthean narrative had been appointed as Jesus' designated successor in Palestine.

Underlying Principles of New Testament Teaching

An important theological principle and an important anthropological principle lie behind what the New Testament has to say about wealth. The theological principle is that everything that is, including wealth, ultimately belongs to God. Render to God what is God's, said Jesus to the Pharisees and Herodians. Nothing that exists lies beyond the sovereignty of God. Those who consider wealth as an idol in competition with God are simply guilty of idolatry. They reject the sovereignty of God.

The anthropological principle is multifaceted. At bottom, it is rooted in a vision that the Creator God made the earth and all that is on it and that God entrusted his creation to the human race, symbolized by the primal couple, Adam and Eve, as his vicegerents. Ultimately, solidarity exists among all human beings. Among believers, brothers and sisters as they are called throughout the New Testament, there is a family bond. Brothers and sisters have a special relationship that involves love but also requires working together for the benefit of the entire family.[43] To the extent that resources are not shared among members of the family, the family suffers in its togetherness. The rank individualism of contemporary Western society is incompatible with a biblical anthropology that underscores the social nature of the human being and the solidarity of all human beings from the standpoint of both creation and redemption.

Wages

"Wages are not reckoned as a gift but as something due," says Paul in writing to the Romans.[44] His statement represents the commonsense proverbial wisdom of the ages, otherwise represented in the aphorism, "The laborer deserves to be paid." This axiom of basic

---

[43] Cf. Trevor J. Burke, *Family Matters: A Socio-Historical Study of Kinship Metaphors in 1 Thessalonians*, JSNTSup 247 (London: T & T Clark, 2003), 126.

[44] Cf. Rom 4:4.

social justice occurs three times in the New Testament, namely, in Matthew, Luke, and 1 Timothy.[45] The authors of these three books cite the maxim in arguing that those who preach the gospel deserve to be compensated for this work. Paul does not cite the adage, but he presupposes its reality in the defense of his apostolic rights in 1 Corinthians 9. Arguing that he deserves his food and drink, he gives the example of soldiers, vintners, and shepherds as people who deserve just payment for what they do according to their station in life.[46]

The citation of this basic economic principle does not of itself suggest how much the worker deserves to be paid, but the way in which Luke cites the principle in the Mission Discourse addressed to the seventy disciples suggests that what the worker deserves to be paid is a basic subsistence wage, in coin or in kind, that is sufficient enough to cover lodging, food, and drink. Typically, a coin in the amount of a denarius was the wage paid to a day laborer. Jesus asked to see the coin in his discussion with the Pharisees and Herodians about paying taxes.

The denarius, the usual daily wage, is featured in Jesus' powerful story about the Laborers in the Vineyard.[47] The story begins in typical "once upon a time" fashion. A landowner goes out to a place where day laborers seeking work are gathered. He hires workers for his vineyard, agreeing with them that they should receive the usual daily wage, the denarius. At three different times later in the day, the landowner returns to the gathering place and meets unemployed workers. He hires all of them, and at the end of the day he instructs his manager to pay all of the workers the usual daily wage, the denarius.

That these day laborers received their wages at the end of the day is in keeping with a principle of economic justice expressed in Deuteronomy 24:15,[48] that workers are to be paid daily before sunset because their livelihood depends on their earnings. Deuteronomy

---

[45] Cf. Matt 10:10; Luke 10:7; and 1 Tim 5:18, albeit in a slightly different form in the Matthean version of the saying.

[46] Cf. 1 Cor 9:4, 7-8.

[47] Cf. Matt 20:1-16.

[48] Cf. Lev 19:13. Deut 24:14 stipulates that the day's wages are to be paid not only to Israelites but also to "aliens who reside in your land in one of your towns."

suggests that if day laborers are not adequately paid at the end of the day, they will cry out to the Lord, and the employers will be found guilty. The author of the Epistle of James reprises this tradition in his condemnation of rich employers who defraud laborers of their wages.[49]

Jesus' story about the workers in the vineyard is a powerful teaching on economic justice: wages are to be paid promptly and should be sufficient to provide adequate support for workers. The operative principle is adequate financial compensation for workers, not maximum profit for employers.

And the Wealthy

Scattered throughout the New Testament are the names of more than a few men and women who used their wealth in a godly manner. We can think of men like Joseph of Arimathea who provided a burial place for Jesus;[50] Joseph Barnabas who, having sold his land, gave the profits to the apostles to distribute to the poor;[51] and Gaius who hosted the whole church of Corinth.[52] We can also think of women like Mary Magdalene, Joanna, and Susanna who provided financial support for Jesus and his band of disciples/missionaries;[53] Mary of Bethany who was extravagant in preparing Jesus' body for burial;[54] and Phoebe who was a benefactor not only of Paul but also of untold others.[55]

Difficulties Confronting the Wealthy

On the other hand, the New Testament often speaks of the difficulties of the wealthy. The story of the "rich young man" dramatically illustrates the fact that riches are an impediment to discipleship.[56] But

---

[49] Cf. Jas 5:4.
[50] Matt 27:57-60.
[51] Acts 4:36-37.
[52] Rom 16:23.
[53] Luke 8:1-3.
[54] John 12:3-8.
[55] Rom 16:1-2.
[56] Mark 10:17-22; Matt 19:16-22; Luke 18:18-23.

other statements are even more troubling. In God's plan of salvation, so the *Magnificat* proclaims, the rich are to be sent away empty.[57] This is not simply an affirmation of the commonplace truth that "you can't take it with you." It has to do with the values of the kingdom of God and their consequences. In the first beatitude Jesus seems to threaten the rich with his "Woe to you rich, for you have received your consolation."[58] This ominous warning is almost a funeral dirge; it says that the accumulation of riches leads to death, a point that the evangelist stresses in his stories of the Rich Man and Lazarus and Ananias and Sapphira.

Perhaps the most challenging statement is Jesus' utterance, "How hard it will be for those who have wealth to enter the kingdom of God. . . . It is easier for a camel to go through the eye of a needle than for someone who is rich to enter the kingdom of God."[59] The underlying issue is that the rich rely on their wealth rather than on God, as the story about the rich fool illustrates too well.[60]

To enter the kingdom of God is to embrace the reign of God, God's dominion over all that exists, including people and their possessions. Amassing wealth can be self-destructive insofar as it leads the rich person to rely on their possessions rather than on God. It is a matter of making choices for the goods of this earth rather than amassing treasures in heaven.

A First Challenge: Failure to Take Care of the Poor

The New Testament highlights three faults to which the wealthy are particularly prone. The first is a failure to provide for the poor.[61] The rich young man was called to a life of radical discipleship by selling all that he had and giving to the poor, but he was unable and/ or unwilling to do that.[62] Ananias and his wife[63] were willing to give

[57] Cf. Luke 2:53.
[58] Luke 6:24.
[59] Mark 10:23, 25.
[60] Luke 12:13-21.
[61] Cf. Jas 5:2-3c.
[62] Cf. Matt 19:16-22; Mark 10:17-22; Luke 18:18-23.
[63] Acts 5:1-11.

to the poor but held back some of the proceeds of what they had ostensibly sold in order to support the poor, attempting to conceal what they did from the community, but they could not fool God. Most dramatic perhaps is the story of the Rich Man and Lazarus.[64] The rich man lived elegantly and sumptuously; he would not even share the table scraps with the poor man who sat at his gate.

All four individuals—the rich young man, the married couple Ananias and Sapphira, and the rich man of Luke 16—do not belong to Jesus' company because of their failure to provide for the poor. Luke's narrative dramatically describes how the woe that threatens the rich with death[65] applies to Ananias and his wife as well as to the rich man who neglected Lazarus. Their fate is the emptiness announced in the *Magnificat*.[66] Echoing the strong words of James, one can say that those who fail to provide for the poor are irreligious blasphemers.[67]

A Second Challenge: Defrauding Workers of Their Wages

A second fault to which the rich are particularly prone is defrauding laborers of their wages. Israel's biblical tradition had long condemned the practice, but the tradition is rarely echoed in the New Testament. The singular exception is the Epistle of James. James is a text whose principal topic is the discrepancy between the rich and the poor. Echoing the Torah,[68] the epistle says with a prophetic voice, "Listen! The wages of the laborers who mowed your fields, which you kept back by fraud, cry out, and the cries of the harvesters have reached the ears of the Lord of hosts."[69] The author's "listen" echoes

---

[64] Luke 16:19-31.

[65] Luke 6:24.

[66] Luke 1:54.

[67] Cf. Jas 1:27; 2:7. The words of Pope Francis are apropos: "Any Church community," he writes, "if it thinks it can comfortably go its own way without creative concern and effective cooperation in helping the poor to live with dignity and reaching out to everyone, will also risk breaking down however much it may talk about social issues or criticize governments. It will easily drift into a spiritual worldliness camouflaged by religious practices, unproductive meetings and empty talk" (*Evangelii Gaudium* 207).

[68] Lev 19:13; Deut 24:14-15.

[69] Jas 5:4.

the prophetic warning of the biblical prophets of social justice. It is a call for conversion and a threat to those who fail to listen.

Closely related to defrauding workers, for the most part day laborers, of their wages is the manipulation of the poor so that what they have is taken from them. This was a well-known problem in the Roman Empire. Rich landowners schemed to put poor farmers in difficult financial circumstances and then seized their small plots of land in payment of the contrived debt. This issue apparently lies behind James's denunciatory words as the author begins his accusations against the rich in James 5:16.

A Third Challenge: Misuse of the Judicial System

A third form of evil to which the rich easily fall victim is the exploitation of the judicial system to their own advantage and to the disadvantage of the poorer members of society.[70] It is all too easy for believers to accept the status quo, to tolerate the privileged position of the affluent in judicial proceedings. In James 2:1-4, the writer graphically describes the unequal treatment afforded to the rich and to the poor in judicial proceedings. The rich are favored; the poor dishonored. The author warns the community not to tolerate this discrepancy and asks his audience this poser, "Is it not they [the rich] who drag you into court?"[71]

The date of composition of this epistle is disputed, but there is little doubt about the approximate date of composition of 1 Corinthians. By any computation, it is one of the earliest texts of the New Testament. Paul devotes a relatively long passage of the epistle, 1 Corinthians 6:1-11, to lawsuits among believers. In the social circumstances of his times, the impoverished could not expect to receive justice in a court of law; it would have been futile for them to attempt

---

[70] Pope Francis spoke of this situation when he addressed the General Assembly of the United Nations on September 25, 2015, to wit: "The effective distribution of power (political, economic, defense-related, technological, etc.) among a plurality of subjects and the creation of a judicial system for regulating claims and interests are one concrete way of limiting power. Yet today's world presents us with many false rights and—at the same time—broad sectors that are vulnerable, victims of power badly exercised."

[71] Jas 2:6.

to do so. Those who made use of the judicial system were the rich, who often assured the results of the proceedings by means of well-placed bribes, offered to the judge or to witnesses.[72]

Given this situation, we must read this passage in Paul's First Letter to the Corinthians as having been written by the apostle in order to shame the rich[73] who would use the secular judicial system to solve whatever grievances they might have had against the less well-off members of the community. Paul confronted those richer members of the community of believers with these words: "To have lawsuits at all with one another is already a defeat for you. Why not rather be wronged? Why not rather be defrauded? But you yourselves wrong and defraud and believers at that."[74]

Epilogue

The witness of the New Testament with regard to wealth, wages, and the wealthy is clear and consistent. Yet it is rarely the subject of a Sunday sermon by Christian pastors or of commentary by Christian religious leaders. Their silence supports Yoder's assertion that Christian ethical teaching has largely ignored Jesus.

A voice crying in the wilderness trying to redress this shameful situation is that of Francis, the Bishop of Rome. This study is offered as a witness that he is on the right track. The Good News of Jesus Christ, the Christian gospel, has much to say about wealth, wages, and the wealthy. What it has to say can be summed up under the term "justice," the New Testament's *dikaiosynē* that echoes the biblical mishpat, so important to Jesus of Nazareth.

[72] Cf. Matt 25:59-61.
[73] Cf. 1 Cor 6:5.
[74] 1 Cor 6:7-8.

Bibliography of Scriptural Commentaries

Achtemeier, Paul J. *1 Peter*. Hermeneia. Minneapolis: Fortress, 1996.

Aletti, Jean-Noël. *Saint Paul: Épître aux Colossiens*. EBib. Paris: Gabalda, 1993.

Allison, Dale C., Jr. *The Epistle of James*. ICC. New York: Bloomsbury T&T Clark, 2013.

Allo, Ernest-Bernard. *Saint Paul: Première Épître aux Corinthiens*. EtBib. 2nd ed. Paris: Gabalda, 1956.

Aune, David E. *Revelation 6–16*. WBC 52B. Nashville: Thomas Nelson, 1998.

Barnett, Paul. *The Second Epistle to the Corinthians*. NICNT. Grand Rapids: Eerdmans, 1997.

Barrett, Charles Kingsley. *The Acts of the Apostles*. Vol. 1: *Acts 1–14*. ICC. London: T&T Clark, 1994.

———. *The Acts of the Apostles*. Vol. 2: *Acts 15–28*. ICC. London: T&T Clark, 1998.

———. *The Second Epistle to the Corinthians*. BNTC. London: A&C Black, 1973.

Barth, Joel. *Mark 1–8*. AB 27. New York: Doubleday, 2000.

———. *Mark 8–16*. AYB 27. New Haven: Yale University Press, 2009.

Barth, Markus. *Ephesians 4–6*. AB 36A. Garden City, NY: Doubleday, 1974.

Beale, Gregory K. *The Book of Revelation*. NIGTC. Grand Rapids: Eerdmans, 1999.

Best, Ernest. *Ephesians*. ICC. London: T&T Clark, 1998.

Betz, Hans Dieter. *2 Corinthians 8 and 9: A Commentary on Two Administrative Letters of the Apostle Paul*. Hermeneia. Philadelphia: Fortress, 1985.

———. *Galatians: A Commentary on Paul's Letter to the Churches in Galatia*. Hermeneia. Philadelphia: Fortress, 1979.

Blount, Brian K.. *Revelation*. NTL. Louisville: Westminster John Knox, 2009.

Boring, M. Eugene. *Mark*. NTL. Louisville: Westminster John Knox, 2006.

Bovon, François. *Luke 1: A Commentary on the Gospel of Luke 1:1–9:50*. Hermeneia. Minneapolis: Fortress, 2002.

————. *Luke 2: A Commentary on the Gospel of Luke 9:51–19:27.* Hermeneia. Minneapolis: Fortress, 2013.

————. *Luke 3: A Commentary on the Gospel of Luke 19:28–24:53.* Hermeneia. Minneapolis: Fortress, 2012.

Brown, Raymond E. *The Epistles of John.* AB 30. Garden City, NY: Doubleday, 1982.

Bruce, F. F. *Commentary on Galatians.* NIGTC. Grand Rapids: Eerdmans, 1982.

Byrne, Brendan. *Romans.* SP 6. Collegeville, MN: Liturgical Press, 1996.

Bultmann, Rudolf. *The Johannine Epistles.* Hermeneia. Philadelphia: Fortress, 1973.

————. *The Second Letter to the Corinthians.* Minneapolis: Augsburg, 1985.

Caird, G. B. *Paul's Letters from Prison (Ephesians Philippians, Colossians, Philemon) in the Revised Standard Version.* London: Oxford University Press, 1976.

Ciampa, Roy E., and Brian S. Rosner. *The First Letter to the Corinthians.* Pillar New Testament Commentary. Grand Rapids: Eerdmans, 2010.

Collins, Adela Yarbro. *Mark.* Hermeneia. Minneapolis: Fortress, 2007.

Collins, Raymond F. *I and II Timothy and Titus: A Commentary.* NTL. Louisville: Westminster John Knox, 2002.

————. *First Corinthians.* SP 7. Collegeville, MN: Liturgical Press, 1999.

————. *Second Corinthians.* Paideia Commentaries on the New Testament. Grand Rapids: Baker Academic, 2013.

Conzelmann, Hans. *Acts of the Apostles.* Hermeneia. Philadelphia: Fortress, 1987.

Davies, William D., and Dale C. Allison Jr. *The Gospel according to Saint Matthew.* Vol. 1: *Introduction and Commentary on Matthew I–VII.* ICC. Edinburgh: T&T Clark, 1988.

————. *The Gospel according to Saint Matthew.* Vol. 2: *Commentary on Matthew VIII–XIII.* ICC. London: T&T Clark, 1991.

————. *The Gospel according to Saint Matthew.* Vol. 3: *Commentary on Matthew XIX–XXVIII.* ICC. London: T&T Clark, 1997.

De Boer, Martinus C. *Galatians.* NTL. Louisville: Westminster John Knox, 2011.

Dibelius, Martin. *James: A Commentary on the Epistle of James.* Hermeneia. Philadelphia: Fortress, 1976.

Donahue, John R., and Daniel J. Harrington. *The Gospel of Mark.* SP 2. Collegeville, MN: Liturgical Press, 2002.

Donelson, Lewis R. *I & II Peter and Jude: A Commentary.* NTL. Louisville: Westminster John Knox, 2010.

Dornier, Pierre. *Les Épîtres pastorales.* SB. Paris: Gabalda, 1969.

Dunn, James D. G. *The Acts of the Apostles.* Valley Forge, PA: Trinity Press International, 1996.

————. *The Epistles to the Colossians and to Philemon.* NIGTC. Grand Rapids: Eerdmans, 1996.

————. *Romans.* Vol. 2. WBC 38B. Dallas: Word, 1988.

Elliott, John H. *1 Peter.* AB 37B. New York: Doubleday, 2000.

Fee, Gordon D. *The First and Second Letters to the Thessalonians.* NICNT. Grand Rapids: Eerdmans, 2009.

————. *The First Epistle to the Corinthians.* NICNT. Grand Rapids: Eerdmans, 1987.

Fiore, Benjamin. *The Pastoral Epistles: First Timothy, Second Timothy, Titus.* SP 12. Collegeville, MN: Liturgical Press, 2007.

Fitzmyer, Joseph A. *The Acts of the Apostles.* AB 31. New York: Doubleday, 1998.

————. *First Corinthians.* AYB 33. New Haven: Yale University Press, 2008.

————. *The Gospel according to Luke I–IX.* AB 28. Garden City, NY: Doubleday, 1981.

————. *The Gospel according to Luke X–XXIV.* AB 28A. Garden City, NY: Doubleday, 1985.

————. *The Letter to Philemon.* AB 34C. New York: Doubleday, 2000.

Focant, Camille. *The Gospel according to Mark: A Commentary.* Eugene, OR: Pickwick, 2012.

France, Richard T. *The Gospel of Matthew.* NIBCNT. Grand Rapids: Eerdmans, 2007.

Furnish, Victor P. *II Corinthians.* AB 32A. Garden City, NY: Doubleday, 1984.

Garland, David E. *2 Corinthians.* NAC 29. Nashville: Broadman & Holman, 1999.

Gloer, W. Hulitt, and Perry L. Stepp. *Reading Paul's Letters to Individuals: A Literary and Theological Commentary on Paul's Letters to Philemon, Titus, and Timothy.* Macon, GA: Smyth & Helwys, 2008.

Greeen, Gene L. *The Letters to the Thessalonians.* Pillar New Testament Commentary. Grand Rapids: Eerdmans, 2002.

Gundry, Robert H. *Mark: A Commentary on His Apology for the Cross.* Grand Rapids: Eerdmans, 1993.

Haenchen, Ernst. *The Acts of the Apostles: A Commentary.* Philadelphia: Westminster, 1971.

Hagner, Donald A. *Matthew 1–13.* WBC 33. Dallas: Word, 1993.

Harrington, Daniel J. *The Gospel of Matthew.* SP 1. Collegeville, MN: Liturgical Press, 1991.

————. "Jude and 2 Peter." In Senior and Harrington, *1 Peter, Jude, and 2 Peter*, 161–299.

Harrington, Wilfred J. *Revelation.* SP 16. Collegeville, MN: Liturgical Press, 1993.

Hartin, Patrick J. *James.* SP 14. Collegeville, MN: Liturgical Press, 2003.

Jewett, Robert. *Romans*. Hermeneia. Minneapolis: Fortress, 2007.

Johnson, Luke Timothy. *The Acts of the Apostles*. SP 5. Collegeville, MN: Liturgical Press, 1992.

———. *The First and Second Letters to Timothy*. AB 35A. New York: Doubleday, 2001.

———. *The Gospel of Luke*. SP 3. Collegeville, MN: Liturgical Press, 1991.

———. *The Letter of James*. AB 37A. Garden City, NY: Doubleday, 1995.

———. *Hebrews*. NTL. Louisville: Westminster John Knox, 2006.

Käsemann, Ernst. *Commentary on Romans*. Grand Rapids: Eerdmans, 1980.

Keener, Craig S. *The Gospel of Matthew: A Socio-Rhetorical Commentary*. Grand Rapids: Eerdmans, 2009.

Klaiber, Walter. *Der zweite Korintherbrief*. BNT. Neukirchen-Vluyn: Neukirchener Theologie, 2012.

Koester, Craig R. *Hebrews*. AB 36. New York: Doubleday, 2001.

———. *Revelation*. AYB 38A. New Haven: Yale University Press, 2014.

Krause, Deborah. *1 Timothy*. London: T&T Clark, 2004.

Longenecker, Richard N. *Galatians*. WBC 41. Dallas: Word Books, 1990.

Luz, Ulrich. *Matthew 1–7*. Hermeneia. Minneapolis: Fortress, 2007.

———. *Matthew 8–20*. Hermeneia. Minneapolis: Fortress, 2001.

MacDonald, Margaret Y. *Colossians. Ephesians*. SP 17. Collegeville, MN: Liturgical Press, 2000.

Malherbe, Abraham J. *The Letters to the Thessalonians*. AB 32B. New York: Doubleday, 2000.

Marcus, Joel. *Mark 1–8*. AB 27. New York: Doubleday, 2000.

———. *Mark 8–16*. AYB 27A. New Haven: Yale University Press, 2009.

Marshall, I. Howard. *The Gospel of Luke*. NIGTC. Grand Rapids: Eerdmans, 1978.

Martyn, J. Louis. *Galatians*. AB 33A. New York: Doubleday, 1997.

Matera, Frank J. *II Corinthians*. NTL. Louisville: Westminster John Knox, 2003.

———. *Romans*. Paideia Commentaries on the New Testament. Grand Rapids: Baker Academic, 2010.

Meyers, Carol L., and Eric M. Meyers, *Zachariah 9–14*. AB 25C. New York: Doubleday, 1993.

Minor, Mitzi L. *2 Corinthians*. Smyth & Helwys Bible Commentary. Macon, GA: Smyth & Helwys, 2009.

Mitchell, Alan C. *Hebrews*. SP 13. Collegeville, MN: Liturgical Press, 2007.

Moloney, Francis J. *The Gospel of Mark: A Commentary*. Peabody, MA: Hendrickson, 2002.

Neyrey, Jerome H. *2 Peter, Jude*. AB 37C. New York: Doubleday, 1993.

Nineham, Dennis E. *Saint Mark*. PGC. Baltimore: Penguin, 1963.

Nolland, John. *Luke 9:21–18:34*. WBC 35B. Waco, TX: Word, 1993.

O'Brien, Peter T. *Colossians, Philemon*. WBC 44. Waco, TX: Word, 1982.

———. *The Letter to the Ephesians.* Pillar New Testament Commentary. Grand Rapids: Eerdmans, 1999.

Painter, James, and David A. de Sliva. *James and Jude.* Paideia Commentaries on the New Testament. Grand Rapids: Baker Academic, 2012.

Parsons, Mikeal C. *Luke.* Paideia Commentaries on the New Testament. Grand Rapids: Baker Academic, 2015.

———. *Acts.* Paideia Commentaries on the New Testament. Grand Rapids: Baker Academic, 2008.

Perkins, Pheme. *First Corinthians.* Paideia Commentaries on the New Testament. Grand Rapids: Baker Academic, 2012.

Pesch, Rudolf. *Das Markus-evangelium.* HTKNT II, 1. Freiburg: Herder, 1976.

Propp, William C. *Exodus 19–40.* AB 2A. New York: Doubleday, 2006,

Quinn, Jerome D., and William C. Wacker. *The First and Second Letters to Timothy.* Eerdmans Critical Commentaries. Grand Rapids: Eerdmans, 2000.

Quinn, Jerome D. *The Letter to Titus.* AB 35. New York: Doubleday, 1990.

Roetzel, Calvin J. *2 Corinthians.* ANTC. Nashville: Abingdon, 2007.

Polhill, John B. *Acts.* NAC 26. Nashville: Broadman, 1992.

Reicke, Bo. *The Epistles of James, Peter, and Jude.* AB 37. Garden City, NY: Doubleday, 1964.

Rigaux, Béda. *Saint Paul: Les épîtres aux Thessaloniens.* EBib. Paris: Gabalda, 1956.

Roloff, Jürgen. *Der erste Brief an Timotheus.* EKK 15. Zurich: Benziger—Neukirchen-Vluyn: Neukirchener Verlag, 1988.

Ryan, Judith M. "Philemon." In Thurston and Ryan, *Philippians & Philemon,* 167–261.

Senior, Donald P., and Daniel J. Harrington. *1 Peter, Jude, and 2 Peter.* SP 15. Collegeville, MN: Liturgical Press, 2003.

Senior, Donald P. "1 Peter." In Senior and Harrington, *1 Peter, Jude, and 2 Peter,* 4–158.

Smith, Dwight Moody. *First, Second, and Third John.* Interpretation. Louisville: Westminster John Knox, 1991.

Sumney, Jerry L. *Colossians.* NTL. Louisville: Westminster John Knox, 2008.

Talbert, Charles H. *Ephesians and Colossians.* Paideia Commentaries on the New Testament. Grand Rapids: Baker Academic, 2007.

———. *Matthew.* Paideia Commentaries on the New Testament. Grand Rapids: Baker Academic, 2010.

Taylor, Vincent. *The Gospel according to St. Mark.* London: Macmillan, 1963.

Thiselton, Anthony C. *The First Epistle to the Corinthians.* NIGTC. Grand Rapids: Eerdmans, 2000.

Thompson, James W. *Hebrews.* Paideia Commentaries on the New Testament. Grand Rapids: Baker Academic, 2008.

Thrall, Margaret E. *The Second Epistle to the Corinthians*. ICC. 2 vols. London: T&T Clark, 1994, 2000.

Thurston, Bonnie B., and Judith M. Ryan. *Philippians & Philemon*. SP 10. Collegeville, MN: Liturgical Press, 2005.

Thurston, Bonnie B. "Philippians." In Thurston and Ryan, *Philippians & Philemon*, 3–163.

Wall, Robert W., with Richard B. Steele. *1 and 2 Timothy and Titus*. Two Horizons New Testament Commentary. Grand Rapids: Eerdmans, 2012.

Weima, Jeffrey A. D. *1–2 Thessalonians*. Baker Exegetical Commentary on the New Testament. Grand Rapids: Baker, 2014.

Weiser, Alfons. *Der zweite Brief an Timotheus*. EKK 16/1. Zurich: Benziger— Neukirchen-Vluyn: Neukirchener Verlag, 2003.

Weiss, Johannes. *Der erste Korintherbrief.* KEK 9. Göttingen: Vandenhoeck & Ruprecht, 1910.

Witherington, Ben, III. *Conflict and Community: A Socio-Rhetorical Commentary on 1 and 2 Corinthians*. Grand Rapids: Eerdmans; Carlisle: Paternoster, 1995.

———. *Letters and Homilies for Hellenized Christians*. Vol. 1: *A Socio-Rhetorical Commentary on Titus, 1–2 Timothy and 1–3 John*, Downers Grove, IL: IVP Academic, 2006,

———. *Letters and Homilies for Jewish Christians: A Socio-Rhetorical Commentary on Hebrews, James and Jude*. Downers Grove, IL: IVP Academic, 2007.

Bibliography

Adams, Edward. *The Earliest Christian Meeting Places: Almost Exclusively Houses?* Library of New Testament Studies. JSNTSup 430. London: Bloomsbury T&T Clark, 2013.

Adams, Samuel L. *Social and Economic Life in Second Temple Judea.* Louisville: Westminster John Knox, 2014.

Alkier, Stefan. "'Frucht bringen' oder 'Gewinnmaximierung'? Überlegungen zur Gestaltung des Lebens und des Wirtschaftens im Anschluss an des Mattäusevangelium." *ZNT* 16 (2013): 11–20.

Anderson, Gary A. "Forgive Us Our Debts." In Frechette, ed., *Biblical Essays,* 56–67.

Arzt-Grabner, Peter. "How to Deal with Onesimus? Paul's Solution within the Frame of Ancient Legal and Documentary Sources." In Tolmie, *Philemon in Perspective,* 113–42.

Ascough, Richard S., Philip A. Harland, and John S. Kloppenborg. *Associations in the Greco-Roman World: A Sourcebook.* Waco, TX: Baylor University Press; Berlin: de Gruyter, 2012.

Aslan, Reza. *Zealot: The Life and Times of Jesus of Nazareth.* New York: Random House, 2013.

Bailey, Kenneth E. *Paul through Mediterranean Eyes: Cultural Studies in 1 Corinthians.* Downers Grove, IL: IVP Academic, 2011.

Barbero, Mario, "A First-Century Couple: Priscilla and Aquila; Their House Churches and Missionary Activity." PhD diss. The Catholic University of America, Washington, DC, 2001.

Barrick, W. Boyd. "The Rich Man from Arimathea (Matt 27:57-60) and 1QIsa[a]." *JBL* 96 (1977): 235–39.

Bassler, Jouette. *God and Mammon: Asking for Money in the New Testament.* Nashville: Abingdon, 1991.

Batey, R. *Jesus and the Poor.* New York: Harper, 1972.

Beavis, Mary Ann. "Ancient Slavery as an Interpretive Context for the New Testament Servant Parables with Special Reference to the Unjust Steward (Luke 16:1-8)." *JBL* 111 (1992): 37–54.

Belezos, Constantine J., ed. *Saint Paul and Corinth: 1950 Years since the Writing of the Epistles to the Corinthians; International Scholarly Conference Proceedings (Corinth, 23–25 September 2007).* 2 vols. Athens: Psichogios, 2009.

Bennemma, Cornelis. *A Theory of Character in New Testament Narrative.* Minneapolis: Augsburg Fortress, 2014.

Blanton, Thomas R., IV. "The Benefactor's Account Book: The Rhetoric of Gift Reciprocation according to Seneca and Paul." *NTS* 59 (2013): 396–414.

Blasi, Anthony J. *Early Christianity as a Social Movement.* Toronto Studies in Religion 5. New York: Lang, 1988,

Bloomberg, Craig L. *Neither Poverty Nor Riches.* New Studies in Biblical Theology 7. Downers Grove, IL: IVP, 2000.

Borg, Marcus J. "A New Context for Romans xiii." *NTS* 19 (1972–1973): 205–18.

Boring, M. Eugene, Klaus Berge, and Carsten Colpe, eds. *Hellenistic Commentary to the New Testament.* Nashville: Abingdon, 1995.

Bornkamm, Günther. "The Lord's Supper and Church in Paul." In *Early Christian Experience.* New York: Harper & Row, 1969.

Bradley, Keith, and Paul Cartledge, eds. *The Cambridge World History of Slavery.* Vol. 1: *The Ancient Mediterranean World.* Cambridge: Cambridge University Press, 2011.

Briones, David E. *Paul's Financial Policy: A Socio-Theological Approach.* LNTS 494. London: Bloomsbury T&T Clark, 2013.

Brown, Raymond E. *The Birth of the Messiah: A Commentary on the Infancy Narratives in the Gospels of Matthew and Luke.* Rev. ed. ABRL. New York: Doubleday, 1993.

Bultmann, Rudolf. *The History of the Synoptic Tradition.* Rev. ed. New York: Harper & Row, 1968.

Burke, Trevor J. *Family Matters: A Socio-Historical Study of Kinship Metaphors in 1 Thessalonians.* JSNTSup 247. London: T&T Clark, 2003.

Cadbury, Henry J. "Erastus of Corinth." *JBL* 50 (1931): 42–58.

Callon, Callie. "*Adulescentes* and *Meretrices:* The Correlation between Sqandered Patimony and Prostitutes in the Parable of the Prodigal Son." *CBQ* 75 (2013): 259–78.

Caragounis, Chrys C. "A House Church in Corinth: An Inquiry into the Structure of Early Corinthian Christianity." In Belezos, *Saint Paul and Corinth,* 1:365–418.

Chester, Stephen. *Conversion at Corinth: Perspectives on Conversion in Paul's Theology and the Corinthian Church.* SNTW. London: T&T Clark, 2003.

Chow, John K. *Patronage and Power: A Study of Social Networks in Corinth.* JSNTSS 75. Sheffield: Sheffield Academic Press, 1992.

———. "Patronage in Roman Corinth." In Horsley, ed., *Paul and Empire,* 104–25.

Clarke, Andrew D. *Secular and Christian Leadership in Corinth: A Socio-Historical and Exegetical Study of 1 Corinthians 1–6.* AGJU 18. Leiden: Brill, 1993.

Collins, Adela Yarbro. "Revelation 18: Taunt-Song or Dirge." In Lambrecht, *L'Apocalypse johannique,* 185–204.

Collins, John J. "Toward the Morphology of a Genre." *Semeia* 14 (1979): 1–19.

Collins, Raymond F. *The Birth of the New Testament: The Origin and Development of the First Christian Generation.* New York: Crossroad, 1993.

———. "The Case of a Wandering Doxology: Rom 16:25-27." In *New Testament Textual Criticism and Exegesis,* edited by Adelbert Denaux, 249–59. BETL 161. Louvain: University Press; Peeters, 2002.

———. "The Church in the House." *Corpus Reports* 40, no. 4 (2014): 21–29.

———. "The Origins of Church Law." *The Jurist* 61 (2001): 134–56.

———. "Paul's Damascus Experience: Reflections on the Lukan Account." *LS* 11 (1986): 99–118.

———. "How Not to Behave in the Household of God." *LS* 35 (2011): 7–31.

———. *Letters That Paul Did Not Write: The Epistle to the Hebrews and the Pauline Pseudepigrapha.* Good News Studies 28. Wilmington, DE: Glazier, 1988. Reprinted, Eugene, OR: Wipf & Stock, 2005.

———. "The Man Who Came to Dinner." In *Luke and His Readers,* edited by R. Bieringer, G. Van Belle, and J. Verheyden, 151–72. BETL 182. Leuven: University Press; Peeters, 2004.

———. "Obedience, Children and the Fourth Commandment: A New Testament Note." *LS* 4 (1972–1973): 157–73.

———. *The Power of Images in Paul.* Collegeville, MN: Liturgical Press, 2008.

———. *Sexual Ethics and the New Testament: Behavior and Belief.* Companions to the New Testament. New York Crossroad, 2000.

———. "Servant of the Lord, The." *NIDB.* 5:192–95.

———. "The Ten Commandments and the Christian Response." *LS* 3 (1970–1971): 308–22.

———. "The Ten Commandments in Current Perspective." *AER* 161 (1969): 169–82.

———. "'Who Are You?' Comparison/Contrast and Fourth Gospel Characterization." In Skinner, *Characters and Characterization,* 77–93.

Crossan, John D. "Hidden Treasure Parables in Later Antiquity." SBLSP (1976): 359–79.

Crossley, James G. "The Damned Rich (Mark 10:17-31)." *ExpTim* 116 (2005).

Countryman, L. William. *The Rich Christians in the Church of the Early Empire: Contradictions and Accommodations.* New York: Edwin Mellen, 1980.

Coutsoumpos, Panayotis. *Paul and the Lord's Supper: A Socio-Historical Investigation.* Studies in Biblical Literature 84. New York: Peter Lang, 2005.

Dahl, Niels A. "Paul and Possessions." In *Studies on Paul.* Minneapolis: Augsburg, 1977.

Deissmann, Adolf. *Light from the Ancient East: The New Testament Illustrated by Recently Discovered Texts of the Graeco-Roman World.* New York: George H. Doran, 1927.

Derrett, J. Duncan M. *Law in the New Testament.* London: Darton, Longman & Todd, 1970.

———. "The Parable of the Great Supper." In *Law in the New Testament,* 126–55.

Descamps, Albert-Marie. *Les Justes et la Justice dans les Évangiles et le Christianisme primitif, hormis la doctrine proprement paulinienne.* Louvain-Gembloux: Duculot, 1950.

Dewey, Joanna. "The Literary Structure of the Controversy Stories in Mark 2:1–3:6." *JBL* 92 (1973): 394–401.

———. *Markan Public Debate: Literary Technique, Concentric Structure and Theology in Mark 2:1–3:6.* SBLDS 48. Chico, CA: Scholars, 1980.

Donahue, John R. "The Lure of Wealth: Does Mark Have a Social Gospel?" In Skinner and Iverson, eds., *Unity and Diversity,* 70–93.

Drake, Lyndon. "Did Jesus Oppose the *Prosbul* in the Forgiveness Petition of the Lord's Prayer?" *NovT* 56 (2014): 233–44.

Dunn, James D. G. "Romans 13:1-7—A Charter for Political Quietism." *Ex Auditu* 2 (1986): 55–68.

Dupont, Jacques. *Les Béatitudes.* Vol. 1. Ebib. Paris: Gabalda, 1969.

———. *The Sources of Acts.* London: Darton, Longman & Todd, 1964.

Elliott, Neil. "Romans 13:1-7 in the Context of Imperial Propaganda." in Horsley, *Paul and Empire,* 184–204.

Ellul, Jacques. *Money and Power.* Downers Grove, IL: Intervarsity Press, 1985.

———. *On Being Rich and Poor: Christianity in a Time of Economic Globalization.* Toronto: University of Toronto Press, 2014.

Eubank, Nathan. "What Does Matthew Say about Divine Recompense? On the Misuse of the Parable of the Workers in the Vineyard (20.1-16)." *JSNT* 35 (2013): 242–62.

Fiensy, David A. "Assessing the Economy of Galilee in the Late Second Temple Period: Five Considerations." In Fiensy and Hawkins, *Galilean Economy,* 165–86.

Fiensy, David A., and Ralph K. Hawkins, eds. *The Galilean Economy in the Time of Jesus.* ECL 11. Atlanta: SBL, 2013.

Fitzgerald, John T., Thomas H. Olbricht, and L. Michael White, eds. *Early Christianity and Classical Culture: Comparative Studies in Honor of Abraham J. Malherbe.* NovTSup 110. Leiden: Brill, 2003.

Fitzmyer, Joseph A. "The Aramaic Qorban Inscription from Jebel Hallet et-Turi and Mark 7:11/Matt 15:5." *JBL* 78 (1959): 60–65.

Ford, R. Q. "Jesus' Parable of the Unforgiving Slave and the Wall Street Crisis of 2008." *FR* 24 (2011): 15–20, 22.

Fortna, Robert. "Exegesis and Theology." *Journal of Theology for Southern Africa* 72 (1960): 66–72.

France, Richard T. "God and Mammon." *EvQ* 51 (1979): 3–21.

Frechette, Christopher G., Christopher R. Matthews, and Thomas D. Stegman, eds. *Biblical Essays in Honor of Daniel J. Harrington, SJ, and Richard J. Clifford, SJ: Opportunity for No Little Instruction.* Mahwah, NJ: Paulist, 2014.

Friedrichsen, Timothy A. "The Temple, a Pharisee, a Tax Collector, and the Kingdom of God: Rereading a Jesus Parable (Luke 18.10-14a)." *JBL* 124 (2005): 89–119.

Fusco, Vittorio. *Povertà e Sequela. Le Pericope sinottica della Chiamata del Ricco (Mc. 10-17-311 Parr.).* Brescia: Paideia, 1991.

Georgi, Dieter. *Remembering the Poor: The History of Paul's Collection for Jerusalem.* Nashville: Abingdon, 1992.

Gillman, Florence M. *Women Who Knew Paul.* Zacchaeus Studies: New Testament. Collegeville, MN: Liturgical Press, 1992.

Goodrich, John K. "Voluntary Debt Remission and the Parable of the Unjust Steward (Luke 16:1-13)." *JBL* 131 (2012): 547–66.

Hamel, Édouard. "Le Magnificat et le renversement des situations: Réflections théologico-bibliques (Lc 1, 51-53)." *Greg* 60 (1979): 55–84.

Hamm, Dennis. "Luke 19:8 Once Again: Does Zacchaeus Defend or Resolve?" *JBL* 107 (1998): 431–37.

———. "Zacchaeus Revisited Once More: A Story of Vindication or Conversion?" *Bib* 72 (1991): 248–52.

Handayani, M. "Understanding the Concept of Sin as Debt in the Lord's Prayer." *Stulos Theological Journal* 16 (2008): 85–93.

Harb, Gertraud. "Matthew 17.24-27 and its Value for Historical Jesus Research." *JournStudHistJesus* 8 (2010): 254–74.

Hay, David M., and E. Elizabeth Johnson, eds. *Pauline Theology: Romans.* Minneapolis: Fortress, 1995.

Hengel, Martin. *Property and Riches in the Early Church.* Philadelphia: Fortress, 1974.

Hellerman, Joseph H. "Wealth and Sacrifice in Early Christianity: Revisiting Mark's Presentation of Jesus' Encounter with the Rich Young Ruler." *TJ* 21 (2000): 143–64.

Hentschel, Anni. *Diakonia im Neuen Testament. Studien zur Semantik unter besonderer Berücksichtguing der Rolle von Frauen.* WUNT 2/226. Tübingen: Mohr Siebeck, 2007.

Hezser, Catherine. *Lohnmetaphorik und Arbeitswelt in Mt 20, 1-16.* NTOA 15. Gottimgen: Vandenhoeck & Ruprecht, 1990.

Hills, Julian V., ed. *Common Life in the Early Church: Essays Honoring Graydon F. Snyder.* Harrisburg, PA: Trinity Press International, 1998.

Hock, Ronald F. "The Parable of the Foolish Rich Man (Luke 12:16-20) and Graeco-Roman Conventions of Thought and Behavior." In Fitzgerald et al., *Early Christianity and Classical Culture*, 181–96.

Hofius, Gottfried. "The Lord's Supper and the Lord's Supper Tradition: Reflections on 1 Corinthians 11:23b-25." In Meyer, *One Loaf, One Cup*, 75–115.

Holmberg, Bengt. *Paul and Power: The Structure of Authority in the Primitive Church as Reflected in the Pauline Epistles.* Lund: Studentlitteratur AB, 1978.

Horrell, David G. "Farewell to Another Wealthy Patron? Reassessing Philemon in the Light of Recent Scholarly Discussion of Socio-Economic Level and Domestic Space." A paper delivered at the 2014 Ecumenical Pauline Colloquium held at Rome's Abbey of St. Paul's Outside the Walls, September 15–20, 2014.

Horsley, Richard A., ed. *Paul and Empire: Religion and Power in Roman Imperial Society.* Harrisburg, PA: Trinity Press International, 1997.

Horsley, Richard A. "1 Corinthians: A Case Study of Paul's Assembly as an Alternative Society." in Horsley, *Paul and Empire*, 242–52.

Huizenga, Annette Bourland. *Moral Education for Women in the Pastoral and Pythagorean Letters.* NTSup 147. Leiden: Brill, 2013.

Hutt, Curtis. "'Be Ye Approved Money Changers!' Reexamining the Social Contexts of the Saying and Its Interpretation." *JBL* 131 (2012): 589–609.

Jeremias, Joachim. *Jerusalem in the Time of Jesus: An Investigation into Economic and Social Conditions during the New Testament Period.* London: SCM, 1969.

———. *The Parables of Jesus.* 2nd ed. New York: Scribner, 1963.

———. *Unknown Sayings of Jesus.* London: SPCK, 1958.

Johnson, Luke Timothy. *The Literary Function of Possessions in Luke–Acts.* SBLDS 39. Missoula, MT: Scholars Press, 1977.

———. *Sharing Possessions: What Faith Demands.* 2nd ed. Grand Rapids: Eerdmans, 2011.

Judge, Edwin A. "The Early Christians as a Scholastic Community." *JRH* 1 (1960–1961): 4–15, 125–37.

Karris, Robert. "Poor and Rich: The Lukan Sitz im Leben." in Talbert, *Perspectives*, 112–25.

Käsemann, Ernst. *New Testament Questions of Today.* Philadelphia: Fortress, 1969.

———. "Principles of the Interpretation of Romans 13." In *New Testament Questions*, 196–216.

Keck, Leander E. "The 'Poor among the Saints' in Jewish Christianity and Qumran." *ZNW* 57 (1966): 54–78.

———. "What Makes Romans Tick?" In Hay and Johnson, *Romans*, 33–29.

Keller, Marie Noël. *Priscilla and Aquila: Paul's Coworkers in Christ Jesus.* Paul's Social Network: Brothers and Sisters in Faith. Collegeville, MN: Liturgical Press, 2010.

Kidd, Reggie M. *Wealth and Beneficence in the Pastoral Epistles: A "Bourgeois" Form of Early Christianity?* SBLDS 122. Atlanta: Scholars Press, 1990.

Kiley, Mark C. *Colossians as Pseudepigrapha.* Biblical Seminar 4. Sheffield: JSOT, 1986.

Kilgallen, John J. "The Foolish Rich Man (Luke 12, 16-20 [15-21])." In *Twenty Parables*, 39–49.

———. "The Rich Man and Lazarus (Luke 16, 19-31)." In *Twenty Parables*, 123–32.

———. "The Sower and the Seed—8, 5-8 (8, 4-15)." In *Twenty Parables*, 17–27.

———. *Twenty Parables of Jesus in the Gospel of Luke*. SubBi 32. Rome: Pontifical Biblical Institute, 2008.

Kim, Kyoung-Jin. *Stewardship and Almsgiving in Luke's Theology*. JSNTSup 155. Sheffield: Sheffield Academic Press, 1998.

Kloha, Jeffrey. "Elizabeth's Magnificat (Luke 1:46)." In *Texts and Traditions: Essays in Honour of J. Keith Elliott*, edited by Peter Doble and Jeffrey Kloha, 200–19. NTTSD 47. Leiden: Brill, 2014.

Koch, Dietrich-Alex. "Die Kontroverse über die Steuer (Mt 22,15-22 / Mk 12, 13-17 / Lk 20,20-26)." In Van Belle and Verheyden, *Christ and the Emperor*, 203–28.

Kovacs, Judith L. *1 Corinthians: Interpreted by Early Christian Commentators*. The Church's Bible. Grand Rapids: Eerdmans, 2005.

Kremer, Jacob, ed. *Les Actes des Apôtres: Tradition, rédaction, théologie*. BETL 48. Gembloux (Belgium): Duculot, 1979.

Lachs, Samuel T. *A Rabbinic Commentary on the New Testament: The Gospels of Matthew, Mark, and Luke*. Hoboken, NJ: KTAV, 1987.

Lambrecht, Jan. *Once More Astonished: The Parables of Jesus*. 2nd ed. New York: Crossroad, 1983.

———. "Paul's Farewell-Address at Miletus (Acts 20:17-38)." in Kremer, *Actes*, 307–37.

———. "Three More Notes in Response to John P. Meier: Mark 1,7-8; 3,27 and 10,1-10." *ETL* 89 (2013): 397–409.

———. *Understanding What One Reads III: Essays on the Gospels and Paul (2011–2014)*. Annua Nuntia Lovaniensia 71. Leuven: Peeters, 2015.

Lambrecht, Jan, ed. *L'Apocalypse johannique et l'Apocalyptique dans le Nouveau Testament*. BETL 53. Louvain: University Press, 1980.

Lampe, Peter. "Keine 'Sklavenflucht' des Onesimus." *ZNW* 76 (1985): 135–37.

Le Donne, Anthony. "The Improper Temple Offering of Ananias and Sapphira." *NTS* 59 (2013): 346–64.

Lightfoot, J. B., and J. R. Harmer. *The Apostolic Fathers*. Grand Rapids: Baker, 1984.

Levine, Amy-Jill. *A Feminist Companion to the Acts of the Apostles*. London: T&T Clark, 2004.

———. *Short Stories by Jesus: The Enigmatic Parables of a Controversial Rabbi*. New York: Harper Collins, 2014.

Lindemann, Andreas. "The Beginnings of Christian Life in Jerusalem according to the Summaries in the Acts of the Apostles (2:42-47; 4:32-37; 5:12-16)." In Hills, *Common Life*, 202–18.

Lohfink, Gerhard. *Jesus of Nazareth: What He Wanted, Who He Was.* Collegeville, MN: Liturgical Press, 2012.

Longenecker, Bruce, and Kelly Liebengood, eds. *Engaging Economics: New Testament Scenarios and Early Christian Reception.* Grand Rapids: Eerdmans, 2009.

MacMullen, Ramsey. "Women in Public in the Roman Empire." *Historia: Zeitschrift für Alte Geschichte* 29 (1980) 208–18.

Malina, Bruce. "Wealth and Poverty in the New Testament and Its World." *Int* 41 (1987): 354–67.

Malherbe, Abraham J. "Gentle as a Nurse: The Cynic Background to 1 Thessalonians 2." *NovT* 12 (1970): 203–17; reprinted in *Paul and the Popular Philosophers*, 35–48.

———. *Paul and the Popular Philosophers.* Minneapolis: Fortress, 1989.

———. *Paul and the Thessalonians.* Philadelphia: Fortress, 1987.

———. *Social Aspects of Early Christianity.* Philadelphia: Fortress, 1983.

Manson, T. W. *The Sayings of Jesus.* London: SCM, 2012.

Marguerat, Daniel. *Dieu et l'argent. Une parole à oser.* Parole en liberté. Bière, Switzerland: Cabédita, 2013.

Matera, Frank J. *New Testament Ethics: The Legacies of Jesus and Paul.* Louisville: Westminster John Knox, 1996.

Matthews, Shelley. "Elite Women, Public Religion, and Christian Propaganda in Acts 16." In Levine, ed., *A Feminist Companion*, 111–33.

Mealand, David L. "Hellenistic Historians and the Style of Acts." *ZNW* 82 (1991): 42–66.

McNeel, Jennifer Houston. *Paul as Infant and Nursing Mother: Metaphor, Rhetoric, and Identity in 1 Thessalonians 2:5-8.* ECL 12. Atlanta: SBL Press, 2014.

McRay, John. *Archaeology and the New Testament.* Grand Rapids: Baker, 1991.

Meeks, Wayne A. *The First Urban Christians: The Social World of the Apostle Paul.* New Haven: Yale University Press, 1983.

Meggitt, Justin J. *Paul, Poverty and Survival.* Edinburgh, T&T Clark, 1998.

———. "The Social State of Erastus (Rom 16.23)," *NTS* 38 (1996): 218–23.

Meier John P. *A Marginal Jew: Rethinking the Historical Jesus.* Vol. 3: *Companions and Competitors.* AYBRL. New Haven: Yale University Press, 2001.

———. "The Parable of the Wicked Tenants in the Vineyard: Is the Gospel of Thomas Independent of the Synoptics?" In Skinner and Iverson, eds., *Unity and Diversity*, 129–42.

Metzger, Bruce M. *A Textual Commentary on the Greek New Testament.* 2nd ed. Stuttgart: Deutsche Bibelgesellschaft, 1994.

Meyer, Ben F., ed. *One Loaf, One Cup: Ecumenical Studies of 1 Cor 11 and Other Eucharistic Texts; The Cambridge Conference on the Eucharist, August 1988.* New Gospel Studies 6. Macon, GA: Mercer University Press, 1993.

Michiels, Robrecht. "The 'Model of Church' in the First Christian Community of Jerusalem: Ideal and Reality." *LS* 10 (1985): 303–23.

Miller, Amanda C. "Bridge Work and Seating Charts: A Study of Luke's Ethics of Wealth, Poverty, and Reversal." *Int* 68 (2014): 416–27.

Miller, Patrick D. *The Ten Commandments.* IBC. Louisville: Westminster John Knox, 2000.

Mitchell, Alan C. "1 Corinthians 1:6-11: Group Boundaries and the Courts of Corinth." PhD diss., Yale University, 1986.

———. "Rich and Poor in the Courts of Corinth: Litigiousness and Status in 1 Corinthians 6.1-11." *NTS* 39 (1993): 562–86.

———. "Zacchaeus Revisited: Luke 19:8 as a Defense." *Bib* 71 (1990): 153–76.

Mitchell, Margaret M. "Concerning *peri de* in 1 Corinthians." *NovT* 31 (1989): 221–56.

Morgan, B. *Christians, the Church, and Property.* Philadelphia: Westminster, 1963.

Murchie, David. "The New Testament View of Wealth Accumulation." *JETS* 21 (1978): 335–44.

———. "The New Testament View of . . ." *CBQ* 57 (1978): 710–28.

Nel, M. J. "The Forgiveness of Debt in Matthew 6:12, 14-15." *Neot* 47 (2013): 87–106.

Nickle, Keith F. *The Collection: A Study in Paul's Strategy.* SBT 48. London: SCM; Geneva, AL: Allenson, 1966.

Niederwimmer, Kurt. *The Didache.* Hermeneia. Minneapolis: Fortress, 1988.

Nowell, Irene. "The Call to Economic Justice." *TBT* 52 (2014): 271–76.

Oakman, Douglas E. "Execrating? or Execrable Peasants!" in Fiensy and Hawkins, *Galilean Economy*, 139–64.

———. *Jesus, Debt, and the Lord's Prayer: First-Century Debt and Jesus' Intentions.* Eugene, OR: Cascade, 2014.

O'Day, Gail R. "Jeremiah 9:22-23 and 1 Corinthians 1:26-31: A Study in Intertextuality." *JBL* 109 (1990): 259–67.

Ogereau, Julien M. "The Jerusalem Collection as Koinonia: Paul's Global Poliics of Socio-Economic Equality and Solidarity." *NTS* 58 (2012): 360–78.

———. "Paul's Koinonia with the Phillipians: *Societas* as a Missionary Funding Strategy." *NTS* 60 (2014): 360–78.

Osiek, Carolyn, and David L. Balch. *Families in the New Testament World: Households and House Churches.* The Family, Religion, and Culture. Louisville: Westminster John Knox, 1997.

Padgett, A. "Wealthy Women at Ephesus: 1 Tim 2:8-15 in Social Context." *Int* 41 (1987): 19–31.

Paya, Christophe. "Le discours d'envoie en mission de Matthieu 10. État de la recherche et perspectives." *RHPR* 90 (2010): 479–99.

Peppard, Michael. "Brother against Brother: *Controversiae* about Inheritance Disputes and 1 Corinthians 6:1-11." *JBL* 133 (2014): 179–92.

————. "Torah for the Man Who Has Everything: 'Do Not Defraud' in Mark 10:19." *JBL* 134 (2015): 595–604.

Perotti, Pier Angelo. "La parabola degli' operai della vigna (Mt 19,30-20,16)." *BibOr* 53 (2011): 19–42.

Peterman, G. T. W. "Romans 15.24: Make a Contribution or Establish fellowship." *NTS* 40 (1994): 457–63.

Piper, O. A. *The Christian Meaning of Money*. Englewood Cliffs, NJ: Prentice Hall, 1986.

Pippin, Tina. "Of Metaphors and Monsters: The Body of the Whore of Babylon in the Apocalypse of John." *Classical Bulletin* 86 (2010): 156–72.

Powell, Mark Allan. *Introducing the New Testament: A Historical, Literary, and Theological Survey*. Grand Rapids: Baker Academic, 2009.

Rapske, Brian. *The Book of Acts and Paul in Roman Custody*. The Book of Act in Its First Century Setting 3. Grand Rapids: Eerdmans, 1994.

Reasoner, Mark, *Roman Imperial Texts: A Source Book*. Minneapolis: Fortress, 2014.

Redalié, Yann. *Paul après Paul: Le temps, le salut, la morale selon les épîtres à Timothée et à Tite*. MdB 31. Geneva: Labor et Fides, 1994.

Rindge, Matthew S. "Luke's Artistic Parables: Narratives of Subversion, Imagination, and Transformation." *Int* 68 (2014): 403–15.

Rodriguez, José David. "The Parable of the Affirmative Action Employer." *CTM* 15 (1988): 418–24.

Sampley, J. Paul. *Pauline Partnership in Christ: Christian Community and Commitment in Light of Roman Law*. Philadelphia: Fortress, 1980.

Sanger, Dieter. "Die *dynatoi* in 1 Kor 1,26." *ZNW* 76 (1985): 285–91.

Scheidel, Walter. "The Roman Slave Supply." In Bradley and Cartledge, *The Cambridge World History of Slavery*, 1:287–310.

Schneider, John R. *The Good of Affluence: Seeking God in a Culture of Affluence*. Grand Rapids: Eerdmans, 2002.

Schnelle, Udo. *Apostle Paul: His Life and Theology*. Grand Rapids: Baker Academic, 2005.

Schottroff, Luise, "Give to Caesar What Belongs to Caesar and to God What Belongs to God: A Theological Response of the Early Christian Church to the Social and Political Environment." In Swartley, *The Love of Enemy*, 223–57.

Seim, Turid K. *The Double Message: Patterns of Gender in Luke–Acts*. SNTW. Edinburgh: T&T Clark, 1994.

Sihombing, Batara. "A Narrative Approach to God and Mammon (6:19-34) and Its Relevance to the Churches in Indonesia." *AJT* 26 (2012): 25–43.

Skinner, Christopher W., ed. *Characters and Characterization in the Gospel of John*. Library of New Testament Studies. JSNTSup 461. London: Bloomsbury, 2013.

Skinner, Christopher W., and Kelly R. Iverson, eds. *Unity and Diversity in the Gospels and Paul: Essays in Honor of Frank J. Matera.* ECL 7. Atlanta: Society of Biblical Literature, 2012.

Smith, Dennis E. *From Symposium to Eucharist: The Banquet in the Early Christian World.* Minneapolis: Fortress, 2002.

———. "Meals and Morality in Paul and His World." SBLSP (1981): 319–39.

Soards, Marion L. *The Speeches in Acts: Their Content, Context, and Concerns.* Louisville: Westminster John Knox, 1994.

Spencer, F. Scott. *Salty Wives, Spirited Mothers, and Savvy Widows: Capable Women of Purpose and Persistence in Luke's Gospel.* Grand Rapids: Eerdmans, 2012.

Stegman, Thomas D. "Paul's Use of Scripture in the Collection Discourse (2 Corinthians 8–9)." In Frechette, *Biblical Essays,* 153–69.

———. "Reading Luke 12:13-34 as a Elaboration of a Chreia: How Hermogenes of Tarsus Sheds Light on Luke's Gospel." *NovT* 49 (2007): 328–52.

Strecker, Georg. *The Sermon on the Mount: An Exegetical Commentary.* Nashville: Abingdon, 1988.

Strelan, John G. "Burden-Bearing and the Law of Christ: A Re-examination of Gal 6:2." *JBL* 94 (1975): 266–76.

Swartley, Williard M., ed. *The Love of Enemy and Nonretaliation in the New Testament.* Louisville: Westminster John Knox, 1992.

Szsesnat, H. "What Did the *Skēnopoios* Paul Produce." *Neot* 27 (1993): 391–402.

Talbert, Charles H. *Perspectives on Luke–Acts.* Danville, VA: Association of Baptist Professors of Religion, 1978.

Tannehill, Robert C. *The Sword of His Mouth.* Philadelphia: Fortress, 1975.

Taussig, Hal. *In the Beginning Was the Meal: Social Experimentation and Early Christian Identity.* Minneapolis: Fortress, 2009.

Teevan, John Addison. *Integrated Justice and Equality: Biblical Wisdom for Those Who Do Good Works.* Grand Rapids: Acton Institute, 2014.

Theissen, Gerd. *The Social Setting of Pauline Christianity: Essays on Corinth.* Philadelphia: Fortress, 1982.

Thompson, James W. *The Church According to Paul: Rediscovering the Community Conformed to Christ.* Grand Rapids: Baker Academic, 2014.

Tolmie, D. François, ed. *Philemon in Perspective: Interpreting a Pauline Letter.* BZNW 169. Berlin: De Gruyter, 2010.

Udoh, Fabian E. *To Caesar What Is Caesar's: Tribute, Taxes, and Imperial Administration in Early Roman Palestine (63 B.C.E–70 C.E.).* BJS 343. Providence: Brown Judaic Studies 2005.

Ukpong, Justin. "The Parable of the Talents (Matt 25:14-30): Commendation or Critique of Exploitation? A Social-Historical and Theological Reading." *Neot* 46 (2012): 190–207.

Van Belle, Gilbert, and Jos Verheyden, eds. *Christ and the Emperor: The Gospel Evidence.* Biblical Tools and Studies 20. Leuven: Peeters, 2014.

Van der Merwe, Dirk G. "Rich Man, Poor Man in Jerusalem according to the Letter of James." *Acta patristica et byzantina* 21 (2010): 18–46.

van Eck, Ernest. "When Patrons Are Not Patrons: A Social-Scientific Reading of the Rich Man and Lazarus (Lk. 16:19-26)." *Hervormd Teologiese Studies/ Theological Studies* 65 (2009): 11 pages on line.

Vearncombe, Erin K. "Redistribution and Reciprocity: A Socio-Economic Interpretation of the Parable of the Labourers in the Vineyard (Matthew 20:1-15)." *JournStudHistJesus* 8 (2010): 199–236.

Verbrugge, Verlyn D. *Paul's Style of Church Leadership Illustrated by His Instructions to the Corinthians on the Collection.* San Francisco: Mellen Research University Press, 1992.

Verhey, Allen. *Remembering Jesus: Christian Community, Scripture, and the Moral Life.* Grand Rapids: Eerdmans, 2002.

Wan, Sze-kar. "Collection for the Saints as an Anti-colonial Act." In *Paul and Politics: Ekklesia, Israel, Imperium, Interpretation: Essays in Honor of Krister Stendahl*, edited by Richard A. Horsley, 191–215. Harrisburg, PA: Trinity Press International, 2000.

Ward, Roy Bowen. "Partiality in the Assembly: James 2:2-4." *HTR* 62 (1969): 87–97.

Weima, Jeffrey A. D. *Neglected Endings: The Significance of the Pauline Letter Closings.* JSNTS 101. Sheffield: JSOT Press, 1994.

Welborn, Lawrence L. "'That There Be Equality': The Contexts and Consequences of a Pauline Ideal." *NTS* 59 (2013): 73–90.

Wheeler, Sondra Ely. *Wealth as Peril and Obligation: The New Testament on Possessions.* Grand Rapids: Eerdmans, 1995.

Winter, Bruce W. "Civil Litigation in Secular Corinth and the Church: The Forensic Background to 1 Cor 6:1-8." *NTS* 31 (1991): 559–72.

Witherington, Ben, III. *Friendship and Finances in Philippi.* The New Testament in Context. Philadelphia: Trinity Press International, 1994.

Wong, Kasper Ho-Yee. *Boasting and Foolishness: A Study of 2 Cor 10 12-18 and 11, 1a.* JDDS 5; Bible and Literature 3. Hong Kong: Alliance Bible Seminary, 1998.

Wray, Tina J., and Gregory Mobley. *The Birth of Satan: Tracing the Devil's Biblical Roots.* New York: Palgrave Macmillan, 2005.

Young, E. M. "'Fulfil the Law of Christ': An Examination of Galatians 6.2." *StBibT* 7 (1977): 31–42.

Young, Frances. "The Pastoral Epistles and the Ethics of Reading." *JSNT* 14 (1992): 105–20.

Scripture Index

Index of Classical, Jewish, and Patristic Sources

Index of Modern Authors

341

Index of Topics

Lightning Source UK Ltd.
Milton Keynes UK
UKOW01f0332310817
308298UK00003B/366/P